IN THE BOSOM OF ABRAHAM

IN THE BOSOM OF ABRAHAM

How Three Ancient Promises Embrace the Biblical Story

PART ONE

From Creation to the Morning Star of New Creation

GEORGE R. EVES

WIPF & STOCK · Eugene, Oregon

IN THE BOSOM OF ABRAHAM
How Three Ancient Promises Embrace the Biblical Story
Part One: From Creation to the Morning Star of New Creation

Copyright © 2015 George R. Eves. All rights reserved. Except for brief quotations in critical publications or reviews, no part of this book may be reproduced in any manner without prior written permission from the publisher. Write: Permissions, Wipf and Stock Publishers, 199 W. 8th Ave., Suite 3, Eugene, OR 97401.

Scriptures taken from the Holy Bible, The World English Bible (WEB). The World English Bible is in the Public Domain. However, "World English Bible" is a Trademark of eBible.org.

Wipf & Stock
An Imprint of Wipf and Stock Publishers
199 W. 8th Ave., Suite 3
Eugene, OR 97401

www.wipfandstock.com

PAPERBACK ISBN: 978-1-62564-775-7
HARDCOVER ISBN: 978-1-4982-7988-8
EBOOK ISBN: 978-1-4982-7987-1

04/06/21

This book is dedicated to the glory of God, first of all, and to my brother, mentor, and friend, Henry Janicki, a scholar and a gentleman.

Listen to me, you who follow after righteousness,
    you who seek Yahweh.
Look to the rock you were cut from,
    and to the quarry you were dug from.
Look to Abraham your father,
    and to Sarah who bore you;
for when he was but one I called him,
    I blessed him,
    and made him many.
For Yahweh has comforted Zion.
    He has comforted all her waste places,
    and has made her wilderness like Eden,
    and her desert like the garden of Yahweh.
Joy and gladness will be found in them,
    thanksgiving, and the voice of melody.

(ISAIAH 51:1–3)

And it came to pass, that the beggar died, and was carried by the angels into Abraham's bosom.
(LUKE 16:22, KJV)

Contents

List of Illustrations | ix
Foreword by Stephen G. Dempster | xi
A Note to the Reader | xiii

1 Introduction: Jerusalem Is Built as a City that Is at Unity with Itself. | 1
2 The Beginning: The Gift of Paradise (The Way Things Are Supposed to Be) | 20
3 Paradise Lost | 39
4 Noah: Paradise Restored? | 51
5 Abram: Called, Confirmed, and Confused | 64
6 Abraham: Laughter, *Laughter*, and *More Laughter* | 75
7 Isaac, Jacob, and Joseph: Two More Promise Keepers and a Savior | 88
8 Moses (Part One): The Birth of a Nation | 108
9 Moses (Part Two): Dead Men Walking | 141
10 Joshua: Into Canaan's Fair Land | 169
11 Here Come the Judges: An Unsettling Experience | 190
12 Israel Under the Kings (Part One): The United Kingdom | 210
13 Israel Under the Kings (Part Two): The "House" of Jeroboam | 240
14 Israel Under the Kings (Part Three): The "House" of David | 265
15 Morning Star of New Creation: The Prophetic Vision | 294
16 Conclusion | 325

Works Cited | 361
Index | 363

Illustrations

Progressive Revelation | 5
Stages of Progressive Revelation | 7
Three Promises: One Story (1) | 10
The Three Promises and Jesus? | 12
The Transformed Promises of the Prophetic Vision | 13
Three Promises: Three Manifestations | 13
The Three Promises Before Abraham | 14
Three Promises: One Story (2) | 15
Abraham's Fingerprints | 19
Covenantal Diagram 1: Abraham–Creation (1) | 35
Covenantal Diagram 2: Abraham–Creation (2) | 37
Covenantal Diagram 3: Abraham–Moses | 133
Covenantal Diagram 4: Abraham-David | 215
Covenantal Diagram 5: Abraham–New Creation | 316
The Story So Far | 324
Eden and Canaan | 337
All Nations "in Adam" and "in Abraham" | 341

Foreword

It was not that long ago that many were saying that the biblical theology movement was dead. If that was ever the case, then there has been a remarkable resurrection and resurgence of the movement in the last few years, to judge from the spate of recent studies. It is true that biblical theology has been defined differently by various theologians, but the study of the theology of the Bible itself, its narrative storyline, and its global structure have largely dominated the field in this movement. George Eves' *In the Bosom of Abraham* takes a legitimate place within this field, and promises to be a significant contribution.

Eves writes concisely and communicates powerfully. His helpful illustrations and diagrams are added highlights which provide a handy method of communicating simply some of the profound ideas of the book. This book is written by a teacher who has a passion for communicating with his students, and it has been the result of a long journey of teaching the message of the Christian Scriptures over the years. I have had the privilege of teaching some of his students and they have been both inspired by the content of this book in its early stages and challenged to go deeper into the truths of the Bible.

Eves' thesis is that the Bible is Abraham shaped, that its fundamental plot structure is based on the Abrahamic covenant, and that this structure can be traced back to the beginning of the biblical story and can be found even in the creation narratives. In stating the matter like this Eves shows the necessity of understanding the Old Testament Scriptures of which the pastors, teachers, leaders and consequently members of the contemporary Christian Church are woefully ignorant. But part of the reason for this ignorance is the lack of an overarching framework to understand the vast amount of detail in the Old Testament. Understanding the fundamental contours of the Abrahamic shape can help remedy this problem.

Jesus once described the true teacher of the Torah who had become a disciple in the kingdom of heaven to be like the owner of a house who brings out of his storeroom new treasures as well as old (Matt 13:52). This has been my experience when reading George's manuscript. He brings out the old treasures of the faith but with new insights and new perspectives that make you stand up and take notice. It is because he has

FOREWORD

been a disciple of the Master Interpreter and thought long and pondered much over His teaching.

As George was in the final stages of bringing *In the Bosom of Abraham* to birth, he was awaiting the birth of a grandson. I mentioned the similarity of the two births to him and have pondered over the coincidence of these new arrivals and the title of his book. Given the subject matter of the book and one of the promises of the Abrahamic covenant that a descendant would someday bless the world, I thought that the book might not only be entitled *In the Bosom of Abraham* but also might be aptly named *Eve's Womb*. Although this book is not to be considered on the same level as the birth of a child, it is about the birth of The Child, the wonder of the birth of The Messiah, who makes every birth worth celebrating. May you rejoice in the wonder of His Salvation as you read, reflect and most of all worship. Come let us adore Him!

Stephen G. Dempster
Professor of Religious Studies
Crandall University

A Note to the Reader

No author is an island. It is impossible to determine all the sources and influences that have come together in my experience in order to produce this volume. But I want to acknowledge a few.

I think of my Grade 1 teacher, Mrs. Robinson, who encouraged my ability to read by having me do so in front of the Grade 2 class. Had she any idea of what she was starting?

I remember my father, William Roy Eves, who faithfully led our family in the daily reading of Scripture and prayers. One day when I was very young he was calling my younger brother home for supper and, not getting a response, he asked me if I knew where he was. Quite cleverly, I thought, I quoted Scripture to him: "Am I my brother's keeper?" He was not amused, however, and impressed upon my person the need never to misuse God's Holy Word! I hope he is smiling now.

And then there is Henry Janicki, an electrician by trade, who faithfully taught Sunday School for years at Evangel Pentecostal Church in Oakville, Ontario. For assisting him, one year he gave me a copy of Dewey Beegle's *God's Word Into English*, and in so doing changed my life forever. I was electrified (pun intended) by its scholarly approach to the issues of textual criticism. Who knew one could really think this way about the Bible and still be faithful?

I have dedicated this book to Henry, but he represents all the others, known and unknown. It is a debt that I simply cannot repay. But I *can* say "Thank you!" That is what you will really find between these covers.

This project has its specific origin in a series of sermons at St. John's (Stone) Church that then evolved into my teaching notes for "God's Unfolding Plan," a course I taught at Taylor College of Mission and Evangelism in Saint John, New Brunswick. Being unable to find a textbook for this course as I envisaged it, I began to think seriously of putting my thoughts into a book of my own. Many encouraged me in this.

Another major push toward publication came from Dr. Stephen Dempster, Professor of Religious Studies at Crandall University, who had some kind things to say about an early manuscript and has become my mentor in this effort. We are "kindred spirits" in seeking ways to understand the Bible as a connected Story.

A Note to the Reader

My wife, Deborah, besides being my most constant support, has proofread the text and provided the diagrams that I believe enhance it considerably. The Venerable Kim Salo was kind enough to read the manuscript and I have benefited significantly from his input. In addition, Bea Mealey and Rebecca Ellis took on the onerous task of checking the many biblical citations.

I am humbled by the opportunity to invite others along on the journey I have been on and share in its discoveries. Many times I found myself at a dead end only to find that seeing things through Abraham's eyes provided a way forward to new insights. These experiences give me the sense that God is in this and the confidence to place it before a wider audience.

As the author, I must take responsibility for what is said in this volume. If it resonates with the faithful and proves helpful to them in their own quests for understanding, then thanks be to God. If it fails to do so, at least the paper is recyclable.

In the service of Christ,
George R. Eves
Spring, 2015

1

Introduction

Jerusalem Is Built as a City that Is at Unity with Itself.[1]

THE NATURE OF BIBLICAL UNITY

Most Christians have a sense that the Bible is a unified whole. This stems from a conviction that it is the inspired Word of God on the one hand, and the way that the Story it tells has a sense of continuity from Beginning to End, on the other. However, if asked how this continuity shows itself, many would be unable to provide much of an answer beyond "Well, it's all about Jesus, isn't it?" and have to fall back on the trump card of divine authorship as adequate reason for their belief.

But would it not be more helpful if that continuity could actually be demonstrated in such a compelling way that it would serve to confirm divine inspiration? After all, the Bible is not a single book. It is a compilation of sixty-six books by a variety of mostly unknown authors, compilers, editors, and revisers who wrote in a number of different languages in a variety of cultural and historical settings stretching over perhaps two thousand years. If such a "book" could be shown to hang together, surely its claim to be the Word of God would be strengthened. On the other hand, to undertake such a demonstration is a truly daunting task and should not be undertaken lightly. But that is precisely the goal of what is presented in these pages. As such, it is a work of what is known in the scholarly world as "biblical theology."[2] Although I am a pastor and a teacher, not a scholar, I have benefitted greatly from labors in this recently revitalized discipline.[3]

---

1. Ps 122:3, *Book of Common Prayer* (Coverdale's Translation), 498.

2. Charles H. H. Scobie provides a useful introduction to the scholarly debates in this area for those who are interested, in his book *The Ways of Our God*, 3–102.

3. Two of these scholars that I am especially indebted to are Geerhardus Vos and Willem VanGemeren. The former's *Biblical Theology*, first published in 1948, must surely be regarded as the classic in this field. The latter's *The Progress of Redemption*, 1988, can be regarded as a very important update

Ironically, it is divine authorship, of course, that makes it possible even to imagine that the Bible is a unified whole. Indeed, for purposes of this enquiry it is necessary to read the biblical accounts more or less "as they stand" without scholarly or critical reconstruction. This is the functional equivalent of considering them to be the product of divine inspiration. Without getting into a long discussion about the precise nature of that inspiration,[4] it will be assumed throughout this work that the canonical books of the Old and New Testaments in their present form can be relied upon to tell us the truth, even if questions remain about some of the details and the way in which they came to be recorded. Thus, for example, passages about Moses or Jesus tell the truth about them no matter who the human author/editor was or when or where he or she wrote them down.

Of course, this approach begs a host of questions and may frustrate some readers. But if it results in the emergence of a Bible that can actually be demonstrated to be "at unity with itself," the end will have justified the means. That is, reading the Bible in this fashion reveals a structural unity that can be explained only by divine inspiration and indicates that this is indeed the correct way to read the Bible. The structure *is* there. To say that it just "happens" to be present in such a widely diverse collection of writings is harder to believe than the stubborn Christian instinct that the Bible is the Word of God.

Given this methodology, it is necessary to consider a number of other underlying issues.

Unity and Harmonization

First of all, it is critical that we do not impose a false harmony upon the text. While the instinct to harmonize passages that seem contradictory is deeply Christian and has often yielded significant insights, there are reasons for being very careful when we do so. Perhaps most importantly, in our present state of knowledge, harmonizing too often threatens to compromise the integrity of the texts that we wish to reconcile.

As inheritors of the Greek-influenced Western intellectual tradition, our minds naturally seek precision; but the Hebrew mind, which God used for his revelatory purposes, was able and willing to let what we might see as "contradictions" simply stand side by side. Where the Bible does this clearly and consistently we need to yield to its rough embrace of "opposing" ideas. That is, at these points we would do well to accept the Hebrew "both/and" over the Greek "either/or" as the proper way of expressing realities that may not fit into our more precise categories. After all, we surely need to admit the possibility that the human mind may be unable to fully comprehend spiritual realities.

---

and development of Vos.

4. Cf. J. I. Packer, *Fundamentalism and the Word of God*.

Introduction

One of the most famous and divisive debates in Christianity serves as an excellent case in point: the sovereignty of God vs. the freedom of human will. To our mind these concepts seem incompatible: if God has his way, then humans cannot be free to choose, and if humans are free to choose, then God cannot be in control. Locked into this kind of dilemma Christians have developed rival theologies that stress one side or the other.[5] It is impossible to overestimate how much time, energy, and brotherly love has been sacrificed to this issue. And, unfortunately, it is sacrifice to a false god. The Bible consistently and clearly affirms both sides and we need to recognize and fully accept this fact. An approach more faithful to Scripture would hold such truths together in a kind of tension. It is not either/or, but both/and.

Generally speaking, then, we must come to terms with our human limitations when seeking the unity of Scripture and not impose a kind of cohesiveness it does not possess. We must allow it, when it speaks clearly, to form us, rather than the other way around. This is a complicated business and there are no easy answers. Sometimes a seeming contradiction can be resolved when we know more about ancient culture or history. At other times, especially when dealing with human or divine nature, our own world view must be challenged and revised when necessary. Finally, we may simply have to live in unresolved tension between opposing themes or ideas.

It is along these lines that we need to address the particular and often pressing question of how the Bible and modern science or history might be harmonized. While this is especially applicable to the creation account, there are many other points of intersection as well. It is surely instructive that the Bible has again and again proved itself accurate, especially in light of new evidence supplied by modern historical and archaeological research. This should encourage the task of such harmonization.

However, this needs to be tempered with the awareness that we are dealing with two moving targets. On the one hand we have the current consensus of scientific opinion. By definition science is always open to new evidence and/or new theories, constantly changing. On the other hand, the task of interpreting the Bible is also an ongoing process. It is not always easy to distinguish a statement of literal fact from one that was figuratively intended, for example. We may discover that our way of recording "history" is different from that of ancient cultures. Thankfully, most of the time it is clear how a passage is intended to be read and, when it is not, the context usually alerts us to the fact we need to reconsider our assumptions.

Perhaps the best attitude to maintain is that of Francis Schaeffer, who asserted that when the facts of science are fully known and our interpretation of Scripture is finally perfect, there will be "no final conflict" between them.[6] At the very least, adopting this attitude will enable us to proceed through the Bible taking its history and "science" at face value, confident that whatever questions might arise in the modern

---

5. Calvinists put the accent on God's sovereignty while Arminians prefer to emphasize human freedom.

6. Francis Schaeffer, *No Final Conflict*.

mind here and there will find resolution in ways that do not greatly disturb what we are able to discern in the text as written.

These principles will inform the discussion in the chapters that follow. Premature harmonization may satisfy those who feel the need to tie up every loose end in order to defend the complete truthfulness of the Bible. But it does so at the risk of failing to allow a particular text to tell us what *it* wants to say. The fact that it does not seem to "fit" with other statements of Scripture is not a reason to hurriedly smooth over its rough edges but rather to examine it more carefully in the hope of discovering a fuller truth. It may be our doctrinal template or our world view that needs adjusting instead.

We have, then, on the one side an assumption of the unity of the Bible, while on the other there are serious reasons to be cautious about our ability to discover the nature of that unity. Recognizing the temptation to impose an alien order on the text, we must instead let the Biblical choir sing to us in its own several voices and listen for the harmonies of the composer.

THE NATURE OF THE BIBLICAL RECORD

The Bible as "Story"

In proceeding in this manner, we must also recognize that the Bible is not primarily a collection of timeless truths, spiritual insights, or lists of what is right and wrong. While it certainly contains these things, for the most part the Bible presents them in the context of what appears to be a more or less continuous story. Like all stories it has a beginning, a middle, and an end. It also proposes to be telling a true story in the sense that the events it presents actually happened. This makes it an historical narrative as well, one which, in the end, includes all of history within its sweep. From this perspective it is evident that history itself also must have a Beginning, a Middle, and an End.

There is one important truth that makes all this even a possibility: the "author" of the Story is himself the Lord of history. When a human author creates a story she either imposes her own interpretation upon certain historical events if she is writing history or she makes up the entire plot if she is writing fiction. In the one case she has little control over "what happened" and in the other she has total control, but the events are not real.

Because God is sovereign, he can, unlike a human author, bring real events about and have them occur inside a narrative framework he himself has devised. The sovereignty of God can turn history from a series of seemingly random events into a genuine story with a plot. A breathtaking idea, is it not? And since the purpose of his activity can be summed up as "salvation," the whole process is often called "salvation history."

INTRODUCTION

Progressive Revelation

Approaching the Bible as a story allows us to see another important feature of the revelation it contains. Stories are actually made up of smaller stories built on top of one another as the plot develops toward its climax. The author of a story can be compared to a card dealer who distributes the cards one at a time until each player has a full hand. This is why reading the end of a mystery novel first is so dissatisfying: you may know "who done it" but you don't really care! And you do not care because you cannot understand its implications. Meaning and significance come through the context created by the characters and events portrayed in the earlier chapters.

As a story, the Bible can only be properly seen for what it is at the end, when all the cards have been dealt. Every stage along the way builds on what has already taken place until the whole is finally in view. George Montague provides a vivid analogy:

> [It] is like climbing a mountain. At the start of the journey what looms before us may be the brook we cross or the crest immediately before us. We would never pretend we could judge the whole lay of the mountainous area on the basis of the limited view at the beginning. But each stage is enjoyable in its own right. As we climb, new vistas appear and the old ones, while never completely lost from view, recede into a broader perspective, our earlier impressions being corrected by what we later see. When finally we reach the top, we find that nothing of what we saw along the way has been lost, but it is now only part of a vast panorama in which we see the parts in terms of the whole. To climb the mountain may take effort, but it is rewarded by the surprise of new discovery at every step, and at the summit a splendid vision.[7]

In other words, the story of the Bible unfolds in a "progressive" fashion. As we move through the account more and more details are added until the whole is complete. Because this Story is also part of God's revealing activity, it is necessary to speak of the Scriptures as "progressive revelation." The following triangle diagram serves as a simple illustration of this point:

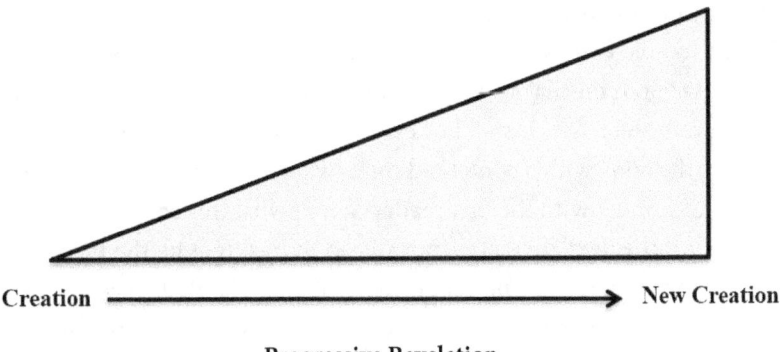

Progressive Revelation

---

7. Montague, *The Holy Spirit*, viii.

In the biblical Story we move through time from Creation to the New Creation. As we do so more and more "data" is accumulated as represented by the increasing area generated in the triangle as the time line is extended. Later events obviously take place in a wider context than do earlier ones, making their meaning somewhat easier to ascertain. At the same time the significance of earlier events develops as more data becomes available.

It is a cardinal rule of biblical interpretation that the primary meaning of a passage arises out of its original context. The first question to ask is: how would this text be understood by those to whom it was first addressed? With this in hand we can then go on to determine how it fits in wider and wider contexts. Eventually, of course, this would include the entire Bible and therefore all of salvation history. It is critical to retain the original meaning because it is the fundamental building block for the entire edifice.

For example, in Genesis 3 God simply promises that someday a descendent of the woman, at some cost to himself, will destroy the serpent who has deceived her. That is all we are told at this point and that is all that the woman would have taken to the grave. The fuller meaning of this Promise only comes into view much later in the Story. Moses uses the bronze serpent to deliver the people from a plague of snakes, which, much later, Jesus said was a precedent for his death on the cross. After Jesus' life, death, and resurrection from the dead, St. Paul proclaims that it is through the cross that Christ has gained the victory over opposing "powers and authorities."[8] But there is more. The book of Revelation's account of Satan being thrown into the lake of fire[9] supplies the last piece of the puzzle. Now the meaning of the passage in Genesis can finally be seen in all its fullness. We are at the top of Montague's mountain at last.

While the view is exhilarating and even essential, it also threatens the nature of the Story as it unfolds. It is all too easy to read the Bible from back to front like that detective novel mentioned earlier. And just like with the detective novel, the sense of biblical story is severely damaged in the process. We are tempted to import all we know from later revelation into a passage and we can lose sight of what the passage itself is actually saying. It is all too easy to allow the premature imposition of an interpretive framework to distort a text and cloud our vision.

In our example from Genesis, reading this Promise as primarily a reference to Jesus and focusing upon that would dull or even eliminate the sense of tension that it introduces into the Story. Instead of eagerly turning the page to see what happens next, we close the book with a contented sigh. By already solving the mystery, mystery dies. We do not wonder with the first readers about what this could possibly mean. We do not wonder if the next character introduced to us might be the Promised One. In fact, we do not wonder at all. And that is the problem. The Bible may be a wonder-full Story, but not to us. And we miss a significant aspect of all the stories along the way.

8. Col 2:13–15.
9. Rev 20:10.

INTRODUCTION

Thinking Inside the Triangle

For these reasons this work will try to help the reader encounter the Story for the first time, again. A lot can be gained from seeing through fresh eyes, including a sense of wonder.

Each segment of the biblical Story will be approached in a way that allows it to speak for itself first. This usually means that we will be able to look backwards to what has already been revealed but not forward to what revelation ultimately discloses. Our goal will be to understand passages "from the inside" and wait (patiently) for the more complete picture that will eventually present itself when the full context is finally given. This method honors the original authors by trying to see things as they saw them and intended them to be seen.

Although, unlike the original audience or reader, we have the complete Story in both Testaments available to us, the temptation to bring it to the table must be resisted as much as possible if we are to remain "inside" the "Story so far." Undoubtedly this will leave a lot of questions to be answered and a lot of rough edges to be smoothed out. However, it is precisely these qualities that will draw us further into the text and open up new treasures of meaning. Let the text speak with its own voice as much as possible first. We can better see how it contributes to the whole from a later perspective.

To return to our "triangle" diagram for visual assistance, as we move through time the triangle increases in size, representing the increasing amount of revealed material we have to work with:

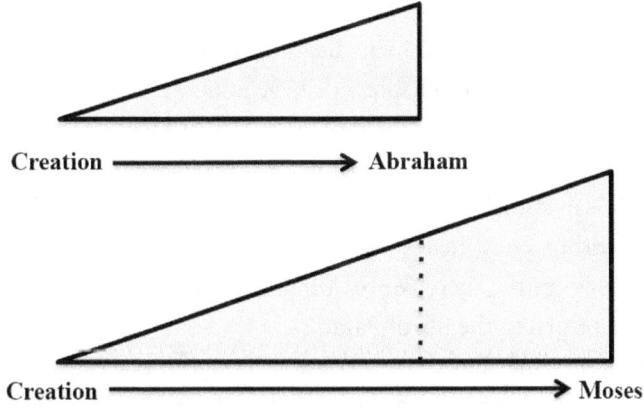

Stages of Progressive Revelation

For Abraham we have just the tip, but by the time of Moses the triangle has grown much larger, encompassing the time from Creation through Abraham and up to Moses. At each stop along our journey we will try to think only "inside" the newly expanded triangle that has been created. In this fashion we will be able to recapture the sense of story and its progressive nature and once again experience something of its drama and mystery. And who knows what we might discover in the process.

The Promise-Fulfillment Dynamic

In the beginning of many a medieval tale a soothsayer foresees greatness for a newborn child and the rest of the story is about how this eventually becomes a reality. The reader "knows" that the story will be shaped by the prediction. When things are going badly s/he will hang in there anticipating better things to come. When events begin to conform to the prediction s/he will understand that they are finally coming to their proper end.

The Bible is full of divine promises and they share this dynamic ability, only for real. As soon as God makes a promise a tension immediately arises between that promise and present reality. Because it is God who has made the promise, people and events are directed toward its fulfillment. The promise sets things in motion and determines their course.

It is the Promise of salvation, of course, which gives direction and focus to the overall narrative of the Scriptures. It is in this direction that human hope must be focused. We are lost in the world and this great Promise turns us in the right direction and even draws us ever closer to its realization. But what is this Promise, specifically? What does this "salvation" actually look like?

The Bible as Abraham's Story

The biblical Story is clearly framed by its Beginning in the first three chapters of Genesis and its End in the last three chapters of Revelation. It moves from the creation of the heavens and the earth, the placement of humanity in a wonderfully fruitful garden in perfect communion with God, and the loss of it all because of human disobedience. It concludes with "salvation," humanity restored to the presence of God in a new Jerusalem that is set within a new heaven and a new earth. The End comes full circle, in a way, back to the Beginning, thereby providing us with at least a basic understanding of "salvation" as a return to the life of Paradise.

Although many Christian thinkers down through the ages have noted this Beginning-End correspondence and have presented the Story from this perspective,[10] there are, as we shall see later, significant discontinuities between the Beginning and the End as well. But we get the drift: the course of salvation history is a journey from Creation to the New Creation, from what was lost in the old to its recovery in the New.

This "Return to Eden" theme is clearly one of the strands of biblical DNA binding the Story together, providing us with an indication of its fundamental unity. We have

---

10. Cf. John Milton, *Paradise Lost* and *Paradise Regained*, from the 17th century.

Introduction

a definite relationship between the Beginning and the End. Even with only these two points on our compass we can get a good sense direction for the biblical narrative.

Having a beginning and an end is necessary, but it is not enough for a complete story. It is like standing at the top of a large bridge abutment on one side of a great river and staring across an empty space to another abutment barely visible on the other side. You see the Beginning and the End and know what direction to go in, but you have no means of getting across. The construction site at your feet is full of the material for the bridge, but how does it all go together? What you need is the designer's blueprint so that a structure can be built to span the distance between the abutments. Similarly, a story cannot emerge from random events: they must be held together in a connected whole, by a "plot."

Upon further consideration, the Return to Eden theme might still serve as a strong candidate for the overall plot of Scripture. It would be possible to see how the Story moved along from pier to pier by gauging how and to what degree each episode bears the stamp of Eden. Our question might be: does this segment bear witness to a special and fruitful place in which humanity enjoys a harmonious relationship with God? By "measuring" this we could determine whether we were going in the right direction and even how close we were to the end.

While this approach has obvious merit, it is not able by itself to bear the weight of the entire biblical narrative. For one thing, the Return to Eden theme, while strongly implied in Scripture, is never explicitly endorsed either. It cannot be considered a promise of God and so lacks the ability to move the Story along. For another, the Return to Eden motif is actually best seen as a subsection of another greater and overarching motif that *is* explicitly supported by the Word of God and does come in the form of a Promise.

These pages will attempt to demonstrate that the Covenant that God made with Abraham provides the basic framework for God's entire plan. Its provisions will be seen to undergird the sweep of the biblical narrative, supplying its fundamental structure and joining each portion to the others, supplying connective tissue to the entire Story.[11] *Incorporating, as has been noted, the Return to Eden strand, this great Promise provides the whole of Scripture with its "direction and focus."*

The main reason for concentrating on the Abrahamic Covenant is simply that the Bible itself repeatedly points us in this direction. God's saving activity is seen in his unfailing faithfulness to one or more of its basic terms: Abraham will possess many

---

11. This is an admittedly bold claim and should be read in the context of the following helpful comments from Paul House: "We should give up arguing that one theme and one theme only is the central theme of the Bible and highlight major themes that allow for other ideas as subpoints. . . . Any theme that links much of the Bible must be broad and must not be rejected for being broad. A broad theme is not the canon's only theme: it is a centering theme. As long as the major theme is clearly discernible in several parts of the canon, as long as it is charted alongside other major themes, as long as it is treated as an important part of a whole instead of being the whole, then it should be welcomed, used and critiqued." House, Paul R., "Biblical Theology," 276.

offspring, they will possess the land of Canaan and the nations will be blessed through them.[12] For the purposes of this book, the covenantal provisions will be referred to in rather shorter form as: 1) Land 2) Many Descendants and 3) Blessing to All Nations. Adding these to our triangle diagram we have the following simplified representation of the idea that the provisions of this Covenant underlie the entire Story:

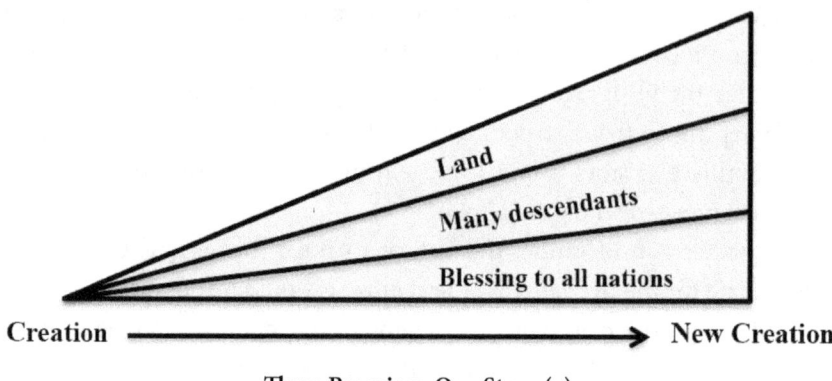

Three Promises: One Story (1)

In the Old Testament narrative, almost all of which is the focus of this volume, it is the first of these, the Land, that is most on the surface most of the time: indeed, it dominates the narrative in a kind of refrain, as in this example:

> I will bring you into the land which I swore to give to Abraham, to Isaac, and to Jacob; and I will give it to you for a heritage: I am Yahweh. (Exodus 6:8)

This is taken from the central story of the Exodus, which is especially concerned with the Promised Land. Its theme is how the children of Abraham are brought out of captivity in Egypt and set on their way back to Canaan. And this focus on the Land continues for the rest of the Old Testament portion of the Story. The Land has to be conquered, occupied, and governed. Eventually it is divided and then lost as the people of Israel go into exile, only to straggle back some seventy years later. It is clearly a connecting theme.

This is not to say that the other two Promises are entirely absent, but that their presence in the Story is more visible at some points than it is at others. For example, if we refer to Land-dominated Exodus once again, we note that its narrative is nevertheless set in motion by the fact that Many Descendants has reached a point of significant fulfillment (making the Egyptians anxious), a fact that then recedes largely into the background. As for Blessing to All Nations, we can see it come to some fulfillment during the world-famous reign of Solomon, but it also quickly fades away. Later still, both "fulfillments" prove to be mere tastes of what the prophets envision as the final reality for the nation. Indeed, as the diagram above implies, all of the Promises

---

12. Cf. Gen 12:1–3; 15:4–20; 17:1–8; 22:15–18.

INTRODUCTION

develop over time, filling in more and more of the blanks in our understanding until the end, when they reach their full and final expression.

There, suddenly and vividly, what had previously been glimpsed only in hints and shadows erupts into brilliant Technicolor as the inclusion of the nations in God's glorious future for Judah and Israel is envisioned! Indeed, it shall be argued in these pages that this event has been the primary goal of the divine purpose for Israel all along and that the other two Promises are best seen as means to that end, even though they, too, are transformed in the end.

In this context, it seems especially ironic that the prophetic revelations of this future come just as "the nations" devastate the Land and most of the few survivors are about to be exiled to Babylon. All Three Promises no doubt strike them as terribly hollow at this moment, but through the prophets they are emphatically assured that fulfillment will come in God's time.

When we turn to the New Testament and look for its links to the Promises made to Abraham we are presented with a somewhat different situation. In general terms, at least, the connection is made perfectly clear: the New Testament explicitly witnesses that the salvation that Jesus brings is the outworking of the Abrahamic Covenant.

St. Luke records that the earliest responses of faithful Jews to the coming of Jesus coupled this event to Abraham. Mary, for example, sings in what has become known as the "Magnificat":

> [God] has given help to Israel, his servant, that he might remember mercy,
>> as he spoke to our fathers,
>> to Abraham and his offspring forever. (1:54–55)

Similarly, John the Baptist's father, Zechariah, proclaims that the time of salvation has arrived, the time for God

> to to show mercy toward our fathers,
>> to remember his holy covenant,
> the oath which he swore to Abraham our father,
> to grant to us that we, being delivered out of the hand of our enemies,
>> should serve him without fear,
> in holiness and righteousness before him all the days of our life. (1:72–75)

Jesus himself, again according to Luke, characterizes those introduced into the kingdom as (true) children of Abraham[13] and St. Paul tells the Galatians:

> If you are Christ's, then you are Abraham's offspring and heirs according to promise. (3:29)

These and many other references establish that the New Testament teaches that the Christ-event is the fulfillment of the Covenant with Abraham, proclaiming

---

13. Luke 19:9 (Zaccheus) and 13:16 (the woman bent double).

especially that those who believe in Jesus are the true inheritors of "the promise" of salvation. It is obtained not by the works of the Law, but by grace alone, through faith.

While all of this is widely understood by most Christians, if we remind ourselves that the salvation promised to Abraham *comes in the form of the Three Promises*, we might wonder what happened to *them* in the New Testament. In the Old Testament they constitute what "salvation" *is*, but where are they in the New? Perhaps it sees its continuity with Abraham in another sense altogether and has another definition of "salvation." We certainly seem to be confronted with something that might look like this:

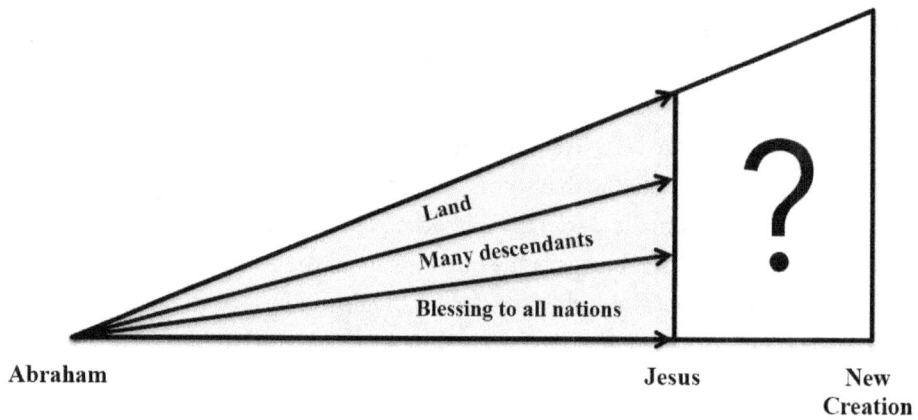

The Three Promises and Jesus?

Do the Promises really only carry the Story up to Jesus and then mysteriously disappear, perhaps eclipsed by the "Behold I make all things new" of Christ? While this is possible, of course, it would seriously weaken the Christian claim of continuity between the Testaments. It would also certainly be a shock to Abraham, not to mention the rest of the Old Testament saints! It would make more sense all around if the Promises find specific expression in the message of the New as well as the Old Testament.

The second volume of this work will demonstrate just how this is, in fact, the case. In so doing we will gain: a) specific content to our understanding of just how Abraham and Jesus/NT are connected; b) a deeper knowledge of the connecting tissue between the Old Testament and Jesus/NT; and c) a broadened perspective on the Christian meaning of salvation when Land, Many Descendants and Blessing to All Nations are duly factored in.

The present volume will show how the Promises are actually already reimagined within the Old Testament itself. Toward the end of the period it covers, the prophets put before Israel a vision of a New Creation to be initiated by God at some point in the future. In it, the Promises can be seen to be amazingly transformed but still very

INTRODUCTION

much recognizable as Land, Many Descendants, and Blessing to All Nations. Visually we might represent this very simply as follows:

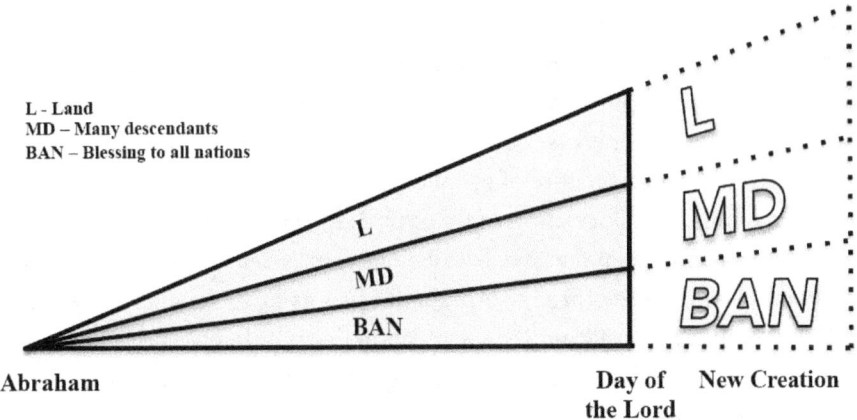

The Transformed Promises of the Prophetic Vision

It is this transformation that provides the best clue for understanding how the Promises are changed with the coming of Jesus. Reading the teachings of the New Testament about salvation in Christ through the lens of the prophetic vision enables us to see that they, too, are in continuity with the Promises. They emerge, as it were, from the waters of baptism as new creatures in Christ but still very much identifiable as Land, Many Descendants, and a Blessing to All Nations. The Promises have not come to an end, but to a wonderful transformation that itself anticipates an even more wonderful change to be undergone in the New Creation. From this perspective we can begin to see more clearly the possibility that the Abrahamic Covenant gives structure to the Story from Abraham all the way through Christ into the New Creation. The following diagram seeks to express all this in visual form:

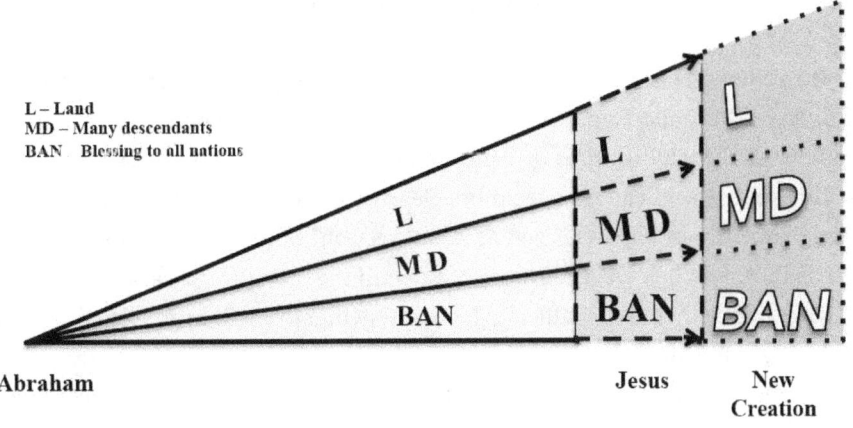

Three Promises: Three Manifestations

13

This understanding of the transformation of the Promises is consistent with the New Testament witness that fulfillment of prophecy is not to be understood simplistically. That is, the relationship of a prophecy to its fulfillment is not necessarily, or even usually, one-to-one. The New Testament itself shows us repeatedly that a fulfillment often transcends its original meaning. That is, the fulfillment goes beyond a strictly literal reading of the prophecy but not so far as to lose connection with it altogether. You can still see how the one arises out of the other, even if it is in an unexpected way. This just seems to be in the nature of prophecy. It should come as no surprise that we find it evident in the transformation of the Promises by the prophets themselves.

There is one more step that needs to be taken in order to complete the picture. Once we have begun to see through Abraham's eyes as he looks ahead, we can turn around to face the Beginning and see the creation in a new light. And what we notice is that the Three Promises are already there, giving their distinct shape to "the way things are supposed to be" in the earliest chapters of the Bible. The Promises, it turns out, are in fact operative from the get-go, built into the very fabric of creation. When they are given to Abraham, they simply bring to the surface and define for the first time what God had in mind for humanity in the Beginning.

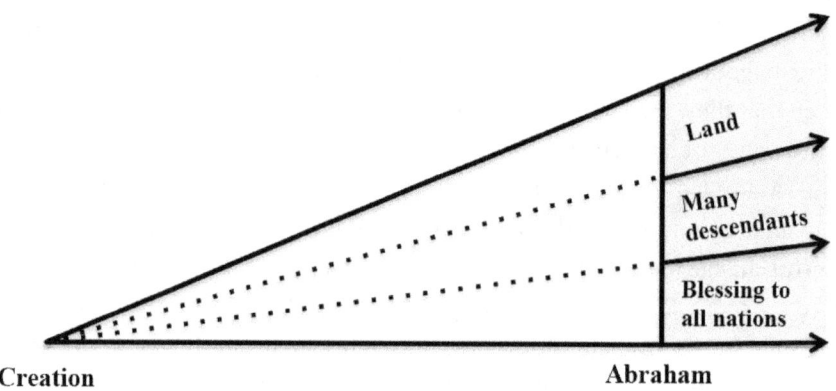

The Three Promises Before Abraham

We can now see the entire picture of what is being suggested in this book. The Beginning, Middle, and End of the Story are *all* Abraham-shaped, each deeply resonating with the Three Promises of Land, Many Descendants, and Blessing to All Nations. This being so, we can now see more clearly why, as was stated earlier, the Return to Eden theme is best characterized as a "subsection" of the overarching structure of the entire Bible.[14] When we find traces of Eden in the Story, we are also finding Abraham's DNA. Since these two naturally belong together, we will be explicitly including both in our approach.

The following illustration incorporates Creation into the now-complete picture:

---

14. See 9, above.

Introduction

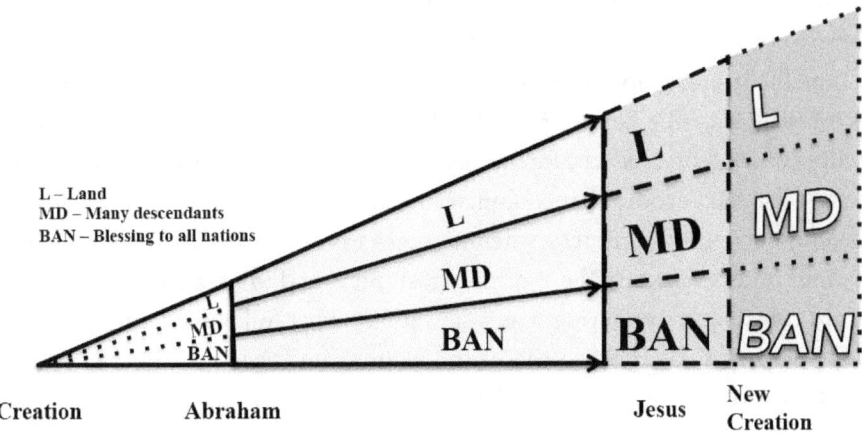

Three Promises: One Story (2)

Here is our bridge, complete, in the bosom of Abraham—at least in theory. But will it bear the weight of the biblical evidence?

THE SHAPE OF THINGS TO COME

Now that the main thrust of this book has been outlined, a word needs to be said about the procedure that will be followed.

The Story, the Whole Story, and Nothing but the Story

In seeking to show how the Bible is linked together as a Story we will necessarily confine ourselves primarily to the narrative portions of Scripture. Other material will be incorporated only when it has direct impact upon the course of the Story. Of necessity, much of the Bible, such as Psalms and Wisdom literature, will remain beyond the scope of this work. It is to be hoped that the reader will be encouraged to read the entire Bible and understand it better once s/he has grasped its essential narrative shape. It is all the Word of God and we can ill afford to ignore any of it. The fact that we have done so here is legitimate cause for concern and an opportunity to remember that all human endeavors are provisional. It is, however, a beginning. And, I would argue, a necessary one.

Each chapter in what follows will cover a major episode of the biblical Story. While the determination of what is "major" is always somewhat subjective, in most cases I am confident that the choice has been suggested by the form of the narrative itself. In any event, the entire sweep of the Story will eventually be under consideration and this will help to provide any necessary corrective.

For the purposes of this telling of the Story, the divine name will often be rendered as YHWH. This is the way it appears in the original Hebrew, a language which used only consonants when written, the vowels being supplied by the reader. Within the Jewish community the Name became considered so holy that it was never said and over time the language forgot what vowels to insert! Although most English translations translate it as "the Lord," I have decided mostly to leave it in its original form in my telling of the Story. Its very foreignness may help inject a sense of fresh encounter into a text that has become all too familiar to many. It also has the very great advantage deepening our sense of mystery when it comes to the Divine. However, the biblical quotations in this work use the World English Bible and this translation includes the standard consonants, rendering it as "Yahweh." In what follows, an attempt has been made to employ YHWH when that is the divine name used in the biblical material under discussion.

Each chapter of this work is presented under headings that are explained below. A reader in a hurry could read only "Major Developments" and "Perspectives" in each chapter and get a fair sense of how the Bible hangs together as a story. But that, of course, would be cheating! For reasons that will become obvious, chapters 15 and 16 will vary from this format.

Suggested Reading

It is extremely important to the author that the reader sees that what is being said in this book arises out of the biblical text itself. A "Suggested Reading" is therefore included at the beginning of each chapter in order to reference the portion of the biblical narrative under consideration. It is strongly recommended that this be read before, and maybe even after, the chapter itself is read. For this same reason, when the Bible is quoted, the chapter and verse is bracketed in the text itself, rather than being footnoted. To lessen distraction, whenever a heading within a chapter indicates that a particular book of the Bible is under consideration, biblical citations from that book do not include its name.

Major Developments

Each chapter begins with a bulleted summary of the main events and characters that will be covered. This is intended to orient the reader to what is coming and provide something of a basic context.

Perspectives

This unit is intended to provide the reader with a broad overview of the events covered in the chapter and how they might be seen from "inside the triangle." The emphasis will be on how the narrative is being developed, on continuing themes and on major "connective tissue" joining it to the preceding narrative.

Introduction

The Story

This main section of each chapter outlines the current section of the Story in some detail, emphasizing the central characters and events and relating them to one another in an orderly fashion. As this latter task sometimes involves blending one scriptural account into another, care has been taken to ensure, as much as possible, that the picture that emerges reflects what actually happened from the Bible's perspective. The more important elements of story, especially drama and mystery, will be highlighted in the process.

In the Bosom of Abraham

Each chapter will conclude with an analysis of how the current segment of the biblical Story has borne the image of the Abrahamic Covenant. Entitled "In the Bosom of Abraham", this section will provide cumulative evidence for our main thesis. Probing a little further beneath the surface and asking specific questions of the biblical text, it will progressively lay bare its underlying structure. Given their importance, it is necessary to understand how these critical questions were developed.

The first three simply represent the terms of the Abrahamic Covenant itself. We will be asking "Where in this portion of the narrative can we see the Promises of 1) Land; 2) Many Descendants; and 3) Blessing to All Nations, and how are they at work?" If they are absent it may be possible to discover reasons for their absence in the Story itself.

We will also be testing for the Return to Eden theme throughout the biblical narrative, keeping in mind our contention that it is an expression of the Abrahamic Covenant. As such, it can provide a fuller sense of how that Covenant underlies the biblical Story. Our inquiry will therefore include three questions designed to detect Edenic qualities in the Story.

The first of these will be an additional feature added to the "Land" category already discussed. We rightly think of "Eden" as a special place in which God and humanity dwell in accord. Are there any places (e.g. Mt. Sinai) in this narrative that share this feature? If so, we could have a sense of how close we are to Eden. Therefore the "Land" discussion will expand to "Land/Place."

Two other full Edenic qualities will be explored in their own sections: "Fruitfulness" will look for appearances of the abundance that so evidently characterized Eden. And, given the atmosphere in the garden, "Relationship" attempts to measure the degree of harmony between God and humanity evident in each segment of the Story. Again, both of these are measures of how far we are along the road home, providing at least provisional answers to those perennial backseat questions: "Are we there yet? How far is it?"

Finally, "In the Bosom of Abraham" addresses a somewhat more theological question. As mentioned above, the connection between Christ and Abraham has commonly been expressed in terms of "salvation by grace alone." For generations of Christians, God's Covenant with Abraham has been identified as the covenant of "grace." That is, Abraham was blessed of God without any reference to his "earning" that blessing: it was pure gift. It is upon this foundation that St. Paul builds his famous doctrine that we are justified by faith and not by works.[15]

At the same time, throughout both Old and New Testaments God's people are constantly being called to a life of obedience. In fact, disobedience is so serious that, if not dealt with, it can lead to exclusion from the blessing. Many have noted the tension this creates: if we are saved by grace alone and not by works, why are these works (of obedience) then necessary? How does obedience fit into our salvation?

This study, focused as it is on discovering Abraham's influence on the entire message of the Bible, provides an ideal opportunity to address this important issue. The specific question we will ask arises out of a dispute among contemporary New Testament scholars over the nature of the religion in the Holy Land in the time of Christ. Was it truly characterized by "legalism," or "salvation by works," as many Christians believe? Various scholars now hold that many Jews of the day typically held, rather, that "We are saved or made righteous by grace but are called to maintain this condition through obedience."[16] In this understanding, obedience properly *follows* salvation by God's act and keeps us saved once we are saved.

While the historical question regarding first-century Judaism will ultimately be settled only by scholars, here this formulation can serve to help us clarify the relationship between grace and works that is presented throughout the biblical Story. We will be asking: *to what extent do the various segments of the Story conform to this pattern of "saved by grace, maintained by obedience"?* This will be our sixth and final question, addressed under the heading "Grace/Obedience." It is to be hoped that in so doing our understanding of what it means to be "in the bosom of Abraham" will be enhanced.

Summary

"In the Bosom of Abraham," as the last section of each chapter, will examine each segment of the Story in reference to:

1. The Land/Place
2. Many Descendants
3. A Blessing to All Nations

---

15. See Rom 4.

16. This idea, referred to as "covenantal nomism," can be found in the so-called "new perspective on Paul" and traced back to E.P. Sanders in his book *Paul and Palestinian Judaism*.

4. Fruitfulness

5. Relationship

6. Grace/Obedience

The following diagram incorporates all of these categories into our familiar triangle in order to illustrate how, from this perspective, Abraham's fingerprints are indeed all over the entire biblical Story:

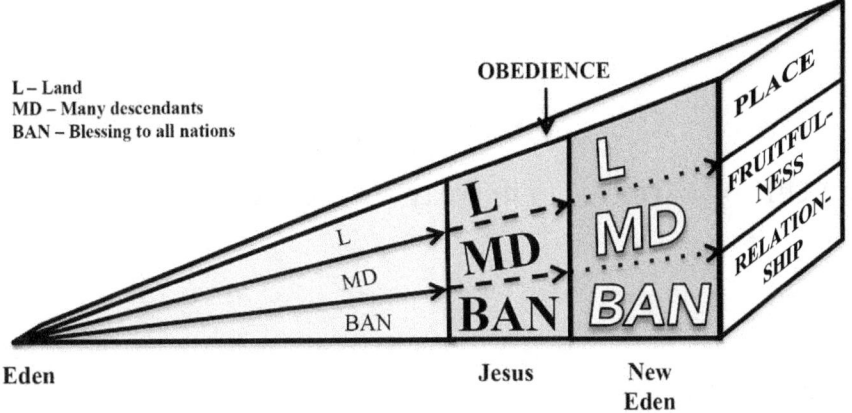

Abraham's Fingerprints

In this diagram we see the that the Return to Eden motif gives depth and dimension to the Abrahamic Covenant through the specific relationships of the categories to one another. The strong affinity between Land and Place suggests such a scheme: the Land being enhanced by Eden's sense of being a special Place where God and humans enjoy harmonious relationship. "Many Descendants" with "Fruitfulness" go hand in hand as well, the former being somewhat dependent on the latter. Connecting "Relationship" with "Blessing to All Nations," while admittedly less obvious than the other pairings, reflects the general truth that the fundamental blessing bestowed on humanity is a proper relationship with YHWH, seen originally in Eden. As far as "Obedience" is concerned, to one degree or another it is present through the entire Story, as we shall discover.

However, it must be kept in mind that the one to one relationships depicted between the various categories are only tentative. The categories themselves are abstracted out of biblical material that is extremely complex and often resistant to easy classification. In reality they intertwine, overlap, and blend into each other in a bewildering variety of ways.

2

The Beginning
The Gift of Paradise (The Way Things Are Supposed to Be)

Suggested Reading

Genesis 1–2.

MAJOR DEVELOPMENTS

- Creation of heaven and earth
- Creation of humankind in the image of God
- Human Mandate to be fruitful and rule over the earth
- Seventh day blessed as a day of rest
- Provision of Eden
- Prohibition against eating the fruit of the Tree of the Knowledge of Good and Evil
- Creation of the woman
- Institution of marriage

PERSPECTIVES

Introduction

The beginning of any good story sets the scene, introduces the main characters and places before the reader the issue or situation that needs to be resolved. So it is with the Bible. Its first three chapters set its overall direction much like a primitive rocket's trajectory is determined by its orientation on the launching pad.

The "lift off" can be divided into two basic movements. The first, related in the first two chapters of Genesis, tells the story of the creation of the world just the way God intended it. The scene is set with impressive and direct simplicity while the central characters of the Story are introduced and provided with the "stage" upon which the drama will unfold. The second movement, related in Genesis 3, tells how that original Creation came to be spoiled through human sin. It also records God's hint that eventual triumph will come through the "seed" of the woman, cuing the reader to begin to look for the arrival of this person. Because both movements are essential to a full understanding of the Beginning of the Story, this chapter deals extensively with the first and chapter 3 with the second.

The narrative respecting the first movement, the creation of the way things are supposed to be, is also given in two distinct segments. First, we have an overview of the Creation up to and including the appearance of the man and woman. The Story then zeroes in on the first couple and their situation in some detail. In this way the reader naturally gets the impression that humanity is the end of Creation, both as its final act and its purpose.

The Creator God

With the story of Creation we are plunged into the action. At first God is the sole actor upon the stage, going about the work of creation, starting with the building blocks of life and then various life-forms in ascending order of kind. This culminates with the creation of humans who are distinguished from all others by being made in the image of God himself and given a special "place" both literally and figuratively: in the garden and in personal relationship with the Creator. They are also set over all the other creatures and given the fruit of the earth for their food. Clearly the entire purpose of the Creation is to be "for" humanity.

God, in the very act of creation, is beginning to define himself. Beyond the obvious fact that he is "the God who creates," these verses also reveal that he is a "transcendent" God who exists independently of his creation and is not bound to it. That is to say, "biblical theism" is to be distinguished from "pantheism" (everything is God) and "panentheism" (God is in everything). Other aspects of his character reveal themselves in the nature of the various acts of Creation and are detailed as they arise in "The Story" below.

All that God creates is pronounced "very good" and we are ready for "happily ever after." Into this idyllic picture, however, is introduced an element of uncertainty and tension. We are told that in order for this situation to persist, the humans are required to obey just one simple rule. The question then becomes: will they, or won't they?

The Nature of the Creation Account

Before moving on into the shape of the Story here, we need to note that it bears the sign of having been very carefully crafted, so much so that it is difficult to escape the conclusion that we are dealing with something which is ". . . more than simple straightforward narration" as Andy M. Reimer puts it. He goes on to elaborate, referring to the original Hebrew text:

> For example, the narrator's play with sevens in a story that covers seven days: seven words in the opening sentence, fourteen words in the second, thirty-five words to narrate the first day, "God" used thirty-five times, "earth" and "heaven" twenty-one times respectively, "God saw that it was good" seven times.[1]

We may well concur with Reimer's conclusion that the orderliness of Creation is reflected in the orderliness of this account and, in fact, ". . . represents the narrator's tribute to a God of design and beauty."[2] At the same time it may constitute a hint that such an account is not meant to be read in a "scientific" or literalistic fashion. If we do, we will be puzzled by the fact that the creation of days (morning and evening) as well as vegetation takes place before the creation of the sun, which, as we know, is needed for both. But the language itself is so straightforward and normal that we are reluctant to conclude that we are simply dealing with poetry adrift on its own metaphors.

Indeed, figurative and ordinary elements are often intertwined. This is no ordinary garden. The only plants actually mentioned are trees. Some seem to be normal trees while others, specifically the "tree of life and the tree of the knowledge of good and evil" (2:9), have a decidedly symbolic element. This same odd mixture of literal and symbolic may also be reflected in the description of the garden's location. We know of the Tigris and the Euphrates rivers, but of the Pishon and the Gishon we can only guess. Are they to be taken symbolically?

It seems to this writer that there is especially an irreducible element of symbol about Eden and the events that took place in it. We see it most forcibly in the talking serpent of ch. 3, the only animal in the Bible that has this ability.[3] At the same time this serpent is, in the passage under consideration, the "father" of all the ordinary serpents with which we are familiar. All of this seems to signal that the actions portrayed are somewhat symbolic in nature but represent real events nevertheless. It is therefore possible to derive proper implications from this text while at the same time avoiding

---

1. Reimer, "In the Beginning," 33. Reimer's article is an excellent short introduction to the issues of interpreting the creation account and is based on the work of the Old Testament scholar, Bruce K. Waltke.

2. Ibid., 34.

3. In the Story of Balaam's donkey in Num. 22, the unusual quality of the event is highlighted and we are told specifically that "Yahweh opened the donkey's mouth" (v.28); in 2 Pet. 2:16 the same animal is said to be "mute" This is not a talking animal but an animal miraculously enabled to speak on one occasion.

dogmatism regarding its literary nature. In this way one can be faithful to the double-sided quality of the narrative.[4]

THE STORY (PART ONE—THE BIG PICTURE [1:1—2:4])

Six Days of Creation (1:1—2:1)

INTRODUCTION

In remarkably concise order this passage sets before us the entire sweep of God's creative activity. The very first verse serves nicely to both introduce and summarize what is to follow: "In the beginning God created the heavens and the earth." In fact, it is basically repeated as a bookend for the entire section (2:1, 4).

The use of "the heavens and earth" in this way suggests that the whole of creation falls into one or the other category. Clearly the author also intends to convey the idea that whatever "is," is a result of what God has done. He existed before the creation and

---

4. The unusual juxtaposition of realistic and symbolic language seen in Gen 1–3 is more characteristic of the prophetic portions of the Bible. For example, the Tree of Life reappears in the book of Revelation in what seems to be a highly symbolic description of the new Jerusalem: "He showed me a river of water of life, clear as crystal, proceeding out of the throne of God and of the Lamb, in the middle of its street. On this side of the river and on that was the tree of life, bearing twelve kinds of fruits, yielding its fruit every month. The leaves of the tree were for the healing of the nations." (22:1–2)

Such language does not surprise us in this context. After all, how else is a prophet to describe a reality (in this case, the world to come) that lies beyond his normal range of understanding (this present world)?

Of course, this makes our task of interpretation that much more difficult. It is often impossible to determine what is symbolic and what is to be taken literally. At the very least, our views should be tempered with a significant degree of provisionality, not to mention humility.

Could it be that the "prophetic" language of Gen 1–3 provides an important clue as to the genre of the passage, and thus how it should be approached by the interpreter? That is, it is "prophecy," and should be treated as such.

This may seem like a startling suggestion at first glance because we are accustomed to think of prophecy as looking *forward* to a different world. But surely the same linguistic and conceptual challenges would face a "prophet" who looked *back* to a different world. Most of what we read in these chapters must have been received through a vision or a direct revelation of some sort. There were no eyewitnesses to Creation! Just as there are no eyewitnesses to the future.

Another argument in favor of this view is that there are a wide variety of interpretations of this portion of Scripture among Christians who are committed to its inspiration as the very Word of God. What can account for this? When we look for a similar pattern of disagreement we find it constantly hovering over the prophetic passages.

What is being suggested here is, that for these reasons at least, Gen 1–3 should be considered as a kind of prophecy-in-reverse and thus subject to the same set of rules by which other prophecy is interpreted.

Taking this approach would have the advantage of helping Christians to relax about the strangeness of the passage. It is not history, it is prophecy. We should expect this kind of language.

We could also relax about the difficulties of interpretation and our subsequent differences of opinion. Just as we seem to be learning to hold onto our interpretations of prophecy more loosely while still recognizing the validity of others, so also we could agree to disagree in this area.

Creating Order Out of Chaos

When creation began the earth was already in existence although "formless and empty" (v. 2). The exact meaning of this phrase is obscure. We might think of the chaotic opening scene from the film *Terminator 2: Judgment Day*, set in a world devastated by a nuclear holocaust, but with the distinction that here it appears to refer to a watery wilderness. We are told of "darkness over the surface of the deep," a darkness that is now confronted by the RUACH (Heb. "wind," "breath" or "spirit") of God hovering over the scene.

And then God begins to create: light, sky, dry ground, and vegetation; planets, sea creatures, and birds; land creatures and humans—all on successive days. Here the reader gets the strong impression that God is in each case creating something out of nothing, speaking things into existence as it were. Traditionally this idea has been expressed in the Latin phrase: *'creatio ex nihilo.'* R. K. Harrison points out that it rightly

> ... rules out the idea that matter is eternal, and also rejects any kind of dualism in the universe in which another entity, power or existence stands over against God and outside his control.[5]

Such implications must be ruled tentative at this point, however, because, as we have seen, the Creation does not begin with "nothing" but with "something," something that is at the same time "formless and empty," dark and watery. The account itself emphasizes rather that God is bringing order out of disorder. As Rolf Rendtorff puts it:

> In Genesis 1 the concern is not with the contrast between Nothing and Created but with the Chaos-Cosmos polarity.[6]

That which is "formless and empty" is transformed into a purposeful and harmonious universe. It is an orderly conversion of disorder into order. Thus God emphatically shows himself to be the God of order.

Speaking Things into Existence

It must also be noted that God's first recorded act is to speak. He is "the God who speaks," whose nature it is to communicate. But his speaking is also acting, for his word has the power to bring about whatever it proclaims. In turn, this shows that God is all-powerful, omnipotent. What could be more powerful than a being who merely

---

5. Harrison, "Creation," I:1023.
6. Rendtorf, *Canonical Hebrew Bible*, 418–19.

commands and the entire universe comes into existence? Awe is surely the only appropriate response.

Fill It Up

God's creative activity is cumulative as well. It begins with three great divisions: light from darkness (morning from evening), water from water (with an expanse, or "sky," between), and land from sea. The resulting land, sky, and sea are then filled in turn: the land with vegetation, the sky with sun, moon, stars, and birds, and the sea with "every living and moving thing with which the water teems" (1:20). On the sixth day the land is the focus again as it produces livestock, creeping things, and wild animals at God's command. The natural environment is now ready for the creatures for whom it was made.

The Creation of Humanity

In a separate act of creation, but still on the sixth day, humanity enters the scene. It is impossible, first of all, to ignore the way in which the formation of the man and woman (1:26–30) is distinguished from the other acts of Creation. Even its literary form is different as the author switches here (v. 27) to poetry in the Hebrew (its first occurrence in the Bible).

In addition, God clearly takes a more "personal" interest in this aspect of Creation. Instead of "Let there be . . ." we have "Let us make man in our image, in our likeness . . ." (v. 26). Many have suggested that the mysterious use of the plural hints either at some kind of undefined "plurality" in God, but perhaps he is simply addressing the angelic hosts.[7]

IN THE IMAGE OF GOD

Introduction

Just what "made in the image of God" means has been the subject of much discussion down through the centuries, much of which reflects then-current ideas of what distinguishes humans from other animals (such as reason or language or the possession of a "soul"). This approach often fails to take seriously the evidence provided in the narrative itself and therefore must be considered more speculative than exegetical (i.e., arising out of the text). A careful examination of the passage reveals that this "image of God" manifests itself in two important aspects of human existence.

---

7. Skarsaune, *In the Shadow of the Temple*, 343, points out that in Jewish literature the reference is to God talking to his "Wisdom." Countless Christian commentators have naturally seen here an intimation of the Holy Trinity.

As Rulers

Verses 26 and 28 proclaim humanity as having "dominion" over the earth and all its creatures.[8] The overall weight of this narrative, of course, shows that God is the ultimate ruler, but here he gives a kind of "regency" to human beings in order that they might serve as his agents, ruling on his behalf and responsible to him for how they carry out their Mandate. In other words, the context suggests that the image of God which humanity bears is seen in the fact that both are rulers over creation. Psalm 8 both celebrates and wonders at this exalted position (esp. v. 5–8 which are, of course, drawn from the Creation account):

> For you have made him a little lower than the angels,
>   and crowned him with glory and honor.
> You make him ruler over the works of your hands.
>   You have put all things under his feet:
> All sheep and cattle,
>   yes, and the animals of the field,
> the birds of the sky, the fish of the sea,
>   and whatever passes through the paths of the seas.

From the point of view of the Bible, then, humanity, while very much a part of the environment, is nevertheless to be distinguished from it by being "over" it as ruler and, as such, to "subdue" it (v. 28) in order that it may fulfill its Mandate to be fruitful. Apparently the earth is somewhat wild and needs taming in order to fulfill its purpose. In this way our ordering of chaos reflects the image of God in us, but it is always secondary to God's ordering.

As Male-and-Female

Verse 27 ties the image of God to the male-and-femaleness of "man." This suggests that it is not the male alone or female alone that is made in the image of God, but both *in their togetherness*. It is as if God has drawn a picture of the divine self, torn it in half, and given one part to the male and the other to the female. Each bears something of that image but it is incomplete until combined with the other. Humanity, God-like in its constitution as male-and-female, creates other humans in its own image so that the divine Mandate will be fulfilled:

> Be fruitful, multiply, fill the earth, and subdue it. Have dominion over the fish of the sea, over the birds of the sky, and over every living thing that moves on the earth. (v. 28)

---

8. Cf. Rendtorf, *Canonical Hebrew Bible*, 428.

Whereas the aspect of "dominion" sets humanity somewhat apart from the other creatures, in this instance, the image of God binds humanity to all the other creatures, also made male and female.

A Life-Support System

It is no coincidence that this account indicates that not just humans, but all living creatures are to thrive on the earth. The same is true of the great fruitfulness implicit in the way the author calls attention to the way in which plants bear seeds within themselves to reproduce "after their kind" (1:12) and then repeats this latter phrase in reference to sea creatures, birds, and animals. For all of these are part of a world intended as a life-support system for humanity and, as such, must keep pace with its growth. It is clear from vv. 28–30 that this is all a gift of God to humanity for its own thriving. At first only its vegetation is "given" as food for both the humans and their subjects, the animals.

It's All Good

Each element of this creation is pronounced good through a connecting refrain, repeated seven times: "God saw that it was good," concluding at the end with the emphatic affirmation that "God saw everything that he had made, and, behold, it was very good." (1:31). This should not be taken in the moral sense, but as an affirmation that all is in accordance with the divine purpose. Everything is just as it is supposed to be.

The Seventh Day, God's Day of Rest (2:2–3)

The first section of the Bible comes to a conclusion with this passage. Again, the note changes from what has preceded. God has now finished his creative activity and commemorates his success by blessing the seventh day.

What does it mean for God to rest? John H. Walton, after examining the Hebrew terms that are used, puts it this way:

> In summary, [they] suggest that the seventh day is marked by God's ceasing the work of the previous six days and by his settling into the stability of the cosmos he created, perhaps experiencing refreshment as he did so. By blessing it, he extends the favor to us.[9]

Although the "Sabbath day" as a day of rest for humanity is not mentioned here as such, it is declared holy or set apart as a blessed day. There remains a suggestion that the omnipotent God was made weary by all his creation "work." Although this may

---

9. *Genesis*, 147.

seem strange or even contradictory to us, it does not appear to embarrass the writer of Genesis in the least. Later on in our story, the people of Israel are commanded to keep holy the Sabbath day precisely because God rested on it when he ceased his own work.[10]

To return to our passage, it is interesting to note that the closing refrain of "There was evening and there was morning, the *n*th day" in the accounts of the previous six days is missing for the seventh. Some have speculated that this implies that the seventh day has no end, but again the text is silent on the point.

THE STORY (PART TWO—THE CREATION OF HUMANKIND- UP CLOSE AND PERSONAL [GENESIS 2:5-25])

The Man is Created (2:5-7)

What's In a Name?

Many have noted that the Creator's name in this passage changes from "God" to "YHWH God" (following a change in the Hebrew) and have proposed a variety of explanations for this fact. If we come at this question in terms of the flow of the Story itself, however, one possibility makes perfect sense. If the first chapter is the big picture of entire act of Creation, then the second zooms in on one small but critical part of that picture. It is a "picture within the picture."[11] As such, we are "up close and personal" with the characters and even the animals, who acquire names in the process. In this context it should come as no surprise that this seems to apply to God as well.

Another Creation Story?

The account begins by noting the absence from creation of certain shrubs and plants that are described as "of the field" in Hebrew (cf. 3:5, KJV) and may be a reference to their being cultivated vegetation.[12] A little later the text, by using the same phrase, may allude to the introduction of domesticated animals into the picture as well (3:19).[13] If this reading is correct, these newly created entities relate directly to the presence of the man on the scene: without him they have no reason, or means, to exist. At the same

---

10. Exod 20:11.

11. From this perspective v. 4 is not the introduction to another version of Creation but the "bookend" (echoing 1:1) to the panoramic view just described. It is important to note the chapter divisions of the Bible are not part of the original text. See Harrison, *Introduction*, 542–49, for a discussion of the structure of Genesis.

12. Cf. Hamilton, "Genesis, 1–17," 154.

13. Cf. Keil and Delitzch, *Commentary*, 88. The NIV adds "wild" as an interpretive gloss, but it is not part of the Hebrew text.

time, it must be acknowledged that the Hebrew could simply be taken as referring to plants and animals generally.

Scholars have had a field day (pun intended) trying to relate this account to what is said in chapter 1 regarding the creation of the plants and animals. Some have assumed that we have here differing Creation accounts. While this is not the place to attempt a harmonization of the two,[14] it is important to note that this section is dealing with a special creation (the garden of Eden) within the Creation and this will no doubt account for many of the differences.[15]

The other environmental note is that the earth was watered by mists (or streams) rather than by rainfall. This is an indication that we are not to assume that the creation just described functions the same way now as it did then. "As it was in the beginning, is now, and ever shall be, world without end" does not apply to creation!

Body and Soul

In this account of the creation of the man we learn a little more about the process as the camera zooms in. Earlier, we learned he was made in the image of God. Here we discover that he is constructed out of the "dust of the ground."[16]

Whatever else this might mean, it at least underlines the connection between the man and the earth. They are part of the same reality. A few verses later (v. 19) a similar understanding is expressed regarding the animals. So, to triangulate, both humans and animals share the same bodily nature and so are bound together in their common "earthness."

Furthermore, they are both characterized as "living creatures/beings" (NEPHESH in 2:7 for the man and 1:24 for the animals). The King James Version leads us astray a bit at this point by translating NEPHESH as "soul" in the case of the man and "creature" in the case of the animals. This leaves the impression that a "soul" was imparted to humanity but not to animals. However, the idea that human beings are comprised of an animal body inhabited by a spiritual soul as two distinct entities is foreign to this text.[17]

At the same time there is a great gulf fixed between the man and the animals. It is *how* life is imparted to the man that establishes the distinctiveness. He is created not simply by God's command as the other creatures were, but by receiving the very breath (NESHAMAH, the equivalent of RUACH) of God into his body. What does it

---

14. Cf. Hamilton, "Genesis, 1–17," 150–52.
15. Cf. Ibid., 1, 176.
16. Cf. Montague, *Holy Spirit*, 5.
17. This is not at all to deny that human beings have a spiritual aspect as well as a physical one. As we will have occasion to note, the biblical view would hold them together, seeing humans as ensouled bodies or embodied souls.

imply that "... man's breath of life is a direct gift from God to him"?[18] George Montague puts it well:

> YHWH puts more of himself into this work, with the result that man is more personally oriented to God than is the rest of the universe...
>
> [The author] was greatly interested in showing that man, a living being like but above the animals, lives in a twofold relationship—he is brother to the earth and all that springs from it. But he is also the breath of YHWH, or 'spirit' if you will, and thus the source of his life not only in its beginning but in every breath he takes, is God.[19]

Again, one is reminded of the language of Psalm 8 which refers to man as "a little lower than the angels" (v. 5) and "ruler over the works of your hands" (v. 6). This is our proper place in the created order: we are not equal with God, on the one hand, nor simply animals on the other.

The Garden of YHWH (2:8–16)

A Garden within the Garden

Unlike what happened in the "big picture" where God simply directed the earth to produce vegetation, here he himself "plants" a garden and then places the man therein to "cultivate and keep it" (v. 15). The parallels are clear. Just as the earth was given into the care of the humans so the garden is given into the care of the man. It, too, is a gift of paradise. And God is the Gardener and the man is a sub-gardener, echoing the roles of Ruler and sub-ruler.

In yet another strong parallel with the earlier account in which "every" plant and tree of the whole earth is given to the man for food (1:29–30), in the garden the man is told, "You may freely eat from every tree..." (v. 16). The man, as before, is made responsible for the whole and although it is paradise he has to "cultivate and keep it." But this is not the "much labor"[20] that it will soon become and with which we are all too familiar.

From these hints we understand that in some sense the garden is a microcosm of the entire earth. It is as if the creation with all its beauty and fruitfulness is too immense for the first humans to comprehend and is therefore recast on a smaller scale to put it within reach. At the same time, it is clear that the garden is but a portion of the earth. The exact relationship is elusive, but as the focus shifts from the earth to the garden we are clearly moving from the general to the particular.

---

18. Montague, *Holy Spirit*, 6.
19. Ibid., 6–7.
20. Gen 3:17.

Two Special Trees

Eden is filled with all kinds of beautiful and fruit-bearing trees. The author takes pains to point out that two special trees stood at its center: the Tree of Life and the Tree of the Knowledge of Good and Evil. No explanation of their nature and purpose is given but a few things can be inferred from their names. To eat of the fruit of the Tree of Life would presumably impart life. As long as the man ate of it he would live.

As for the other tree, it has something to do with knowing right from wrong. So far in the Story, all is "good" and the very idea of "wrong" strikes a new and discordant note. The suggestion seems to be that if the man eats of this tree he will in some way encounter "evil"[21] and thereby for the first time understand "good" as its opposite. If he does not, he will simply remain without experience of evil, in a state of innocence. We might think of a child before he is aware of right and wrong. Perhaps, at first glance, this tree could be seen as an invitation to maturity, to become human in full. We are told that the river that watered the garden divided into four great tributaries, including the mighty Tigris and Euphrates. This information has the effect of underlining the amazing fertility of Eden.

On Probation (2:17)

The Exception Clause

The gift of paradise, however, has a catch. There always seems to be a catch. Here it takes the form of a restriction that YHWH God imposes on the man:

> . . . you shall not eat from the tree of the knowledge of good and evil, for in the day when you eat of it you will surely die. (v. 17)

No fooling around here: it is a matter of life or death. Standing at the very center of the garden with the Tree of Life, is, as it were, the Tree of Death. YHWH God has put before the man life or death. We can almost hear him say "Choose life!" The man is being put to the test: he is now on probation, enjoying the blessings of paradise and life itself, but not as a guaranteed permanent possession.

The first element in the "drama" of redemption is now in place as a cloud threatens to rain on the magnificent parade of creation. The reader is naturally drawn into the tension. Will the man meet the test? That is the question.

Free Will?

From all this we can infer that the man was created with "free will." Without getting too deeply into a very complicated discussion, here this must at least mean that the

---

21. In Hebrew, "knowledge" is experiential, not just intellectual.

man is responsible for his own actions. He is not merely a robot programmed to obey God in all circumstances. Many have also remarked that without the ability to choose, there can be no real freedom or love, let alone a genuine relationship between God and his creature. It is also worth noting the clear implication that it is in choosing to obey God that humans find their proper place in his created order.[22]

The Woman is Created (2:18–25)

Help!

Perhaps this challenge to obey explains YHWH God's realization of the man's need for help in order to succeed! However, God seems a bit puzzled and tentative himself about what to do. Something seems to be missing: the man is "alone" and this is "not good" (v. 18). From what follows, it appears that the man was created to be in relationship with a fellow creature. But which one? The job description is simply a "helper comparable/suitable for him" (v. 18).

In what appears to be a special creation (or is this day 6 up close?) YHWH God forms "every animal of the field, and every bird of the sky" (v. 19) and brings them to the man for naming (again, a feature of this account). Naming seems to be a function of the man's having been made ruler over these creatures. YHWH God grants this privilege to him and even waits patiently to see how it goes. Unfortunately for the man, no "suitable helper" is found.

In terms of story, going up this blind alley has the effect of increasing the tension and emphasizing the gap that does exist between the man and the other creatures even though they share a bodily nature. Of course, the reader may also be tempted to defend God from the charge of seeming to lack in complete knowledge (omniscience). Since our text shows no sign of being embarrassed perhaps we should put this into the same file we created for God's need for a rest and let it provoke us to further thought on the matter.

Man and Woman, Husband and Wife

Instead of simply forming another creature from the dust, YHWH God then puts the man to sleep and, from his body or side (the Hebrew is not as precise as "rib"), fashions a woman and then presents her to the man. Success at last!

> This is now bone of my bones, and flesh of my flesh. She will be called 'woman,' because she was taken out of Man.(23)

---

22. The paradox is that we find our greatest freedom by obeying God! The Bible recognizes no absolute independence of God's creatures, only their proper or improper place in his created order.

Besides the obvious delight of the man, the emphasis here is on the way in which the woman is not so much "other than" the man as she is an extension of him, part of him. In being constructed out of him she becomes both separate from and united with the man at the same time. She is the same but different.[23] Here the earlier hints of male-female complementarity, in bearing the "image of God" together, find fuller expression. The woman was subsequent to the man, it is true, but more as a completion than an afterthought. Pressing just a bit, she may even be considered the crown of Creation as she is the last to be created.

In a remarkable aside the author tells us that the formation of woman in this manner provides the foundation and nature of the institution of marriage:

> Therefore a man will leave his father and his mother, and will join with his wife, and they will be one flesh. (24)

The Edenic unity of the first man and woman is "recreated," as it were, when every man and woman come together as husband and wife. The author, by rooting marriage in "the time of man's innocency,"[24] asserts that marriage is "good" and part of God's original plan for humanity. It is not a mere human institution, a social construct for the channeling of sexual energy in a positive direction (although it does do that!). It is a gift of God, a part of his created order, the way things are supposed to be.

The essence of marriage is not seen as a partnership of two people, complete in themselves, but as the union of two complementary "incompletes." Attraction to the opposite sex is thus partly an expression of yearning for the wholeness found in male-and-female. Bonded into "one flesh" in marriage, human beings are a step closer to reflecting the image of God that each bears less fully as an individual.

The new reality brought into being by marriage is so real that it transcends the natural affinity of blood, of parent and child. Indeed, in some way the latter must "leave" the former in order to find his or her "other half." This last expression, commonplace as it is, perfectly captures the sense of this passage.

There can also be no mistaking the note of fundamental equality in Adam's elated outburst. It is true that the woman is to be his helper and so has something of a subordinate role to play but as far as her essence is concerned, she is equal to the man.[25]

---

23. Vive la différence!

24. *Book of Common Prayer*, 564.

25. In our day, when our social status is bound up so powerfully with our function (what we do), it is difficult to imagine that these two categories can be treated independently. However, in the doctrine of the Holy Trinity Christians have a model that helps us understand how this could be. Here we see a hierarchy of function among the persons of the Godhead combined with an equality of status of each as fully God. For example, the Holy Spirit is only to witness to the Son (not himself) and the Son is only to say what the Father has told him to say. The Son is in this way subordinate to the Father and the Spirit to the Son. And yet all three are equally God. Within such a framework it becomes possible to imagine the full equality of man and woman while at the same time holding to an element of hierarchy and subordination. From this perspective, St. Paul's teachings on the husband-wife and believer-believer relationships fit into a wider biblical world view.

That this has long been recognized by some Christian commentators, at least, is illustrated by the following quotation from the Puritan Matthew Henry, writing around the beginning of the eighteenth century:

> That the woman was made of a rib out of the side of Adam; not made out of his head to rule over him, nor out of his feet to be trampled upon by him, but out of his side to be equal with him, under his arm to be protected, and near his heart to be beloved.[26]

Finally, Genesis points out that the first couple, although naked, feels no shame. To us this comment may seem a bit odd but it no doubt reflects the more significant place of shame and honor in ancient culture. Its effect is certainly at least to underscore the sense of innocence we have already noted. Young children, for whom being naked is a matter of indifference, may again provide a valuable insight.

Conclusion

Creation is now complete. Its main purpose is to serve as a life-support system for humankind. It is given to them to "rule" over and "have dominion" to that end. They are given a wonderful garden, planted just for them by the Creator as their dwelling place. There they are put on notice to obey YHWH God regarding the Tree of the Knowledge of Good and Evil or die. In something of a flashback, YHWH God, in his final act of creation, fashions the first woman, and with her the institution of marriage comes into being. The command to "Be fruitful and increase in number" has now become a possibility.

IN THE BOSOM OF ABRAHAM

Introduction

It was stated in chapter 1 that:

> These pages will attempt to demonstrate that [the Covenant that God made with Abraham] provides the basic framework for God's entire plan. Its provisions will be seen to undergird the sweep of the biblical narrative, supplying its fundamental structure and joining each portion to the others, supplying connective tissue to the entire Story.[27]

The following section will now show how this is true for the Creation account even though it describes events that obviously took place long before the Covenant with Abraham was in existence. Here we are guided by the insight that the Covenant

---

26. "Genesis," on Genesis 2:21–25 (no page number).
27. See 9, above.

The Beginning

with Abraham brings to the surface what was already implied in the original design for all creation. In other words, the various elements of the Three Promises to Abraham actually reflect what God intended for the entire human race "in the beginning." Another way of putting it is that in Abraham the universal is made particular.

All this might suggest that it is the creation "covenant," if we can call it that, which should take precedence over Abraham's in our thought. However, the former is never actually articulated and, indeed, can only be brought into focus and seen for what it is only once the latter provides the proper lens. The Abrahamic Covenant therefore takes a kind of conceptual primacy even though it comes later in the narrative and seems smaller in scale, only applying to one man's family and one small nation out of all the inhabitants of the earth. And, unlike the creation "covenant," it takes the form of an explicit divine Promise that provides a dynamic to the narrative, setting it in motion toward its end. Indeed, as we encounter the various biblical covenants we will see that they *all* conform to this same shape.

Using another kind of triangle diagram, the first of a series of Covenantal Diagrams, it is possible to visualize the basic conceptual relationship between the Covenant with Abraham and Creation itself. Using a more substantial outline for Abraham's Covenant indicates something of its primacy:

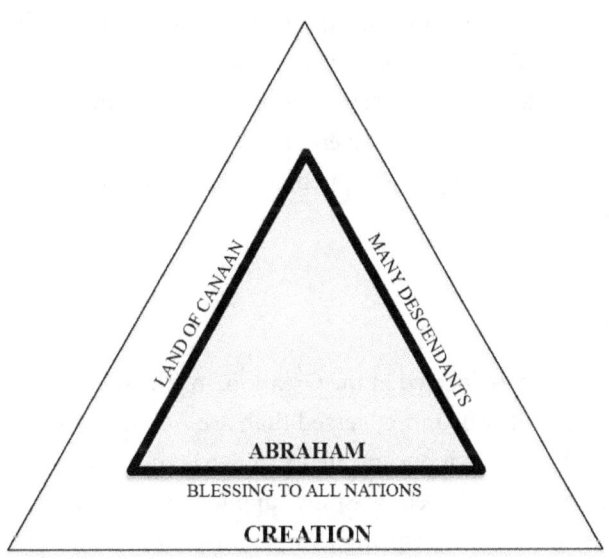

Covenantal Diagram 1
Abraham–Creation (1)

We now turn to the details of just how Adam is "in Abraham."

1. The Land/Place

This Promise finds itself embedded in the "earth" segment of the Creation. The parallel is precise: where Abraham is given the Land of Canaan, Adam is given the whole earth. Of course, the scale is different, but the concept is the same: both men and their offspring are given territory as their domain, presumably forever. It is interesting that Adam and the earth are bound to each other in several important ways. Adam is made "from the earth, made of the dust"[28]: he *is* earth. At the same time, he has dominion over it and a vocation to serve it. In fact, the earth is his life-support system: he cannot survive without it. As it flourishes, he will flourish. Humanity was created for a "place" and this reality is intensified a hundredfold when the man is put in the garden of Eden. This is his special place within the enormity of the earth. Abraham knows what that is all about.

2. Many Descendants

This Promise is "built in" to the Creation, but again, on an enormous scale. Adam and Eve are told to "Be fruitful and multiply; fill the earth . . ." (1:28). Until very recently in human experience this Mandate must have seemed almost beyond human imagining. The "many descendants" of Abraham's Covenant hardly begins to describe it! Did Adam feel a bit like the still-childless Abraham and Sarah at that moment, the impossibility of the idea simply overwhelming? Was he tempted to laugh out loud at the prospect like they did? In any event, it is easy to see that what happened with Adam is the same kind of thing that happened to Abraham, but on a greatly increased order of magnitude.

3. Blessing to All Nations

Again, this Promise can be located in the Creation, in "the way things are supposed to be." No one could possibly be more blessed than are Adam and Eve. The entire earth and all it produced is theirs (concentrated in Eden), and can be had simply for the taking. All of their wants and needs are fully supplied. But it is not just for them alone, of course: it is for all of their offspring as well, offspring that would one day fill the earth. That is, all humans, and thus all the nations into which they might be grouped, would come to share in these abundant blessings. In St. Paul's language, they are all "in Adam" and so receive what he received, if only in principle. This functions much like the Promise to Abraham in that its realization lies in the distant future.

It is now possible to summarize the way in which the Three Promises appear in the creation story by amplifying the previous diagram as follows:

---

28. 1 Cor 15:47.

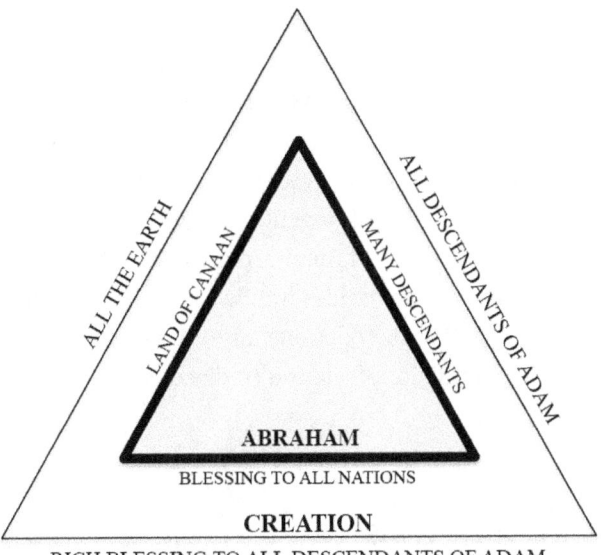

Covenantal Diagram 2
Abraham–Creation (2)

A Suggestion Regarding the Inner Relationship of the Three Promises

These observations regarding the Three Promises were enabled by looking at Creation/Adam through Abraham's eyes. Reversing the process and looking through the creation narrative to the Three Promises allows us to see a bit more clearly how the three of them may be organically interrelated. The Land produces the Blessing which is enjoyed by the Descendants who, in turn care for the Land, etc. This suggests that the Promises have an inner logic to them, even a kind of symbiotic relationship with each other. This will bear keeping an eye on as the Story unfolds.

4. Fruitfulness

We have already seen that fruitfulness/abundance is the predominant feature of the whole Creation. There can be no mistaking that it is a fundamental characteristic of all living things as they are "supposed to be," vegetation and creatures alike.[29] All the Promises made to Abraham are clearly in continuity with this truth, bringing it explicitly into the life experience of one particular branch of the human family, and, through them, to all. Again, we can see in this that the Creator is reorienting the whole of a somewhat wayward creation back towards its original configuration.

---

29. See 27, above.

5. Relationship

There are a number of ways in which this section of the Story demonstrates that God and humans are in close relationship from the Beginning. Most importantly, perhaps, is the fact that they are made in the image of the Creator, clearly distinguished from the other animals as a special creation. As we have seen above, this "image" is seen in the fact that humans are installed as his regents and given the earth as their dominion. It is also reflected in the "one flesh" of the marriage relationship. YHWH God shows concern for the solitary man and provides him with a suitable mate, a relationship of peers. It is essential to note that the relationship of the humans with YHWH God is up close and personal with no hint of friction or distance.

6. Grace/Obedience

Does the idea that our relationship with God is "established by grace but is maintained by our obedience" fit into this segment of the Story? That seems to be exactly what we find here in the creation account. The humans find themselves in a harmonious relationship with God entirely at his initiative. Here is pure grace. Obedience regarding the fruit of the Tree of the Knowledge of Good and Evil is clearly the condition, not only for remaining in that relationship, but also for continuing to live. As far as conforming to what we might call our testing formula is concerned, so far, so good.

3

Paradise Lost

Suggested Reading

Genesis 3:1—4:24

MAJOR DEVELOPMENTS

- Satan's first appearance
- First temptation
- First act of disobedience/sin
- The Fall of humanity
- Introduction of death
- A deteriorated environment
- Humans estranged from God
- A hint of ultimate victory over evil
- Humans estranged from each other (jealousy and murder)

PERSPECTIVES

Introduction

A story is all about the resolution of conflict, and we will now observe the latter injected full force into our narrative. Up to this point harmony has reigned but the prohibition against eating the forbidden fruit has the potential of upsetting the applecart, so to speak. With the main characters in place and facing the possibility of disaster, the Story does not leave us hanging for very long.

The Nature of Sin

The name of the tree in question, "the Knowledge of Good and Evil," signals the nature of the struggle that will dominate the rest of the Story. While "good" has had the stage to itself, now "evil" steps in from the wings in the form of the serpent.

The Story, of course, turns on whether or not the humans will obey the command of God. Indeed, neither good nor evil is defined except in relation to this one question. While it is clear even at this point that doing good is beneficial (continuing to live) and that doing evil is not (death), such considerations are always secondary in Scripture: the main thing is one's "yes" or "no" to God. The latter is the definition of sin. It is that simple.

Temptation

Before sin, however, comes temptation. In Eve's confrontation with the serpent we may have before us a kind of working model of temptation itself. This possibility is worth considering when we look at it in detail below. Although temptation is an admittedly complex process, it revolves around the simple question of whether or not we are prepared to take God at his Word.

Furthermore, it is important to recognize that the serpent tells the truth about YHWH God's motivation for the prohibition against the Tree of the Knowledge of Good and Evil. It really *was* because it would make the humans like him, knowing good and evil (3:5). As well, the serpent takes the ban on the fruit of only one tree and expands it to "any" tree (3:1). He twists the truth rather than fabricating it out of whole cloth. In the art of deception half-truths are more effective than whole lies. And it is the nature of serpents to twist.

The Wages of Sin

The choice of Eve and Adam to disobey leads directly to their banishment from God's intimate presence, the loss of the garden of Eden, and a deteriorated life situation on the outside. Cut off from the Tree of Life, the humans have stumbled out into death's dark domain. This is evident immediately in the pain and hard labor that now weigh them down, but there is more, much more, to come. In fact, it is all downhill from here: death arrives full-blown early in just the second generation of human beings when jealousy leads to murder.

Fallen Humanity

No wonder theologians traditionally refer the "Fall of man" when considering the series of events in the garden. However, at this point it is important to note that there are clearly elements of both discontinuity and continuity between the pre-Fall and post-Fall worlds: the Fall changed everything but everything was not changed completely. The tasks given in Creation are still to be done: the man is still to care for the earth, the woman is still to produce children, the earth is still to produce food. But these have all been made much more difficult. The overall environment of human existence has been compromised and this means that we can never assume that the way things are now is the way things ought to be. Our present experience of the world is of a fallen world, with all its ambiguities and shortcomings included.

By far the most important change brought about by the Fall is undoubtedly in the relationship between God and the humans. The disobedience of the latter has led to their banishment from the garden, from God's very presence. However, God continues to interact with them as is demonstrated in the story of Cain and Abel and, indeed, the rest of the Bible. But the purpose of the interaction is no longer simply to enjoy fellowship. It is now a rescue mission to bring humanity back into proper relationship with himself, to restore that which has been lost.

Speaking of Cain and Abel, it is important to note that the setting of their story is the presenting of "offerings" to Yahweh, likely meant to express thanksgiving. Worship therefore got an early start in the history of humankind, even if the first fight and the first shedding of blood were over how it should be conducted. Fortunately, we have made much progress since then.

The Immanent and Transcendent God

So far the biblical Story has revealed a God who is not simply aloof from his creation, as if he is content to get the whole thing started, like winding up a watch, and then walking away from it. Here is a God who clearly remains involved with his creation. The technical term is that he is an "immanent" God. This carries a sense in which God is in a very real but complicated interrelationship (partnership?) with what he has made. Donald G. Bloesch captures this well:

> . . . the true God is essentially independent of the world though he makes himself dependent in his relationship to his children. God needs man only in relation to the realization of his plan for the world, not because there is any deficiency in himself.[1]

Therefore we properly speak of God as *both* "transcendent" (above and beyond creation) and immanent.

---

1. *Essentials*, 45.

CONCLUSION

The stage for the biblical Story is now set. The main characters have been introduced and the problem to be resolved is clearly before the audience. How this comes about is the subject of the rest of the Bible. While the way back to Eden seems forever barred there is here also the promise of One who will crush the agent provocateur even though there may be a significant number of twists and turns along the way. Perhaps he will also open the gates to paradise.

THE STORY

Temptation and Sin (3:1–6)

Enter the Serpent[2]

The serpent in this account is characterized as "more subtle" than any of the other animals (3:1). This quality may be a positive one, as in "clever," or a more negative one, in the sense of "cunning." Both meanings show themselves in this episode. Although we are clearly to take the serpent as just one of the wild animals, the Story makes clear that he is not a serpent as we know them today.[3] As the account opens he is talking and thinking and possibly walking as well. No wonder he is described as "more subtle" than the other creatures. At the same time no one can read this account without being aware that the serpent represents something like evil incarnate.

The Serpent and the Woman

The serpent begins by asking the woman if God had really forbidden eating from *any* tree in the garden. He makes it sound like it was a rumor that was going around Eden and he simply wants to confirm whether or not it is true. The woman corrects him: it is only the one tree that is forbidden. The fact that she adds a prohibition against even touching the tree may simply be her way of emphasizing the ban but it may also express some resentment at being restricted in this manner.

The subtle approach having failed, the serpent directly denies the truth of God's word that they would die if they ate the forbidden fruit. He then suggests that God's

---

2. While central to this account, is the serpent/devil/Satan a "main character" in the larger Story itself? I would argue that, as far as the actual telling of the Story is concerned, he is not. After his brief appearance here, except for the book of Job, Satan virtually disappears from the Old Testament. As we shall soon see, however, he remains a central character in the mind of the reader. In the New Testament Satan is more present, but often only in the background as well, not as an active participant. While he is presented as God's adversary, the Bible does not support the idea of "dualism": that from the beginning there was a good god and an evil god striving for superiority. Satan is always subject to God and as such his schemes are doomed. In more ways than one he is a third-rate character at best.

3. Cf. the many artistic representations of this scene in which the serpent looks like an ordinary snake.

real motive was to keep the humans from equality with himself, knowing good and evil. This comes across as an attack on God's character and reveals the serpent as his adversary. For the woman, the serpent's version has double-sided drawing power. The possibility of terrible punishment is negated and in its place she is given an opportunity to be like God.

You can almost follow the woman's eyes as they turn toward the Tree of the Knowledge of Good and Evil, seeing it in a new light. Suddenly it has enormous appeal: as delicious food, as a beautiful object, and as something able to make her wise. All are integral to the original Creation and good in and of themselves. But here, located in a forbidden object, they pull the woman completely away from obedience to the word of God.

> So it is that "she took some of its fruit and ate." (3:3)

And nothing happened! The serpent was right! It *is* good. So good that she is eager to share her discovery with her mate who is apparently present, silent beside her as she eats. It was only when both had disobeyed that the consequences of their sin begin to make themselves known. They do not know it, but they are dead men walking.

Death as Shame, Fear, Guilt and Blame (3:7–13)

The Naked Truth

First of all, Adam and Eve become aware of being naked. In this moment, they experience "wrong" for the first time, moving out of the theoretical/potential and into the real/actual. Where once it was just natural to be naked, now it becomes an issue. Given the earlier comment (2:25) that they had known no shame in their nakedness we are led to conclude that now they do. Both texts assume that it is obvious why nakedness is wrong and therefore shameful. In response, the two carry out history's first cover-up.

Enter YHWH God

The next scene reveals something more of the relationship between YHWH God and the humans up to this point. We see the Creator walking in the garden in the cool of the evening, expecting to encounter the man and the woman whom he had placed there. It is the picture of harmony and intimacy. But this time he fails to encounter them and he has to call them out of hiding. Adam has to confess that he is afraid because he is naked. Apparently he felt the fig leaves were insufficient covering, or perhaps he was still intensely aware of his underlying nakedness. Going from bad to worse, his original shame had escalated to fear in the presence of God.

> God said, "Who told you that you were naked? Have you eaten from the tree that I commanded you not to eat from?" (v. 11)

Adam seeks to avoid taking responsibility by shifting the blame to his wife and, breathtakingly, even to God himself:

> The man said, "The woman whom you gave to be with me, she gave me fruit from the tree, and I ate it." (v. 12)

The woman immediately joins the "blame game," saying the serpent deceived her (v. 13). It is almost comical. It is all too human.

And it does not work. All three parties to the crime, the serpent, the woman and the man, are guilty as charged. Only their sentences await.

The Effects of the Fall (3:14—14:26)

On the Serpent

The serpent, perhaps because he took the initiative in this whole mess, is the first to go down as a result. Literally. He is now to "crawl on his belly" and "eat dust" (3:14). The only one of the trio to be cursed directly, he seems to have the greatest fall. He goes from being the most crafty to being the most cursed of all the animals, the lowest of the low. It is humiliation of the first order. Presumably it also involves a change in his bodily form.

Fittingly, the serpent's conspiratorial relationship with the woman is replaced by "enmity." A certain alienation/rivalry sets in between them and also between their "seed" (Hebrew, lit.). But there is more:

> . . . (he/they/it) will *sup* your head, and you will *sup* his heel. (v. 3:15b)

I have put it like this to highlight some of the problems that scholars have encountered in translating and interpreting this passage.[4] The Hebrew word *sup* can have various meanings including "strike at" and "crush." Some translations, such as the NIV, translate:

> . . . he will crush your head and you will strike his heel.

While this is a possible translation, Victor Hamilton reasonably argues that it involves an illegitimate change of meaning for the same word in the same context. It should read either "crush" or "strike" in both clauses, as does the WEB. In either case, he nevertheless finds here a promise that the seed of the serpent will ultimately be subject to the seed of the woman. This certainly fits the general sense of the passage, even if it is primarily a reference to the ongoing relationship of the human and the serpent. One has his heel at risk, while the other, his head. A lethal difference!

---

4. I am indebted especially to the discussion of this issue by Hamilton, "Genesis, 1–17," 197–200.

Enter the Serpent Crusher

The reader therefore comes to expect an ongoing human-serpent conflict that will end with the ultimate triumph of the former over the latter through the agency of a particular descendant of the woman. Thus arises the compelling expectation of the eventual arrival of a Serpent Crusher/Striker. This hope inevitably comes to lie at the center of this Story in the mind of the reader even if it is not explicitly present in the subsequent narrative. At this point the identity of the Serpent Crusher is a very open question, but it is clear that the reader is to be on the lookout for his appearance.

On the Woman

The woman is dealt with next. While no curse is actually mentioned as such, one is pronounced upon her nevertheless. She is told that from now on giving birth will bring her greatly increased pain. This, by the way, seems to imply that there was some pain in paradise! In the context of an ancient culture in which woman's greatest calling was to bring children into the world, this pronouncement is especially poignant: from now on it can only be hers at great cost.

Again, there is more. In the fallen world now descending, the woman will find herself subject to her husband and will be held in that subjection by the chains of her own desire. This is not the way it was in the Beginning, but it is the "natural" way of the world in its post-Edenic state. One cannot help but wonder what this relationship was like before sin entered. Both equality of men and women and their freer association are clearly implied.

On the Earth/Man

Last, but not least, comes the man. The very earth is cursed as a result of his sin. The ground, which had been his to till and care for, would no longer yield its increase without "much labor" (v. 17). Presumably, in its original state the earth produced its fruit with minimal effort from the man. From now on it will produce weeds along with produce, making the man's task infinitely harder.

The direct inclusion of the earth itself in the curse is of great significance. It con firms in a final way that the Fall is not just spiritual. The entire life situation of the three protagonists is affected. We have also seen its direct effect upon the bodies of the serpent and the woman: now we see that it effects the environment as well and thus, indirectly, the body of the man. The humans and their world are bound together, for good and for bad.

This point is underlined in the last and worst part of the curse. The man is told that he will return to the ground from which he was taken. Here the stated penalty of eating the forbidden fruit, "you will surely die," comes ominously into view. The man does not die immediately (to give the serpent his due) but his death is now inevitable, and his own dust will be mingled with that of the earth in a kind of de-creation. The serpent might "eat dust" but the man will *be* dust. What tragic irony.

Labor Union

It is worth noting that each of the guilty parties receives what is in effect the same immediate sentence: hard labor. The man will have to labor the earth, the woman will have to endure the labor of childbirth, and the serpent will have to move laboriously across the earth. In each case, their resultant exhaustion heralds their ultimate mortality. Solidarity forever!

The Naming of Eve

The fallout continues as the Story continues. Adam ("the man") now names his wife. At first this might seem insignificant until we remember that the earlier naming of the domestic animals implied that they were subject to the man. Here, the woman's naming may signify her new status as subject to her husband. At the same time, she is honored by her name, Eve ("living"), as the mother of the entire race.

A Better Cover

Next, in what appears to us as a bit odd, perhaps, we read that YHWH God himself made garments of animal skin to clothe Adam and Eve. Clearly we are to take it that this is a better covering than the fig leaves, but the reason why remains obscure to the modern reader. Perhaps they were simply more permanent. No doubt in the culture of the author the reason is perfectly obvious. The fact that it is YHWH God himself who provides the covering suggests that the wrong has been righted and the humans should be comfortable in their new skins.

Expulsion from the Garden

But not all is well:

> Yahweh God said, "Behold, the man has become like one of us, knowing good and evil. Now, lest he reach out his hand, and also take of the tree of life, and eat, and live forever—" (3:22)

The sentence of death requires "access denied" to the tree of life and this means, given his tendency to disobedience, that the man (and his mate) have to be removed from the garden altogether. They cannot be trusted. Simply knowing good and evil, while perhaps a step up (an inner sense of morality, or a conscience?), hardly qualifies them for eternal life. The implication is that they will have to "do" good as well as "know" it. And therein lies the rub.

Understandably reluctant to leave the garden, Adam and Eve have to be driven out. Adding further emphasis to the finality of this act, YHWH God

> . . . placed cherubim at the east of the garden of Eden, and a flaming sword which turned every way, to guard the way to the tree of life. (3:24)

One can almost hear a jarring clang as the gate to the grand estate is slammed shut, leaving the former occupants as outcasts, longing for what was once theirs. True, the promise regarding the eventual triumph of the seed of the woman perhaps gives the reader hope of a restoration. But for now it is looking grim.

Murder One

This prognosis is confirmed by what happens next in the story of the first two sons, Cain and Abel. Both give offerings to YHWH from what they have produced, fruits of the soil from Cain and the fat portions from the firstborn of his flock from Abel. The latter is accepted while the former is not. Ignoring YHWH's warning, Cain murders his innocent brother in cold blood. This act is so shocking to the reader, accustomed as we are by now to the ways of Eden, that we know that we have entered into an altered malevolent world for sure. Sin now abounds. In fact, it is universal.[5] In a few short pages we read the following indictment:

> Yahweh saw that the wickedness of man was great in the earth, and that every imagination of the thoughts of man's heart was continually only evil. (6:5)

We are not in Eden anymore.

In fact we are in the land of Nod, east of Eden. That is where Cain is doomed to wander and have his family, working the stubborn earth. The latter is made even more

---

5. Somehow each human being participates in Adam's "original sin" and thus is subject to the Fall. What has been said above in reference to how sin is universal in scope is not controversial among biblically minded Christians, but there is debate on many related issues. G. W. Bromiley, "Sin," IV:519, points out that there is much scope for the opinions of dogmatic theologians because the Bible itself is silent on most of them:

> It does not state how original sin is transmitted, whether by hereditary taint, environment, or a recurrent Fall. It does not state how individual sin is related to original sin, whether by necessary consequence, concurrence, or influence. It does not state what measure of guilt attaches to original sin if it stands alone, e.g., in the day-old baby who dies without committing actual sin of its own. It does not state in what form original sin persists in the regenerate, whether as sin that is guilty, sin that stands under pardon, or as no more than a scar or weakness that easily leads to sin.

That is a lot of silence! Whatever views we have on such subjects should be held with an appropriate degree of tentativeness. That is, the theologians dealing with them should not be *too* dogmatic!

stubborn by another curse imposed upon it by YHWH, just for Cain. His line quickly disappears from the narrative entirely and he is gone.

IN THE BOSOM OF ABRAHAM

Introduction

This portion of the biblical narrative deals with the way in which the original state of blessing was compromised but not entirely lost by the introduction of the curses into the picture. As the examination below demonstrates, those curses are largely the flip side of the blessings. When God blesses, he blesses in terms of the Covenant with Abraham, and when he curses, he does so in the same categories. But, at least in this case, the curse does not have the power to negate the blessing entirely.

1. The Land/Place

As a result of the man's disobedience, the ground itself is cursed. While it will continue to yield the desired fruit it will now also produce weeds. To a farmer this means that the land will necessarily be less productive. Not only will the weeds compete with the crop for the nutrients of the soil and water, it will take extra resources to deal with them. As well, the land serves as a constant reminder of the man's mortality, his being under the judgment of death and his subsequent return to dust.

As far as place is concerned, the humans lose the right to occupy the garden, their original "place." We read that Cain "went out from the presence of YHWH and lived in the land of Nod, east of Eden" (4:16). From now on, wherever they are on the earth, humans will be in exile. If they could just find another place, another land, another garden.

2. Many Descendants

There is nothing said in this narrative that explicitly dictates a lessening number of descendants for the humans. We read that there will be a running battle between the descendants of the woman and the serpent, and so we know that she will "be fruitful and multiply," at least to some degree. Indeed, we see that sexual intercourse and childbirth are the first acts recorded after the expulsion from Eden. The blessing of children is, however, effectively conditioned by the fact that each newborn child will enter the fallen world through a corridor of motherly pain. To the extent that the earth has become less fruitful, those children will undoubtedly be fewer in number than they would have been otherwise.

3. Blessing to All Nations

As this section in the last chapter pointed out, there is a universal relevance to the experience of Adam. All human beings, and thus all nations, are "in Adam." Just as they, in principle, share in the blessing, so also do they share in the curse. It is clear that they, too, will be excluded from Eden and the Tree of Life and have to work hard to squeeze a living out of a reluctant earth. Given what we see between Cain and Abel, we can well anticipate that nations will not likely live in harmony together. In fact, the very existence of nations in the first place implies divisions and discord in the human family. One nation just will not do for all, it seems. This is now just part of the human condition.

4. Fruitfulness

As indicated above, the introduction of "thorns and thistles" lessens the productivity of the land. Although there is no mention of a curse on flocks and herds, their fruitfulness would undoubtedly be negatively impacted by the diminished capacity of the earth to provide fodder. All this is to say that there is still the possibility of fruitfulness after the Fall, but it is not to be compared to that of Eden.

5. Relationship

The most obvious and important effect here is that a significant degree of alienation has come between humans and God because of sin. The story is told in such fashion that it must be taken that not only Adam and Eve, but also all of their descendants, are banned from the presence of YHWH. The curses are an obvious expression of this. Generally, the relationship is marred but not destroyed because God continues to take a keen interest in humanity. But it is now of a different nature. Once the humans are barred from the garden God appears mostly in judgment and then almost disappears into the background. It is only in the third generation that "men began to call upon the name of YHWH" (4:26). Judging from what follows this may represent not the beginning of a new relationship, but a longing for the old one.

6. Grace/Obedience

This narrative conforms nicely to our testing formulation that we are saved by grace and maintained in that condition by our obedience. By "saved," here we mean "in a harmonious relationship with God" and we can easily see that it is human disobedience that has caused this relationship to be damaged and both spiritual and physical distance put between Creator and creature. Now the question becomes: how can all this be restored? What did YHWH say to Cain?

If you do well, won't it be lifted up? If you don't do well, sin crouches at the door. Its desire is for you, but you are to rule over it. (4:7)

Perhaps it is a matter of giving the humans a second chance. Just try harder next time.

4

Noah
Paradise Restored?

Suggested Reading

Genesis 4:25—11:9

MAJOR DEVELOPMENTS

- The line of Seth is introduced
- Wickedness increases in the earth
- God decides to destroy all creatures
- Righteous Noah finds God's favor
- The ark is built
- The Flood begins
- Noah, his immediate family, and breeding pairs of animals survive in the ark
- The Flood ends
- Humankind is given a fresh start
- Animals now to be considered food
- Through the first covenant God promises to never again flood the earth
- Wickedness continues
- The tower of Babel is planned but God brings it to an end
- Humankind is scattered over the earth

PERSPECTIVES

Introduction

After the passing of Adam and Eve from the scene God seems to step behind the curtain while generations come and go.[1] During this time he is not an active participant in the Story and humanity, left to its own devices, falls deeper and deeper into wickedness. Then Noah is born.

The story of Noah and the Flood is fascinating from almost any angle. In terms of the Story, it is a vivid and somewhat perplexing sidebar. It also marks the final stage of the process that produced the natural environment as we know it and reveals the true nature of the human predicament.

A New Adam?

With paradise lost and Cain dealt with, the reader's attention naturally shifts to the line of Seth, the replacement for the murdered Abel, the good son. When the author points out that Adam now has a son in his own image the implication seems to be that the hope for redemption will lie in Seth and his descendants. Noah is one of them.

Noah serves as a kind of second Adam through whom YHWH populates the world after the Flood is sent as judgment upon sinful humanity. The way in which he is introduced into the Story strongly encourages the reader to assume that he is the expected Serpent Crusher. Even though we are soon disabused of that idea, the account leaves behind it the strong impression that it is indeed a single individual that we are to look for. The eye turns inevitably to the approaching horizon.

Indeed, before this episode is finished Noah pronounces a blessing on his son Shem that seems to exalt him above his brother Japheth while relegating his grandson Canaan, the son of the third brother, Ham, to be the slave of other two. From this the reader will naturally look for the subsequent narrative to flow toward Shem for redemption.

A Covenant for the New Beginning

In the meantime, after the Flood and a few creative tweaks that follow, the earth is ready for a new start and for a brief moment it seems that all is well again. This sense is underlined by the introduction of the notion of "covenant" into the Story. A covenant

---

1. A careful reader would note that because of the long life attributed to humankind before the Flood the actual gap between the death of Adam and the birth of Noah is in fact only 126 years. However, the way in which the Story is told (our focus) leaves the impression that the period of God's inactivity is much longer. God's "withdrawal," indeed, may well have begun long before Adam's death, extending its duration accordingly. For a chronology of this period following a straightforward reading of the text the reader is referred to Scroggie, *Unfolding Drama*, Vol. 1, 137.

is a particular kind of promise, one that is usually of greater importance and more formal in nature than others. In the Bible, the most important covenants are those that God himself makes between himself and a portion of humanity (like the Jewish people), or with one person (like David).[2]

In our text the parties to the covenant are God on the one hand and all the living creatures on the other. It is, in fact, God's unconditional promise never to "cut off" all life by means of a flood again. This may leave open the possibility that another method of destruction (e.g., fire) might be used. That is to say, it is not necessarily a question of whether or not the world will again be destroyed, but by what means it will be accomplished. Nevertheless, there is a lingering sense that the world has been given a permanent reprieve.

In terms of "story" it is important to note that this covenant is essentially negative in nature and, as such, cannot provide a dynamic to the narrative. That is, God promises *not* to do something and, while this conveys a sense of his general benevolence towards his creatures and an assurance of stability in nature, it does not direct the reader to anticipate some future event. In failing to impart a goal for the Story, the "Noahic" covenant stands in marked contrast to the Covenant with Abraham. There, as we shall soon see, God sets redemptive history more clearly in motion toward his Promises.[3]

In line with this thought, Noah's covenant effects no real change in the narrative direction. Sin again shows itself in the generation after Noah and we are back to square one. This section therefore presents the reader with something of a false (new) beginning. Even after a massive clean-up operation sin still persists and even dominates the human condition. The serpent has managed to slither off the ark unmolested. Any hope for a new world anytime soon has gone with him. Except that the line of Shem, of course, continues.

Lessons Learned

The general effect of these developments is to help the reader to orient him or herself toward the spiritual problem at the core of the Story's central conflict. Sin not only persists in the social and natural environment but also deep within the makeup of every child of Adam. This is the beginning of one of the most important lessons of the

---

2. Biblical covenants, in both form and content (to some extent) are rooted in the culture of the Ancient Near East. For a more technical discussion of the background and significance of this concept the reader is referred to a good "Introduction" to the Old Testament. (Cf. Harrison, *Introduction*, 648–50) From there one can gain access to the vast body of scholarly material on this subject. At its root a covenant is an agreement between two parties in which the terms of their relationship are established. Promises are made and usually a "sign" or symbol is used to be a visual reminder that the covenant is in effect. As such, covenants are still with us. An example is the wedding service. The bride and groom make promises to each other, promises that define not only their relationship with one another, but even their very self-understanding as "husband" or "wife." They also exchange rings as a sign of this covenant.

3. See 9, above.

Bible and the life of faith. Without it we might imagine that all we need is a change of environment or different circumstances in order to live as God would have us live. This story is the antidote to such illusions. For salvation to be truly effective it must include nothing less than a "renovation of the heart," as Dallas Willard puts it.[4]

Even though ultimately a failure, this first movement toward redemption illustrates another truth: judgment and salvation are two sides of the same coin. For the unrighteous the Flood was an unmitigated disaster and destruction, but for the righteous it was the context for survival and new hope. Judgment and salvation: the same event, differently experienced.

Questions Anyone?

The Sinfulness of Sin

How can it be that a God of love could carry out such a terrible judgment? This raises, for the first time in the Story, the age-old question of the relationship between God's love and his justice. It is difficult to see how they fit together in this case, outside of simply (!) trusting whatever he does, he does for reasons that do not contradict either aspect of his character.

Perhaps we can learn something from this episode that will help our understanding as we struggle with this issue. For whatever else the story of the Flood does, it brings absolute clarity to the truth that YHWH God is utterly opposed to sin. Death is a *judgment* for sin, not something "natural." To put it more positively, he is a holy God who has no tolerance for sin. As sinful human beings we have the tendency to see sin as a mere character flaw, a regrettable but understandable shortcoming, a tiny speck in our eye. Not so with God. He cannot just shrug his shoulders and walk away. If we could see sin as he sees sin, we might see his justice in another light. And tremble. And realize that it is to him that we must turn for hope.

Does God Know All?

Another dilemma confronts us when we ponder other questions forced on us by this account. Does God make a mistake with the creation of humankind, change his mind and then change it again? Did he not foresee Noah's ultimate failure? Can this depiction of God be reconciled with our understanding of him as both unchanging and knowing all things?

Some recent controversy has swirled around this question with the suggestion of several prominent evangelical theologians that the traditional understanding of God's omniscience needs modification precisely because of passages such as ours.[5]

---

4. Willard, *Renovation of the Heart*.
5. This view is generally known as "Openness" theology. Cf. Pinnock, *Openness of God*.

While this approach is commendable in that it takes seriously the biblical witness, it runs up against the fact that the traditional understanding reflects the overwhelming Scriptural emphasis.

Again, it might be best simply to allow these two understandings to coexist side by side in a state of tension, remembering that the Hebrew mind is quite happy with holding such opposites together.[6] While such puzzles may occupy us as modern readers, they do not seem to embarrass the ancient author in the least: he or she is just telling the story and letting the theological chips fall where they may.

THE STORY

Unto Adam a Son is Born (4:25—25:27)

This section of the Story opens with the birth to Adam of another son, Seth, who was born "instead of Abel" (4:25). He is described as being in Adam's own image as Adam himself was in God's image (5:1–3). It is difficult to escape the impression that this is the line on which to keep one's eye, especially as the rest of this section concentrates only on his line, down to Lamech, the father of Noah.

In the ninth generation of Seth's family (and the tenth of Adam's) Noah is born. He, we are told by his father, will:

> . . . comfort us in our work and in the toil of our hands, caused by the ground which Yahweh has cursed. (5:29)

There is here a hint of an alleviation of the effects of the curse, at least, and perhaps even its reversal through this "comforter," as Noah means in English.[7]

---

6. A curious passage in the Gospel of John opens up the possibility of an explanation based upon our Lord's own method of teaching. This is found in chapter 11 when Jesus at first delays his departure for Bethany until after Lazarus has died. He says:

> "Our friend Lazarus has Fallen asleep; but I am going there to wake him up." His disciples replied, "Lord, if he sleeps, he will get better." Jesus had been speaking of his death, but his disciples thought he meant natural sleep. So then he told them plainly, "Lazarus is dead, and for your sake I am glad I was not there, so that you may believe. But let us go to him." (11–15)

Following the raising of Lazarus we read:

> So they took away the stone. Then Jesus looked up and said, 'Father, I thank you that you have heard me. I knew that you always hear me, but I said this for the benefit of the people standing here, that they may believe that you sent me.' (41–42)

In these passages we find Jesus seeming to act inconsistently with what we know of his character and person as the Son of God. He himself tells us this in order to engender belief in others even though he could have acted differently. Could it not be, then, that those passages which portray God acting in ways that seem to be at odds with what we know of him are moments when he similarly portrays himself as less than he really is in order to lead us to faith?

7. Cf. Hamilton, "Genesis, 1–17," 259.

A Second Adam (5:28—26:12)

Chaos, Again

Paradoxically, as Noah the comforter comes on to the scene, the general population is experiencing a fatal moral meltdown. This degeneration is highlighted by corruption and widespread violence (6:11) and seems to involve an unhealthy preoccupation with sexual matters. Ironically, this happens just as humanity is beginning to fulfill their God-given Mandate to "Be fruitful and increase in number; fill the earth . . . " (1:28, cf. 6:1). Here again we see the effect of the Fall: the good gift of sexuality has been perverted and twisted into a snare. While the precise nature of this degeneration may remain unclear, there is no mistaking that the underlying cause is a deep-seated sinfulness that now has humanity firmly in its grasp.

Divine Distress

God is almost driven to despair by this development, even seeming to toy with the idea of giving up completely on the creature he has made in his own image.

> My Spirit will not strive with man forever, because he also is flesh; (6:3)

> Yahweh saw that the wickedness of man was great in the earth, and that every imagination of the thoughts of man's heart was continually only evil. Yahweh was sorry that he had made man on the earth, and it grieved him in his heart. (6:5–6)

God's grief and pain helps to explain the severe judgment that he now plans, determining to destroy not only the entire human race but also all of the animals and birds. These are all the creatures that have "the breath of life" in them (6:17). The fact that sea dwellers are not included no doubt reflects the fact that they are not "breathers," and as such, they will survive the coming destruction because they are at home in the water. Perhaps we are to infer that the creation clock is being set back to about the middle of day five and a new start made from there.

Just One Just Man

And then, in a bit of a surprise, we read:

> But Noah found favor in Yahweh's eyes. (6:8)

This was a big "but" indeed! It seems to stop God in his tracks and cause him to alter his strategy. Noah was a "righteous man, blameless among the people of his time," who "walked with God" (6:8). For the sake of this one just man God is prepared to start all over again, with Noah as the new progenitor of the human race. Judgment will still be meted out but Noah, his immediate family, and representatives of all the animals would be saved and then set free in a freshly scoured environment. Humanity will be given a second chance. Its hope would lie in Noah's (righteous) DNA. Hopefully it would be better than Adam's.

The Flood: Planned and Executed (6:13—17:14)

The familiar story then unfolds as Noah is brought into God's confidence about what is going to happen. He is given precise instructions about what to do: build an ark of a certain size, enter it with his wife, his three sons, and their wives, along with a breeding pair of all the living creatures. He is also to store enough provisions for them all. In this way they will be saved from the coming devastation. In a very simple statement, said three times, the reader is told that:

> He did all that God commanded him. (6:22, 7:5. 16)

Simple, perhaps, but it surely reveals that Noah looks to be a man who took God at his word. To build a giant boat on dry land was an act of great faith. Anyone who has heard Bill Cosby's comedy routine ("You want me to do what? . . . What's an ark?") will understand how ridiculous this must have seemed to the other residents of the neighborhood, not to mention Noah himself!

The great Flood then comes in the wake of forty days and nights of intense rain as "the fountains of the great deep burst open, and the sky's windows opened" (7:11). It is, at its peak, twenty feet higher than earth's highest mountains, snuffing out almost all air-breathing creatures.

> Only Noah was left, and those who were with him. . . (7:23)

In due course the waters recede and the ark is deposited on the dry land again.

A New Beginning (7:15—19:19)

The Same

One gets the impression that the whole world has been scoured clean. Creation will have a second chance, as indicated by the animals and the humans being granted a mandate in terms identical to the first one:

> Be fruitful, multiply and replenish the earth. (9:1)

But Different

Different Humanity

Things are not altogether the same as it was for Adam, as our text makes abundantly clear. For one thing, YHWH seems to be under no illusions about the human condition:

> I will not again curse the ground any more for man's sake because the imagination of man's heart is evil from his youth. (8:21a.)

Clearly humanity has not returned to a state of Eden-like innocence.

Different Environment

In spite of this, God makes a gracious promise:

> I will never again strike every living thing, as I have done. While the earth remains, seed time and harvest, and cold and heat, and summer and winter, and day and night will not cease. (8:21.b–22)[8]

It is important to understand that the environment changed after the Flood. For one thing, the above verses, placed where they are, may well suggest that the cycle of the seasons is only now introduced into the world.

For another, the relationship of the human race to the other creatures is radically changed:

> The fear of you and the dread of you will be on every animal of the earth, and on every bird of the sky. Everything that moves along the ground, and all the fish of the sea, are delivered into your hand. Every moving thing that lives will be food for you. As I gave you the green herb, I have given everything to you. (9:2–3)

The clear implication is that until the Flood, human beings were (or were supposed to be) vegetarians. Now God gives them the animals for food as well. Naturally this will cause the latter to be wary of the hunter now among them, and, perhaps for the first time, wary of one another as predators and meat eaters. Presumably this is a new note of disharmony in creation—but one that is God-ordained.

This new situation generates a further command:

> But flesh with its life, that is, its blood, you shall not eat. I will surely require accounting for your life's blood. At the hand of every animal I will require it. At the hand of man, even at the hand of every man's brother, I will require the

---

8. Some have plausibly argued that the understanding of the constancy of the cosmos which this verse expresses enabled the rise of science in the first place. That is, as long as people saw the world as subject to the whims of the gods or magic manipulation they would have no reason to search out any laws by which it might run.

life of man. Whoever sheds man's blood, his blood will be shed by man, for God made man in his own image. (9:4–6)[9]

Clearly the taking of life, especially human life, is a very serious matter.

It is at this point that God then sets his rainbow in the clouds as "the token of the covenant" (9:12), indicating that he will never again destroy the earth by flood. Interestingly, it is not (primarily) to remind humanity of God's promise, but to remind himself of it! In this case he is the only one who is obliged to keep the covenant, so it is appropriate that he is the one to be reminded. But, again, does God need reminding?

Within the context of the Story, the rainbow is a further indication that atmospheric conditions themselves have been altered by the Flood. We are told in the creation account that there was water above the expanse of the sky (1:7) and in the Flood account that "the sky's windows opened" (7:11). It may be that this is the first time water was released wholesale into the atmosphere, making it possible for the sun's rays to be refracted through it, forming that first rainbow. From this perspective the Flood, with the introduction of the seasons and a system of precipitation, was actually the last act in the creation of the environment as we know it today.[10]

Noah, like Adam before him, steps into a new world to become the father of us all. The unspoken question on the mind of the reader is: Will he do any better? Not likely, given God's own observation that even after the Flood, the heart of human beings "is evil from childhood" (8:21a).

Nakedness Exposed, Again (9:20—10:32)

Immediately we learn that Noah planted a vineyard and then got himself drunk on its wine, opening the door to sin. His youngest son, Ham, sees him lying naked in his tent and gets his brothers to cover him up without themselves looking. Ham's having seen his father naked, apparently an outrageous thing in those days, results in Noah pronouncing a curse upon the guilty party: he is to be a slave to his brothers Shem and Japheth, who themselves receive a blessing that hints that the former will

---

9. Whatever else this might mean, it is clearly the point of origin for the biblical linkage of "life" and "blood." Out of respect for life, the blood is to be drained out of meat that is to be eaten. In addition, human life is (again) put above that of other animals, even to the point of animals being held to account for killing humans! Furthermore, this higher value put on humans, rooted in the fact that they are made in the image of God, is here used as justification for capital punishment. Interestingly, in modern debates on this subject this unique status is often used instead to justify the *abolition* of capital punishment! And as far as this debate is concerned, it is important to note that this commandment is part of the "new world order," given long before the Law.

10. A change in the air itself might also explain the fact that it was around this time that the lifespan of human beings began to drop. By the time of the patriarchs it had reached more-or-less modern levels. Could the water above the expanse have served to protect earthly creatures from the harmful effects of the sun? The text makes it clear that the reduction in life span was the result of the sinfulness of pre-Noahic civilization (Gen 6:3). Was the Flood God's instrument of judgment in this sense too?

predominate. Indeed, the Story will soon narrow down to the descendants of Shem, the father of the Semites.

It is hard not to see the parallels here with what happened with Adam and Eve. After the Fall, awareness of their nakedness was the first sign something was wrong. With Noah after the Flood nakedness is the issue as well. Sin, with its resulting curse, marks the second generation along with hope from the good brother: Adam–Cain–Seth, Noah–Ham–Shem. We are also informed that from Noah's offspring "the nations divided from these in the earth after the flood" (10:31). Just as we are all descendants of Adam and Eve, so are we all descendants of Noah and his wife.

YHWH Brooks No Babel (11:1–9)

After the nations that eventually develop are listed (ch. 10), we then are apparently taken back, in kind of a flashback, to the time when there was but one language (11:1), perhaps as a way of explaining the emergence of the different peoples:

> They said, "Come, let's build ourselves a city, and a tower whose top reaches to the sky, and let's make a name for ourselves, lest we be scattered abroad on the surface of the whole earth." (11:4)

YHWH is mightily displeased at this development. Perhaps it is because humanity is doing the opposite of their Mandate to fill the earth by gathering in one place. Perhaps it is because the motive was pride. Perhaps it is because it appears to be another attempt (like Eve's) to be like God: "Now nothing will be withheld from them, which they intend to do" (11:6). Perhaps it is all three.

God "confused the language of all the earth" (v. 9), making the common project unworkable. The place was called Babel, a word that sounds like the Hebrew verb that means "to confuse." It is interesting to observe that this is the word for Babylon as well: that area was famous for its great "wedding cake" towers or "ziggurats," and the ruins of a number of them remain to this day. And even in modern English, incoherent speech is known as "babble."

We seem to be back to square one. The off-ramp of the ark has led to Babel, not to Eden, to a tower that fails reach the heavens, not to mention the Tree of Life. Time for Plan C.

IN THE BOSOM OF ABRAHAM

Introduction

Because the story of Noah and the Flood is so unmistakably reflective of the original creation there is naturally a degree of similarity in the ways in which they exhibit the

Promises. At the same time there is development from one to the other due largely to the fact that now the curses are in play as well.

1. The Land/Place

This theme is manifest once again in the Story's focus on the whole earth. It and its inhabitants are subject to the judgment of the cleansing Flood and the anticipated salvation includes the ground itself. Eden as a specific place seems lost from view in this narrative—but another temporary one, the ark, is added as a place of order, safety, and provision in the chaos of the Flood. It could also be argued that the tower of Babel, as a place where heaven and earth came together, was an attempt to provide a man-made alternative to Eden. Its failure leads to a diffused sense of place as humanity is scattered over the face of the whole earth and divided into nations. Noah and his descendants are still in exile from Eden. Paradise eludes their grasp.

2. Many Descendants

This portion of the Story opens with "When men began to multiply on the surface of the ground" (6:1). Unfortunately, so also did their wickedness increase, to the point where YHWH was "sorry that he had made man on the earth, and it grieved him in his heart." (6:6) Until he noticed Noah it looked as if this Promise was stillborn: all of the creatures were to be destroyed. Of course, the Flood reduced the total population to a mere eight persons, putting "many descendants" at some risk. However, upon emerging from the ark Noah and his sons receive the same Mandate as Adam and Eve: "Be fruitful, multiply, and replenish the earth." (9:1b) Perhaps the changed diet with its increase in protein from meat was meant to be a means to this end. In any event, within a few generations the sons of Noah had multiplied accordingly into "their families, according to their languages, lands, and nations." (10:4, 20 & 32) The game was still on.

3. Blessing to All Nations

At first glance, the effect of the Flood on the nations is a curse: almost the entire population of the earth has been destroyed. Another picture can be seen, however, when we consider that salvation for the nations works here much in the way it did with Adam. That is, because all humanity is "in Noah," the new Adam, all share in the blessing of the salvation that he experienced through the Flood. Furthermore, "nations" (Hebrew "goyim"—the largest group or "family" [WEB] of humanity[11]) first make their appearance right after the Flood in the so-called "Table of Nations" (10:1ff.). This is evidence

---

11. Cf. Hamilton, "Genesis, 1–17," 334.

of a certain maturing (in social structure, at least) and expanding of the human race as it spreads out over the face of the earth. After the Flood they are scattered, but this, too, seems more of a judgment than a blessing. But at least there are now nations to be blessed!

4. Fruitfulness

We hear God repeat the Creation Mandate again, this time to the animals as they are released into the renewed earth: "be fruitful and multiply on the earth" (8:17). Although it is not said explicitly, the clear implication is that the earth itself, as the life-support system for all creatures, will also exhibit an appropriate degree of fruitfulness. Indeed, this seems to be guaranteed by the commitment YHWH then makes:

> I will not again curse the ground any more for man's sake because the imagination of man's heart is evil from his youth... While the earth remains, seed time and harvest, and cold and heat, and summer and winter, and day and night will not cease. (8:21–22).

The fresh olive leaf brought back by the dove was no accident. It was a promise of more to come, firstfruits of a New Creation.

5. Relationship

As it begins, this narrative has God and humanity decidedly at odds. God observes their wayward behavior and determines that "My Spirit will not strive with man forever" (6:3a). His pain at humanity's disobedience is both intense and personal, showing the depth of his desire to be in relationship with them. He is willing to start over with Noah, the one just man he can find, who "walked with God" (6:9). God actually talks to him, breaking a long silence (since the conversation with Cain), giving rise to hope for a restored relationship. God enters into a covenant with his creatures never again to destroy the earth by flood. This seems to signify his good will toward humanity but, by the end of this episode, it turns it's back on him in the story of the tower of Babel and we seem to be back where we started.

6. Grace/Disobedience

Although no specific moral code has been mentioned in this narrative, there is a clear inference that that the people of Noah's day knew right from wrong and were responsible for their own "wickedness." They are destroyed, while Noah, who is "righteous," is saved. Both cases verify that it is "obedience" that is required in order to please God and so continue to be on good terms and enjoy the creation (a gift of grace?). The account provides a straightforward example of how disobedience leads to alienation from God and utter destruction. In that sense it validates at least the second part of the idea that we are "saved by grace and maintained by our obedience." On the other hand, it also manages to bring even the possibility of obedience into question: no sooner is Noah "saved" (by his obedience?) than he (or his son) staggers into sin. Indeed, both before and after the Flood humanity is described as having hearts inclined only to evil. The tower of Babel can be seen as an attempt to reach heaven on the basis of human ingenuity and power and God's disapproval of the same. Things are already not looking good for "obedience."

5

Abram
Called, Confirmed, and Confused

Suggested Reading

Genesis 11:10—16:16

MAJOR DEVELOPMENTS

- Abram is born to Terah in the line of Shem
- YHWH calls Abram to leave his home and extended family
- The Threefold Promise is given for the first time: Land, Many Descendants, and a Blessing to All Nations
- Abram takes his childless wife, along with his nephew, to the land of Canaan
- YHWH appears to Abram, who worships him at Shechem in Canaan
- Abram escapes Canaan's famine by going down to Egypt, gains favor and thrives there, and then gets in trouble and is ordered to leave by Pharaoh
- Abram dwells successfully in Canaan
- Abram learns that his own flesh and blood will be his heir
- YHWH confirms the Promise by entering into a solemn Covenant with Abram, affirming the Promise and extending the Land portion to cover most of the Ancient Near East (ANE)[1]

---

1. The area roughly extending over modern Iraq, Turkey, Syria, Lebanon, Palestine, Israel, Egypt, Jordan, and the Arabian Peninsula.

- In order to produce an heir of his own Abram takes Hagar, Sarai's servant, who gives birth to Ishmael

PERSPECTIVES

A Call to Action

Just as in God's first move toward redemption through Noah, the events of this section have been preceded by a long period of divine inactivity.[2] The reader's attention is instead simply directed to the line of the favored son of Noah, Shem, from his son Arphaxad down to Abram, nine generations.

Abram has settled in Haran after travelling from Ur of the Chaldeans with his father when, out of the blue, YHWH commands him to depart for another country. The last person YHWH had spoken to was Noah, generations ago. Why Abram? Why now? We are simply not told. All we know is that God has ended his long silence. Lights! Camera! Action!

Promises! Promises!

But what kind of "action" is this? It is really just the *promise* of action: three promises, in fact. *We* might say, "Promises! Promises! All I ever get is promises!," but what *Abram* said is not recorded. Perhaps he is stunned into silence by what YHWH told him. Not only would he come into another country, but he is also assured that a great nation will come from him and all the earth's inhabitants will be blessed through him.

To a man without any prospects of even one descendant these promises are staggering in their implications. A land? Maybe. A great nation? Impossible. A blessing to all peoples? Unimaginable! No wonder he is silent. What could he possibly say?

Inner Logic?

Once again we can observe an aspect of the "inner logic" of the Promises: the specific promise of a Blessing to All Nations has universalistic implications for the others. A nation without a territory is an anomaly and, as the nations are incorporated into the Blessing, so also, naturally, is their land. "All nations" implies "all land," hinting at the eventual possible inclusion of the whole earth into the Land. And, of course, "all nations" implies huge numbers of people being brought into the Blessing as well. While they are not descendants of Abram in the literal sense, they are sharing in the Blessing, suggesting some kind of broadened redefinition of "descendants" may be in

---

2. While the length of that previous "absence" before the Flood is not specified, this one, from the Flood to the call of Abraham, is recorded as 427 years long. YHWH does enter the Story more directly regarding the tower of Babel, but even then it is from behind the curtain.

view. Given these effects, Blessing to All Nations seems to be something of the driving force within the Promises.

The Dawn of World Redemption

In any event, the universal scope of YHWH's plan has not been seen since Noah began to chop down trees under a darkening sky. At that time humanity had been marked for destruction, but now it is marked for blessing. Instead of merely saving a few and providing humanity with another chance, YHWH himself now takes over the course of history in order to take humanity to a blessed destination. Something new, something wonderful, is stirring. A corner has been turned and a destination has been sighted, if only from afar and against all odds.

For the reader, a great redemptive vista has opened up that reaches from this ancient encounter all the way up into his or her own life. Each of us becomes part of the Story in this one moment, for we are all included in the grand sweep of YHWH's intentions for humanity. At first glance we are bound to assume that Abram is the One, the long-expected Serpent Crusher, but a second glance reveals that such cannot be the case. The Promises, especially Many Descendants, by their very nature, look to fulfillment well beyond the lifetime of this man, however critically important he may be to the Story. Abram's role may "only" to be the father of the family from whom that promised One will eventually come. Indeed, as the attention of the Story begins to shift toward the extraordinary birth of Abram's own son it is difficult not to assume that he will be the One instead.

Abram's more precise role in the Story is that of being what might be called the first "Promise Keeper," not in the sense that he is a person who does what he says he will do, but in the sense that he has the Promise, *as promise*, in his possession. He is to preserve it intact and pass it along to the next generation until it is eventually fulfilled and thereby ceases to be *promise* altogether.

A Promising Progression

In the meantime, the tale hangs on the immediate obstacles to God's plan and how they are overcome. In a remarkable example of "progressive revelation" YHWH only gradually reveals his intentions to Abram, thereby drawing the reader in step by step. The drama is further heightened by Abram taking things into his own bed, as it were, at least partly no doubt because God did not at first reveal the full extent of his Promise. In response to Abram's serial misunderstandings, God gradually but graciously clarifies his plan. In so doing, the reader is assured that God is truly committed to it. There will be no other way this time. No Plan D.

Abram Believes God

Abram's responses to God's revelations are almost equally compelling. At first he simply obeys and keeps his mouth shut. Then he complains that his servant is the only one who will inherit and when he is told he will have a son of his own, he colludes with his wife to have such a son by Hagar, the servant girl. And then there is the intriguing statement that when Abram believed God's promise of a son YHWH "credited it to him for righteousness" (15:6).

Although the Hebrew in the phrase is difficult to pin down precisely, it does seem to imply that Abram's trust in YHWH led to his being declared righteous. It is even possible that Abram makes the very first confession of faith.[3] Only one man before him, Noah, is called "righteous" and the context tells us that he was "blameless among the people of his time. Noah walked with God." (6:9). To be righteous, then, at least means to be acceptable to God.[4] Whereas Noah was said to be "righteous" because he lived uprightly, it seems YHWH simply declares Abram to be "righteous" because he believed the Promise. Something new seems to have been injected into the biblical bloodstream.

Blessed Assurance

This part of the narrative also links itself securely to the promised future by means of a more specific prophecy from YHWH himself.[5] Abram is told that his offspring will someday be enslaved in a foreign country, but after four hundred years will be set free in great triumph and then take possession of the Promised Land. By this means Abram is reassured that nothing will negate the Promise and the reader's attention is primed for a future mighty act of salvation that begins in slavery and ends in freedom.

THE STORY

Called (11:9—12:9)

With the scattering of humanity after the tower of Babel came an extended period in which God is essentially absent from the Story. He appears only in the mention of Nimrod as "a mighty hunter before YHWH" (10:9). Perhaps the dislocation of the Babel story is meant to enhance this sense of estrangement between Creator and creature in the immediate post-Noah period. Indeed, research on the meaning of the names

---

3. Cf. Hamilton, "Genesis, 1–17," 424.

4. On this definition Adam and Eve would also qualify as "righteous" although the term is not used of them.

5. Gen 15:13–16.

of Shem's descendants suggests that even Abram himself came from a family of moon worshippers in either southern or northern Mesopotamia.[6]

It is all the more startling, then, when we read of God speaking to this man out of the blue. Abram, we have already been told, was one of three sons of Terah (in the line of Shem) whose entire family had set out from Ur to go to Canaan but settled in Haran instead. We have also been informed that Sarai, Abram's wife, is barren and has no children (11:30).

God commands Abram to leave Haran and go to the "land that I will show you" (v. 1). At the same time he is told that "I will make of you a great nation" (v. 2) and that "All the families of the earth will be blessed through you" (v. 3). The predominant note in this telling is that God's abundant blessing is being poured out on Abram and through him upon his descendants and ultimately even the entire world population.

Although Scripture fails to record what Abram was thinking at this stage, he was certainly aware of the problem: he had no descendants at all and his wife could have no children. Nevertheless, he is submissive to the command, and leaves all his extended family behind him except for his wife and his nephew Lot. Coming from a nomadic family, he is on the road again, but this time to an apparently unknown destination. This is a serious act of faith and obedience.

Abram, perhaps resuming the path his family had been on earlier, sets out immediately, and, being led somehow by God, he arrives in Canaan in due course. It is already occupied but in the face of this obvious difficulty YHWH affirms that this is indeed the land that he is going to give to Abram.

The Story makes it clear at this point that Abram would not himself possess this land. It would be given instead to his offspring (v. 7). It turns out that God really meant it when he told him earlier that he would simply "show" him the land (v. 1). Abram's response is one of worship: he builds an altar to God there at Shechem, by the great tree of Moreh that marked the site. He builds another between Ai and Bethel as he makes his way south through the land. Significantly, it is there that he "called on Yahweh's name" (12:8).

Confirmed (12:10—14:24)

Down into Egypt

After a preliminary reconnaissance of the Land, Abram leaves for Egypt as a result of a local famine. While there it is made clear that YHWH is indeed with him. Pharaoh takes the still-attractive Sarai into his palace and Abram into his favor, but then discovers that Sarai is not merely Abram's sister as he had been told. As a result, the

---

6. Cf. Hamilton, "Genesis, 1–17," 363. The exact location of Ur is a matter of considerable scholarly debate.

foreigner and his wife are sent packing back to Canaan along with his nephew Lot, but not before he had become very prosperous in Egypt.

More of the Promise

They arrive back at Bethel where he had earlier worshipped YHWH. Because both Lot and Abram have herds too large for one territory, they decide to split up in order to prevent any quarrelling. At Abram's insistence, Lot gets first choice, picking the valley of the Jordan River because it "was well-watered everywhere, . . .like the garden of Yahweh, like the land of Egypt." (13:10). Lot leaves for his area, and then Abram raises his eyes to what has been left to him.

God tells him that he and his descendants would someday possess the entire Land as far as he could see in all four directions (v. 14–15). In this way Abram is shown the Land, as was promised (v. 1). At the same time, the promise of fathering a great nation now includes so many descendants that they would be like "the dust of the earth" (v. 16). It is important to observe that two of the Promises have now been progressively fleshed out.[7]

Blessed by a King/Priest

While in Canaan, Abram and Lot become entangled in the conflicts of the local inhabitants. At one point, Lot is captured and, after Abram manages to rescue him and recover his possessions, he is blessed by the mysterious Melchizedek, king of Salem and priest of "God Most High" (14:18). This has the effect of once again confirming that God's hand is upon Abram. The episode ends with Abram demonstrating his integrity by refusing to accept any of the spoils of victory.

Confused (15 & 16)

Who's In the Will?

YHWH once again affirms to Abram that he will care for him and be his "exceedingly great reward" (15:1). Abram points out the ultimate futility of this assurance because he is childless and his servant Eliezer will inherit all his estate, not his own flesh. What good will God's blessing be if there is no child to carry on the family? Behind this is the ancient world's view of the importance of having offspring, no doubt reflecting

---

7. In a pattern that will mark much of the Old Testament perspective on the Promises, the third, the Blessing to All Nations, recedes into the background of the narrative for the time being. As we shall see it is, however, strongly implied in chapter 17 and explicitly affirmed in chapter 22. Interestingly, the Story of Abraham is "bookended" with the Promise in all three dimensions. It may well be that the Many Descendants and the Land components are highlighted because they have a more immediate relevance to the Story, whereas the Blessing to All Nations is still far over the horizon at this point.

both the Creation Mandate to increase in number and the ancient idea that one goes on living through one's descendants.[8]

To this God responds with the word that "he who will come out of your own body will be your heir" (15:4), not Eliezer. From this son will come offspring as numerous as the stars in the heavens. What is fascinating about this account is that Abram is not told that the child will actually be Sarai's as well. It is as if God is testing Abram at each juncture in the story, stringing him along to see if he will remain faithful while in possession of only partial knowledge. Again, we are dealing with progressive revelation and its inherent tensions are heightened even further by key omissions all the more compelling within such a condensed narrative.

Bound by Covenant

In response to this new information, Abram believes YHWH who "credited it to him for righteousness" (15:6). This verse dramatically focuses the reader's attention on the exceptional quality of Abram's trust in YHWH, only to be brought up short by his immediate demand for verification of the Promise! Instead of being angry, as we might expect, however, God responds graciously by submitting to a covenant-making ceremony, binding himself in no uncertain terms to keep his word (the smoke and fire of 15:17 are undoubtedly symbolic of the divine presence[9]). At YHWH's command, Abram brings a heifer, a goat, a ram, a dove, and a pigeon. He then proceeds to cut the first three in two, laying the halves opposite one another. In order to understand what is going on here it is necessary to set this event in its cultural context.

The world of the ANE offers widespread evidence that animals were slaughtered in treaty contraction ceremonies. Some of these texts–but not all of them–suggest that the two parties to the treaty walked between the rows of freshly killed animal flesh, and in so doing placed a curse upon themselves if they should prove disloyal to the terms of the treaty: may they too be torn apart if they are responsible in any way for violating the arrangement.[10] Significantly, here we observe only one party to the Covenant, YHWH, making this commitment to do as promised. Abram is merely a passive observer/recipient.

Expect Delays

At this point God reveals to Abram yet more details about what lies ahead:

---

8. See especially the interesting discussion in Levenson, *Resurrection and the Restoration*, 108–22.

9. The same symbolism can be seen in the cloud and the flame, which led the Israelites through the wilderness (cf. Exod 13:21 etc.).

10. Hamilton, "Genesis, 1–17," 430. See also Jer 34:18.

> Know for sure that your offspring will live as foreigners in a land that is not theirs, and will serve them. They will afflict them four hundred years. I will also judge that nation, whom they will serve. Afterward they will come out with great wealth; but you will go to your fathers in peace. You will be buried at a good old age. In the fourth generation they will come here again, for the iniquity of the Amorite is not yet full. (15:13–16)

From this Abram would discern that the road ahead was long and uneven, but nonetheless certain. Many of his offspring can expect to live in promise rather than fulfillment. He himself will have been long in his grave before any of these critical events would take place. There are strong hints here, however, that they would form the crucible in which his family would finally be forged into the promised great nation. Oddly, it seems that this long delay is an act of divine forbearance toward the wicked Amorites who currently possess at least some of the Land.

The World at His Feet

One more detail of the Promise is now added. The full extent of the Land will stretch from the Nile to the Euphrates, a huge territory, perhaps even the whole of what Abram would understand as the "world." It certainly encompasses all the territory on which he had ever set his feet. Will this Promise ever stop expanding?

His Own Son!

Certainly Abram's confusion persists as he tries another tack, now that he knows that his own son would inherit. In an account that perhaps reminds us a bit of Eve's encouraging of Adam to eat the forbidden fruit, Sarai (blaming God for her barrenness?) urges Abram to sleep with her servant Hagar so that "I will obtain children by her." (16:2). This was apparently in keeping with ANE custom in the case of a wife who was infertile.[11]

Immediately Hagar becomes pregnant and begins to lord it over her mistress, who in turn mistreats her and causes her to run away into the desert. There she encounters an angel of YHWH who counsels her to return to Sarai and gives her a promise that she will be blessed with descendants who "will not be counted for multitude" (v. 10). The angel also instructs her to name her son Ishmael ("God hears"). And so, it seems, at age eighty-six, Abram finally has his heir and the necessary bridge to "many descendants."

What other conclusion could he or the reader come to? Undoubtedly Hagar had told him what the angel had said about many descendants coming through Ishmael

---

11. Cf. Hamilton, "Genesis, 1–17," 444–46.

and the fact that the angel had named him.[12] These two facts go only in one direction: Ishmael is the chosen one. On the other hand, the angel also predicted that Ishmael, far from being a blessing to the nations, would live in hostility with everyone, including his brothers. In spite of appearances, something doesn't quite add up.

IN THE BOSOM OF ABRAHAM

1. The Land/Place

In this section of the Story the famous "Promised Land" is introduced into the narrative. It is first described to Abram as "the land I will show you," then, "all the land that you see" (Canaan) in all directions from where he was in Shechem and finally the whole of the ANE. This last description, with its inclusion of the Euphrates, may allude to Eden itself. Abram lives and prospers in the Land but does not possess it for himself. However, a profound sense of "place" is evoked when Lot's choice of part of it is likened explicitly to the garden of Eden. Are we there yet? No, but we are getting close. You can almost see it from here.

2. Many Descendants

This episode is preoccupied with the tension between the repeated emphatic promise (in several forms) of many descendants and the similarly repeated fact that Sarai is barren. At first it seems that the fulfillment will have to come through Abram's servant Eliezer and then, more satisfactorily, through Ishmael, his son by Sarai's servant girl. By its very nature this Promise will have to wait many generations before becoming a reality. However, this is one rocket that is very wobbly on the launching pad and we are not yet sure what direction it is going to go.

3. Blessing to All Nations

This Promise, while an explicit part of the original Promise (12:2–3), recedes almost entirely into the background of the narrative. Indeed, it is not even mentioned during the actual covenant-making ceremony. A glimpse of it is to be seen, however, in the positive interactions of Abram with several of the nations with which he comes into contact. Experiencing its flip side, Egypt suffers serious diseases because Pharaoh had taken Sarai into his harem. Already the principle outlined in the original Promise is beginning to work:

> I will bless those who bless you, and I will curse him who treats you with contempt. (12:3a)

---

12. Before this only Adam had been named by God (Gen 5:2). This is auspicious company indeed for Ishmael.

Positively, when Abram rescues Lot he ends up blessing the king of Sodom by refusing to take any of the spoils himself. When we see Abram being blessed by the king of Salem, Melchizedek, we cannot help but think of the above principle. Abram then gives him a tenth of the spoils. More of this Blessing can be anticipated, perhaps, in the extension of the Promised Land to include most, if not all, of the nations then known to Abram.

4. Fruitfulness

Our narrative abounds with this quality. Whether it is the nature of the Promised Land (like Eden) or in the fact that the territory of all the nations is part of the Land, the predominant note is abundance. Even Abram's flocks and herds grow by leaps and bounds while in Egypt and he and Lot have to go their separate ways in Canaan because they just keep increasing. No reader can miss this dimension of the account.

5. Relationship

This, too, is a prominent feature of this section. Anyone in covenant with God is by definition in relationship with him. And it is "covenant" which dominates in this section. In terms of its nature, clearly God is once again entering into a friendly relationship with a member of the human race. Where his benevolent presence had been missing in the immediately preceding narrative, he steps dramatically into the life of Abram and is with him each step of the way. It is up close and personal between them. For the first time since Adam, intimacy and genuine dialogue are present. Things are looking up.

6. Grace/Obedience

YHWH's calling of Abram is naturally seen as the classic example of grace in the Old Testament. There is no discernable reason offered in the text for God's choice of this particular man for these extravagant Promises. He does not appear to be responding to anything in Abram's character or life situation, suggesting that the great program outlined for humanity comes entirely at his own initiative. In fact, later on in the story Abram shows points of both good character (particularly with reference his generous treatment of Lot in the division of the Land) and bad (he lied to Pharaoh about Sarai being his wife). To see grace at work here is both inevitable and perhaps even unremarkable.

It must also be noted that Abram is immediately called to obey YHWH:

> Leave your country, and your relatives, and your father's house, and go to the land that I will show you. (12:1)

Here, it seems, is a classic example of obedience following grace. The same pattern is seen later after Lot takes the better portion of the Land. YHWH reassures Abram that all of it will someday be his and commands him to:

> Arise, walk through the land in its length and in its width; for I will give it to you. (13:17)

It must not be assumed, however, that the Promise is in any way *contingent* upon Abram's obedience. The last quote makes this perfectly clear: it does not say: "In order to maintain your inheritance you must go." The emphasis here, as always for these Promises, is on the certainty of their fulfillment.

Furthermore, the obedience called for here is not that of righteousness or morality but of taking a certain action. It is really the former that is part of our governing question about salvation being maintained by our "obedience." And it is missing altogether in this section. The kind of obedience on exhibit is better seen as an expression of Abram's trust in YHWH, a faith, we have been told, that is counted to him for righteousness.

Here, then, seems to be a new reality: salvation that is a sure thing, based on a sure Promise and responded to by a righteousness-engendering faith that expresses itself in obedience. On the other hand, this may not be so much a new reality than it is a straightforward and definitive expression of "saved by grace." While earlier manifestations of this idea may not have been obvious at first glance (as, for example, in Eden), here it arises unmistakably out of the text itself. The idea that righteousness is achieved simply through believing the Promise also sharpens our understanding that "works" have no place in *becoming* righteous. But as to their role in *maintaining* that status the Story here is largely silent. That itself may be significant, but we will be in a better position to judge after the next section completes our consideration of Abraham.

6

Abraham
Laughter, *Laughter*, and *More Laughter*

Suggested Reading

Genesis 17:1—22:19

MAJOR DEVELOPMENTS

- YHWH appears to Abram and:
    1. gives him the new name of "Abraham"
    2. confirms the Covenant Promises
    3. gives circumcision as the sign of the Covenant
    4. gives Sarai the new name of "Sarah"
    5. promises Abraham a son *by Sarah*, the true son of Promise

- YHWH appears again to Abraham in the context of the 3 Visitors and:
    1. explicitly brings Sarah into the picture
    2. confirms in an aside his covenantal intentions regarding Abraham
    3. negotiates with Abraham over the fate of Sodom
    4. destroys Sodom and Gomorrah as judgment upon their terrible wickedness, while providing for the escape of Lot and his family

- Abraham deceives a local king named Abimelech concerning Sarah but manages to come through unscathed

- Isaac is born at the appointed time
- Hagar and Ishmael are sent away, but remain under God's care
- Abraham is tested at Moriah when God commands him to sacrifice Isaac
- A ram is provided as a substitute for Isaac
- God confirms the covenant Promises in response to Abraham's obedience

PERSPECTIVES

Introduction

In this section of the Story, the progressive revelation of YHWH's plan for providing Abram with an heir finally reaches its climax with the promise and realization of the birth of a son to Sarai herself. The way the reader has been ushered step by step to this moment naturally leads to the assumption that with the birth of Isaac we have finally found the One, the Serpent Crusher. Even the fact that both parents receive a new name from YHWH underlines for them (and the reader) that something new and of utmost significance is now being brought into the world.

In this account the repeated confirmations of the covenant Promises in the face of present reality far short of them pile up into a mountain of unresolved tension. Then, when both Abraham and Sarah laugh at the idea of her becoming pregnant, the reader catches his or her breath. The stories that follow, of Abraham's bargaining with God over Sodom, its destruction, and the Abimelech affair, all serve to prolong the agony to the point where the short and simple account of the birth of Isaac becomes almost anticlimactic. This serves as a hint that his role in the Story to follow may not be as important as it might have seemed, given the dramatic build-up to his birth.

Three or One?

This section of the Story includes the arrival of three visitors to Abraham. At several points they talk to him in the normal fashion but in the next breath it is YHWH himself who is speaking, leaving the impression that the three of them and YHWH are somehow one and the same. There is a definite "oddness" about the passage that defies easy explanation, but the ancient writer offers no explanation.[1] As W. M. Alston Jr. puts it, that itself may be the point:

---

1. Over the centuries many Christians have seen this as an appearance of the Holy Trinity in the Old Testament text. It is an intriguing but ultimately speculative interpretation.

Obscurity is the story's way of telling us of God's hiddenness, of the concreteness of God's revelation, and of the impossible possibilities that are open to all that believe.[2]

Certainly, the God of the Bible cannot be confined within our human understanding. He is who he is.[3]

A Real Bargain

The above-mentioned negotiating episode over Sodom raises a number of important issues, not the least of which is its portrayal of God changing his mind in response to human pleading. As we shall have occasion to note, this is not the only time in the Bible that a similar thing happens.[4] Whatever else it might mean, it certainly denotes a dialogue between God and a man who is treated as a genuine, if not equal, partner.[5] Not since Eden have we seen anything like this, and even there it did not reach such heights. The net effect is to underscore the special place of Abraham in the grand scheme of things, perhaps even signaling a new stage in the divine-human encounter.

Intimations of a Royal Line

It is easy to overlook the new revelation in this section that not only will nations come from Abraham and Sarah, but also kings (17:6, 16). At the moment this may seem simply part of the package of having nations as one's progeny but it may hint that the coming Blessing (and, in the reader's mind, the coming One) will have something to do with these royal progeny.

The Death and Resurrection of the Beloved Son

The incident of Isaac's near sacrifice at Moriah, the occasion of the last in the series of Promise confirmations, is vividly and movingly portrayed. On first reading, Abraham's answer to Isaac's question about the missing lamb seems the wrenching but evasive response of a heartbroken father:

> God will provide himself the lamb for a burnt offering, my son. (22:8)

From the perspective of the end of the account, when God really did provide a sacrifice, this seems an affirmation of profound faith on Abraham's part. After all his

---

2. Quoted in Hamilton, "Genesis, 18–50," 8.
3. Cf. Exod 3:14.
4. See 97, 148–49, below.
5. It is little wonder that in all of Scripture it is only Abraham who is called God's "friend" (2 Chr 20:7; Isa 41:8, and Jas 2:23), although Moses comes very close (Exod 33:11).

ups and downs with God, Abraham finally trusts completely in his word. The Threefold Promise is confirmed again at this point and the reader definitely gets the impression that this is finally the seal on the deal.

Jon Levenson has drawn attention to this account as the primary example of "the death and resurrection of the beloved son," a theme that he finds throughout Genesis.[6] Expanding "resurrection" to refer to events in which someone could be said to "die" and/or "rise" in a metaphorical sense, he finds this motif beginning in the death of Abel and the birth of Seth, his replacement brother.[7] In our story Isaac certainly qualifies as "the beloved son," while his death and resurrection on Moriah, while "only" symbolic, skate very close to the literal meaning of the terms. Levenson does us the favor of pointing out the persistence of this pattern and we will have further occasion to note its development as the Story progresses.

Substitutions Allowed

It should also not be overlooked that the climactic drama played out on Moriah provides the reader with a kind of heads-up with reference to "substitution" as a theological category. Presumably YHWH could have simply stopped Abraham from sacrificing his son and ended the episode at that point. Instead, however, he provides a substitute animal for the boy and a sacrifice takes place. This almost incidental detail offers a first opportunity to peer over the edge of the Story into a great mystery: a substitute, at least one that he himself provides, is clearly acceptable to YHWH and fulfills his demand for a sacrifice.

Who's Laughing Now?

Finally, a word needs to be said about the role of "laughter" in this segment. This would no doubt be more obvious to anyone reading the Hebrew text than it is for those of us who read it only in translation but, even so, it is hard to miss. The word's transformation from being a sign of unbelief to a sign of profound joy comes across to all readers as the Story moves from God's promise of a son for Sarah to her reaction to the child's birth. That "Isaac" means "laughter" or "he laughs" only adds another wonderful level of irony to the narrative. And it may be that "he laughs" refers most appropriately to God himself, now that his ultimate plan of salvation has finally been set in motion.

---

6. Levenson, *Death and Resurrection*.
7. Levenson, *Death and Resurrection*, 78.

THE STORY

Laughter (Gen 17)

A New Name is Given

For thirteen long years Abram lives with the misunderstanding that Ishmael was the Son of Promise. Just about the time the boy is to become a man, YHWH suddenly appears again to the 99-year-old patriarch:

> I am God Almighty. Walk before me and be blameless. I will make my covenant between me and you, and will multiply you exceedingly. (v. 1b–2)

In order to underline this commitment YHWH gives Abram ("exalted father") a new name. All by itself this act sets the old man apart as special. And then there is the new name itself: Abraham, (literally, "father of many"). Furthermore, this "many" will include both nations and kings (v. 6). For the first time a plurality of nations from Abraham (and even royalty) is introduced into the Promise. It just keeps getting better and better.

A New Relationship is Promised

And then God spells out the essential meaning of all his extravagant benevolence to Abraham:

> I will establish my covenant between me and you and your offspring after you throughout their generations for an everlasting covenant, to be a God to you and to your offspring after you. I will give to you, and to your offspring after you, the land where you are traveling, all the land of Canaan, for an everlasting possession. I will be their God. (vv. 7–8)

Up to this point, Abraham had every reason to imagine that his descendants would participate in the blessing being promised to him by themselves having many descendants, possessing the Land, and being a blessing to the nations. Now it is made clear that their blessing will include a special intimate relationship with God himself. It just keeps getting better and better, indeed.

A Sign is Given

Besides giving Abram a new name, YHWH institutes a sign (or token [WEB]) of the Covenant (v. 11), commanding that each male child in his line be circumcised on the eighth day after birth.[8] This is to apply to slaves as well, even if they are foreigners. The text fails to indicate the precise significance of this particular sign but it certainly was

---

8. This is the second such sign of the covenant, Noah's rainbow being the first. See Gen 9:12–17.

not unique to Abraham's household. Indeed, it was common among the inhabitants of Canaan with the clear exception of the "uncircumcised" Philistines along the coastal plain. Therefore, it could not simply serve to mark off Abraham and his descendants from all their neighbors. Given its nature, however, there is a strong suggestion that it is to be associated with the fertility by which the Promise of Many Descendants will be fulfilled.[9]

Whatever its meaning, it certainly is made an absolute requirement in order to be part of the covenant people: if a male child was not "cut" he is to be "cut off" from the community. How an adult could be held accountable for the failure of his parents to have him "done" when he was but a helpless infant is not explained. It may be that our modern preoccupation with the autonomous self blinds us to a more corporate understanding of how sin (and salvation) actually work.[10]

Another New Name is Given

At this point Abraham is instructed to call his wife "Sarah" ("princess") from now on, although he is not told why. While this name is not significantly different from "Sarai," which also means "princess," it may signify that now she is going to be a princess for real in that "kings of peoples will come from her" (v. 16). Perhaps her old name had become to her a faded hope from her parents but has now taken on substantial reality: kings are born to princesses, after all.

You're Joking

Abraham's response to all of this is to laugh. In fact, he fell down he was laughing so hard. What an absurd idea! For him and Sarah to have a child at such an advanced age! Impossible! Ridiculous!

God, however, is not amused at this lack of faith from the man of faith. Just when he has been given the last and most important piece of the puzzle this "believer" responds by laughing in YHWH's face! Still clinging to the idea that Ishmael is his heir, he simply cannot comprehend this news. Incredibly, God responds by reaffirming the Promise and even confirms the blessing for Ishmael.[11] And then he commands

---

9. Cf. Hamilton, "Genesis, 1–17," 471.

10. Cf. the disciples' question to Jesus about the man born blind in John 9:1, "Rabbi, who sinned, this man or his parents, that he was born blind?"

11. Latent in this text is the ancient animosity between Jew and Arab, and later between Judaism and Islam. Both religions trace their roots back to Abraham, but one through Isaac and the other through "Isamail." Muslims seem to deliberately misread this text to make Ishmael the true son of Promise. From their point of view the nation of Israel became proud and disobeyed God, thus losing out on his blessing. Muhammad considered himself a son of Isamail. This interpretation obviously contradicts the plain statements of Scripture, but Ishmael is not to be lightly dismissed from the narrative.

Abraham to name his son "Isaac," which means "laughter" in Hebrew. His true Son of Promise will thereby become a constant reminder of his unbelief. The joke is on Abraham, but he isn't laughing. Yet.

Laughter (Gen 18–19)

Sarah Laughs Too

This is the final installment of the dramatic story leading up, finally, to the birth of the Son of Promise. Abraham is told that the boy will be born to Sarah in about a year. Sarah, eavesdropping at the door of the tent, overhears this, apparently learning for the first time of her impending motherhood, and laughs to herself at the absurdity of the idea. She, like her husband before her, finds it extremely funny. Again, YHWH is not amused, and directly challenges her lack of faith:

> Is anything too hard for Yahweh? (18:14)

Sarah is frightened and denies her laughter, but she is left with God's parting words ringing in her ears:

> Yes, you did laugh. (18:15)

If we cringe at Sarah's response, we obviously get the point. The divine question still hangs in the air for us all. It is a central question of the life of faith and will come to us all.

Abraham Bargains over Sodom

In the meantime, the three "men" proceed towards Sodom while YHWH wonders out loud if he should take Abraham into his confidence regarding his intent to obliterate that city because of its great sinfulness. He does so, but Abraham, knowing that Lot is living there, boldly tries to talk him out of it, asking if it was fair to so destroy the righteous who dwell in Sodom along with the wicked. When YHWH states his willingness to spare the city if fifty righteous persons can be found within it, Abraham, perhaps aware that this is not likely, dares to bargain with the Almighty! Even more startling, YHWH actually enters into the negotiation! Abraham does get the required number reduced to ten, but that apparently is still too many, given what happens next.

A Study in Contrasts

The rest of the story of Sodom and its destruction, vividly told as it is (ch. 19), is somewhat of a tangent to the main story but it does add to our understanding of Abraham's character. Two "angels" (supernatural messengers) are sent to Sodom where Lot takes them in as guests. Some of the inhabitants surround his house demanding that they be surrendered to them for wicked sexual purpose. The way in which both Abraham and Lot have welcomed these same "men" stands out in stark contrast to this outrage.[12] Perhaps that is why the story is included in the first place, to highlight Abraham's righteousness once again. In any event, the "messengers" save Lot and his family from the mob and the coming obliteration of the wicked city.

Abraham, Sarah, and Abimelech

Abraham then leaves the area of Sodom to live at Gerar on the border of Philistine territory and while there he once again passes Sarah off as his sister (a half-truth) for his own protection. When she is claimed by a local king named Abimelech, YHWH comes to the ruler in a dream to warn him that Sarah is a married woman. Protesting his innocence, he then presents gifts to Abraham and Sarah while the former prays that the wombs of Abimelech's women, having been closed by an angry YHWH, might be healed. And so they are. We are assured through this story that YHWH is still with Abraham in spite of his backsliding, and that all will be well.

And More Laughter (Ch. 21)

The Birth of Laughter

A year later the promised son is born as predicted. He is named Isaac ("Laughter") and Sarah finally gets the joke:

> God has made me laugh. Everyone who hears will laugh with me. (v. 6)

This joyful laughter will undoubtedly sustain Sarah the rest of her days. But will the name not also remind both parents that they had failed to believe the word of YHWH? Perhaps the reader is being invited to laugh as well: what irony inhabits this name!

The Fate of Ishmael

Not everyone is laughing *with* Sarah. Ishmael, in fact, laughs *at* her (or Isaac), mocking when the child is weaned and thereby making both him and his mother Hagar personae non gratae in Sarah's household. Reluctantly, Abraham sends them away after God reassures him that they will survive and even that a nation will come from Ishmael "because he is your child" (v. 13). This is confirmed by the story of how God provides for Hagar and Ishmael in the desert. The reader, however, has noted God's

---

12. The homosexual nature of the assault is probably what is considered "wicked." The literature is extensive, but Hamilton, "Genesis, 1–17," gives a nice overview of the biblical evidence, 33–34.

word to Abraham that "your offspring will be named through Isaac." (v. 12). His will be the story to follow. He is the One.

Putting it All to the Test (Ch. 22)

An Aweful Command

The reader would imagine that at this point the Covenant is signed, sealed, and delivered. But one final and dramatic episode still remains. It seems that Abraham's faith in YHWH must be tried in the fire before the Covenant is finalized. We have seen him waver under pressure before. What will happen this time?

> Now take your son, your only son, Isaac, whom you love, and go into the land of Moriah. Offer him there as a burnt offering on one of the mountains which I will tell you of. (22:2)

So comes the awful command of God to Abraham. Talk about being conflicted! What an impossible thing! But Abraham remains silent, much as he did when YHWH first called him in Haran and he obediently makes his way to the place of sacrifice with Isaac his son. "Laughter" is at his side, but there is no laughter in his heart. Indeed the name must have been mocking him on that interminable uphill climb. All the other impossible promises of God rested on the boy, and yet . . . . Would he, could he, believe that God would keep his clear Promise to provide offspring through *this* child, even if he was sacrificed? Was it this hope that somehow enabled him to put one reluctant foot in front of the other?

YHWH Provides the Sacrifice

The story is told with beautiful poignancy as the son innocently questions his father about the missing lamb. Abraham's reply that "God will provide himself the lamb" (v. 8) may indicate something of his faith, even at this stage. But when he raises the knife in the final climatic scene, there can be no doubt regarding his obedience, at least. Unlike Adam and Eve before him, he has no reason to hide when God's voice booms out from above:

> Abraham, Abraham! (v. 11)

His simple reply provides a model for the ages[13]:

> Here I am. (v. 11)

Abraham is instructed to cease and desist:

---

13. Cf. The Story of Samuel in 1 Samuel 3:16, and that of Mary in Luke 1:38.

> Now I know that you fear God, because you have not withheld your son, your only son from me. (v. 12)

It is then that the patriarch notices a ram nearby, caught by its horns in a thicket. He sacrifices the animal instead of his son.

> Abraham called the name of that place "Yahweh Will Provide." As it is said to this day, "On Yahweh's mountain, it will be provided." (v. 14)

The critical lesson has finally been learned: God will indeed provide. Three times this story has repeated the point (v. 8, v. 14) just to make sure that we get it. The author, while not uninterested in the testing of Abraham, is focused on another even more important point.[14] He has been driving toward the definitive answer to God's earlier question of Sarah (and of the reader):

> Is anything too hard for Yahweh? (18:14).

YHWH will provide. You can count on it. It really was a rhetorical question, after all.

Three at Last

Fittingly, it is at this point in the narrative that the Threefold Promise is reiterated to Abraham for the final time. It is done so clearly in response to his demonstration of obedience (and no doubt the faithful trust that would engender such obedience):

> 'I have sworn by myself,' says Yahweh, 'because you have done this thing, and have not withheld your son, your only son, that I will bless you greatly, and I will multiply your offspring greatly like the stars of the heavens, and like the sand which is on the seashore. Your offspring will possess the gate of his enemies. All the nations of the earth will be blessed by your offspring, because you have obeyed my voice.' (vv. 16–18)

The text fails to mention the laughter that must have filled the camp that night. But we can hear it nevertheless.

IN THE BOSOM OF ABRAHAM

1. The Land/Place

The Land remains a strong focus, but still only as promise and not as possession. With the institution of circumcision as the sign of the Covenant comes a reaffirmation that the "whole land of Canaan" will be given to Abraham's offspring (17:8). However, in spite of the fact that this Promise in its final form is an affirmation that his "offspring

---

14. See Greidanus, *Preaching*, 292ff.

will possess the gate of his enemies" (22:17), Abraham himself remains an alien in the Land. His relationship with the inhabitants is shown to be one of mutual respect (cf. the story of Abimelech in ch. 20–21) but actual possession of the Land is not his lot. At the same time, as Abimelech puts it, "God is with you in all that you do" (21:22). In this way the Land and its inhabitants are blessed to some degree through Abraham's presence.

2. Many Descendants

As a Promise, this feature is mentioned explicitly three times: during the initiation of the covenant of circumcision (17:6 & 19); indirectly as part of God's soliloquy (18:18); and in God's response to Abraham on Moriah where both metaphors previously used (stars and sand) are combined for emphasis (22:17). The narrative itself, of course, is preoccupied with the progressive resolution of the tension between Sarah's barrenness and this Promise. Temporary relief is achieved when Isaac is born, but anxiety heightens again at God's command to sacrifice the boy. Final resolution is delayed until all doubt is removed by the emphatic demonstration that "God will provide" assuring both Abraham and the reader of ultimate fulfillment. As the episode closes, however, Abraham has only two sons as far as we know: Ishmael and Isaac. But it only takes One.

3. Blessing to All Nations

This Promise is stated twice, once in YHWH's soliloquy over Sodom (18:18) and again after the episode on Moriah (22:18). However, as we noted of the last chapter, it remains largely in the background of the story. But there are a number of hints made: the inclusion of foreigners (those in Abraham's household) within the Covenant (17:12–13); the generous hospitality that Abraham shows to strangers (18:1–8); the concern of Abraham for the fate of Sodom (or is it just Lot that he wants to save?) (18:22ff). These, along with the Abimelech episode, all point, if only indirectly, in the same way: blessing comes to the nations through Abraham.

4. Fruitfulness

Like the Promise of Many Descendants, fruitfulness is something that is largely held in suspense. But if we read carefully between the lines, it is already part of Abraham's reality as he continues to prosper from the produce of the Land. His prosperity is definitely enhanced by the sheep, cattle, slaves, and silver that Abimelech gives to him (20:14; cf. 24:35).

5. Relationship

The permanent nature of the covenant relationship is established once and for all in this part of the Story. YHWH commits himself to Abraham *and his offspring* in significant simplicity: "I will be their God" (17:8). The alienation experienced by post-Edenic humanity is clearly not the final answer. As far as the main characters in this section are concerned, the up close and personal relationship between God and Abraham (and Sarah) is made abundantly clear. In the short space of five chapters, we note no less than four "face-to-face" conversations between them. One, the bargaining session over Sodom, is a remarkable demonstration of Abraham's being admitted into the very council of God. This intimacy is nothing short of breathtaking. God and man are talking again for the first time since the aftermath of the Fall.

6. Grace/Obedience

This part of the Story is clearly moved along at God's initiative: he simply keeps appearing "out of the blue" to Abraham, each time revealing only the next step in the divine plan. In the face of skepticism and laughter he still persists. All this climaxes with the birth of Isaac as an act of pure grace. Nothing could be more clear. At the same time there is a strong undercurrent throughout of the need for obedience:

> I am God Almighty; walk before me and be blameless. (17:1b)

Perhaps the relationship between these two themes is best expressed by YHWH just before the Sodom and Gomorrah incident:

> . . .since Abraham will surely become a great and mighty nation, and all the nations of the earth will be blessed in him. . . For I have known him, to the end that he may command his children and his household after him, that they may keep the way of Yahweh, to do righteousness and justice; to the end that Yahweh may bring on Abraham that which he has spoken of him. (18:18–19)

This is an almost perfect expression of the idea that we are saved by grace and maintain that salvation through obedience. However, a careful reading might suggest that things are not quite so simple. The first line states that the Promises will come to effect. Period. Then it goes on to introduce with the words "so that," an element of contingency. While our Greek minds try to fit this statement into either one category or the other ("contingent" or "noncontingent," "for sure," or "it depends"), the Hebrew mind is once again content with a "both/and" approach.

This pattern appears again when we set the fulfillment of the Promises in no uncertain terms from chapter 17:4–9 against the clear statement a few verses later that dire consequences will follow unless the people keep the covenant of circumcision. Again we struggle with certainty on the one hand and uncertainty on the other.

It is instructive that when both Abraham and Sarah laugh at the promise of a son by means of their own bodies, their skepticism has no effect at all on the Promise itself. In addition, the account of God and Abraham bargaining over Sodom may provide a useful insight into how grace is dominant. That story is about what we might call the *quantity* of righteousness that will forestall judgment. What emerges is that it only takes a little! God's fundamental orientation is toward his Promises (as the discussion above indicates) and it will take almost unimaginable human disobedience to bring them to naught. Even then, one suspects, he will find a way, at least for his covenant people. After all, Lot and his family were saved in spite of being under even the ten-person requirement, when "God remembered Abraham" (19:29).

It is this last thought which lingers at the end of day: God will save whom he saves because of Abraham. Period. The final confirmation of the Covenant on Moriah even states that "because you have done this . . . I will bless you greatly" (22:16–17), suggesting that his absolute obedience on the mountain has sealed the deal for all time.

Here the obedience in view is again one of action arising from faith, not adherence to moral law. It is faith as trust, absolute trust. And it wins the world. While there are earlier indications that ethical living would be demanded of Abraham's descendants and even that the Blessing would be in some sense contingent upon their performance, here, in its final climactic form, the Promise is simply unqualified. It would seem that Abraham's great act of trust-induced obedience was all-sufficient. While the need for obedience from that point on cannot be overlooked, the salvation here before us cannot, in the end, be dependent upon it. God will make it happen. Somehow.[15]

---

15. Cf. Hamilton, "Genesis, 1–17," 465–66.

7

Isaac, Jacob, and Joseph
Two More Promise Keepers and a Savior

Suggested Reading

Genesis 23:1—50:26

MAJOR DEVELOPMENTS

- Sarah dies in Canaan and Abraham purchases a family plot at Machpelah for her burial
- Abraham sends a servant back to his relatives in Haran to obtain a wife for Isaac. He returns with Rebekah, a granddaughter of Abraham's brother Nahor.
- Abraham dies and is buried with Sarah at Machpelah
- Twins Jacob and Esau are born to Rebekah, whose barren womb was opened by YHWH
- Jacob takes advantage of his brother and obtains the latter's birthright as firstborn
- YHWH confirms to Isaac that the Promises will flow through him
- Jacob tricks the elderly Isaac into giving him the firstborn's blessing, enraging Esau
- Jacob flees to Haran to obtain a wife from among Rebekah's brother Laban's daughters
- At Bethel, YHWH confirms to Jacob that the Promises will flow through him
- Jacob marries Leah and Rachel, agreeing to work for Laban for 14 years as a

bride-price

- God blesses Jacob with a miraculous increase in flocks and herds as well as 11 sons, but only Joseph is by his favorite, Rachel
- Jacob and family return to Canaan and God encounters him again at Bethel, gives him a new name, Israel, and confirms the Covenant a second time
- Rachel dies while giving birth to Benjamin, Jacob's 12th and final son
- After Jacob arrives back at his father's home, Isaac dies at 180
- Joseph's jealous brothers sell him into Egyptian servitude, where, through his ability to interpret dreams, he rises to become Pharaoh's chief administrator
- Joseph reconciles with his family and saves them by bringing them down to Egypt during a terrible famine
- The children of Israel settle in Egypt
- Israel blesses all 12 of his sons, dies in Egypt at age 147, and is buried in the family plot at Machpelah back in Canaan
- Joseph dies at age 110 in Egypt but makes his brothers promise to take his bones with them when they finally return to the Land

PERSPECTIVES

Introduction

The drama definitely gets turned up to "high" for this part of the Story. The camera, as it were, remains zeroed in on the actions of the three main characters and portrays them in considerable detail, thereby alerting the reader to their overall significance. Covering the turbulent three generations after Abraham, the narrative includes intrigue, sibling rivalry, fear, betrayal, reconciliation, and even romance. But it ends with the children of Israel firmly settled in Egypt, far away from the Promised Land.

A Corporate Promise Keeper

From the careful attention given to each in turn, the reader is led to expect that Isaac, then Jacob, and finally Joseph, might be the expected Serpent Crusher. The winding narrative, instead, proves the first two to be Promise Keepers only, like Abraham before them, while the third has a different role altogether. He is not even simply the next link in the chain descending from Abraham: instead he is the savior through whom *all of the children of Israel* are brought into the role of Promise Keeper.

This is an important moment marking the first phase of expansion of this function beyond a single person in each generation. When Jacob blesses all his sons, the gate leading to "many descendants" now seems to have swung wide open. And it seems clear that the expected One will be among those who will go through it.

Isaac Not the One?

Abraham fades remarkably quickly into the background once the curtain falls on Moriah. His main purpose has no doubt been fulfilled now that the Covenant is solidified. All eyes now naturally turn to Isaac, the son of Promise. After all, a great deal of consideration has been given to the circumstances leading up to his birth, naturally building up our expectations. Oddly, however, he turns out to be a relatively minor character in the Story. With the exception of how he came to obtain Rebekah for his wife and an interlude with Abimelech, the story of Isaac focuses on how, at the end of his life, he was deceived into blessing the wrong son! It turns out that he is but a link in the chain, and a weak one at that. But critical, nevertheless.

A Rogue is Blessed?

His son Jacob is the antihero of this story. Right from the womb he is a person who reaches out and grasps whatever he can get his hands on. He cheats his brother Esau out of his proper inheritance and God, instead of punishing him, blesses him outrageously! The narrative makes it abundantly clear that this "grasper" is the one through whom the Promises will come. Indeed, both he and his father experience YHWH's personal affirmation of this fact!

How can a scoundrel like Jacob be so favored by God? The narrator, who unflinchingly shows him warts and all, seems untroubled by this question. At the same time, he is careful to ascribe Jacob's good fortune to YHWH's commitment to the covenant relationship he had established with his grandfather Abraham. God is simply keeping his Promise. This is clearly the overriding theme throughout all the serpentine convolutions in the plot line.[1] Even the least attentive reader will grasp the essential truth that God is sovereign over all of history and that nothing, not even Israel, will thwart his purpose.

YHWH the Womb Opener

This same lesson is well taught by another theme that begins with the story of Abraham: even barren wombs are no obstacle to the Almighty. The wives favored by his son Isaac (Rebekah) and his grandson Jacob (Rachel) are both barren. And, like Sarah, YHWH grants to them the sons who become the narrative's focus of attention. This

---

1. Cf. Gen 28:13–15.

repetitive pattern hammers away at the same point: nothing will stand in the way of YHWH's Promise. He will provide.

Enter Joseph

"Death and Resurrection of the Beloved Son," Again

The thin line of Promise Keepers may be about to expand to the entire nation of Israel, but the narrative line continues the pattern of concentrating on only one son as Joseph, Israel's favorite, first comes to center stage. While YHWH speaks to him through dreams, he never appears to him or affirms him as the son of Promise. However, he still has a decisive role to play in the Story. It is through him that the entire clan is preserved intact and saved from certain starvation. Although it is especially tempting to see him as the expected Serpent Crusher, it soon becomes evident that this is not his calling.

Joseph's story is nevertheless beautifully told. It must be counted among the masterpieces of literature from any age, let alone the world of the Ancient Near East. Furthermore, the account of Joseph's apparent death, descent into Egypt, subsequent rise to power, and his appearing alive to his father, is, according to Jon Levenson, the clearest example of a pattern he drew our attention to earlier in connection with Abraham and Isaac on Moriah[2]:

> The story of Joseph in Genesis 37–50 is not only the longest and most intricate Israelite exemplar of the narrative of the death and resurrection of the beloved son, but also the most explicit. In it is concentrated almost every variation of the theme which first appeared in the little tale of Cain and Abel and has been growing and becoming more involved and more complex through the book of Genesis. . . . It is the crescendo to the theme of the beloved son, which it presents in extraordinarily polished form. It is arguably the most sophisticated narrative in the Jewish or Christian Bible.[3]

Whatever else we may make of this remarkable motif, it seems to be moving more and more toward the center of the Story.

YHWH, Transformer of Evil

The story of Joseph also makes another significant contribution to our understanding of the power of God. After the death of their father Israel, Joseph's brothers fear that he will take vengeance upon them for having sold him into exile as a young man. In reassuring them he draws the following conclusion from the events of his life:

---

2. See 77–78, above.
3. Levenson, *Death and Ressurection*, 142.

> As for you, you meant evil against me, but God meant it for good, to save many people alive, as is happening today. (50:20)

God can actually convert evil into good! Not only can he shape events, not only can he use a scoundrel: he can even transform wickedness into something positive. This does not mean that sin is not sin, but that God can gather its malevolent effects together as means to his glorious ends. Such is his awesome power. The so-called "problem of evil," which finds an absolute contradiction between God's goodness and the persistence of evil, simply evaporates in the presence of YHWH.

THE STORY

Preamble

As they appear in the Bible, the stories of Isaac, Jacob, and Joseph are intertwined and can be confusing. What follows will, as much as possible, treat each patriarch separately in the interest of clarity. This will involve some minor dislocations of the biblical text.

Sarah Dies and is Buried in the Land (23:1–20)

Once the Covenant is firmly established, Abraham rapidly exits from the scene, leaving the vivid impression that his role in the Story is largely as the one through whom the Promises are established and is their initial Keeper. We do read that he settles in Beersheba and that, when Sarah dies at Hebron about 25 years later, he acquires a field with a cave in Machpelah for her burial. The story of its purchase draws our attention to the unquestionable legality of the transaction, perhaps in order to signify that this is the only portion of the Land that Abraham ever actually possessed as his very own. It seems especially poignant that it is a burial ground. But at least it is his. Otherwise, as he himself admits, he is but "a stranger and a foreigner" among his neighbors (v. 4).

Isaac: Keeper of the Promise

The Woman at the Well (24:1-67)

The Story then shifts rapidly to Isaac, the son of Promise. The reader naturally expects that a significant amount of attention will be focused upon him, his accomplishments, and the affirmation of his unique status as the Keeper of the Covenant. Not so much: his life story actually proves of relatively little interest to the author. The exception is the wonderfully romantic account of how he obtained Rebekah for his wife.

Because he wants no Canaanite blood in his line, Abraham instructs his servant to go all the way back to "to my country, and to my relatives, and take a wife for my son

Isaac, Jacob, and Joseph

Isaac" (24:4). Underneath all the romance, however, is the central message that God is as active in the life of the son as he was in that of the father. The Promise is holding through to the second generation: of that there can be no doubt. Even the fact that Rebekah is barren proves no obstacle. For Sarah this had been almost a lifelong burden, but when Isaac's prays to YHWH on her behalf, Rebekah immediately becomes pregnant and the next generation of Promise Keepers is assured.

Isaac Inherits the Promises (26:1–6)

During a famine, God appears to Isaac for the first time. He is instructed to stay in the Land and not to go down to Egypt:

> Live in this land, and I will be with you, and will bless you. For I will give to you, and to your offspring, all these lands, and I will establish the oath which I swore to Abraham your father. I will multiply your offspring as the stars of the sky, and will give all these lands to your offspring. In your offspring all the nations of the earth will be blessed, because Abraham obeyed my voice, and kept my requirements, my commandments, my statutes, and my laws. (v. 3–5)

Isaac has come into the full inheritance of the same Threefold Promise given to his father.

Like Father, Like Son (26:1–16, 26–31)

Curiously, just as his father did on two occasions, Isaac then passes off his wife as his sister for his own safety's sake. On this occasion, even more curiously, Abimelech is involved again, and again it ends well: ultimately the two swear to do no harm to each other. This is the second major episode of Isaac's life and YHWH's similar involvement serves as a way of underlining the fact that the torch has indeed been passed to another generation.

A Blessing at Beersheba (26:23–25)

It is around this time that YHWH appears a second time to Isaac, assuring him that he will be blessed and have many descendants. In response he builds an altar at that place, Beersheba, where he calls upon the name of YHWH. Isaac prospers but Esau marries two Hittite women, an act which "grieved Isaac's and Rebekah's spirits" (26:35).

Abraham's Last Days (25:1–11)

After Sarah's death, Abraham takes another wife by whom he has 6 more sons, but these are sent away somewhere to the east because he "gave all that he had to Isaac"

(vv. 5–6). There can be no question of the proper line of descent in this Story, although, poignantly, Ishmael joins his half-brother in burying their father when he dies at age 175.[4] Sadly, there is no mention of Hagar. Abraham is placed in his cave at Machpelah with his wife Sarah and so, in the end, the Land has taken possession of him.

Jacob the Deceiver

Getting a Grip (25:19–34)

Rebekah gives birth to twins, having been told by YHWH that the jostling babies in her womb are two nations and that the older will serve the younger. As we will see, she is not above making sure that this is, in fact, what happens. And so it is that Esau ("hairy") and Jacob ("he grasps the heel" or "deceiver") are born. Later, "despising his birthright" (v. 34b), a famished Esau gives up his proper place as first son to his brother in exchange for some food. It was a bargain he would come to regret. Jacob, in the meantime, has begun to live up to his name big time.

Wronging the Birthright (27:1–40)

Continuing his deceitful ways, Jacob, at his mother's instigation, disguises himself and tricks his almost-blind father into giving him the patriarchal blessing that he had earlier bargained away from Esau. While this blessing lacks the precise form of the Three Promises, it clearly resonates with them and the related themes we have been following:

> God give you of the dew of the sky,
>   of the fatness of the earth,
>   and plenty of grain and new wine.
> Let peoples serve you,
>   and nations bow down to you.
> Be lord over your brothers.
>   Let your mother's sons bow down to you.
> Cursed be everyone who curses you.
>   Blessed be everyone who blesses you. (27:28–29)

Esau is beside himself with rage upon discovering the ruse. He pleads with his father for a blessing of some kind and he duly receives the following:

---

4. Interestingly, the Bible here uses the phrase "was gathered to his people" (v. 8) to describe Abraham's death. Such language implies a belief in the afterlife as does God's reference in 15:15 to Abraham going "to your fathers in peace." This usage is found in the Pentateuch (the first five books of the Bible) only and, while not explicit, is remarkable at such an early stage in the biblical narrative: it only gradually comes to a more full-blown understanding of life after death. Cf. Hamilton, "Genesis, 1–17," 168.

> Behold, your dwelling will be of the fatness of the earth,
> and of the dew of the sky from above.
> You will live by your sword, and you will serve your brother.
> It will happen, when you will break loose,
> that you will shake his yoke from off your neck. (27:39–40)

His reaction to this "blessing" is hardly surprising:

> Esau hated Jacob because of the blessing with which his father blessed him. Esau said in his heart, "The days of mourning for my father are at hand. Then I will kill my brother Jacob." (27:41)

This sets in motion a series of dramatic events that focus almost exclusively on Jacob and make it clear that he is now the one through whom the Promise will be kept. His brother Esau is basically set aside and his father Isaac is mentioned again only upon his death some years later.

Jacob Flees to Haran (27:41—31:55)

A Stairway to Heaven in the House of God

Meanwhile, Rebekah, hearing of Esau's intent, gets Isaac to send Jacob back to Paddan Aram (Haran) to obtain a wife from among the daughters of her brother Laban. Familiar with the drill and already upset with Esau's Canaanite wives, Isaac readily agrees. He sends Jacob away with a blessing that comes even closer to the threefold format and makes it absolutely clear once again that the line of Promise goes from Abraham to Isaac to Jacob:

> May God Almighty bless you, and make you fruitful, and multiply you, that you may be a company of peoples, and give you the blessing of Abraham, to you and to your offspring with you, that you may inherit the land where you travel, which God gave to Abraham. (28:3–4)

The fact that this is all under the hand of God is made certain when Jacob reaches a "certain place" (28:11) not long after he sets out for Haran. There he has his famous dream of ". . . a stairway resting on the earth, with its top reaching to heaven, and the angels of God ascending and descending on it" (28:12). But that is not all:

> Behold, Yahweh stood above it, and said, "I am Yahweh, the God of Abraham your father, and the God of Isaac. I will give the land you lie on to you and to your offspring. Your offspring will be as the dust of the earth, and you will spread abroad to the west, and to the east, and to the north, and to the south. In you and in your offspring, all the families of the earth will be blessed. Behold, I am with you, and will keep you, wherever you go, and will bring you

again into this land. For I will not leave you until I have done that which I have spoken of to you. (28:13–15)

Here is the Promise in its precise threefold Abrahamic form, confirming that Jacob is indeed its true heir. Awestruck, he awakens and calls the place "Bethel," or "house of God," because of YHWH's presence there. It is, he says, "the gate of heaven" (v. 17). He sets up a memorial pillar and then he has the audacity to hold the deity to account, proclaiming that *if* God keeps his word then ". . . Yahweh will be my God" (v. 21). The "one who grasps" indeed!

SISTER WIVES

Jacob then journeys on to Haran and, in a romantic interlude reminiscent of his parents, meets Rachel, his beautiful cousin. He falls in love with her and offers to work for her father Laban seven years in exchange for her hand. A wedding night switch by Laban, however, finds him married to Leah her sister, instead. Once he agrees to work for Laban another seven years he is allowed to marry Rachel as a second wife. The trickster is himself tricked and the seeds of favoritism are sown once again! The irony is obvious.

RACHEL HAS A SON

It turns out that Rachel, like Sarah and Rebekah before her, is barren. In contrast, because Leah is unloved, YHWH ensures that she is fruitful. Each wife also provides a servant girl to Jacob, by which he has more children. Eventually we are told that "God remembered Rachel; he listened to her and enabled her to conceive" (30:22) and she bears her son Joseph. His miraculous birth, like the others before it, serves to alert the reader to his coming importance for the Story.

PROSPERITY TO JEALOUSY TO DEPARTURE

In the meantime, Jacob is clearly being blessed of God during his fourteen-year sojourn in Haran. Once Laban realizes that his own prosperity is due to God's blessing of Jacob, he attempts to dissuade his son-in-law when it looks like he is going to leave for Canaan with all his family and possessions. Jacob agrees to stay and proposes conditions that should be favorable to the herds of Laban who readily accepts the arrangement. But it is Jacob's herds that increase wildly instead. Again, God is at work.

> The man increased exceedingly, and had large flocks, female servants and male servants, and camels and donkeys. (30:43)

With these developments the sons of Laban become jealous of Jacob and the relationship becomes even more strained. In the wake of their false accusations against Jacob, YHWH directs him to return to Canaan, assuring him that "I will be with you" (31:3), echoing the earlier promise at Bethel (28:15). In such circumstances the long journey home begins with a hurried clandestine departure, perfectly in keeping with Jacob's character.

Laban pursues, but when he receives a warning from God his attitude changes. Jacob and Laban end up making a covenant, agreeing to a kind of nonaggression pact, with God called as witness. Laban kisses his daughters and grandchildren goodbye and goes back home.

Jacob Wrestles Under a New Name (32:1-32)

As Jacob turns and heads towards Canaan, he is aware of yet another problem lying in that direction: Esau, his aggrieved brother. He sends messengers ahead who return with the unwelcome news that Esau is coming with 400 men to meet them. This panics Jacob, who prays to God and then makes preparations to appease his brother with gifts that he sends on ahead.

That night, however, he has a strange encounter at the ford of the Jabbok. We are told that he got into an intense all-night wrestling match with another "man" (32:22-32). Jacob prevails until daybreak when the man wishes to be let go, but Jacob insists on a blessing first. The man asks him for his name and then announces:

> Your name will no longer be called Jacob, but Israel; for you have fought with
> God and with men, and have prevailed. (v. 28)

While the man declines to give his name, he does end up blessing Jacob there.

> Jacob called the name of the place Peniel; for he said, "I have seen God face to
> face, and my life is preserved." (v. 30)

Strange encounter indeed! But details in the account, including Jacob's new name, make it necessary to conclude that it is somehow God himself who appears in the person of this "man." One thinks immediately of the three men who visited with Abraham and the subsequent bargaining over Sodom. Once again, the narrator offers no explanation to his curious readers.[5]

The new name ("he struggles with God") is, of course, perfectly suited to what we know of Jacob: he has struggled with Esau right from the womb, with Isaac, with Laban, and now with God himself. And he has prevailed each time. Curiously, the narrator continues to call him "Jacob" until he reaches Bethel once again and God

---

5. One explanation is that God is "accommodating" himself to the human condition in order to make himself understood. In this way he could retain all of his divinity while only seeming to be something less.

confirms the change. From that point on, the names seem interchangeable: he is, fittingly, *both* "deceiver" and "he struggles with God."

A Final Divine Encounter (35:1–15)

After Jacob's meeting with Esau proves unexpectedly amicable he settles at Shechem in Canaan and then, directed by God, at Bethel. He builds an altar there and God appears to him yet again, confirming his new name and then the Promises again:

> I am God Almighty. Be fruitful and multiply. A nation and a company of nations will be from you, and kings will come out of your body. The land which I gave to Abraham and Isaac, I will give it to you, and to your offspring after you I will give the land. (35:11–12)

And Benjamin Makes Twelve (35:16–29)

While the family is returning from Bethel, the beloved Rachel dies near Bethlehem in giving birth to Benjamin, the last of Jacob's twelve sons. They are all then tabulated:

> The sons of Leah: Reuben (Jacob's firstborn), Simeon, Levi, Judah, Issachar, and Zebulun. The sons of Rachel: Joseph and Benjamin. The sons of Bilhah (Rachel's servant): Dan and Naphtali. The sons of Zilpah (Leah's servant): Gad and Asher. These are the sons of Jacob, who were born to him in Paddan Aram. (35:23–26)

This is the first generation from Israel and he has gone from one to twelve. At this rate it becomes possible to imagine the kind of growth that could be likened to the stars of the sky.

Isaac's Burial (35:27–29)

It is about this time in the story that Isaac dies at age 180. In a scene reminiscent of his father Abraham's own burial about a hundred years earlier, Isaac is buried by *his* two sons, Esau and Jacob. Interestingly, the text, perhaps in an effort to restore to Esau something of his birthright, follows the correct birth order by naming him first (35:29). In terms of the Story, Isaac's adult life serves more as a foil for the wily Jacob than anything else. Except for one all-important thing: he is the necessary genetic link by which the Abrahamic Blessing is passed on to those who follow in the line of Promise Keepers.

Esau Gets His (36:1–43)

While our text makes it crystal clear that Jacob is the chosen one, it is important to note that just after Esau is named first at his father's burial, a whole chapter is devoted to his descendants. They settle southeast of the Dead Sea and become the Edomites, and in so doing confirm the "blessing" Esau had wrung out of his father, that his dwelling would be in a poor and dry area. Remembering that strife between him and his brother was also predicted means we can no doubt expect trouble for Israel from that quarter in the future.

Joseph

Introduction

Now the Story shifts to Joseph, Rachel's firstborn, and how it is that the Israelites come to find themselves living in Egypt (and no longer resident, even as aliens, in the Promised Land). At first the familiar pattern seems to be repeating itself as the Story again narrows down on the one son through whom the Promise is transmitted. But it emerges that Joseph's chief role is to ensure that all twelve sons and their families are preserved and come into the Promises *as a group*. Now, for the first time, we can see before us the actual multiplication of descendants within the Promise.

That Joseph does not become a Promise Keeper like his father, grandfather, and great-grandfather, is underlined by the fact that God makes no appearances to him or has any conversations with him, communicating more indirectly through dreams instead. Furthermore, he is in no way affirmed as the special recipient of the Blessing. As we have noted above, Joseph has been chosen for another critical role: he becomes nothing less than the savior of Abraham's offspring and hence of the entire line of Promise.

It is a story many are familiar with, one of great adventure that is told with considerable skill. The scene toward the end in which Joseph finally reveals his identity to his brothers is surely one of the most deeply moving in the whole Bible. It is best to read these chapters in their entirety in order to fully appreciate the richness of the narrative. For our present purposes, however, a summary will suffice. Before we proceed, it should be noted that the narrator repeatedly makes it clear that God was behind everything that happens to Joseph, both good and bad.

Killing the Dream (37:1–36)

Already made jealous by their father's blatant favoritism toward Joseph, his brothers boil over when he naively tells them of his prophetic dreams that portray him as their superior. Seizing an opportunity to be rid of this "dreamer" they sell him to a caravan of Ishmaelites on their way to Egypt and convince their father that he has been killed by a wild animal. Jacob is completely devastated by the loss of his Beloved Son.

Following the Dream (39:1—41:57)

One of Pharaoh's officials, Potiphar, purchases Joseph, who then quickly proves his worth and is put in charge of the whole household. However, when he resists the advances of Potiphar's wife she arranges to have him imprisoned. While there he correctly interprets the dreams of two fellow prisoners who served in the royal household, one as Pharaoh's cupbearer and the other as his baker. The former is restored to his old job, just as Joseph had predicted, but forgets to advocate on his behalf.

Pharaoh himself then has two disturbing dreams no one could interpret and this finally triggers the memory of his cupbearer. Joseph is brought up out of the dungeon to do his thing. He says the dreams mean that the land is facing a severe seven-year famine that will follow seven years of abundant harvests. He then suggests a plan to store up during the good years in order to prepare for the lean ones. Pharaoh is impressed and puts this obviously wise man in charge of all the necessary preparations, making him the number two man in Egypt.

Joseph is given the daughter of an Egyptian priest as wife and has two sons by her, Manasseh and Ephraim. Their names reflect Joseph's thankfulness to God for making him forget all his previous troubles by making him fruitful in the very place of his difficulties. As we shall see, these two boys are destined for a special blessing in the plan of God.

Living the Dream (42:1—45:18)

Once the predicted famine is underway it proves to be so extensive that inhabitants of all the countries around have to go hat in hand to buy food from Joseph in Egypt. This includes ten of his brothers still in Canaan who are sent by their father Jacob. He keeps Joseph's full brother Benjamin, Rachel's other son, at home out of fear of losing him as well. Joseph recognizes his brothers immediately, but they remain ignorant of his true identity. He toys with them, taking Simeon as hostage and sending them back to their father with the demand that they return with Benjamin in order to prove they have been telling the truth. At first Jacob refuses to let his youngest son out of his sight, but the famine persists to the point where he is forced to let him go.

Again, Joseph arranges things that implicate his brothers as thieves and they fear for Benjamin's safety. But when he sees Benjamin in the flesh, his only full brother, Joseph breaks down in tears and reveals his true identity to his brothers. They are absolutely terrified because they immediately assume he will now take his vengeance upon *them* for what they had done to him years ago. Instead, they cannot believe their ears at what he says:

> Now don't be grieved, nor angry with yourselves, that you sold me here, for God sent me before you to preserve life... God sent me before you to preserve for you a remnant in the earth, and to save you alive by a great deliverance. So now it wasn't you who sent me here, but God... (45:5, 7–8a)

Joseph turns out to be their savior, used by God himself to this end. All his innocent suffering is paradoxically redemptive: betrayed by his own brothers, separated from his father, given up for dead, sold into slavery, imprisoned in Egypt for years. God has bent it all to his own redemptive purpose. The reader is once again assured that the covenant Promises to Abraham, Isaac, and Jacob will not fail. The dream just refuses to die.

Jacob and the Others Come Down to Egypt (45:19—47:31)

The narrative continues with Joseph and his brothers embracing and weeping, after which Pharaoh insists that they go back to get their father and the rest of the family. When they arrive, Israel is dumbfounded at the news, refusing to believe it at first. However, he is eventually convinced by the evidence and agrees to go down to Egypt before he dies. On the way, God encounters him one last time:

> He said, "I am God, the God of your father. Don't be afraid to go down into Egypt, for there I will make of you a great nation. I will go down with you into Egypt. I will also surely bring you up again. Joseph's hand will close your eyes. (46:3–4)

Israel's family is only seventy in number when they arrive in Egypt, having been preserved through the famine by Joseph's supply of grain. They settle in the much-favored land of Goshen apart from the Egyptians because, we are told, "every shepherd is an abomination to the Egyptians." (46:34). This comment also suggests that there may be trouble ahead for the Israelites.

Trickster to the End (48:1–22)

In any event, Jacob lives in Egypt another seventeen years before he dies at age 147. But before he does, he has one last trick up his old sleeve. It is one he knows all too well. In pronouncing a blessing upon Joseph's two sons he deliberately crosses his hands and gives the greater blessing to the younger son, Ephraim. Both will become great, but Manasseh's offspring will be the lesser while his brother's "... will become a multitude of nations." (48:19). Significantly, he also declares that the two "even as Reuben and Simeon, will be mine" (v. 5) and implies that they will each be allotted a full share in the Promised Land (v. 6).

Blessings Upon All, Especially Judah (49:1-28)

Joseph then gives the patriarchal blessing to all twelve sons in the form of a prophetic word for each one. Of particular interest is a portion of that given to Judah:

> The scepter will not depart from Judah,
>   nor the ruler's staff from between his feet,
> until he comes to whom it belongs.
>   The obedience of the peoples will be to him. (49:10)

Here some kind of kingly rule is granted to Judah, to be culminated in the rule of one who rules over the nations! The way it is put almost compels the reader to wonder if this might be the expected Serpent Crusher, especially given the promise made to Abraham (17:6, 16) and Jacob (35:11) that kings would come from them. It is now apparent that these kings will come from the line of Judah. Is the Serpent Crusher one of them?

Jacob Dies and is Taken Back to Canaan (49:29—50:14)

After finishing the blessings, Jacob "gathered up his feet into the bed, breathed his last breath, and was gathered to his people" (49:33). And so it is that Israel's long, grasping journey finally comes to an end. But not quite. His last wish is to be buried back in Canaan, in the Promised Land with his grandparents (Abraham and Sarah), his parents (Isaac and Rebekah), and his first wife Leah.

Accordingly, Joseph has him embalmed, and, with his brothers and many Egyptians, sets off for Canaan and buries him there in the cave at Machpelah. Israel finally comes to rest in the bosom of Abraham.

All Things Work Together for Good (50:15-21)

Joseph's brothers, fearing that he will take revenge on them now that their father is dead, tell him that their father had expressly wanted him to forgive them. Joseph's response reflects his earlier words to them when he revealed his true identity some years earlier:

> "Don't be afraid, for am I in the place of God? As for you, you meant evil against me, but God meant it for good, to save many people alive, as is happening today. Now therefore don't be afraid. I will provide for you and your little ones." He comforted them, and spoke kindly to them (50:19-21)

All's well that ends well.

ISAAC, JACOB, AND JOSEPH

No Grave in Egypt (50:22–26)

When his own time comes, Joseph summons his brothers and assures them that:

> God will surely visit you, and bring you up out of this land to the land which he swore to Abraham, to Isaac, and to Jacob. (50:24)

He makes them swear that when that happens they will take his bones with them. At age 110 Joseph dies and "they embalmed him, and he was put in a coffin in Egypt." (v. 26).

Pointedly, no grave is mentioned. Egypt may become a grave for the rest of Israel's descendants, but not for Joseph, a dreamer to the last! Or is it more than a dream? After all, his other dreams had all come true. He himself had already come back from the dead.

IN THE BOSOM OF ABRAHAM

1. The Land/Place

Although some of the action covered in this chapter takes place in the Land, most of it does not: Haran for Jacob and Egypt for Joseph. The only part of the Land actually owned is a burial site, appropriate for a narrative in which possession recedes further and further into the distance. It is repeatedly affirmed as promise, lastly by Joseph when he commits his brothers to take his bones with them when they return. On a more hopeful note, the account closes with the entire clan happily settled, prospering in a new Eden, the region of Goshen, the most fertile part of their host nation (47:6).

This narrative also displays a gathering sense of "sacred place." This seems especially true of Bethel, where Abraham had earlier "built an altar to Yahweh and called on Yahweh's name" on his first incursion into the Land (12:8). However, it only acquires its name ("House of God") from Jacob after his dream there of a stairway to heaven. It is his first encounter with YHWH and first affirmation of the Covenant, a truly momentous occasion:

> "Surely Yahweh is in this place, and I didn't know it." He was afraid, and said, "How awesome this place is! This is none other than God's house, and this is the gate of heaven." (28:16–17)

On his return to Canaan after his adventures in Haran, Jacob is instructed to go back to Bethel and build an altar there. It has become holy ground because of the presence of YHWH.

2. Many Descendants

This Promise now begins to take more concrete shape, but not until the narrative presents us with the repeated obstacle of barren women. It turns out that Sarah was only the beginning of a series, being followed by Rebekah and then Rachel in the subsequent generations. In each case God intervenes and ensures that the proper line continues. The reader is thereby assured repeatedly that nothing is going to stand in the way of this Promise. When a descendent is required, "YHWH will provide." Indeed.

"Many Descendants" is reaffirmed at least six times as Promise in this portion of the narrative. And, after hanging by the single threads of Isaac and Jacob, there are, in the end, seventy who find themselves safely settled in Egypt. It is there, as God had told Jacob, they would be made into a great nation (46:3). Certainly, their prospects seem excellent in the fertile Goshen district.

3. Blessing to All Nations

Although this aspect is very much present in the story, it is so mainly (again) as promise. It shows itself as such both directly (26:3–5; 28:14) and indirectly (27:28–29; 28:3; 35:11). As in the case of Abraham himself, however the Blessing is entered into by some of those non-Israelites in relationship with Jacob and Joseph. Jacob tells his father-in-law Laban that:

> For it was little which you had before I came, and it has increased to a multitude. Yahweh has blessed you wherever I turned. (30:30)

Laban had already learned that YHWH had blessed him because of Jacob (30:27). Moreover, both Potiphar and Pharaoh grow rich when Joseph is managing their domains. Indeed, the whole land of Egypt and many other nations affected by the famine survive those seven years due to Joseph. Additionally, Jacob blesses Pharaoh twice when Joseph introduces them. From these instances we can see Blessing to All Nations coming precisely as YHWH had told Abraham it would:

> I will bless those who bless you, and I will curse him who treats you with contempt. All the families of the earth will be blessed through you. (12:3)

This promise implies that all the nations will come to bless Israel and because of that they will be blessed themselves. We must add to this the seemingly contrary fact that the promised ruler from the line of Judah will dominate the nations. How these themes fit together is left unaddressed, but we may be given a clue in the notion of a "company" of "peoples" (28:3) or "nations" (35:11) which Jacob is also promised will come from him. This amplification of the Promise seems to suggest that at some point his descendants will be part of an "international" body, perhaps its head, and making their king its king. It is difficult to imagine another interpretation at this point, but future developments may add clarification. Just as the Promise Keeper begins to go corporate, this Promise also takes on greater definition. Both are very intriguing developments.

4. Fruitfulness

During this period, fruitfulness has really come to mark the lives of the Promise Keepers.

In his old age, Abraham is "blessed in all things" and his servant, bearing a number of them, tells Laban how rich his master is in livestock, cash, and servants (24:1,10, 31–35).

We are told that Isaac, even in what may have been a time of famine:

> …sowed in that land, and reaped in the same year one hundred times what he planted. Yahweh blessed him. The man grew great, and grew more and more until he became very great. He had possessions of flocks, possessions of herds, and a great household. The Philistines envied him. (26:12–14)

The Story also stresses how fruitful Jacob was, even in Haran where he labored under trying circumstances for Laban. There, under God's hand, he grew very wealthy himself:

> The man increased exceedingly, and had large flocks, female servants and male servants, and camels and donkeys. (30:43)

As for Joseph, it seems as if he succeeded in everything he put his hand to while he was in Egypt. During the seven good years the land blossomed under his care and even during the seven lean years his wisdom ensured that even greater prosperity came to Pharaoh.

Ironically, it is a lack of fruitfulness in the Land itself, engulfed in a widespread and terrible famine, which plays a key role in this narrative. It is behind Joseph's rise in Pharaoh's administration and motivates his brothers to go down to Egypt in search of relief from its local effects. And then they end up prospering in Goshen, the best land in Egypt.

5. Relationship

In this narrative God's commitment to be in close relationship with the children of Abraham is very much in evidence. YHWH directs the quest for a wife for Isaac and personally appears to him on two occasions. On the second of these he tells Isaac "Don't be afraid, for I am with you. . ." (26:24). This pretty well sums it up for his son and grandson as well. Jacob encounters YHWH at Bethel and is told:

> Behold, I am with you, and will keep you, wherever you go. . . For I will not leave you until I have done that which I have spoken of to you. (28:15)

This is repeated when YHWH tells him to return to Canaan from Haran (31:3). The famous wrestling match with God marks him as especially intimate with the deity and indeed reminds the reader of Abraham bargaining with God over Sodom. The name that Jacob is given, "he who struggles with God," reflects the personal relationship between them. Jacob also affirms that YHWH is his God at this particular moment (28:21). YHWH, we are told, is also with Joseph (39:2) and it is made plain that this is the essential cause of his success.

All in all, it is clear that, with the advent of Abraham's line, YHWH has, of his own initiative, entered into close relationship once again with the human race. True, it is only a select portion for the present, but it is a start. And it contains a specific Promise to include the rest at some point in the future.

6. Grace/Obedience

In spite of the fact that this narrative covers three generations it follows something of a pattern in reference to this question. Unfortunately, in so doing it raises a few questions along the way.

The main thing that emerges is that Isaac, Jacob, and Joseph seem to be recipients of the Blessing simply because God is keeping his Promise to Abraham. The classical expression of this comes in his word to Isaac:

> Live in this land, and I will be with you, and will bless you. For I will give to you, and to your offspring, all these lands, and I will establish the oath which I swore to Abraham your father. I will multiply your offspring as the stars of the sky, and will give all these lands to your offspring. In your offspring all the nations of the earth will be blessed, because Abraham obeyed my voice, and kept my requirements, my commandments, my statutes, and my laws. (ch. 26:3–5)

Here there is no call to Isaac and Jacob for obedience or of the Blessing being contingent upon it. The only obedience mentioned of them in the text occurs when God instructs them to go or not go somewhere. In reference to moral uprightness, they must receive mixed reviews: Isaac lies regarding Rebekah and appears weak in the face of her scheming with Jacob; the latter, except on a couple of occasions, comes across as a lifelong scoundrel; Joseph alone seems entirely of good character. And yet they all inherit the Blessing equally.

This seems especially unjust in the case of Jacob. Turned on its head, however, it is also a paradigm of grace as unmerited favor. Even Jacob himself is aware of this:

> I am not worthy of the least of all the loving kindnesses, and of all the truth, which you have shown to your servant; (32:10a)

It can be argued that Jacob is an even better test case for grace than Abraham. YHWH blesses the latter without any hint at his worthiness but he blesses the former *in spite of* his downright *un*worthiness. What better illustration of YHWH's sovereign grace could there possibly be? However, we should note his awe and even humility at being in the very presence of God both at Bethel on his way to Haran and at the Jabbok on his way back, not to mention his words above. Is it possible that these are these glimpses into a heart that desires God above all? Could it be that this is what YHWH has found in Jacob in spite of his many failings? Noah might agree that we are at least looking in the right direction.

And then there is the question of what we are to make of God's telling Isaac in the quote above that he will be blessed because of Abraham's total obedience to the divine commands. Given all that we have observed earlier, this can only suggest that such obedience was *subsequent* to his call and the establishing of the Covenant. Even then, in the light of Abraham's actual behavior, it seems something of a "Semitic exaggeration"![6] And what does YHWH mean by "my requirements, my commandments, my statutes, and my laws," of which we have heard nothing at all in the text? If Moriah is in view, which seems the most likely reference, perhaps this is simply a way of expressing the absolute commitment to the ways of God that Abraham demonstrated on that occasion, a commitment arising out of his faith that God would keep his promise.

There is yet another question here that should not be overlooked: is it possible for the faithfulness of one man to "stand in" for others? Jacob's blessings, we are told explicitly, come from Abraham's obedience two generations earlier. Perhaps it is our cultural obsession with an absolute individualism that once again blinds us to a biblical truth. God does have grandchildren after all. Even great-grandchildren!

All of this makes it difficult to ascertain the precise relationship between grace and obedience in this narrative. As far as our central actors are concerned, it seems that they experience salvation as pure grace but they are not called, explicitly at least, to obedience in the ways of God. At the same time, the grace they receive is due to the long-ago obedience of Abraham, introducing the idea that through one man's exceptional obedience others who follow him can be saved by grace alone! And immoral behavior does not automatically and immediately negate this salvation once it has been entered into. What seems to matter more is a heart oriented to God as seen in the story of Jacob/Israel who never ceases to relate to YHWH, even if he finds it a struggle to follow in his ways. Bottom line: you don't have to keep a promise to be a Promise Keeper.

---

6. A type of ancient humor according to my Old Testament professor, R. K. Harrison, who was fond of invoking it to explain such seeming inconsistencies.

8

Moses (Part One)
The Birth of a Nation

Suggested Reading

Exodus 1–31; Deuteronomy 1–8; Deuteronomy 27–30 (these last chapters cover the end of Moses's career and will be dealt with from that perspective in the next chapter; but they also relate how the Law, the subject of this chapter, is designed to work). Quotations of Scripture are from Exodus unless otherwise indicated.

MAJOR DEVELOPMENTS

- Four hundred years after the death of Joseph the children of Israel find themselves enslaved in Egypt
- Moses is born, grows up in the house of Pharaoh, escapes to the wilderness, and is called by God to deliver "my people"
- Moses and his brother Aaron confront Pharaoh with YHWH's demand that he "let my people go," but things only get worse
- YHWH inflicts nine plagues upon Egypt but each time Moses asks for his people's freedom, Pharaoh refuses
- The tenth plague, the death of all the firstborn males, is unleashed, but the angel of death passes over the Israelites
- Pharaoh finally relents and lets them go
- The first Passover takes place and is instituted as a memorial for all time
- The Israelites complain to Moses when they are trapped between the pursuing

Moses (Part One)

Pharaoh and the Red Sea

- The Red Sea parts and the children of Israel cross safely, but the Egyptians are destroyed
- The Israelites complain to Moses when they run out of water and YHWH provides it at Marah
- The Israelites complain to Moses when they run out of food in the Desert of Sin and YHWH provides both manna and quail
- The Israelites complain to Moses when they run out of water again and YHWH provides water from the rock at Horeb
- At the suggestion of his father-in-law Jethro, Moses appoints judges to help share the burden of leadership
- YHWH gives the Ten Commandments and other laws to Moses on Mt. Sinai over a period of forty days
- The tent of meeting/tabernacle, the place of YHWH's dwelling among the people, is established

Preamble

The account of Moses, the Exodus, and the giving of the Law so clearly marks a new direction in the biblical narrative that careful attention is needed in order to see how it fits into "the story so far." This is especially true of the covenant that YHWH initiated at Mount Sinai. How does this "new" covenant relate to that made with Abraham and confirmed to Isaac and Jacob? Because this is both so important and so complicated a question it deserves its own extended treatment. Perspectives (Part A) below constitutes our regular treatment and is followed by "The Story" section as usual. We will then be in a position to consider the covenantal implications of what we have learned in Perspectives (Part B).

PERSPECTIVES (PART A)

Introduction

This portion of the narrative is focused on the rise of Moses, Israel's escape from Egypt, and the giving of the Law. Although not quite as intimate as the tale of the patriarchs, it is nevertheless full of high drama and powerful characters. Tumultuous events give birth to what will ultimately become the Jewish faith as God reveals himself to their ancestors and to the world. Alongside the heights of divine disclosure are set the depths of human frailty. Through these events the nation of Israel comes into being and the Promise takes a giant leap forward towards fulfillment.

While it is a story first of all for the Jews, it is also one for the ages, helping to shape human history. Its theme of the transformation of an enslaved people into a free nation resonates deeply in the collective human psyche. Many have found in it both inspiration and hope for a better world. Oppressors and tyrants across the centuries have been unable to stand against its enduring call for freedom and justice: "Let my people go!" Of course this has particular application to the experience of black slaves in America.

The Silence of God

The story begins in the silence of God. Since the passing of the patriarchs four hundred years ago, God has not spoken. The descendants of Jacob/Israel find themselves still in Egypt, but now subject to a terrible captivity. The God who had saved them by the hand of Joseph seems largely forgotten. No doubt Joseph himself is also forgotten, as is their parting promise as he lay upon his deathbed:

> Joseph took an oath from the children of Israel, saying, "God will surely visit you, and you shall carry up my bones from here." (Gen 50:25)

But, against all appearances and in spite of his silence, God has not forgotten *them*. Or Joseph, for that matter. When he finally acts we can be sure that it will not be something that goes unnoticed.

This is his third long silence since the Creation. The good news is that after each of the previous occasions he has rebooted his redemptive activity, first with Noah and then with Abraham. Now he does it again with Moses, tuning the reader to the rhythm of divine activity.

While these silences clearly do not indicate that YHWH has turned his back on humanity in any final sense, they do pose something of a mystery. We get a glimpse of a possible reason for them, however, in what YHWH revealed to Abram long ago about what is now about to happen:

> Know for sure that your offspring will live as foreigners in a land that is not theirs, and will serve them. They will afflict them four hundred years. I will also judge that nation, whom they will serve. Afterward they will come out with great wealth; but you will go to your fathers in peace. You will be buried at a good old age. In the fourth generation they will come here again, for the iniquity of the Amorite is not yet full. (Gen 15:13–16 [my emphasis])

It seems from this that humanity's need has to rise to a particular level of intensity before God takes action. Certainly this was true of the situation in the days of Noah and this present account conforms to this explanation twice over: the sin of the Amorites just mentioned has reached its full measure and the suffering of the Israelites has reached a painful crescendo. While God's silences may often be a mystery to

Moses (Part One)

us, these references indicate that they are not arbitrary. He has his reasons and that should perhaps be reason enough for us.

Something New This Way Comes

There are several important indicators that our narrative represents the beginning of a significant new stage in the history of salvation. Most obvious is the focus upon the birth and semi-miraculous preservation of the infant Moses. The perceptive reader, because of the circumstances surrounding the births of Isaac, Jacob, and Joseph, will be inclined to see this birth narrative as a signal that a person of extraordinary importance has now entered the scene. He may even be the expected One, the Serpent Crusher.

This identification seems only to be verified when Moses commands his brother to throw his staff down before Pharaoh and it becomes a snake, a snake that swallows up the staffs/snakes of the court magicians. Here is finally a man with supreme authority over serpents! Perhaps the time has come.

Another indication that the Story is turning a corner is the attention given to the revelation of God's holy Name.[1] Moses is told that this is a major part of the program just after Pharaoh has responded to Moses's demands by frightfully increasing the workload of the Israelites. Moses dares to complain to God about the situation and he graciously responds as follows:

> I am Yahweh. I appeared to Abraham, to Isaac, and to Jacob, as God Almighty; but by my name Yahweh I was not known to them. I have also established my covenant with them, to give them the land of Canaan, the land of their travels, in which they lived as aliens. Moreover I have heard the groaning of the children of Israel, whom the Egyptians keep in bondage, and I have remembered my covenant. Therefore tell the children of Israel, 'I am Yahweh, and I will bring you out from under the burdens of the Egyptians. . .I will take you to myself for a people. I will be your God; and you shall know that I am Yahweh your God.' (6:2–7a)

Surprisingly, the terrible plagues unleashed against Egypt are not just designed to twist Pharaoh's arm: they are a form of his self-disclosure to Israel as well. YHWH is introducing himself to them as "YHWH" and he is determined to make a lasting first impression:

> . . .that you may tell in the hearing of your son, and of your son's son, what things I have done to Egypt, and my signs which I have done among them; that you may know that I am Yahweh. (Exod 10:2)

---

1. This name is transliterated as "YHWH" from the Hebrew. Peter Enns makes a good case for the new name to mean "I AM" (*Exodus*, 101–7).

This narrative will offer an opportunity to test the old saying about first impressions being lasting impressions.

A further strong indication that the nation is entering a new era is that the moment of deliverance from Egypt becomes the beginning of its calendar:

> Yahweh spoke to Moses and Aaron in the land of Egypt, saying, "This month shall be to you the beginning of months. It shall be the first month of the year to you." (12:1–2)

It is in this month that they are to celebrate both Passover (on the fourteenth day) and the Feast of Unleavened Bread (on the seven following days). Each new year is to begin with a reenactment of their deliverance from Egypt. While it would be going too far to suggest that this event is the beginning of their history, it certainly outranks all others in terms of their relationship with YHWH. Each new year represents their beginning as a nation, another fresh start with YHWH.

A Prelude to Monotheism

When the nature of the plagues is examined it can be seen that YHWH has invested them with an even wider agenda. Scholars have pointed out that they seem to be directed mostly at the gods of Egypt. For example, the Nile was turned to blood and the sun was totally darkened. Both were held to be gods in Egypt. In effect, Moses is demonstrating that "my God is bigger than your god" in each case.[2]

But it goes further. Four times in the subsequent narrative we learn that the power of YHWH demonstrated in the Exodus was meant to convince the Egyptians themselves (and not just the Israelites) that "I am YHWH" (7:5, 17; 14:4, 18). The plagues thus have an "evangelistic" purpose. In them YHWH is asserting his exclusive right to the worship of all humanity: all other gods, wherever or whenever they are found, are of no final significance.

This narrative takes us a giant step toward "monotheism," the understanding that there is really only one God. However, this is not yet explicit. Even the Ten Commandments do not affirm the actual nonexistence of other gods, as a careful reading will confirm:

> You shall have no other gods before me.
>
> You shall not make for yourselves an idol, nor any image of anything that is in the heavens above, or that is in the earth beneath, or that is in the water under the earth: you shall not bow yourself down to them, nor serve them, for I, Yahweh your God, am a jealous God... (20:3–5a)

---

2. Cf. Enns, *Exodus*, 205.

Moses (Part One)

It would have been so easy, we might think, for YHWH simply to deny the very existence of these so-called gods and have been done with it. Indeed, looking back over the Story so far it seems to be pointing in an exclusively monotheistic direction: only one God is acting and speaking, and he is clearly "in charge" of all creation. At the same time it does not deny the reality of spiritual powers that may be arrayed against YHWH. It is nowhere explicitly affirmed that he alone is God. Instead, the Story steadily undermines any other possibility.

The first two commandments just quoted provide an excellent example of this. In the context of the ANE the gods were seen as habitually sharing power in a divine assembly, but these commandments leave them no ground to stand on. John H. Walton puts it well in discussing the first one:

> Although it does not say explicitly that no other gods exist, it does remove them from the presence of YHWH. If YHWH does not share power, authority or jurisdiction with them, they are not gods in any meaningful sense of the word. The first commandment does not insist that the other gods are non-existent, but that they are powerless; it disenfranchises them. It does not simply say that they should not be worshipped; it leaves them with no status worthy of worship.[3]

It is likely that this indirect approach is taken because, again, we are dealing with a "progressive" revelation in which timing is everything. In this case, the full biblical revelation that the idols and gods of the nations are merely the products of human imagination awaits the lofty words of Isaiah and the Psalms.[4] The Bible never affirms that these "other gods" exist in any objective sense. It never presents them acting or speaking. They are simply nonplayers who nevertheless pose a real danger to God's people. Partly this is because they are a means by which loyalty to YHWH might be compromised. And partly this is because they seem to be a means of somehow channeling malignant spiritual forces.[5]

---

3. *Ancient Near Eastern Thought*, 256.

4. Cf. Isa 40:18–20 and Ps 115:1–8. Ps 95:3, on the other hand, expresses perfectly the revelation on Sinai: "For Yahweh is a great God, a great King above all gods." Cf. Enns, *Exodus*, 413–14. The question seems to hang in the OT as to whether these "other gods" exist or not. Certainly, idols, in and of themselves, are but human creations.

5. There is a parallel ambiguity in the NT teaching about idols and it may be helpful to examine its approach briefly. In discussing idol worship St. Paul says that ". . . the things which the Gentiles sacrifice, they sacrifice to demons, and not to God, and I don't desire that you would have fellowship with demons." (1 Cor. 10:20) In other words, there is a spiritual reality behind the idol, which itself is nothing. Are the "demons" of the NT, then, to be equated with the "other gods" of the OT? If they are, the intriguing difference between the NT's presentation of the demonic world and the OT's seeming lack of interest in it might be explained. That is, the same reality is going under a different name in each testament. Other factors are no doubt at work as well, such as the relative inactivity of the demonic in some cultures (North America) as opposed to others (Africa) that we observe in the world today. It almost seems as if demons (and the gods) are able to take on more substance when believed in.

A Corporate Promise Keeper, For Keeps

In the days of the patriarchs God at first entered into covenant only with single individuals, one in each generation: Abraham and then with his son Isaac and his grandson Jacob/Israel. They were the ones through whom the Promise would come.

As we have seen,[6] when Jacob blesses all of his sons the reader gets the idea that they and their descendants are now *together* the inheritors and keepers of the Promise. This becomes explicit in our narrative when God for the first time begins to refer to the children of Israel as "my people" (3:10). The events that follow incorporate them fully into Jacob as they take on his name and even his character as "Israel," the "one who struggles with God." The Promise has gone fully corporate.

Going from the personal to the corporate naturally brings with it a change in the way that YHWH deals with those who bear his Covenant. When it was still one patriarch at a time this largely took the form of direct one-on-one appearances of YHWH, along with his instructions to do this or to go there. This level of divine encounter will continue for a select few but, while the nation as a whole may indeed be the Promise Keeper, its individual members do not generally experience a personal relationship with YHWH (at least in the sense under discussion).

Relating to YHWH Corporately

Appropriately, now that an entire people has become the Promise Keeper, YHWH "appears" to all Israel on a number of occasions. Two of these are at the giving of the Law on Sinai (Exod 19) and at the first sacrifices in the tabernacle (Lev 9:23–24). In response to the former the people tremble in fear, insisting on staying at a distance, while to the latter they react with joy, no doubt because YHWH has come among them this time after their sin has been dealt with.

The nation's Sinai reaction also seems to give rise to the office of "prophet" as a way in which YHWH can speak to the people at arm's length. As Moses tells the people:

> Yahweh your God will raise up to you a prophet from among you, of your brothers, like me. You shall listen to him. This is according to all that you desired of Yahweh your God in Horeb in the day of the assembly, saying, "Let me not hear again Yahweh my God's voice, neither let me see this great fire any more, that I not die." (Deut 18:15–16)

From this point on in the narrative the relationship of the average Israelite with YHWH will be partly mediated through this leader/prophet. I say partly because it will also be mediated through the Law: his or her relationship with YHWH will depend upon their own observance as well as that of the entire community.

---

6. See 89–90, above.

Obviously, appearances of God are momentous occasions, whenever they take place. Technically called "theophanies," people often react to them out of their own humanity with both awe and fear, and sometimes joy, as we have noted. Part of the Sinai experience points in a more unexpected direction when, in a truly remarkable scene:

> . . . Moses, Aaron, Nadab, Abihu, and seventy of the elders of Israel went up. They saw the God of Israel. Under his feet was like a paved work of sapphire stone, like the skies for clearness. He didn't lay his hand on the nobles of the children of Israel. They saw God, and ate and drank. (24:9–11)

Not only did the leadership of Israel see God, they had a fellowship meal with him! Abraham would perhaps not be surprised if we assume that his encounter with the three "men" was a theophany, for we note that it too took place in the context of a shared meal. It is hard to imagine another image that would better signify harmony between the Promise Maker and Promise Keeper.

The Death and Resurrection of the Beloved Son, Once Again

When YHWH refers to Israel as his firstborn son in his instructions to Moses (4:22), and as the special object of his love a little later (Deut 10:15), we have a hint that this story embodies yet another instance of this theme. We saw it most clearly exhibited in the stories of Abraham/Isaac and Jacob/Joseph.[7] Here, the son in question is not merely the son of Jacob, or the son of Abraham, or the son of Adam: it is *the son of God himself* who is "dead" in captivity and is "resurrected" to new life in the Exodus.[8]

All this can also throw a bit of light on an episode back in the life of Abraham. Not only was he given a hint about the Exodus, as quoted earlier—he also lived it, in a fashion. It will be recalled that he went down into Egypt himself in a time of famine and was then expelled due to the anger he begets in the Pharaoh. From this perspective the Exodus is a distant echo of Abraham's story and raises the possibility that perhaps we can regard him, too, as a Beloved Son who experiences resurrection. But, in what sense is he God's son? He is certainly someone uniquely favored by the Almighty. Beyond this it is best not to speculate, but in retrospect his Egyptian sojourn does seem to anticipate that of the nation generations later.

The centrality of this event for Israel, with its annual reenactment in the Passover, ensures that "the death and resurrection of the beloved son" will become integral to the self-understanding of the nation. It still remains somewhat below the surface, but it seems to be coming more and more recognizable as the Story progresses. And it is somewhat more clearly on view in Moses's own prediction regarding another eventual banishment and return in years to come (Deut 30:1–10).

---

7. See 77–78, 91, above.
8. Cf. Levenson, *Death and Resurrection*, 36–42.

Theocracy: Reboot of Creation?

The Law also can be seen as a function of Israel's becoming a nation. A nation needs laws in order to be governed, and so the two go together both naturally and necessarily. This correspondence also helps explain why, as we shall see, the Ten Commandments expand into many other laws in order to cover all aspects of Israelite life.

If laws define *how* a nation is to function, the other question is: *who* is going to do the governing? The dominant role of Moses in this narrative might suggest to a modern reader that Israel is constituted as a dictatorship. It is true that all power flows through Moses and he brooks no opposition. At the same time, and most importantly, he is clearly "under" YHWH who is the actual ruler of the nation. The technical name for this form of government is "theocracy" and it is built into the very fabric of Israel's existence. The fact that God may choose to rule indirectly through a person or an assembly of persons should not obscure this truth.

It is important to recall that the same theocratic structure informs humanity's original Mandate to "rule" over the earth as God's regents, responsible to him.[9] Israel is to deliberately structure itself to reflect what all of humanity is in danger of forgetting. The Creation Mandate is thus, in a sense, renewed in and through Israel. You could even say that what we see in this narrative is a reboot of creation. We saw this earlier with Noah, but this time it is concerned not with a cleansed earth but with a cleansed people, one nation truly "under" God. Upon this, perhaps, hangs the possibility of renovation for the human heart. In this light we would have to see the Law as a means to that end.

Substitution (Again)

In the story of the Passover the concept of substitution, first seen clearly in the almost-sacrifice of Isaac on Moriah, is operational once again. In fact, the parallel is striking: the firstborn male is under threat of death from YHWH but a means of redemption is provided. In this case it is the life of the Passover lamb for the life of the child.

This time, through the yearly reenactment of Passover this notion will be vividly impressed into the consciousness of the entire nation, becoming a living part of their present reality. As we shall see, it will go on to become the key concept in the sacrificial system soon initiated among them. At that point it will have gone the entire journey from the periphery to the center.

---

9. See 26, above.

Moses (Part One)

THE STORY

A Death in Egypt (Exod 1)

Four hundred years have gone by since Joseph died and, as they say, things change. While in their Egyptian exile the seventy descendants of Jacob/Israel have multiplied to the point where it has become a problem for the Egyptians: there are just too many of these untrustworthy foreigners in their midst. They have gone from being an asset to being a liability.

The Egyptians also have a solution: enslave these aliens and order the Hebrew midwives to kill all the male babies as soon as they are born. This primitive method of birth control fails because the midwives were horrified at having to perform such a despicable task. Pharaoh then simply instructs his own people to throw such children into the Nile. As we shall see, this, also, may have been too much to demand of people with normal human feelings. It is in this context that we are presented with yet another extraordinary birth narrative, this time rooted in fertility instead of infertility.

A Savior is Born (Exod 2)

A son is born to an Israelite woman who, in order to save her baby, hides him in a waterproof basket among the reeds at the river's side. He is rescued from this crocodile-infested peril by a daughter of Pharaoh, no less, who not only defies her father but also adopts him as her own son, naming him Moses. Ironically, she hires his real mother to nurse the baby!

When he is a young man, Moses kills an Egyptian he finds mistreating a fellow Hebrew and is forced to flee into the wilderness. There he marries, tending the flocks of his father-in-law Jethro until he is about forty years old. Meanwhile, YHWH is beginning to stir on behalf of the children of Israel:

> . . .the children of Israel sighed because of the bondage, and they cried, and their cry came up to God because of the bondage. God heard their groaning, and God remembered his covenant with Abraham, with Isaac, and with Jacob. God saw the children of Israel, and God was concerned about them. (2:23–25)

The time for action has come.

Moses Answers a Call (Exod 3)

God appears to the exiled Moses at Horeb in the wilderness, calling out to him from a burning bush that refuses to be consumed by the flames. Moses, echoing the response of both Abraham and Jacob to the same call, answers:

> Here I am. (3:4)

In a remarkable exchange, God then identifies himself and gives Moses his marching orders:

> I am the God of your father, the God of Abraham, the God of Isaac, and the God of Jacob. I have come down to deliver them out of the hand of the Egyptians, and to bring them up out of that land to a good and large land, to a land flowing with milk and honey; to the place of the Canaanite, the Hittite, the Amorite, the Perizzite, the Hivite, and the Jebusite. Come now therefore, and I will send you to Pharaoh, that you may bring my people, the children of Israel, out of Egypt. (3:6, 8, 10)

Moses is aghast at this suggestion, triggering the following exchange[10]:

> Moses: Who am I, that I should go to Pharaoh, and that I should bring the children of Israel out of Egypt?
>
> God: Certainly I will be with you. This will be the token to you, that I have sent you: when you have brought the people out of Egypt, you shall serve God on this mountain.
>
> Moses: Behold, when I come to the children of Israel, and tell them, 'The God of your fathers has sent me to you,' and they ask me, 'What is his name?' what should I tell them?
>
> God: I AM WHO I AM. You shall tell the children of Israel this: 'I AM has sent me to you.' God said moreover to Moses, "You shall tell the children of Israel this, 'Yahweh, the God of your fathers, the God of Abraham, the God of Isaac, and the God of Jacob, has sent me to you.' This is my name forever. . .

This call has a number of similarities and differences with that of Abraham. Like the latter, it comes "out of the blue" and involves going to the Land of Promise. But instead of leaving his kinfolk behind, Moses is to take them all with him and, as they are now an enslaved people, this obviously represents a serious obstacle.

Moses's response is certainly unlike that of Abraham. Although neither had any previous recorded encounters with the Almighty, Abraham offers no objections to his calling. Of course, the task he faced was distant and theoretically doable. Not so with Moses! He is charged with an extremely challenging task upfront. It is made even more difficult by his estrangement from his fellow Israelites and his alienation from the Egyptians.

As seen above, his first response is that he is a nobody, without qualifications or credentials. Then he worries that he will not be listened to (4:1) and so YHWH gives

---

10. Taken from 3:10–15.

him the power to perform miraculous signs to get Pharaoh's attention. When Moses next complains that he has no gift for public speaking (4:10), YHWH tells him he will give him the words to say. Finally, having run out of excuses, Moses bursts out with a sentiment many others in a similar situation have shared:

> Oh, Lord, please send someone else. (4:13)

It is almost comical. But YHWH certainly does not see it that way. Angry, he reminds Moses that his brother Aaron is an eloquent man and informs him that he is now coming to help. He will do the public speaking. This finally seems to satisfy Moses who then begins the journey back to Egypt and his encounter with destiny. It has not been a great start, however. The reader wonders about his reluctance, especially in light of YHWH's affirmation that "I will be with you," words that echo those given repeatedly to Abraham, Isaac, Jacob, and Joseph. Should this not have been enough?

Pharaoh Won't Listen (Exod 4–10)

After establishing their credentials with the Hebrew elders, Moses and Aaron go before Pharaoh, perhaps granted an audience because Moses had been adopted into the royal house. In any event, in response to Moses's first request to "let my people go," Pharaoh scoffs:

> Who is Yahweh, that I should listen to his voice to let Israel go? I don't know
> Yahweh, and moreover I will not let Israel go. (5:2)

Instead, he forces them to work under almost impossible conditions, heightening the drama along with the buildings. YHWH then has Moses announce a series of nine terrible plagues upon the land of Egypt in order to encourage Pharaoh to change his mind.

The plagues fail because Pharaoh proves extraordinarily stubborn. Several times we are told that this is because YHWH had hardened Pharaoh's heart. Although we are also told that Pharaoh hardened his own heart, this is said in the context of God's clear and repeated pronouncement:

> I will harden Pharaoh's heart, and multiply my signs and my wonders in the
> land of Egypt. But Pharaoh will not listen to you, so I will lay my hand on
> Egypt, and bring out my armies, my people the children of Israel, out of the
> land of Egypt by great judgments. (7:3–4)

Puzzling as this may be to us, as usual it again warrants no comment from our narrator. However, as in many of our previous instances of bewilderment, it points us firmly in the direction of God's sovereignty. Nothing takes place beyond his control. At the same time, as in this case, the human actors are held responsible and subject to judgment if their actions are contrary to the commands of God. And there the matter rests.

The Tenth Plague and the Passover (Exod 11–13)

The plagues, meanwhile, reach a devastating finale with the death of all the firstborn males in the land of Egypt. However, YHWH provides a means of redemption for the Israelite families, who are told to slaughter a lamb and place its blood on the doorframes of their houses. The angel of death would "pass over" those houses and any child at risk would be spared.

In response to this horror Pharaoh finally lets the people go and so the great act of judgment upon Egypt becomes Israel's redemption. And it is not to be forgotten. First of all, YHWH declares that:

> This month shall be to you the beginning of months. It shall be the first month of the year to you. (12:2)

In this month they are to reenact the event with the Feast of Passover, sacrificing an unblemished lamb and smearing its blood on their doorframes. This is to be followed by the seven days of the Feast of Unleavened Bread to recall how they left Egypt in haste, with no time even to allow for yeast to work.

In other words, their year is always to begin with this great act of remembrance. The effect of this would be like the United States changing the calendar to have New Year's Day on July 4 with each family reading out the Declaration of Independence followed by a week-long celebration. This calendar would mark it off from all the other Western nations and at the same time signal the supreme importance of the Declaration to its own population. "This is where our history begins. Don't forget it."

But this biblical act of deliverance is so important that it cannot be left to merely one week of remembrance. Every firstborn male of man and beast among the Israelites is now to be YHWH's, the animals sacrificed and the humans redeemed.

> It shall be, when your son asks you in time to come, saying, 'What is this?' that you shall tell him, 'By strength of hand Yahweh brought us out from Egypt, from the house of bondage. When Pharaoh stubbornly refused to let us go, Yahweh killed all the firstborn in the land of Egypt, both the firstborn of man, and the firstborn of livestock. Therefore I sacrifice to Yahweh all that opens the womb, being males; but all the firstborn of my sons I redeem.' It shall be for a sign on your hand, and for symbols between your eyes; for by strength of hand Yahweh brought us out of Egypt. (Exod 13:14–16)

By this means the whole Hebrew year will be saturated with reminders of their great redemption. For all time the Israelites will live out their entire lives in the context of this moment. It is that important. No other event even comes close. But it is, even at that, only a beginning.

Not forgetting the bones of the long-dead Joseph, Moses leads the people out of their captivity, guided by YHWH during the day in a "pillar of cloud" and at night in a "pillar of fire" (13:21–22). This expression of the presence of God is similar to the phenomenon of the burning bush that got Moses's attention in the first place.[11]

The truly remarkable thing about the following events is that they clearly portray the people of Israel as not having learned the lesson about who God is any more than Pharaoh did. No sooner are they faced with difficulties than they complain to Moses, preferring "the good old days" of their enslavement!

Deliverance through the Red Sea (Exod 14:1—15:21)

First of all, there is the small matter of the Egyptian army that pursues them almost as soon as they leave. Pharaoh has once again reneged on his promise to let them go and now has them trapped at the shore of the Red Sea. As Pharaoh approaches, the Israelites look up and see the Egyptians coming fast with obvious intent. They are terrified and cry out to YHWH and rage at Moses:

> Because there were no graves in Egypt, have you taken us away to die in the wilderness? Why have you treated us this way, to bring us out of Egypt? Isn't this the word that we spoke to you in Egypt, saying, 'Leave us alone, that we may serve the Egyptians?' For it would have been better for us to serve the Egyptians than to die in the wilderness. (14:11–12)

No heroes here. Except, of course, for One. Moses answers the people:

> Don't be afraid. Stand still, and see the salvation of Yahweh, which he will work for you today; for you will never again see the Egyptians whom you have seen today. Yahweh will fight for you, and you shall be still. (14:13–14)

With the famous parting of the Red Sea, of course, they are saved and the Egyptians are destroyed.[12]

Lodging Complaints in the Wilderness (Exod 15:22—18:27)

But they have not learned their lesson! When they come to the bitter waters of Marah they grumble (15:24) and when they run out of food shortly after that, they grumble again:

---

11. Cf. Enns, *Exodus*, 270. This is now the third time (starting with the "smoking firepot and blazing torch" of Gen 15:17) that the Bible characterizes God in terms of fire and the associated image of light.

12. As with Noah and the Passover itself, what is salvation for some is judgment for others.

> We wish that we had died by Yahweh's hand in the land of Egypt, when we sat by the meat pots, when we ate our fill of bread, for you have brought us out into this wilderness to kill this whole assembly with hunger. (16:3)

And at Rephedim, where they discover no water present, they grumble some more:

> "Give us water to drink." Moses said to them, "Why do you quarrel with me? Why do you test Yahweh?" . . . the people murmured against Moses, and said, "Why have you brought us up out of Egypt, to kill us, our children, and our livestock with thirst?" (17:2–3)

In each case God graciously provides water to drink and manna or quail to eat. The nation is certainly living up to its name Israel, "He who struggles with God."

Will they ever learn to trust in YHWH? Or would he give up on them first? Certainly, Moses's frustration level is rising rapidly. The reader gets a sense that the people may be pushing both him and God just a little bit too far. But, instead, God continues to journey with them.

Fortunately for him, Moses's frustration is relieved somewhat when he meets up with Jethro, his father-in-law, along with his own wife and sons, in the region of Mount Sinai. Jethro conveys a word from God that Moses should share the task of judging the people with a number of worthy subordinates, leaving only the most difficult cases for himself. Moses quickly creates such a body, the beginnings of what we might call "judicial" or even "political" administration for the nation.[13]

The Gift of the Law (Exod 19:1—20:21)

The next series of events once again provides the reader with intense drama. Moses leads the people to the foot of Mt. Sinai, the place where YHWH had first called him from the burning bush. It is quickly becoming clear that this is indeed "holy ground," perhaps the very dwelling place of God. As he proceeds up the mountain, YHWH calls out to him again:

> This is what you shall tell the house of Jacob, and tell the children of Israel: 'You have seen what I did to the Egyptians, and how I bore you on eagles' wings, and brought you to myself. Now therefore, if you will indeed obey my voice and keep my covenant, then you shall be my own possession from among all peoples; for all the earth is mine; and you shall be to me a kingdom of priests and a holy nation.' These are the words which you shall speak to the children of Israel. (19:3–6)

---

13. While these men are not identified any further here, perhaps they are the seventy "elders" mentioned a bit later (in chapter 24).

MOSES (PART ONE)

We are witnessing nothing less than the birth of a nation, a very special nation. From an impotent collection of slaves ignorant of their birthright, they are to become a holy nation, set apart for God's great purpose: the tomb has become a womb. This instruction to Moses is indeed their "Declaration of Independence."

While we must be careful not to assume a modern understanding of "nation" here, clearly this great conglomeration of people is about to enter a higher order of coherence and identity than ever before. To get a sense of what is happening, we might imagine all the slaves in the pre-Civil War American South being unexpectedly released from their various plantations and then assembling together on the far side of the Mississippi River to journey to their own land beyond the Rocky Mountains. Long and viciously oppressed, with little corporate sense of identity, they are suddenly a people, a nation even, alive with bright possibilities.

Here we do well to remember the word that God spoke to the elderly Jacob when he was reluctant to journey to Egypt so many years earlier:

> I am God, the God of your father. Don't be afraid to go down into Egypt, for there I will make of you a great nation. (Gen 46:3)

Until now this promise has been mocking the long-lived experience of Jacob's clan. Things are about to change.

Did any among the people even remember this promise? If they did it might explain (along with all of their pent-up need) why the Israelites immediately commit themselves to this covenant even before they hear all the terms of the contract:

> All that Yahweh has spoken we will do. (19:9)

But this most definitely is not a thing to be rushed into. The people are given three days to consecrate themselves, even to the point of washing their clothes. On "the third day" (repeated three times), they are told:

> Be careful that you don't go up onto the mountain, or touch its border. Whoever touches the mountain shall be surely put to death. (19:12)

Then there is a long blast of the ram's horn, thunder and lightning, thick clouds, and a very loud trumpet.

> All of Mount Sinai smoked, because Yahweh descended on it in fire; and its smoke ascended like the smoke of a furnace, and the whole mountain quaked greatly... the sound of the trumpet grew louder and louder... (19:18–19)

Creation itself seems to be bearing witness that something extraordinary is about to happen. We may well sympathize with the reaction of the Israelites:

> All the people perceived the thunderings, the lightnings, the sound of the trumpet, and the mountain smoking. When the people saw it, they trembled, and stayed at a distance. They said to Moses, "Speak with us yourself, and

we will listen; but don't let God speak with us, lest we die." Moses said to the people, "Don't be afraid, for God has come to test you, and that his fear may be before you, that you won't sin." The people stayed at a distance, and Moses came near to the thick darkness where God was. (20:18–21)

This, then, is the riveting context for the giving of the Ten Commandments. YHWH, needless to say, has their undivided attention:

> God spoke all these words, saying, "I am Yahweh your God, who brought you out of the land of Egypt, out of the house of bondage.
>
> "You shall have no other gods before me.
>
> "You shall not make for yourselves an idol, nor any image of anything that is in the heavens above, or that is in the earth beneath, or that is in the water under the earth: you shall not bow yourself down to them, nor serve them, for I, Yahweh your God, am a jealous God, visiting the iniquity of the fathers on the children, on the third and on the fourth generation of those who hate me, and showing loving kindness to thousands of those who love me and keep my commandments.
>
> "You shall not misuse the name of Yahweh your God, for Yahweh will not hold him guiltless who misuses his name.
>
> "Remember the Sabbath day, to keep it holy. You shall labor six days, and do all your work, but the seventh day is a Sabbath to Yahweh your God. You shall not do any work in it, you, nor your son, nor your daughter, your male servant, nor your female servant, nor your livestock, nor your stranger who is within your gates; for in six days Yahweh made heaven and earth, the sea, and all that is in them, and rested the seventh day; therefore Yahweh blessed the Sabbath day, and made it holy.
>
> "Honor your father and your mother, that your days may be long in the land which Yahweh your God gives you.
>
> "You shall not murder.
>
> "You shall not commit adultery.
>
> "You shall not steal.
>
> "You shall not give false testimony against your neighbor.
>
> "You shall not covet your neighbor's house. You shall not covet your neighbor's wife, nor his male servant, nor his female servant, nor his ox, nor his donkey, nor anything that is your neighbor's." (20:1–17)

Here, in a very few words, the Israelites are presented with the terms of the covenant into which they are entering. These terms constitute YHWH's primary directions for how they are to live and they are all about relationships: first with himself (in the first four) and then with other human beings (in the last six). YHWH claims exclusive rights to their worship along with the honor and attention that goes with it. His people are to be utterly intolerant of other gods, having nothing to do with them. YHWH has hallowed the seventh day as a day of rest and it is to be honored as such. Other human beings and their possessions are also to be treated with the kind of serious respect that is not trumped by one's own self-interest.

Some Reflections on the Commandments

There is much that can be said (and has been!) about the Ten Commandments, but here it is important to note just a few things. First of all, the strong emphasis on who the Israelites are to worship is related to their long sojourn in an extremely idolatrous and polytheistic society. They need to focus. The plagues against Egypt, demonstrating the superiority of YHWH over the indigenous gods, had the same goal. Here on the mountain, with all of the associated phenomena, he has finally gotten their full attention. At least for the moment.

Secondly, in the injunction against images, YHWH says that:

> I, Yahweh your God, am a jealous God, visiting the iniquity of the fathers on the children, on the third and on the fourth generation of those who hate me, and showing loving kindness to thousands of those who love me and keep my commandments.

"Jealous" here should be taken as a way of underlining what he has just been saying about his demand for his people to worship no other gods. Human jealousy is born of insecurity and is often irrational and hurtful. There is none of this in YHWH. He simply wants the people to be totally oriented towards the true source of their blessing for their own good. Not to mention that he, as the sovereign YHWH, really does deserve the credit. It is a reality check to worship him alone. With this understanding all else will follow.

The above quotation, in addition, throws light on God's character as massively predisposed to bless and not to curse. This, in turn, helps to explain something that caused us bewilderment in the earlier sections of the narrative: Why did YHWH bless a scoundrel like Jacob? In being told now that God will show his love to "a thousand generations" of those who prove themselves faithful, we have an answer. Jacob was indeed basking in the warmth of Abraham's faithfulness: that is just how God works.

Finally, it may be helpful to continue the analogy of YHWH's first words to Moses on Mt. Sinai as a kind of "Declaration of Independence." From this perspective the Ten Commandments can be analogous to a "Constitution," in the sense that they set out the general principles by which the nation will be governed in accordance with the "Declaration." That is, these are the laws, which, when followed, will result in Israel being a kingdom of priests and a holy nation. This is their calling and by obedience to these 10 simple rules they will fulfill their end of the covenantal bargain.[14]

---

14. 19:6. For a discussion of the meaning of this calling, see "Blessing to All Nations," 136–37, below.

Commandments without Borders (Exod 20:22—31:18; Deut 11–26)

The Ten Commandments are just the beginning. Still on Mount Sinai, Moses receives a host of other laws which themselves will later be amplified greatly in the rest of Pentateuch.[15] For the most part these further laws fill out how the Israelites are to conduct themselves in their "religious" and "secular" lives. Although this distinction is a modern one, it is helpful in terms of our being able to understand that these regulations encompass the whole of life for the ancient Jewish community. It is worth taking a moment to ponder their relationship to the Ten Commandments.

Our analogy of the Ten Commandments as Israel's Constitution[16] may again be helpful. Many countries have a legislative body (Congress or Parliament) that, at least in theory, enacts laws applying the basic tenets of their Constitution to the circumstances of the day. Through Moses, YHWH "legislates" many laws that expand the first four (the relationship with God) into the rules of worship and many others that expand the second six (the relationship with each other) into the rules of justice. In this way the Ten Commandments find authentic expression within the bewildering variety of subsequent laws whose function is to extend the Ten into all the nooks and crannies of Israelite life. It is all known as the Law (Torah) of Moses and it is all of a piece.

There is another helpful way of understanding the relationship of the Ten Commandments to these other laws. Traditionally, they have been categorized as the moral law (the Ten Commandments), the civil law (laws regulating society), and the ceremonial law (laws regulating worship). The advantage to this approach is that it is easier to see how the moral law could be considered permanent and absolute while the others may be subject to change as circumstances dictate. The disadvantage is that such categories are imposed on a text that does not itself make such neat distinctions.[17] This can readily be seen in the jumble of laws that follow the giving of the Commandments in Exodus: instructions are given concerning idols and altars, the rights of Hebrew servants, protection of property, social responsibility, justice and mercy, the Sabbath, festivals, etc.

The Tabernacle (Exod 25–27)

In the middle of these extended laws are the provisions for the tabernacle as the "house of Yahweh your God" (23:19). It is worth taking a moment here to focus briefly

---

15. This term refers to the first five books of the Bible, traditionally held to have been written by Moses.

16. Rendtorff, *Canonical Hebrew Bible*, 480–81, argues for the primacy of the Ten Commandments on the basis of their being spoken directly to Israel by God himself, whereas the rest of the Law was meditated through Moses.

17. 2 Chr 19:11 indicates that somewhat later on, in the days of the monarchy, distinctions were indeed made between civil and religious matters.

on this important structure. Not only would this be God's dwelling place on earth but also where he would arrange, through priests and sacrifices, to meet with his sinful people.[18] It is altogether "holy" or set aside for God, constructed and decorated by gifted artisans from the finest of materials. The entire structure is made in such a way that it is totally portable and thus able to accompany the Israelites on their journey.

An "outer court" of about 150 ft. by 30 ft. contains a covered structure at one end, 30 ft. by 15 ft., that itself is divided by a curtain into two rooms: the "holy place" and the "most holy place" or "holy of holies." The latter, taking up a third of the space, is where YHWH's very presence dwells between the outstretched wings of the cherubim that adorn the cover of the Ark of the Covenant.[19] The latter is a wooden box overlaid in pure gold, in which are placed the stone tablets of the Law.

On a High (Exod 24)

After receiving a number of these other laws while still on Sinai, Moses relays them to the people, writing them down, along with the Ten Commandments, in the "Book of the Covenant." This he then reads out to the people at the foot of the mountain and for the second time they commit themselves to be fully obedient (24:3–8). As with the Abrahamic Covenant, this one requires repetition in order to be lodged firmly in the psyche of the people.

Moses then sacrifices some young bulls and sprinkles half of their blood on the altar and half on the crowd, reminding us of the animal sacrifices associated with Abraham's Covenant (Gen 17:9ff.). He then goes back up the mountain with Aaron, the sons of Aaron, Nadab and Elihu, and the seventy elders of Israel, while he and Joshua (a promising young general/aide) proceed even higher to receive the tablets of stone inscribed with the Commandments by YHWH himself, leaving Aaron in charge of those left behind. Again we have dramatic special effects:

> . . .and the cloud covered the mountain. Yahweh's glory settled on Mount Sinai, and the cloud covered it six days. The seventh day he called to Moses out of the middle of the cloud. The appearance of Yahweh's glory was like devouring fire on the top of the mountain in the eyes of the children of Israel. Moses entered into the middle of the cloud, and went up on the mountain; and Moses was on the mountain forty days and forty nights. (24:15–18)

The fire and cloud we see here are the same phenomena that lead the Israelites on their wilderness journey, confirming that these, too, represent the very presence of YHWH. And surely the "forty days and forty nights" bring to mind the time Noah

18. In Exod 40 it appears that the tabernacle is also called the "tent of meeting," although this may refer to another structure for God and Moses only. In any event, the idea of a "meeting place" for God and his people is clearly part of the scenario in the post-Sinai wilderness experience. See Feinberg, "Tabernacle," V:581–82, for a discussion of the issue.

19. See also 135, below, regarding the significance of the tabernacle.

and his family spent in the ark while the world was changed forever. The coming of the Law is no less significant an event: the world is being changed forever, again.

Literally and figuratively we have reached the high point in the establishment of the Mosaic covenant. It is like a wedding ceremony when the bride and groom kiss at the altar after completing their vows and everything is perfect. It is wonderful. It is magical. It is also, alas, a passing moment.

PERSPECTIVES (PART B)

Introduction

Now that we have had an opportunity to examine the Mosaic covenant in some detail it is necessary to explore how it is related to that of Abraham. Understanding this connection will, in turn, provide us with a deepened appreciation of how the Bible as a whole is linked together.

New Content

First of all, as Moses himself affirms, the covenant established at Sinai is distinct from the earlier one:

> Hear, Israel, the statutes and the ordinances which I speak in your ears today, that you may learn them, and observe to do them. Yahweh our God made a covenant with us in Horeb. Yahweh didn't make this covenant with our fathers, but with us, even us, who are all of us here alive today. (Deut 1:1–3)

The centerpiece of this covenant is clearly the Law and this is definitely at the root of the difference between the covenants. While the earlier one set forth no explicit moral code, the patriarchs did seem to be aware of YHWH's standards for human conduct. For example, we are told that YHWH chose Abraham:

> . . .to the end that he may command his children and his household after him, that they may keep the way of Yahweh, to do righteousness and justice. . . (Gen 18:19)

The "way of YHWH" or what is right and just are never actually spelled out but when Joseph resists the advances of Potiphar's wife, he does so somehow knowing that adultery is "wickedness" and a "sin against God" (Gen 39:9).

Whatever the patriarchs might have understood as a God-approved life may have been lost to their descendants after 400 years of being immersed in a pagan culture. They have not only forgotten who their God was, they have probably forgotten how he wanted them to live. The two go hand in hand. This may help explain the forceful introduction of the Ten Commandments at this point in the Story.

New Conditions

The advent of the Law leads directly to the essence of the Sinai covenant. Law, by its very nature, demands obedience and stipulates the reward for compliance and the penalty for noncompliance. Law operates only where options exist and choice is required. Just after the Ten Commandments are given, Moses makes it clear to the people that the Promise of the Land is contingent upon their obedience:

> You shall diligently keep the commandments of Yahweh your God, and his testimonies, and his statutes, which he has commanded you. You shall do that which is right and good in Yahweh's sight, that it may be well with you and that you may go in and possess the good land which Yahweh swore to your fathers.... (Deut 6:17–18)

All of a sudden what Abraham had been promised as a sure thing now seems not so sure anymore, having become conditional upon the obedience of Israel. Nothing could more starkly define the difference at the heart of these two covenants.

Old Consequences

The Covenant Mechanism

Not that the content of the Promise itself has been changed, but the way it is to be realized certainly has. Now obedience is explicitly demanded, and Blessings are promised for compliance and Curses for non-compliance. These serve as what we might call a "covenant mechanism" designed to keep the nation on the straight and narrow:

> Behold, I set before you today a blessing and a curse: the blessing, if you listen to the commandments of Yahweh your God, which I command you today; and the curse, if you do not listen to the commandments of Yahweh your God, but turn away out of the way which I command you today, to go after other gods which you have not known. (Deut 11:26–28)

Call it the "carrot and stick" method, if you will. It should also be noted that "mechanism" here is not to be understood in an impersonal sense: enforcement is always YHWH's decision and action.

Nearing the end of his life, Moses, echoing God's address to Adam in the garden, movingly lays it all out once and for all in his great charge to the people:

> I call heaven and earth to witness against you today that I have set before you life and death, the blessing and the curse. Therefore choose life, that you may live, you and your descendants, to love Yahweh your God, to obey his voice, and to cling to him; (Deut 30:19–20a)

This comes after Moses's command that the people write the Law on plaster-covered stones and set them up on Mount Ebal once they have crossed the Jordan. Then six of their tribes are to stand there and pronounce the Curses for disobedience while the other six pronounce the Blessings for obedience on Mount Gerizim opposite (Deut 27:12–13). The Blessings and the Curses become the gateway to the Promised Land. Literally.

The Promises in the Mechanism

But if this is the mechanism by which the Blessings and the Curses "work," it is critical to explore further their relationship with the Promises made so long ago to Abraham. As we have noted above in the quote from Deut 6:18, the possession of the Land is clearly made conditional upon obedience to the Law. *But the Blessings in store for such obedience are not confined just to the Land. In fact they encompass nothing less than the substance of all three Promises together*:

> Yahweh will establish you for a holy people to himself, as he has sworn to you, if you shall keep the commandments of Yahweh your God, and walk in his ways. All the peoples of the earth shall see that you are called by Yahweh's name, and they will be afraid of you. Yahweh will grant you abundant prosperity in the fruit of your body, in the fruit of your livestock, and in the fruit of your ground, in the land which Yahweh swore to your fathers to give you. (Deut 28:9–11)

> Yahweh will make you the head, and not the tail. You will be above only, and you will not be beneath, if you listen to the commandments of Yahweh your God which I command you today, to observe and to do. . . (Deut 28:13)

The Curses, not surprisingly, perhaps, are the direct opposites.

> If you will not observe to do all the words of this law that are written in this book, that you may fear this glorious and fearful name, YAHWEH your God, then Yahweh will make your plagues and the plagues of your offspring fearful, even great plagues, and of long duration, and severe sicknesses, and of long duration. . . You will be left few in number, even though you were as the stars of the sky for multitude. . . You will be plucked from the land that you are going in to possess. (From Deut 28:58–63)

> You will become an astonishment, a proverb, and a byword among all the peoples where Yahweh will lead you away. (Deut 28:37)

In summary, it will be either possession of the Land or expulsion from it; either many descendants or death, disaster and disease; either the ruler of the nations (who would surely be blessed under an obedient and righteous Israel), or a thing of horror and ridicule to them.

This last provision, with the option of ruling the nations, brings to mind Jacob's blessing upon Judah that a leader would come from him who would someday be sovereign over the nations. It seems to fit and at the same time it confirms our presumption that what Jacob said does in fact imply a blessing to the nations, and not mere dominance.[20]

The End of the Law

In a remarkable charge to the Israelites at the end of his life Moses prophesies how all this will actually play out in the life of the nation:

> It shall happen, when all these things have come on you, the blessing and the curse, which I have set before you, and you shall call them to mind among all the nations where Yahweh your God has driven you, and return to Yahweh your God and obey his voice according to all that I command you today, you and your children, with all your heart and with all your soul, that then Yahweh your God will release you from captivity, have compassion on you, and will return and gather you from all the peoples where Yahweh your God has scattered you. If your outcasts are in the uttermost parts of the heavens, from there Yahweh your God will gather you, and from there he will bring you back. Yahweh your God will bring you into the land which your fathers possessed, and you will possess it. He will do you good, and increase your numbers more than your fathers. Yahweh your God will circumcise your heart, and the heart of your offspring, to love Yahweh your God with all your heart and with all your soul, that you may live. (Deut 30:1–6)

In this passage it is possible to discern a number of features that will help us understand more fully the purpose of the Mosaic covenant.

Disobedience Rules

Interestingly, at the beginning of the quote the Curses seem to be merely possibilities in the event of disobedience, but by the end they are more predictions that Israel will, in *fact*, fail to obey, bringing all this disaster upon itself, especially exile from the Land. Perhaps this is not surprising for a nation that is named "he who struggles with God." This will happen not because of any fault in the Law, but because of one in the people who are attempting to follow it. They will show themselves incapable of fulfilling its demands, thus placing the Blessings out of reach. From this perspective it is tempting to see the Law as simply another "false start" towards redemption.

---

20. See 104–5, above.

Blessings Trump Curses

And there is one final twist on this path: as with Jacob, the original Israel, bad behavior somehow does not lead to rejection in the end for the nation. Moses clearly proclaims that the Blessings will ultimately prevail in spite of repeated failures of the people. YHWH himself will do this by bringing them back from their exile and "circumcising" their hearts. In other words, he will intervene at some point and render his people capable of perfect obedience to the Law through an *inner* transformation.

Nothing less than a new "sinless" humanity seems to be in view. And it is difficult to imagine this within the world as we know it. Our entire existence in this environment is conditioned by sin. To err, after all, *is* human. Will not the creation also need to be transformed in order to be compatible with this new humanity? For now, such a vision is not much more than a distant gleam in Moses's eye.

Same Ends, Different Means

It seems that the Mosaic covenant shares the same goal as that of Abraham but attempts to take a different route to get there: obedience to the Law (vs. carried along regardless in the embrace of the Promise). This, however, seems to come to a dead end because of human failure to actually obey its commandments. Ironically, then, the Law ends up exposing the reason for its own inability to deliver on the Promises: the inescapable human proclivity to sin. This truth, in turn, opens us to the understanding that what is required is not another plan but another kind of person. And that is exactly what Moses foresees.

For our present purposes it is important to note that this concept of a changed humanity tends to lessen the tension between the certainty of the Promises under Abraham and their uncertainty under Moses while at the same time affirming the priority of the former. Once God's people have had their hearts circumcised, the issue of the conditionality of the Mosaic covenant becomes a moot point because obedience is now assured. YHWH's Promise on oath to Abraham will carry the day in the end.

It becomes clear, then, that the Mosaic covenant is a function of the Abrahamic and subordinate to it. That is, the newer has no independent purpose, but seeks only to bring about the objectives of the older, a means the same end. It beckons us upward like a stairway to heaven whose individual steps are just too high for us to scale on our own. Here is where a little injection of steroids is necessary but apparently not until we have exhausted ourselves trying. For now, however, the path for Israel to the Promised Land is perfectly straight.

It is possible to see that there is a kind of symmetry to these developments. In the patriarchal period the Promise has been operating more or less unconditionally from one generation to the next. Because obedience did not play a large part in the process it was not necessary to define specifically what "obedience" might mean. The Mosaic covenant, by putting a great stress on obedience, needs to articulate what that involves or remain meaningless. The Law arrives as a necessary corollary, then, to the call for obedience. As we noted above, they go hand in hand.

The following diagram expands our covenantal diagram to include the Mosaic covenant. Its parameters are identical to those of Abraham and because of its conditionality it is rendered in broken lines.

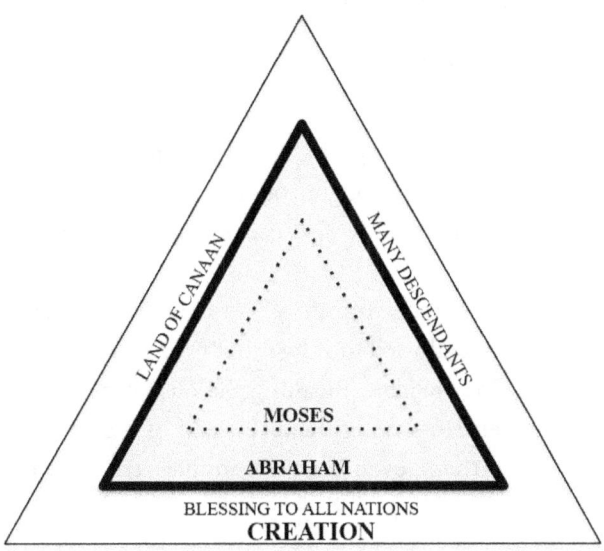

**Covenantal Diagram 3
Abraham–Moses**

IN THE BOSOM OF ABRAHAM

1. The Land/Place

As this narrative opens, the children of Israel are slaves in Egypt and it seems as if this Promise is at the very least lying dormant, if not abandoned altogether. However, when God addresses Moses at the burning bush he announces that he has come down to rescue them and bring them up out of the land of Egypt to the land of Canaan. With the Exodus the wheels of this Promise once more begin to turn.

Of course the people have made it only as far as Mount Sinai for now, but at least they are moving in the right direction. In receiving the Law, the Israelites have been made aware that it is directly tied to this Promise: if they obey, they will possess the Land and if they disobey, they will lose it. Or, as Leviticus 20:22 graphically puts it, they are to keep all of God's laws so that "the land where I am bringing you to dwell may not vomit you out."

With the Law, then, they have been given the spiritual course they have to follow in order to guarantee a successful occupation of the Land. Another step closer.

The whole idea of "exodus" is naturally rooted in this particular Promise. It is the focal point of the story. They have begun the journey through the desert with the Land shimmering just over the eastern horizon, beckoning them at every turn. But they have yet to set a foot upon its soil. Is it just a mirage?

In terms of an Edenic sense of "place," where God and humanity dwell together in harmony, mention must be made here of both Mount Sinai and the tabernacle. It was at Sinai/Horeb, where YHWH first met with Moses and said:

> "Don't come close. Take off your sandals, for the place you are standing on is holy ground." (3:5)

The overwhelming impression given later in the narrative is that God actually dwells on the holy mountain (c.f. "brought you to myself" in 19:4) and is inviting Moses into his direct presence, marked by fire, earthquake and smoke, while the people are kept at a safe distance.

His presence, in a sense, then "transfers"[21] to the holy of holies in the tabernacle and the people are again not allowed too close, but provision for some access, at least, is made. And this "place" is portable, meaning YHWH comes down from Sinai and will go with them and remain among them. Instead of making their way to Eden, Eden has made its way to them, even if significant barriers remain. It is now within reach.

2. Many Descendants

Here we have a Promise that is clearly gaining traction even before this part of the Story gets underway. It drives the beginning of the Exodus narrative: the descendants of Israel have been enslaved precisely because they have become so numerous that they are a threat to the Egyptians. Even the cruel attempts of the Pharaoh to limit their growth fail wonderfully. God may be silent, but it looks like Covenant-related things are beginning to happen, a small but growing cloud on Pharaoh's horizon.

The people leave Egypt in huge numbers: according to the text about 600,000 men plus women and children (12:37). They have grown exponentially in captivity, not only surviving but abounding. In fact, Moses uses a "covenantal metaphor" to describe the nation at this time:

> Yahweh your God has multiplied you, and behold, you are today as the stars of the sky for multitude. Yahweh, the God of your fathers, make you a thousand times as many as you are and bless you, as he has promised you! (Deut 1:10–11)

---

21. While such language is necessary, YHWH's presence cannot be confined to a single place. The moment of "transfer" appears to have been when the first Passover since leaving Egypt was celebrated (Exod 40 and Num 9). See 150, below.

At the same time there are not yet enough of them to occupy a territory as large as Canaan. God tells them that he will take more than a year to drive out the current occupants:

> I will not drive them out from before you in one year, lest the land become desolate, and the animals of the field multiply against you. Little by little I will drive them out from before you, until you have increased and inherit the land. (23:29–30)

Here the possession of the Land is linked explicitly to the Promise of Many Descendants. This goes toward confirming our earlier observation in reference to both the Creation and Abraham: there appears to be an inner logic weaving the Three Promises into a seamless whole.[22] What appear at first to be three disconnected promises, even arbitrary, might actually be the three interdependent and interlocking components of "salvation" or "redemption."

3. Blessing to All Nations

This Promise, except what we have seen in the "Blessings and Curses" discussion above,[23] seems to have gone off the radar screen altogether. However, a few "blips" can be discerned by a well-trained operator.

Undoubtedly what falls to "the nations" in this portion of the narrative is largely negative: the disasters that overwhelm the Egyptians. Not only do they suffer from the ten plagues, but they are also plundered by their former slaves and then their army is swallowed by the Red Sea. Kind of a reverse blessing! But even here there is at least a clue as to how this Promise will work itself out in a positive direction: as the nations treat Israel with favor, they themselves will be blessed. We have already seen this principle at work in the life of Abraham and the other patriarchs.[24]

A more positive clue, if subtle, lies almost hidden in the provisions that YHWH gives to the people regarding the Passover (12:43–49). As long as they are circumcised, foreigners and aliens are welcome at the table: "One law shall be to him who is born at home, and to the stranger who lives as a foreigner among you." (12:49).

It is therefore possible for at least individuals from the nations to enjoy the Covenant Blessings as long as they become members of the covenant community first. While this is a potential bridge to the nations it seems unlikely that it can bear the entire weight of this Promise. But at least a principle is established.

The relationship of blessing between Israel and the nations is yet more clearly observed in her calling as a "kingdom of priests." It is worth quoting again:

---

22. See 37, 65–66, above.
23. See 130–31, above.
24. Eg., see 72–73, 104–5, above.

> You have seen what I did to the Egyptians, and how I bore you on eagles' wings, and brought you to myself. Now therefore, if you will indeed obey my voice and keep my covenant, then you shall be my own possession from among all peoples; for all the earth is mine; and you shall be to me a kingdom of priests and a holy nation. (19:4–6a)

What can this mean? In general, the main role of a priest in antiquity was to be a mediator between the gods and the people. If the whole nation is to function as priest, it must be between YHWH, the true God, and part or all of the rest of humanity. The context ("among all peoples") strongly suggests that Israel is to act as priest to the nations. It is difficult to see what else this could mean, in fact. In this high calling, Israel will bring God to the nations and the nations to God, forming the conduit through which (as the wording of the Promise itself declares) the Blessing will flow to the nations.

If such is Israel's fundamental purpose, something of the "inner logic" of the Three Promises reveals itself even more fully here. The Land and Many Descendants turn out to be *means to this end* of blessing for the nations rather than ends in themselves. They provide the context for Israel to flourish, enabling her to fulfill her true calling which is to be a Blessing to All Nations. The connection between the Promises might now be put in this way: "When a blessed Land is occupied by a blessed (flourishing) Nation all the nations will then be blessed." Interestingly, this turns our narrative's usual emphasis on the Land and the Nation upside down. Or right side up.

It must be kept in mind that the passage itself does not define what is meant by "a kingdom of priests and a holy nation." However, this interpretation fits both the context and our gathering sense of the meaning of the third Promise and how it will be fulfilled.[25]

4. Fruitfulness

It is evident that the same fruitfulness enjoyed by the Israelites themselves also applies to their flocks and herds. When they escape from Egypt we are told that they were accompanied by enormous numbers of animals (12:38). Even in captivity they were actively enjoying this aspect of God's blessing. And further material blessings occurred when they escaped from Egypt taking articles of gold, silver, and clothing given up to them by the Egyptians.

This theme also graces the Promise of the Land. YHWH's first revelation to Moses famously depicted it as:

> ... a good and large land, a land flowing with milk and honey. (3:8)

---

25. It may also help explain why St. Paul, oddly, on the face of it, refers to his ministry to the Gentiles as his "*priestly* duty of proclaiming the gospel of God, so that the Gentiles might become an offering acceptable to God, sanctified by the Holy Spirit." Rom 15:16

Moses (Part One)

This characterization is used fifteen times in the Pentateuch and it has lodged itself firmly in the imagination of countless generations of Jews and Christians. Just after the Law is given, God describes the Land as "good" (echoing his pronouncement upon the original creation) and then adds the following details pointing all the way back to Eden itself:

> . . .a land of brooks of water, of springs, and underground water flowing into valleys and hills; a land of wheat, barley, vines, fig trees, and pomegranates; a land of olive trees and honey; a land in which you shall eat bread without scarcity, you shall not lack anything in it; a land whose stones are iron, and out of whose hills you may dig copper. (Deut 8:7–9)

At the end of Deuteronomy we find the following description as part of the Blessing that would come upon Israel for obedience:

> Yahweh will grant you abundant prosperity in the fruit of your body, in the fruit of your livestock, and in the fruit of your ground, in the land which Yahweh swore to your fathers to give you. Yahweh will open to you his good treasure in the sky, to give the rain of your land in its season, and to bless all the work of your hand. (28:11–12)

At this point in the Story, of course, it is a vision of what could be. However, it has also already started to become reality in their escape from Egypt.

5. Relationship

The Story has in many ways taken a dramatic turn for the better in this regard. The long years spent in Egypt were years apparently spent out of relationship with God: as we have seen they did not even know who YHWH was.[26] It is abundantly clear that at the heart of the Exodus experience is YHWH's stated purpose of reestablishing that relationship.

> I will take you to myself for a people. I will be your God:[27] and you shall know that I am Yahweh your God, who brings you out from under the burdens of the Egyptians. (6:7)

YHWH even calls the people of Israel "my son, my firstborn" (4:22). This identification is first and foremost a clear signal of how God feels towards the people of Israel. They are to him his firstborn son: in the culture of the Ancient Near East there simply could be no more pivotal relationship. The implications for Israel are profound: as God's firstborn son, the nation is set above all others and is the object of his special

---

26. See 111, above.
27. This phrase will soon earn the status of "covenantal language" because of its frequent use in the text to signify the relationship between YHWH and Israel.

concern, the heir.[28] It also has an obligation to be a faithful son, adhering to the will of the Father.

Furthermore, all through this narrative YHWH refers to the Israelites as "my people" (as in "Let my people go"). It will also be noted that when he says he had carried the Israelites "on eagles' wings" he adds "and brought you *to myself*" and refers to them as his "own possession" (19:4–5). Mount Sinai was where God dwelt and that was where he met with the Israelites, entering formally into relationship with them through the covenant. These are all indications that the alienation between humanity and God is being overcome, at least for this one small segment of the race.

As noted above, the Ten Commandments themselves are focused on the relationship with God, first of all, and then on interhuman relationships.[29] We are on the road again, back to Eden. Indeed, the Fourth Commandment calls for keeping the Sabbath day holy specifically because YHWH rested from his creative activity on the seventh day. Here is a taste of the "good"ness of paradise in the midst of the everyday labors imposed by the curse. In fact, it could be argued that Ten Commandments as a whole define the essence of Edenic life in terms of relationship.

The extraordinary relationship between YHWH and Moses is also instructive. At the burning bush they begin a close personal relationship in which Moses is portrayed as quite capable of negotiating with the Almighty, much in the manner of Abraham. We also have the following truly amazing statement:

> Yahweh spoke to Moses face to face, as a man speaks to his friend. (33:11)

While it is true that Moses had a special relationship with YHWH, it needs to be recalled that the seventy elders also drew near to him on Mount Sinai. In fact, as indicated above,[30] they "saw" God and ate and drank in his presence. Through this it is possible to discern in YHWH a willingness to enter into a genuine relationship with even more of his creatures, if not as equals then perhaps as friends.

As we also noted above, however, this type of relationship does not to apply to the nation as a whole, which remains somewhat at a distance.[31] With the institution of the tabernacle YHWH has condescended to come into their midst and dwell among them. But it remains a guarded presence only approachable through the priesthood and the sacrificial system.

---

28. Cf. Deut 15:10.
29. See 126, above.
30. See 114, above.
31. See 115–16, above.

6. Grace/Obedience

This portion of the narrative conforms nicely to the formulation that "we are saved by grace and then maintained in salvation by our obedience." In fact, it probably provides us with the perfect example of this idea, maybe even the paradigm for it.

The story told here, of the deliverance from Egypt and the giving of the Law, was entirely underwritten by grace. The people were absolutely helpless in their slavery. Moses failed miserably when he tried to liberate his people himself and had to flee. When God did act, it was not because the Israelites deserved it somehow, but simply because, as he told Moses, he had long ago made a Promise:

> I am Yahweh. I appeared to Abraham, to Isaac, and to Jacob, as God Almighty; but by my name Yahweh I was not known to them. I have also established my covenant with them, to give them the land of Canaan, the land of their travels, in which they lived as aliens. Moreover I have heard the groaning of the children of Israel, whom the Egyptians keep in bondage, and I have remembered my covenant. (6:2–5)

What we have called Israel's "Declaration of Independence"[32] contains the classic expression of our thesis, starting with grace:

> You have seen what I did to the Egyptians, and how I bore you on eagles' wings, and brought you to myself. (19:4)

And concluding with the need for obedience in order to bring it to completion:

> Now therefore, if you will indeed obey my voice and keep my covenant, then you shall be my own possession from among all peoples; for all the earth is mine; and you shall be to me a kingdom of priests and a holy nation. (19:5–6a)

The Law is set out clearly as the means of remaining in an already established relationship rather than the means of establishing that relationship. The whole "covenant mechanism" of Blessings and Curses is founded upon this understanding as an aid to encourage obedience and discourage disobedience.

However, the reader is here reminded of the earlier discussion in Perspectives (Part B) of how the events of the Exodus and the Mosaic covenant (with its demand for obedience) are generated by and operate inside the Covenant with Abraham.[33] The latter remains primary and it seems that in the end grace will indeed abound, extending itself even into the stubborn ("uncircumcised") human heart and enabling the obedience called for by Moses.

The biblical pattern of "grace" followed by "works" is therefore discerned in the general shape of this part of the Story as well as in its details. However, a new concept of what we might call "grace-enabled works" is introduced when we consider that

---

32. See 123, above.
33. See 132–33, above.

YHWH's ultimate plan includes a redeemed Israel. If the works that are to follow grace are themselves grace enabled, as this suggests, then all will be grace in the End. Those eagles' wings will carry God's people all the way to the gates of Paradise!

9

Moses (Part Two)
Dead Men Walking

Suggested Reading

Exodus 32–40 (Golden Calf –> First Use of Tabernacle); Numbers 9–33 (First Use of Tabernacle –> Plains of Moab); Deuteronomy 8–34 (Golden Calf –> Death of Moses) The Exodus and Numbers portions are roughly sequential while Deuteronomy provides Moses's retrospective overview of this entire period.

MAJOR DEVELOPMENTS

- Tablets of the freshly given Law firmly in hand, Moses descends from Mt. Sinai to discover, to his horror, that the people are worshipping the idolatrous golden calf
- YHWH is furious and it is only through the intervention of Moses that the nation is spared immediate annihilation
- Moses is granted a special glimpse of the glory/presence of YHWH from a cleft in the rock
- A second set of the Commandments is given
- YHWH continues to dwell in the midst of the people and provides several means to make this possible in the context of their continued sinfulness
- The people leave the region of the mountain to continue their journey but complain again about food and again quail arrive
- Spies are sent into the Land, resulting in rebellion among the people who then fear the inhabitants

- Moses again intervenes when this arouses YHWH's great anger and he threatens to destroy them all

- Korah and other leaders rebel against Moses's leadership and are swallowed by the earth

- When the people complain about water again, Moses strikes a rock instead of speaking to it, resulting in his eventual exclusion from the Promised Land

- The complaining continues and YHWH sends venomous snakes among the people and then instructs Moses to erect a bronze serpent for their healing

- The nation arrives at the border to the Promised Land having defeated the nations between the wilderness and the Jordan

- Balaam, with the encouragement of his talking donkey, blesses the people instead of cursing them

- Moses dies having seen the Promised Land only from afar

PERSPECTIVES

Introduction

The reader leans forward in anticipation as Moses descends from Mt. Sinai, the Law in hand. The awesome presence of YHWH on the mountain, the thunder and lightning, the violent shaking of the earth, the blast of the trumpets, the smoke and fire: surely, she says to herself, these are enough to ensure that from now on the nation would walk in faithful obedience and fulfill its calling. What a marvelous moment!

Same Old, Same Old

The utter shock Moses experienced when he encountered the people indulging in revelry and worshipping the golden calf is ours as well. How could they?! From the heights to the depths in a single leap. We wince, even as we sympathize with YHWH's desire to destroy the whole lot of them. They are the same miserable crowd that had stumbled through the wilderness to get to Sinai in the first place. Nothing has changed. Nothing.

This very point is underlined by the fact that the Story goes on to recount almost identical events taking place both before and after Sinai:

- the people complain about not having water and Moses provides it from a rock (Exod 17/Num 20:1–11)

- the people complain about food and YHWH sends in quail (Exod 16:11–13/Num 11:31–34)

- the people long for the "good old days" back in Egypt (Exod 16:3/Num 21:5)
- the people are such a burden that a council of elders is provided to assist Moses (Exod 18:13–26/Num 11:16–17/Deut 1:9–18)

Nothing has changed. Nothing.

Pressing Questions

In terms of our present narrative, two questions demand the reader's attention: "How can these people be so stubbornly disobedient?" and "Why is it that YHWH continues to journey with them in spite of this fact?"

We ask the first question because we fail to recognize ourselves in this story. If we are honest and put ourselves into the picture, we will admit that we would have done no better. The truth is that our common humanity is revealed all too vividly in this story. Like Adam and Eve in the garden, there is nowhere to hide. We, with all of their children, are made aware through this story that we stand naked before God, stripped of any and all pretensions. It is a sobering experience.

For hope, we cling to the mere fact of Israel's survival and the second question becomes more urgent. If people are really this unworthy of YHWH's favor, what is it that keeps him hanging in? To do so almost seems perverse. But that is because we ask the question, naturally, out of our experience as human beings. But it is fundamental mistake to assume that he is like us in all things and thinks like we do. He is "other" and the waywardness of Israel has the happy consequence of revealing yet more of his true character.

When Moses is appealing to YHWH to spare the people in their rebellion after the report of the spies, he says:

> Yahweh is slow to anger, and abundant in loving kindness, forgiving iniquity and disobedience; and he will by no means clear the guilty, visiting the iniquity of the fathers on the children, on the third and on the fourth generation. Please pardon the iniquity of this people according to the greatness of your loving kindness, and just as you have forgiven this people, from Egypt even until now. (Num 14:18–19)

That is, it is obvious that YHWH is fundamentally oriented toward love, forbearance and forgiveness. This is on top of his unswerving commitment to keep his promises, a quality we have already had occasion to note on a number of occasions, but especially in the near-sacrifice of Isaac on Moriah.[1] But he is not a kindly grandfather type who simply overlooks misbehavior. No, sin must be accounted for.

In this particular case, those who actually rebelled in the wilderness are spared immediate death but they will serve out their life sentences within its borders, short of

---

1. See 83–84, above.

the Promised Land. The fact that their children will actually be allowed to enter may be a case of leniency, given that they are second generation! In any case, it would be a new "Egypt-free" generation that would cross over Jordan.

Testing the Tester

If this story reveals something about both ourselves and YHWH, it still raises the question of why Israel itself had to go through such a terrible experience. In his last words to the nation, or "farewell discourse" as these speeches are often called, Moses offers the following explanation to them and to us:

> You shall remember all the way which Yahweh your God has led you these forty years in the wilderness, that he might humble you, to test you, to know what was in your heart, whether you would keep his commandments or not. He humbled you, allowed you to be hungry, and fed you with manna, which you didn't know, neither did your fathers know, that he might teach you that man does not live by bread only, but man lives by every word that proceeds out of Yahweh's mouth. (Deut 8:2–3)

It is all a test! Leaving aside the question of how they grade, its purpose is to transform their verbal commitment to serve YHWH into practice. When a couple marries they make vows to each other but no one really knows if they are going to keep those promises. That becomes evident only when "the honeymoon is over," when reality begins to sink in.

We might wonder about why an all-knowing God would need to test Israel in order to "discover" the truth of her commitment. But a test is useful for both the tester and the one being tested and no doubt it is primarily the latter that is in view here. After all, the proof of the pudding is in the eating. We don't even know what we are made of until circumstances arise to draw our true qualities to the surface. Combat, for example, often has this effect on participants.

So Israel is put to the test in the wilderness. The astounding thing is, however, that they, in their perversity, put YHWH to the test instead, as the Psalmist says:

> Today, oh that you would hear his voice!
> > Don't harden your heart, as at Meribah,
> > as in the day of Massah in the wilderness,
> > when your fathers tempted me,
> > tested me, and saw my work.
> > Forty long years I was grieved with that generation,
> > and said, "It is a people that errs in their heart.
> > They have not known my ways. (Ps. 95:7b–10)

Again, family life can provide an example of this type of testing. Consider children and how they push the limits on what they are allowed to do, driving their parents to distraction. In Israel's case, testing the tester only reveals its own failures.

He Is Good, but He Is Not Safe

The above discussion with its depiction of the tension between a holy God and a sinful people can help us understand another important function of the Law. We have already seen how the people were to remain at a distance on the pain of death when YHWH appeared on Mt. Sinai. In this portion of the narrative YHWH comes to actually dwell in the midst of the Israelites and for this to be "safe" for them, an entire way of life, which we will call living "in the Presence," is set out for them to follow. Although it may be a fragile arrangement given the behavior of the people so far, it is of enormous significance for our Story.

For the first time since the garden, God is living together with (part of) humanity. It will be recalled that after Adam and Eve were expelled from Eden, the way to the Tree of Life was guarded by cherubim and a flaming sword. Now a "way of life" is offered again through the Law: "Do this and live." While this may not necessarily mean the complete absence of death, the Blessings for covenant obedience certainly have an Edenic quality to them. We might be on the road back at last, but we will need to keep our eyes fixed on the road and our hands on the wheel. We are not there yet, but we can see it on the horizon.

Limited Atonement?

One of the means of living "in the Presence" is the provision of the sacrificial system as a way removing sin and restoring the divine-human relationship. In effect, this makes it "safe" for humans to draw near to the divine. But what may come as a surprise is that these sacrifices cover only "accidental" sins and not "deliberate" ones. For the latter, it seems that the only sufficient atonement is the death of the sinner.[2] No substitutes allowed.

It makes sense that more serious transgressions would call for a more serious penalty. But here is an odd thing: in actual practice often even the most grievous sins recounted in this Story are forgiven without any death occurring or even any sacrifice being offered. The wilderness experience of Israel is a case in point. As noted above, when YHWH was about to inflict the death penalty upon a rebellious nation, Moses intercedes and the people are simply forgiven. True, they are not allowed to enter the Promised Land, but the amazing thing is that they are allowed to go on living at all.

---

2. See 152, below.

What is going on here? On what grounds, then, are they forgiven? Our text makes it clear that it involves the appeal of a powerful mediator, Moses, to YHWH, a God whose very nature is inclined to love and forgive his people. But this answer begs the question of why he simply does not forgive all sin all the time for the same reason.

Or, looked at from the other way around, if sin brings about death and even minor sins demand the substitutionary death of an animal without defect, where is the required death in the case of major sins? Should not an even greater sacrifice of perhaps greater perfection be required? Instead we apparently have forgiveness without sacrifice just where it would seem to be most necessary. Something seems to be missing here, but the question is simply left hanging throughout the Old Testament.[3]

Moses is the Man

From his very birth Moses is a man marked by God for greatness. Although his genuine humanity is evident throughout the subsequent narrative, he stands head and shoulders above his peers. In terms of his role in salvation history it may not be quite right to say that "one greater than Abraham is here," but in terms of his character and experiences with YHWH he stands alone.

The scene on Mt. Sinai says it all: Moses alone ascends into the very Presence and it is as if he is admitted into heaven itself. His intimacy with YHWH takes the reader's breath away and yet, by the end of the story it seems almost routine. When he is hidden by YHWH in the cleft of the rock and actually "sees" YHWH, Moses's status is underscored in bold.

Another measure of the man (and subsequently of this period in the Story) is the vast amount of revelation that comes through him. Even if we discount the tradition that he is the author of the entire Pentateuch, much of its content still derives from him. Such a role is entirely without precedent in the Bible. No other character has spoken like this man. In this sense Moses is the first prophet. In fact, no other character before him actually spoke the word of God at all. Not Adam, not Noah, not Abraham, not Isaac, not Jacob.[4]

This is also an important point because it shapes the very narrative itself. It goes from a story in which YHWH occasionally speaks *to* various individuals to one in which he speaks *through* one in particular to a wide audience. It is part of "going corporate," no doubt. The result is an entire body of revelatory material that is to be

---

3. A study of the Psalms, for example, reveals no real appeal for forgiveness on the basis of sacrifice. Rather it is again the character of YHWH that is appealed to on the basis of true repentance. Cf. Ps 51:16–17.

4. The blessings conferred on their sons by Isaac and Jacob may be exceptions but although they are predictive and are presumed to be inspired, they are not the direct word of God we see given to Moses. As "farewell discourses" they are exceptions to the normal patriarchal way of speaking.

regarded as the authoritative Word of God. From this point on the Story will revolve around this "given." The Bible is born, and Moses is its midwife.

So much significance attaches to this man that the reader is naturally drawn further into the assumption that he might be the One, the Serpent Crusher, at last. What other conclusion is possible? After all, he had the power to change a serpent into a staff. On two occasions YHWH even decides to wipe out the nation entirely and start over again with Moses and his descendants. And then he overcomes the deadly venom of attacking snakes by merely having the people look to his own superior snake (in bronze) to be healed. In spite of everything, however, Moses, too, passes from the scene. He is not the One after all. The serpent lives on.

A scribe wrote an addendum to the Law describing the death of Moses, providing this epitaph:

> Since then, there has not arisen a prophet in Israel like Moses, whom Yahweh knew face to face, in all the signs and the wonders which Yahweh sent him to do in the land of Egypt, to Pharaoh, and to all his servants, and to all his land, and in all the mighty hand, and in all the awesome deeds, which Moses did in the sight of all Israel. (Deut 34:10–12)

While this echoes our own assessment, we must defer to Moses himself in the end. He knew that his was not the last word. In fact, he pointed to another "Moses" yet to come:

> Yahweh your God will raise up to you a prophet from among you, of your brothers, like me. You shall listen to him. (Deut 18:15)

Who could this prophet be? When will he come? What will he do? How could he possibly match the deeds of Moses? Would he proclaim the Word of God afresh and establish another Law? The Pentateuch ends, like Moses himself, still looking forward to the One. Along with the reader.

Israel in the Balance

One of the main effects of this story is to cast a pall over the long-term prospects of the Israelites ever being faithful partners in the covenant. In spite of YHWH's provision of an extraordinary leader, a miraculous deliverance, providential care, and the Law itself, they fail the test of obedience again and again.[5] One can appreciate YHWH's reaction:

> Forty long years I was grieved with that generation,
>   and said, "It is a people that errs in their heart.
>   They have not known my ways."

---

5. Cf. esp. Deut 8:1–5.

> Therefore I swore in my wrath,
> "They won't enter into my rest." (Ps. 95:10–11)

Can their children make a fresh start on the other side of the Jordan? Is their fathers' perverse attraction to Egypt more than a simple yearning for the good old days? Is it really a symptom of a deeper problem? Has the son of God truly risen from the dead?

THE STORY

The Golden Calf (Exod 32; Deut 9–10)

After the Ten Commandments are proclaimed, Moses returns to the Presence of YHWH on the holy mountain to receive other rules and regulations. While he is there, the rest of the people are wondering what has happened to him and grow impatient. In one of the most famous incidents of the Bible they ask Aaron to make a golden calf for them, perhaps to represent YHWH, the one who delivered them from Egypt.[6] Aaron agrees, and with his own hands he fashions the abomination out of their melted-down earrings.

This breaks the second commandment about making or worshipping an idol, but it goes deeper. As Enns puts it:

> By constructing a calf of gold and claiming that this pagan symbol can in any way be remotely associated with their deliverance from Egypt, the Israelites are in effect turning the Exodus experience on its head. They are going back to the first words God spoke on the mountain, the heart of the law in Exodus, and saying "No, we see things differently." It is hard to imagine a worse thing they could have done.[7]

With one stroke the Israelites have blown it. Right at the very moment they were receiving the Law and entering into solemn covenant with YHWH through Moses, they were insulting him in the grossest possible manner. YHWH is understandably furious and informs Moses that he is going to wipe out the Israelite people and start all over again. His choice of a new patriarch would be Moses himself. Another "great nation" would come from him.

Amazingly, however, Moses immediately begins to pray for them in a forty day fast![8] Like Abraham before him, he has the temerity to argue with the Almighty in order to get him to change his mind, and, like Abraham, he is successful. This cements his role as the mediator of the covenant of Sinai and ensures his colossus-like stature for generations to come.

---

6. This is probably the best way to take this difficult passage. Cf. Enns, *Exodus*, 569–70.
7. *Exodus*, 570.
8. Deut 9:18.

Moses (Part Two)

Having won his case, Moses descends the mountain, the two stone tablets firmly in hand. However, when he personally comes face-to-face with the reality of Israel's apostasy he boils over in anger and smashes the tablets to the ground. The covenant is shattered, literally. He then destroys the offending idol and demands an accounting from his brother. Aaron suggests, Adam-like, that it wasn't really his fault: the calf just sprang out of the fire into which he had cast the people's gold! Moses has nothing to say to this. Perhaps he is simply dumbstruck at his brother's obvious evasion.

Moses then instructs the Levites to destroy "about three thousand men of the people" (32:28)[9] and then the next day ascends to YHWH to make atonement for the rest, if possible. In an amazing act of solidarity with the sinful nation, Moses challenges God to "blot me out of the book you have written" (v. 32) if he will not forgive their sin. The result is a kind of stand-off: God reserves the right to punish the people, but the punishment is moderated to a plague. The mediator has done his job.

The crisis, however, is not yet over. YHWH commands Moses to lead the people on to the Promised Land but promises to drive out the inhabitants by an angel instead of doing it personally:

> . . . You are a stiff-necked people. If I were to go with you even for a moment,
> I might destroy you. (33:5)

While YHWH's position is understandable it undermines his whole purpose in bringing the Israelites out of Egypt to be "with" him. Of this, Moses is well aware:

> If your presence doesn't go with me, don't carry us up from here. For how
> would people know that I have found favor in your sight, I and your people?
> Isn't it that you go with us, so that we are separated, I and your people, from all
> the people who are on the surface of the earth? (33:15–16)

Once again God responds to Moses's mediation positively and commits himself to not abandon the children of Israel:

> I will do this thing also that you have spoken; for you have found favor in my
> sight, and I know you by name. (v. 17)

Pressing his advantage, Moses then brazenly asks for the ultimate demonstration of YHWH's favor, a personal appearance or theophany. Moses has recently experienced the awesome (and threatening) Presence upon the mountain and must know that this is a dangerous thing to ask for. In any event, reminding him that no one can see him and live (unlike it was in Eden? [v. 20]), YHWH graciously provides Moses with a safe place to stand:

> It will happen, while my glory passes by, that I will put you in a cleft of the
> rock, and will cover you with my hand until I have passed by; then I will take

---

9. Enns suggests in *Exodus*, 577, that these persons are more directly responsible for the apostasy.

away my hand, and you will see my back; but my face shall not be seen. (vv. 22–23)

This signifies both that Moses is a unique recipient of divine favor and that the crisis has clearly passed. YHWH will go with his people, but it was touch and go for a while. In fact, the rift caused by the golden calf episode is so serious that the covenant itself needs to be reestablished. They are back to square one.

The Second Giving of the Law (Exod 34; Deut 10)

Moses takes two new stone tablets up Mount Sinai so that YHWH will inscribe them with the Law. Once again they meet in the cloud, YHWH passing in front of Moses in another theophany and making it clear that, while he possesses deep wells of forgiveness, wickedness will not go unpunished. It is in this sobering context that the substance of the original covenant is rearticulated while Moses remains on the mountain for forty days and nights.[10]

Living in the Presence

By Means of the Veil

When Moses comes down his face is brilliantly radiant as the result of being so fully in the awesome presence of God. He even has to veil his face when standing before the people because they would not be able to endure immediate exposure even to the reflection of the divine glory. From this point on Moses seems finally to have the respect of the Israelites. Is it too much to hope that this is a result of a new attitude toward God himself? Time will tell.

By Means of the Cloud and the Fire (Num 9:15–23)

YHWH continues to dwell personally among the people by means of his presence. When the tabernacle is finished in time for the first celebration of the Passover since the departure from Egypt (one whole year ago), the structure is covered and filled with his glory cloud. This lifts when they set out again on their journey to show them the way during the day, while at night it appears as fire. We are told that this continued to be the case during the entire wilderness trek. Clearly YHWH has not abandoned them and is, in fact, leading their way.

---

10. See Enns, *Exodus*, 585–86, for details.

Moses (Part Two)

By Means of the Tabernacle Sacrifices (Lev 16; Num 15:22–31)

While we have already noted the basic structure of the tabernacle, it is now necessary to look further into its purpose. The tabernacle is the place of God's dwelling and the sacrificial system is provided as the way in which such a deity can be approached by sinful humanity. They must come offering a sacrifice in order to "cover" their guilt and to turn away the righteous anger of YHWH. And so it is that the tabernacle, with its two altars (for incense before the veil and for burnt offerings in the holy place), is also a place for sacrifice.

There are a bewildering variety of sacrifices called for in the Pentateuch,[11] but how do they "work"? How do they resolve the tension between a holy God and sinful humanity? This is perhaps best revealed in the provisions for "the Day of Atonement" in Leviticus 16. This day, the tenth day of the seventh month, is the one day of the year on which the high priest (and he alone) is permitted to enter into the holy of holies. To enter at any other time would result in death because, says YHWH, ". . . I will appear in the cloud on the mercy seat" (v. 2).

By means of sacrifice the high priest makes atonement for himself, his household, the whole community, and even the tabernacle itself, contaminated as it is ". . . because of the uncleanness of the children of Israel, and because of their transgressions, even all their sins . . ." (v. 16). The word translated as "atonement" has a variety of related meanings including "to cover," "to wipe away," and "to reconcile."[12] At its heart is the idea that human sin is removed and, with it, the barrier it presents to fellowship with God (v. 30).

Interestingly, in the case of the community as a whole, two male goats are used. Lots are drawn and one is sacrificed in the usual way so as to make atonement. However, atonement is made through the live goat as well. The high priest is to lay both of his hands on its head and:

> . . .confess over him all the iniquities of the children of Israel, and all their transgressions, even all their sins. . .The goat shall carry all their iniquities on himself to a solitary land, and he shall release the goat in the wilderness. (v. 21–22)

This is the origin of our concept of the "scapegoat" as the innocent person who gets blamed for the offences of others. It also embodies the idea of the transference of the sins of many onto the one.

Both means of atonement, sacrifice and scapegoat, embody the idea of substitution. We have discussed this concept earlier in connection with the provision of the

---

11. Technically there are *expiatory* offerings (sin offerings and guilt offerings), *consecratory* offerings (burnt, cereal, and drink offerings), and *communal* offerings (peace, wave and thank, votive (vows), free will, and ordination . See discussion in Rainey, "Sacrifices and Offerings," V:203–9.

12. See Jewett, "Atonement," I:408–13.

ram to "stand in" for Isaac on Mount Moriah and the lamb for the firstborn son in the first Passover: a life for a life[13]. Leviticus 17:11 articulates the essential principle:

> For the life of the flesh is in the blood. I have given it to you on the altar to make atonement for your souls; for it is the blood that makes atonement by reason of the life...

The Mosaic Law also makes it repeatedly clear that only animals "without defect" qualify for sacrifice.[14] They have to be perfect specimens, the very best from the flocks and herds. Nothing less would be acceptable to God, nothing less could be used for such a holy purpose.

To modern people the sacrificial system no doubt seems at best like cruelty to animals, and at worst to belong to a blood-soaked bygone age. Whatever else it might signify, it certainly is a graphic embodiment of a critical biblical truth about sin: it always results in death. This connection is rooted in the garden when God tells Adam that if he eats of the forbidden fruit, he will "surely die." It can be seen stretching through the Flood all the way to the near destruction of the Israelites in the shadow of Mount Sinai.

To us this may seem extreme, but that may be because we have a trimmed-down idea of sin. YHWH obviously does not. He knows what it is and what it does. Sin kills. YHWH, however, is the giver of life and therefore stands in utter opposition to sin. The latter is fundamentally disobedience, representing a rebellion against God's rule, putting oneself or someone else as supreme in his place. This breaks the first commandment and undermines all the others. No wonder YHWH is upset about sin. It is not a trivial pursuit.

From this perspective it is surely not unwise to have before the people a constant reminder of the depth of God's opposition to sin and the utter seriousness of walking in disobedience. What could make this point more powerfully than the thousands of rams, lambs, goats, oxen, and doves slaughtered day after day, year after year, in the tabernacle?

Furthermore, this whole system of sin and guilt offerings apparently suffices only for "unwitting," or relatively minor, sins according to Numbers 15:22ff. While the exact nature of such sin is somewhat obscure, it is contrasted with sins committed deliberately or "with a high hand" (15:30–31). It seems the latter have no prescribed offering to cover them because they incur the death of the offender.[15] Indeed, a careful reading of the Law as a whole reveals that the death penalty is prescribed for certain violations of each of the Ten Commandments. This suggests that breaking them is in

---

13 See 78, 116, 145–46, above.

14. Stated thirty-seven times in Exodus through Numbers, starting with Exod 12:5.

15. This is the probable meaning of ". . . that soul shall be utterly cut off. His iniquity shall be on him." Cf. Wenham, "Numbers," 131.

fact tantamount to committing a deliberate sin.[16] In any event, the sin-death connection is once again in plain sight for the covenant community and this truth is the key to the functioning of the sacrificial system.

By Means of the Major Feasts (cf. Exod 23:14-19)

The various sacrifices clearly provide a steady and graphic rhythm to Israelite life but they themselves are set within a cycle of feasts celebrated at set times during the year. The major occasions are as follows[17]:

- **March-April:** On the fourteenth day of the first month of each year **Passover** is to be kept in order to remind them of their deliverance from Egypt and slavery. This celebration is to continue for a week. During the week, on the day after Passover, a sheaf of the "**firstfruits**" of the grain harvest is to be waved before YHWH and a sacrifice/offering made. The seven days following Passover is the **Feast of Unleavened Bread**. (Exod 12:1-20)

- **May-June:** The day after seven weeks from Passover brings the **Day of Pentecost/Feast of Weeks** (Pente=50 [the 49 days of the 7 weeks + 1]). This also has a "**firstfruits**" flavor, with two loaves as a wave offering and a sacrifice of seven lambs, one young bull, and two rams. (Lev 23:15-22)

- **Sept-Oct:** As noted above the **Day of Atonement** is on the tenth day of the seventh Hebrew month.

- **Sept-Oct:** Five days after the Day of Atonement marks the beginning of the seven days set aside for the **Feast of Booths/Tabernacles**. By building temporary shelters out of branches and living in them for a week, the Israelites relive the time their forefathers spent in the wilderness. At the same time they are to celebrate the harvest that they will enjoy in the Land. (Lev 23:33-43)

- Add to all this the weekly keeping of the **Sabbath** (with its offerings) and those Sabbaths prescribed for the first of each month. And then there was the **Sabbath Year** (every seventh year) in which no crops are to be sown, the people living off of whatever came up in the fields. To crown it all, the **Year of Jubilee** is to take place every fifty years (after a Sabbath of Sabbath Years: 7 x 7 + 1), in which all land is to lie fallow and be returned to its original family ownership. The idea is that no possession of land is to be seen as permanent because ". . .the land is mine; for you are strangers and live as foreigners with me. . ." says YHWH (Lev 25:23).

---

16. For a discussion of this point, see Rainey, "Sacrifices and Offerings," V:204-5.

17. See especially Deut 16:1-17; Lev 23; Num 28 and 29. The reader will be aware that ancient calendars calculated months differently from the modern ones given in bold here.

Given all this, who could forget YHWH? Multiple remembrances of him are woven into the day-to-day fabric of Israelite existence: a constant state of thanksgiving for God's creation, salvation, and provision, along with petition for their own needs. It is a life that is to be lived from beginning to end "in the Presence."

By Means of the Levites (Num 3)

One last important aspect of this way of life for Israel needs to be considered: YHWH sets aside the whole tribe of Levi (one of the twelve) in order to provide for "religious" functions, especially those in connection with the tabernacle.

> I have taken the Levites from among the children of Israel instead of all the firstborn who open the womb among the children of Israel; and the Levites shall be mine, for all the firstborn are mine. On the day that I struck down all the firstborn in the land of Egypt I made holy to me all the firstborn in Israel, both man and animal. They shall be mine. I am Yahweh. (Num 3:12–13)

Out of these, only the descendants of Aaron and his four sons are qualified to be the priests who offer sacrifice in the tabernacle. It doesn't take long, however, for two of these sons to disqualify themselves (Lev 10) and, accordingly, only the male descendants of Eleazor and Ithamar can be priests in Israel. The high priest (an inherited office, usually) serves as their leader and alone enters the holy of holies on the Day of Atonement. Aaron becomes the first high priest in a line that will take a number of twists and turns along its way down through history.

Alone of all the tribes, the Levites are to inherit no portion of the Promised Land. Instead they are allotted cities and pasture lands scattered throughout its territory. Their consolation rests in the knowledge that "Yahweh is (Levi's) inheritance" (Deut 10:8–9, 18:1–2). They are to be supported through the tithe (Num 18:20–24), one-tenth of the Land's produce, which would correspond roughly with their proportion of the total population. Six of their cities become "cities of refuge" for those accused of murder and seeking to escape immediate retribution at the hands of the victim's relatives (Num 35:6–34).

Conclusion

With this "religious" piece of the puzzle in place we have a fuller understanding of how Israel is to be governed. Again, it is a theocracy: Moses is the human in overall charge, but he and everybody else is under the rule of God. As the place of the Levites, priests and high priest in the society demonstrates (even in the matter of the distribution of the Land), there can be no real distinction between the secular and the sacred. Indeed, such modern distinctions are completely alien to a properly theocratic society.

Although it is not always clear from the way these laws are presented, scattered as they are throughout Exodus, Leviticus, Numbers, and Deuteronomy, it appears that they were all part of the revelation that God gave to Moses on Mt. Sinai after the Ten Commandments were issued. It is to this entire way of life as God's special people that the Israelites heartedly commit themselves. It is now time to pick up the thread of the narrative again to see how they actually perform on the rest of the journey.

Still Complaining about the Food (Num 11:4–34)

Perhaps we can be excused for not being surprised at what we see as the wilderness journey resumes. No sooner are the people out from under the shadow of Sinai than they begin to grumble again. Their focus quickly turns to their stomachs as they rebel at the monotony of having only manna to eat:

> We remember the fish, which we ate in Egypt for nothing; the cucumbers, and the melons, and the leeks, and the onions, and the garlic; (v. 5)

Once more Moses is exasperated and this time he bitterly complains to YHWH in terms similar to the Deity's own words at Sinai:

> Why have you treated your servant so badly? Why haven't I found favor in your sight, that you lay the burden of all this people on me? Have I conceived all this people? Have I brought them out, that you should tell me, 'Carry them in your bosom, as a nurse carries a nursing infant, to the land which you swore to their fathers?' Where could I get meat to give all these people? For they weep before me, saying, 'Give us meat, that we may eat.' I am not able to bear all this people alone, because it is too heavy for me. (vv. 11–14)

YHWH responds by taking the Spirit that was on Moses and putting the same Spirit on seventy elders so that the responsibilities of leadership might be shared. Then YHWH causes such a huge flock of quail to be blown to the ground that it becomes a health hazard and many Israelites die as a result.

Good Spy vs. Bad Spy (Num 13 & 14)

Next, at YHWH'S command Moses sends twelve spies into the Promised Land to determine its fertility and defenses. All report that the Land is indeed fruitful but ten of them are so negative regarding the ability of the Israelites to defeat the inhabitants that, yet again,

> All the children of Israel murmured against Moses and against Aaron. The whole congregation said to them, "We wish that we had died in the land of Egypt, or that we had died in this wilderness! Why does Yahweh bring us to this land, to fall by the sword? Our wives and our little ones will be captured

or killed! Wouldn't it be better for us to return into Egypt?" They said to one another, "Let's choose a leader, and let's return into Egypt." (14:2–4)

At this point the two optimistic spies, Joshua and Caleb speak up, reminding the people that "Yahweh is with us" (v. 9) and point out what should then be obvious: *there is no reason to fear.* The crowd's response is to consider stoning these faithful men. It is déjà vu all over again:

> Yahweh said to Moses, "How long will this people despise me? How long will they not believe in me, for all the signs which I have worked among them? I will strike them with the pestilence, and disinherit them, and will make of you a nation greater and mightier than they." (14:11–12)

For the second time Moses turns down the offer and pleads for the Israelites on the same basis as he did when they had sinned with the golden calf. That is, he argued that if YHWH destroyed the Hebrews, YHWH's own reputation would suffer and his Promise would fail (vv. 13–16). And again YHWH relents, forgiving the people "according to the greatness of (his) loving kindness" (v. 19).

As usual, however, this is not "cheap grace": the whole nation is sentenced to wander in the wilderness until all of those who rebelled die of natural causes, a period that will last forty years. They will not be allowed into the Land. Joshua and Caleb, the two faithful spies, are the only exceptions.

The Earth Moves under Their Feet (Num 16)

Not content merely to complain, a group of 250 community leaders openly challenge Moses's leadership at the instigation of a Levite named Korah. Clearly with ambitions of their own, they accuse Moses and Aaron of setting themselves "above Yahweh's assembly" (v. 3) and assuming unwarranted dictatorial powers over them.

Moses responds by proclaiming that YHWH will make it clear to all who is his chosen leader. The next day Moses warns the people to separate themselves from Korah, his fellow leaders, and their families.

> Hereby you shall know that Yahweh has sent me to do all these works; for they are not from my own mind. If these men die the common death of all men, or if they experience what all men experience, then Yahweh hasn't sent me. But if Yahweh makes a new thing, and the ground opens its mouth, and swallows them up with all that belong to them, and they go down alive into Sheol, then you shall understand that these men have despised Yahweh. (28–30)

Immediately the ground opens up and swallows them up. Dramatic as this is, fire then consumes the rest of the conspirators. Not only that, when the people then accuse Moses and Aaron of having killed "Yahweh's people" (v. 41), a plague breaks out among them as YHWH moves once again to destroy them all. However, under Moses' instruction, Aaron "put on the incense, and made atonement for the people." (v. 47), but not before almost 15,000 lie dead.

Yet another close call for Israel. Yet another successful intercession by Moses. Yet another graphic illustration of YHWH's intolerance for sin. What will it take to make this crowd obey YHWH?

Moses Strikes Out (Num 20:1–13)

When the Israelites arrive in the Desert of Zin, at a place called Kadesh, the people quarrel with Moses and Aaron once again because there is no water there. Moses enquires of YHWH and is told simply to speak to the rock to make it gush forth with the needed water. However, for some reason Moses instead strikes the rock with his staff. While this produces the water, YHWH is nevertheless seriously upset with both Hebrew leaders, labeling their action as "rebellion" (20:24):

> Because you didn't believe in me, to sanctify me in the eyes of the children of Israel, therefore you shall not bring this assembly into the land which I have given them. (20:12)

Thus it transpires that Moses and Aaron join the rest of their generation in being excluded from the Promised Land. It is not long after this that Aaron dies and is succeeded as high priest by his son Eleazar.

The Bronze Serpent (Num 21:4–9)

Amazingly, the nation soon returns to its complaining ways and this time YHWH sends venomous snakes among them and many die. Upon admitting their mistake to Moses, he intercedes for them and God instructs him to fashion a bronze snake, set it up on a pole, and tell the people that all they have to do is look at it and they will live. And that is exactly what happens.

In this odd incident, a symbol of death is transformed into a source of healing and life.[18] Such is the power of YHWH. But it is looking as if the nation will never, ever, learn to be obedient.

Journey's End (Deut 2–3; Num 21)

While in the wilderness of Sinai Israel seems to have been, perhaps with the exception of a prolonged stay at Kadesh (Num 20:1; Deut 1:46), continually on the move. Apparently the nation encounters few other people while in the wilderness proper, but as they move up north toward the Dead Sea and along its eastern shore they begin to

---

18. The same symbol, likely tracing its origins in part to this Story, is used today by the medical community.

bump into other nations. In the region of Seir YHWH instructs them to "pass through the border of your brothers, the children of Esau, who dwell in Seir" (Deut 2:4) and not engage them in battle. Just before the bronze snake episode they come to Edom, whose king refuses their request for safe passage and as a result they detour around his kingdom.

It will be recalled that the borders of the Land promised to Abraham were not firmly defined and, as the Israelites get closer, the narrative seems to regard it as having two sections, one on each side of the Jordan River. On the east side is the Transjordan and on the west is Canaan. Both sections will eventually be incorporated into Israel, but it is Canaan that is the main destination and from which Moses has been excluded. However, he continues to lead the people as they conquer and supplant the current occupants of the Transjordan.

This last process begins with the defeat of two kings of the Amorites, taking over their territory up to the border with the Ammonites. According to Moses, this involved the taking of over sixty cities as well as the complete annihilation of the inhabitants. Then they traveled to the plains of Moab across the Jordan from Jericho.

The Curious Case of the Talking Donkey (Num 22–24)

It is here, according to Num 22–24, that a very odd incident takes place.

> Balak the son of Zippor saw all that Israel had done to the Amorites. Moab was very afraid of the people, because they were many. Moab was distressed because of the children of Israel. Moab said to the elders of Midian, "Now this multitude will lick up all that is around us, as the ox licks up the grass of the field."
>
> Balak...sent messengers to Balaam the son of Beor, to Pethor, which is by the River, to the land of the children of his people, to call him, saying, "Behold, there is a people who came out of Egypt. Behold, they cover the surface of the earth, and they are staying opposite me. Please come now therefore, and curse this people for me; for they are too mighty for me. Perhaps I shall prevail, that we may strike them, and that I may drive them out of the land; for I know that he whom you bless is blessed, and he whom you curse is cursed." (22:2–6)

When Balaam gets the message, God tells him not to proceed with the cursing because the Israelites are a blessed people, but to go with the messengers anyway. He starts off, but his donkey refuses to proceed on three occasions when she sees "the angel of YHWH" standing in the way with a drawn sword. This is in spite of repeated beatings from an infuriated Balaam.

> Yahweh opened the mouth of the donkey, and she said to Balaam, "What have I done to you, that you have struck me these three times?" Balaam said to the donkey, "Because you have mocked me, I wish there were a sword in my hand,

> for now I would have killed you." The donkey said to Balaam, "Am I not your donkey, on which you have ridden all your life long until today? Was I ever in the habit of doing so to you? He said, "No." Then Yahweh opened the eyes of Balaam, and he saw Yahweh's angel standing in the way, with his sword drawn in his hand; and he bowed his head, and fell on his face. (22:28–31)

Realizing what and who he is up against, instead of the curses for which he was hired, Balaam fearlessly pronounces blessings upon Israel in the presence of Balak,. It is both humorous and deadly serious at the same time, signaling the ultimate victory of God's people. No power on earth will be able to resist the God of Israel, even the Israelites themselves. The record also makes it very clear that these victories are bestowed by YHWH alone and not by strength or numbers.

The Death of Moses (Num 27:12–23; Deut 34)

Moses is now 120 years old. He fled Egypt at forty, led the Exodus at eighty, and has now spent forty years with the nation in the wilderness. His time is up:

> Moses went up from the plains of Moab to Mount Nebo, to the top of Pisgah, that is opposite Jericho. Yahweh showed him all the land of Gilead to Dan, and all Naphtali, and the land of Ephraim and Manasseh, and all the land of Judah, to the Western Sea, and the south, and the Plain of the valley of Jericho the city of palm trees, to Zoar. Yahweh said to him, "This is the land which I swore to Abraham, to Isaac, and to Jacob, saying, 'I will give it to your offspring.' I have caused you to see it with your eyes, but you shall not go over there." (Deut 34:1–4)

We may think that this is a sad and perhaps even unjust sentence upon a great man of God. But Moses himself is concerned only with the question of who would look after the people once he is gone. This is the true measure of the man. He asks YHWH to appoint someone so that they ". . . may not be as sheep which have no shepherd" (Num 27:17). In response, YHWH commands him to ". . . take Joshua, son of Nun, a man in whom is the Spirit, and lay your hand upon him" (v. 18). With the succession now assured, Moses can go to his grave in peace.

Like the patriarchs before him, however, Moses has some "famous last words" for the people. In fact, the entire book of Deuteronomy seems to be his "farewell discourse." He looks both backward to the journey they have been on and forward to the occupation of the Promised Land. As the book comes to an end we have the so-called "Song of Moses" and a blessing for his children, the Israelites. The Song (ch. 32) recounts the provision of God for Israel and how they have responded in faithlessness, a response that will one day result in them being scattered. However, God will not abandon them in the end: he will take vengeance on the nations that afflict them. The blessing (ch. 33) is configured like that of Jacob/Israel upon his sons, except that it is pronounced, appropriately now, upon whole tribes.

Even as he gazes wistfully across the Jordan into the Promised Land we can almost hear the final bell. If he also hears it, he does not have to ask for whom it tolls:

> So Moses the servant of Yahweh died there in the land of Moab, according to Yahweh's word. He buried him in the valley in the land of Moab opposite Beth Peor, but no man knows where his tomb is to this day. Moses was one hundred twenty years old when he died. His eye was not dim, nor his strength gone. The children of Israel wept for Moses in the plains of Moab thirty days, until the days of weeping in the mourning for Moses were ended. (Deut 34:5–8)

So it is that Moses, the greatest leader of the Jewish nation, steps rather mysteriously off the stage forever. He leaves behind no possibility of his bones becoming an object of worship or his grave a place of pilgrimage. Instead his legacy is his word, his example, and his Law. He wouldn't want it any other way.

IN THE BOSOM OF ABRAHAM

Introduction

This portion of the Story fairly bristles with references to the Promises, but only rarely are all three encountered together. As noted in the previous chapter, we see them together in the "covenant mechanism" of Blessings and Curses, which chronologically belongs here as part of Moses's farewell discourse. Before that, they also appear collectively, although a bit indirectly, as the basis of Moses's appeal to YHWH in the aftermath of the golden calf incident:

> Yahweh, why does your wrath burn hot against your people, that you have brought out of the land of Egypt with great power and with a mighty hand? Why should the Egyptians talk, saying, 'He brought them out for evil, to kill them in the mountains, and to consume them from the surface of the earth?'. . . Remember Abraham, Isaac, and Israel, your servants, to whom you swore by your own self, and said to them, 'I will multiply your offspring as the stars of the sky, and all this land that I have spoken of I will give to your offspring, and they shall inherit it forever.' (Exod 32:11–13: cf. Deut 9:25–29)

The testimony to the nations (here represented by Egypt), the Many Descendants, and the Land itself would all be lost if YHWH were to proceed with their destruction. Here we see the Promise at work as a restraint upon YHWH himself! That is how strongly he is bound to the terms of the patriarchal Covenant.

Moses (Part Two)

1. The Land/Place

While the Land remains over the horizon in this period, the people of Israel are well aware of it as their destination. Fifteen times in the book of Deuteronomy God reminds them about ". . .the land that Yahweh your God gives you to possess." (e.g., 19:14) and many of the laws given at Sinai are directly related to the Land (such as the one against moving a boundary stone in 19:14). The division of the Land among the tribes is also a critical part of Moses's blessing in ch. 33. In this sense the Land is becoming a greater reality.

Furthermore, one man from each tribe actually sets foot in the Land as a spy. Their detailed report of its fruitfulness elevates its place in the consciousness of the nation, but the general disbelief and rebellion engendered by the nature of its inhabitants end up excluding all but Joshua and Caleb from its borders. Instead of inheriting the Land they inherit the wilderness, or, rather, the wilderness inherits them. Even Moses himself never enters because of his own disobedience. As in the last chapter, we see that possession of the Land is dependent upon covenant obedience.

But even at the end Moses is still hopeful:

> For if you shall diligently keep all these commandments which I command you—to do them, to love Yahweh your God, to walk in all his ways, and to cling to him— then Yahweh will drive out all these nations from before you, and you shall dispossess nations greater and mightier than yourselves. Every place on which the sole of your foot treads shall be yours: from the wilderness and Lebanon, from the river, the river Euphrates, even to the western sea shall be your border. (Deut 11:22–24)

With this assurance shoring up their shaky resolve, the Israelites prepare to turn the next page in their history. Perhaps they are encouraged by the reminder of the true scope of this Promise as well: the Land will not be confined simply to Canaan. As was revealed to Abram, YHWH has something much larger in mind.[19] It looks like Canaan is itself a promise of more to come.

As well, another important but very different sense of place has been introduced into the narrative. We read that YHWH comes to dwell in the holy of holies within the tabernacle, his first earthly "residence" since the garden of Eden. Indeed, the cherubim whose outstretched wings hover over the Ark of the Covenant[20] are bound to remind the people of the cherubim who guarded the approach to Eden after the Fall (Gen 3:24). Eden, the place of God and humanity in harmony, has drawn near. You can almost see its gates.

---

19. See 72, above.
20. See Hamilton, "Genesis, 1–17," 210, for a discussion of the similarities and differences.

2. Many Descendants

This Promise continues to work away beneath the surface as the Israelites leave the region of Sinai and continue on their journey to the Land. We noted in the last chapter that about 600,000 men left Egypt and the two censuses taken in the wilderness confirm that this number was maintained in spite of several plagues sent by God as punishment for rebellion.[21]

The first census (Num 1) is undertaken at Sinai, seemingly for military purposes. The second (Num 26) is done just outside the Land in order to determine the relative size of each tribe in order to ensure its fair division once settlement begins. Since the whole generation of adults who had left Egypt has by now died, the maintaining of their numbers is significant in the light of the need for enough people to properly possess the Land (Exod 23:29–30). But beyond these practical reasons for a census, it may be that it was an awareness of this Promise itself that provided a deeper motivation: to see if the time of fulfillment was at hand. In any event both censuses indicate that their population, at least of men, had been about the same (600,000) at the beginning and at the end of the wilderness experience in spite of many losses along the way.

Moses uses one of the covenantal metaphors to express how well this Promise has been at work in the past:

> Your fathers went down into Egypt with seventy persons; and now Yahweh your God has made you as the stars of the sky for multitude. (Deut 10:22)

He continues to hold out numerical blessing as part of his final charge: if they will obey YHWH, "He will do you good, and increase your numbers more than your fathers" (Deut 30:5b, cf. 7:13). He points out that the obverse also holds true in case of disobedience:

> You will be left few in number, even though you were as the stars of the sky for multitude, because you didn't listen to Yahweh your God's voice. (Deut 28:62)

Here is the covenant mechanism again. Curiously, Balaam, when he pronounces his first oracle after seeing just part of the nation, almost uses covenantal language himself, although it is a natural enough metaphor:

> Who can count the dust of Jacob,
>   or count the fourth part of Israel? (Num 23:10)

The negative side of this Blessing is also in view on the two occasions YHWH becomes so angry with the people that he is about to wipe them out and start all over again with Moses. Of course, he relents upon Moses's intervention in each case, but after the second he makes the guilty wander in the desert for forty years until nature takes its course and they all pass away.

---

21. Num 1:46 and 26:51.

Moses (Part Two)

All in all, this Promise is not a whole lot closer to fulfillment as this episode comes to an end, but Israel's numbers are being maintained in spite of disobedience, a hopeful sign. And as *promise* it is reaffirmed as part of God's ultimate intention for his people.

3. A Blessing to All Nations

The nation spends the entire duration of this narrative in the wilderness out of contact with other peoples until they approach the Land. Here they clash with, and triumph over the Amorites (Num 21:21–35), Moabites, and Midianites (Num 22 –25; 31:1–12). Not much of a blessing here for the nations who oppose the chosen people! But, as we have noted on a number of occasions, that is how this Promise is supposed to work, blessing those nations that blessed Israel and cursing them that dealt poorly with them.[22]

Not only is this principle discerned in the events narrated in this section, but also it is stated outright by our friend Balaam, the seer of Aram, himself a non-Israelite:

> Everyone who blesses you is blessed.
> Everyone who curses you is cursed. (Num 24:9)

The context of this pronouncement is a dire warning that those nations who oppose the Israelites will be devoured by them. Once again, it is clear that how a nation treats Israel will determine their receipt of the Blessing. Of course, Balaam's "blessing" is a distinct echo of that which accompanied the original Covenant given to Abraham (Gen 12:2–3).

And then there are both of Moses's successful pleas to YHWH when he was on the verge of destroying the Israelites. On each occasion Moses appealed to the Almighty on the basis of how this would look to the Egyptians and the nations. It is possible to interpret Moses's strategy merely as an appeal to God's desire to save face before the nations: they would lose all respect for YHWH if he wiped out the nation he had himself chosen and rescued. This understanding assumes, of course, that YHWH is subject to such feelings.

However, another interpretation suggests itself: Moses may be pointing out how this particular Promise becomes more unlikely if the nations come to see YHWH as a God unworthy of their attention. In other words, YHWH's mission to bless the nations by drawing them to himself through Israel is at stake.

In sum, however, this Promise of a Blessing to the Nations has little or no positive expression in this part of the Story. The trouble seems to be that there are no nations inclined either to bless or curse the Israelites at this point in the narrative! But there are plenty who begin to come into the picture as Israel approaches the Land. And we have seen what happens to them.

---

22 22. Eg., see 72–73, 104–5, above.

4. Fruitfulness

This Promise must have seemed particularly at odds with the experience of the Israelites as they trek through a wilderness environment. It would appear that they quickly consume most of the animals they had left Egypt with, given their complaints about the lack of food before they even get to Mt. Sinai. A similar reality faces them during the forty years of wandering in a seriously harsh environment, especially burdened with the knowledge that those who had left Egypt would never experience the Land "of milk and honey." Even slavery looks better than this.

On the other hand, toward the end of the journey they receive great spoils from their victory over the Midianites. According to Numbers 31:32–34, this comes to 675,000 sheep, 72,000 cattle and 30,500 donkeys. This would make a significant contribution to restoring the livestock they had used up in the wilderness.

As far as the fruitfulness of the Land itself is concerned, it, like the Land itself, still remains over the horizon, out of reach. The hopes of the Israelites for a fertile territory and its products must be deferred until they cross the Jordan and actually come into its possession. Their long wilderness experience serves only to intensify their longing for what lies ahead.

This feeling was reinforced, no doubt, by having had a literal foretaste of the fruitful Land. When the twelve spies come back they bring some pomegranates and figs with them along with a single cluster of grapes that took two men to carry suspended on a pole between them (Num 13:21–25). The Israelites are so impressed they forever after called the place it came from "Eshcol," or "cluster" valley. Such excessive fertility is characteristic of Eden itself, and again reminds us of the connection between the land of Canaan and the garden. We are on the road again, back to Eden.

And finally there is Moses's description of what YHWH has in store for an obedient Israel:

> You shall be blessed in the city, and you shall be blessed in the field. You shall be blessed in the fruit of your body, the fruit of your ground, the fruit of your animals, the increase of your livestock, and the young of your flock. Your basket and your kneading trough shall be blessed. You shall be blessed when you come in, and you shall be blessed when you go out. (Deut 28:3–6[23]; cf. Num 24:6–7)

But they are not there yet. Almost, but not quite. And it is not just the Jordan River that forms a barrier: there is still the little matter of covenant obedience.

---

23. See also Deut 7:13–15.

5. Relationship[24]

In this segment of the Story the tide of Relationship seems to be running in different directions at the same time. In spite of this, a major step forward has indeed been taken.

First of all, we return to the two occasions on which YHWH confronts the unfaithfulness of the Israelites and threatens to destroy them altogether, starting over again with Moses. But these are just the lowest points in a journey in which the people are all too consistent in their unbelief/disobedience, putting repeated and serious strain on their relationship with YHWH. He is like a parent whose son has fallen into drug addiction but who somehow cannot bring herself to throw him out of the house, in spite of all the lies, stealing, and self-destructive behavior. An outsider may shake his head in perplexity, but YHWH is clearly deeply committed to his relationship with Israel and it will take a great deal of misconduct indeed to undo it.

Astoundingly, it is into the midst of these same people that YHWH comes to make his dwelling in the tabernacle! One would expect that his Presence between the cherubim of the holy of holies would result in an impossible tension but, because this structure also embodies the sacrificial system, it provides the means by which the sinfulness of the people can be covered. In this way YHWH can be "with" them even without fully resolving the inevitable tension in the relationship.

The willingness of YHWH to enter into negotiations with Moses on two occasions also reveals what the divine-human relationship could look like. It is not of equals, but neither is it that of master and servant. Something much more profound is at work here. These points are confirmed in the theophany Moses experiences while hidden in the cleft of the rock: this appearance of YHWH, unlike any since the garden itself (even that with the elders on Sinai), has a directness that is truly awesome. Is this really possible for a human being, even one as unique as Moses?

A partial answer to this question is offered when we consider the significance of the giving of YHWH's Spirit to Moses, the seventy elders, Joshua, and Bezalel.[25] In all but the last instance, this endowment has to do with enabling them to lead God's people. At the very least this must mean that something of God's very person had bonded with these individuals: God and human beings together in a new and startling way. True, this has happened to only a few, but the fact that it happened at all is remarkable and, we might hope, a sign that more will someday be brought into this circle of intimacy.

---

24. Aspects of relationship were also discussed in the Perspectives section of this chapter. See 145-46, above.

25. Num 11:21-30; Num 27:18, Deut 34:9; Exod 31:3, 35:31.

6. Grace/Obedience

Much of the content of the present chapter is relevant to this question and what follows will attempt to gather the various strands to discern something of a coherent pattern. It will be recalled that we are exploring the idea that we are saved by grace and then called to maintain ourselves in that condition by our works of obedience.

The last time we tackled this question we began to see more clearly that, while this concept is clearly operative, "obedience" itself is, in the end, "grace-enabled," suggesting that the whole equation is a matter of grace.[26] The narrative now before us supports a similar conclusion, albeit from a slightly different perspective.

Our formula in its original form is evident in the book of Deuteronomy, as Moses addresses the people who are about to cross into the Land. Here we find, first of all, a very explicit indication that Israel has been "saved" by grace alone followed by an equally explicit demand for obedience:

> Yahweh didn't set his love on you nor choose you, because you were more in number than any people; for you were the fewest of all peoples; but because Yahweh loves you, and because he desires to keep the oath which he swore to your fathers, Yahweh has brought you out with a mighty hand and redeemed you out of the house of bondage, from the hand of Pharaoh king of Egypt...*It shall happen, because you listen to these ordinances and keep and do them, that Yahweh your God will keep with you the covenant and the loving kindness which he swore to your fathers.* (Deut 7:7–8, 12, italics added)

And, if that is not clear enough, he makes the same point when he warns them about the dangers lurking in their future successes against the inhabitants of the Promised Land:

> Not for your righteousness or for the uprightness of your heart do you go in to possess their land; but for the wickedness of these nations Yahweh your God does drive them out from before you, and that he may establish the word which Yahweh swore to your fathers, to Abraham, to Isaac, and to Jacob. Know therefore that Yahweh your God doesn't give you this good land to possess for your righteousness, for you are a stiff-necked people. (Deut 9:5–6)

> ... Now, Israel, what does Yahweh your God require of you, but *to fear Yahweh your God, to walk in all his ways, to love him, and to serve Yahweh your God with all your heart and with all your soul, to keep Yahweh's commandments and statutes, which I command you today for your good?* (Deut 10:12–13, italics added)

Once again it is crystal clear that works have nothing to do with redemption but, as the italicized verses attest, obedience is still required to stay redeemed.

---

26. See 140, above.

Moses (Part Two)

If we find our template pattern confirmed in these affirmations, it is once again the actual events in the narrative that move us beyond it. The people of Israel repeatedly fail the test of obedience in the wilderness (ten times according to YHWH's own reckoning [Num 14:22]) and yet the covenant continues to hold! How much disobedience will it take to nullify the agreement altogether?

The golden calf and the good spy/bad spy incidents seem to push YHWH over the edge and he readies himself to make an end of this stubborn rabble. But even then he is not prepared to utterly abandon the covenant. He wants to substitute the children of Moses for the current members of the children of Israel, once again narrowing the line to a presumably more obedience-inclined DNA. When he relents upon Moses's intercession we are left with the overall impression that the Promises will be fulfilled in spite of disobedience.

This idea is confirmed in the Song of Moses found in Deut ch. 32 where Israel's redemption is celebrated:

> He found him in a desert land,
>   in the waste howling wilderness.
> He surrounded him.
>   He cared for him.
>   He kept him as the apple of his eye.
> As an eagle that stirs up her nest,
>   that flutters over her young,
> he spread abroad his wings,
>   he took them,
>   he bore them on his feathers. (vv. 10–11)

But:

> They have dealt corruptly with him.
>   They are not his children, because of their defect.
>   They are a perverse and crooked generation.
> Is this the way you repay Yahweh,
>   foolish and unwise people?
> Isn't he your father who has bought you?
>   He has made you and established you. (vv. 5–6)

And in the end?

> I said that I would scatter them afar.
>   I would make their memory to cease from among men;
> were it not that I feared the provocation of the enemy,
>   lest their adversaries should judge wrongly,
>   lest they should say, 'Our hand is exalted,
>   Yahweh has not done all this.' (vv. 26–27)

Grace prevails once again.

It must be noted, however, that there is a complex interplay between grace as extended to individuals and grace extended to the nation. This comes out in the (delayed) sentence of death on the people who had rebelled. They were allowed to live out their natural lives and so perpetuate the nation, ensuring that it continue and enter into the Promised Land. The corporate seems to have something of the upper hand over the individual.

We earlier noted that the scoundrel Jacob was able to bask in the faithfulness of Abraham because YHWH's very nature was "massively predisposed to bless and not to curse."[27] Apparently there is no bottom to this deep well of grace.

---

27. See 125, above.

10

Joshua
Into Canaan's Fair Land

Suggested Reading

Joshua 1–24. Quotations of Scripture are from Joshua unless otherwise indicated.

MAJOR DEVELOPMENTS

- YHWH commissions Joshua to lead Israel across the Jordan and occupy the Land
- Joshua sends in spies who report that the natives are fearful of the invaders
- Three tribes settle east of the Jordan but send their fighting men across with the others
- Led by the Ark of the Covenant, the Israelites cross over the stopped-up Jordan into the Land
- Passover is celebrated in the Land for the first time
- Jericho's walls come tumblin' down and it is destroyed along with all its inhabitants
- Ai is taken, plundered, and all its citizens put to death
- The covenant is renewed at Mt. Ebal
- YHWH causes the sun to stand still so that Israel can wreak havoc on the Amorites
- The Land is taken city by city (thirty-one in total), but much of it remains unconquered

- The tribes are allotted their various territories and the Levites are given their towns throughout the Land
- The warriors from the Eastern tribes return to their portions in the Transjordan
- An elderly Joshua challenges the nation to covenant obedience
- The covenant is renewed at Shechem
- Joshua dies and is buried within his tribe's territory

PERSPECTIVES

Introduction

With the great Moses passed from the scene, the reader can only wonder what is in store next for the Israelites. True, Moses appointed Joshua to succeed him, but even under Moses the nation has proven fickle in its obedience to YHWH. Nevertheless, the Story has been leading up to this moment when the Promised Land will become the possession of Israel at last. It is a moment filled with glorious possibilities and dangerous pitfalls. Which will it be?

New Mission/ New Leader

With the death of Moses the revelatory voice is silenced. While Joshua is clearly guided by YHWH throughout this narrative, and speaks for him on several occasions, he does not receive the kinds of revelations his mentor did. No new laws, no new covenant, no theophanies, no mediations: all that is over. Now is the time for a valiant warrior, a man of action. The Serpent Crusher?

His name is Joshua, which means, appropriately, "YHWH is salvation." Joshua had already distinguished himself by the time Moses commissions him, accompanying Moses when he ascended Mt. Sinai to receive the Law and being one of the two faithful spies that had been sent into the Land. We are told that he was "filled with the spirit of wisdom for Moses had laid his hands on him."[1] The man for the job.

It is important to note, at least in passing, that YHWH is continuing his pattern of working through one man at a time. Only when Moses has passed from the scene does Joshua himself begin to hear from YHWH. And, like Moses, while he is living no one else shares this role.

Theocracy still rules: God is leading through his chosen servant. In this sense Israel's leadership style has not changed in any fundamental way: it is still one man, chosen by God, who leads for life as God's regent. The office of overall leader does not pass from father to son as it does in the Levitical priesthood. Rather it is "charismatic"

---

1. Deut 34:9; cf. Num 27:18.

in the sense that each candidate possesses gifts of leadership which are either recognized and/or endowed at the time of commissioning.

New Era/New Leader

In a reversal of the Exodus experience, Israel's new commander leads them out of the generally disappointing experience of the wilderness, across the Jordan, and into the Promised Land. This marks a major new phase of the Story, one in which the wandering and disobedience of the desert are left behind and a new faithfulness and direction emerges. They begin to settle into their new territory and do not rebel against Joshua as they did against Moses. It seems as if the children of Jacob have finally learned their lesson and have entered the long-promised time of blessing.

Not that it is an easy transition. Repeatedly, Joshua has to rally the troops in the face of a truly daunting task. The Land is presently occupied by a number of nations organized as city-states and they naturally resist the advance of this foreign people into their territory. However, theirs is a lost cause because YHWH is fighting on behalf of the Israelites. This is not to say that the latter are entirely virtuous either, but in the main they stay faithful to YHWH.

Banning the Ban?

If there is any part of the Bible that many would like to see removed, it would be those portions of the book of Joshua that deal with the complete extermination of the men, women, and children who were conquered by the Israelites. What is especially difficult is that the text repeatedly emphasizes it was YHWH himself who issued the "ban," as it is sometimes called, marking all under it for destruction. Since this study is committed to the text as it stands, however, banning the ban is not an option. But how can we even begin to understand it?

Many have offered "explanations" for the ban, but most modern people, Christians included, find them wanting. We read these accounts in our own context of genocide or ethnic cleansing done out of racism, revenge, or some other kind of blind hatred. How can there be any justification for this and how can we reconcile it with our understanding of God himself? While a fully satisfactory explanation may elude us, it is possible to at least glimpse some hints of one when we consider the wider context of the Story.

A number of things need to be taken into account. First of all, the overall picture suggests that the Conquest, while an act of redemption for the Israelites, is also an act of judgment upon the Canaanites for gross and persistent sin. YHWH had told Abraham long ago that the reason why he could not possess the Land back then was that "the iniquity of the Amorite is not yet full" (Gen 15:16).[2] The nations being destroyed were not simply innocent bystanders, in the wrong place at the wrong time when a powerful and land-hungry hoard arrived and wiped them out. It is actually an act of forbearance on YHWH's part that withholds the destruction of these nations until the Conquest. The Scripture on many occasions both warns and illustrates that there is a limit to God's patience and severe judgment awaits those who continue in refusing to turn away from their sin.[3]

In this regard Israel enjoys no immunity whatsoever. Even though they are the chosen people of YHWH, they enter the Land having heard these words from Moses himself:

> You shall not go after other gods, of the gods of the peoples who are around you, for Yahweh your God among you is a jealous God, lest the anger of Yahweh your God be kindled against you, and he destroy you from off the face of the earth. (Deut 6:14–15)

Israel is thus acting as an instrument of judgment throughout the Conquest. Those people and their possessions that are under the ban are, in a curious phrase, "devoted" to Yahweh. It is used in regard to Jericho as the Israelites are given the following instructions:

> The city shall be devoted, even it and all that is in it, to Yahweh. Only Rahab the prostitute shall live, she and all who are with her in the house, because she hid the messengers that we sent. But as for you, only keep yourselves from what is devoted to destruction, lest when you have devoted it, you take of the devoted thing; so you would make the camp of Israel accursed and trouble it. (6:17–18)

It almost has the sense of these people and things being analogous to the firstborn male child born to an Israelite, who "belongs to" YHWH but is to be redeemed, and thus escape death.[4] In any case, the ban at least supplies the Israelites with a motive other than greed or even savagery. In fact, when Achan confiscates some of the plunder of Jericho for himself, YHWH's anger is directed at the entire nation, putting them all at risk until he and his family are put to death. It was expedient for them that one man and his family should die for the people.

As far as being motivated by ethnic hatred is concerned, the problem with the Israelites is generally just the opposite. They tend to admire the degenerate cultures and religions around them and have a persistent inclination to assimilate into them.

---

2. Deut 9:5 also sees the Conquest as judgment for sin.

3. Certainly, the New Testament indicates that it is possible to reach a point of no return (cf. Hebrews 6:4–6; 10:26–31). In a remarkable parallel to "the sin of the Amorites," St. Paul talks about God's wrath Falling upon the Jews directly responsible for killing Jesus because their sins had gone over the limit (1 Thess 2:14–16).

4. Cf. Exod 13:1–13.

This is a direct threat to their covenant commitments and, if pursued, will result in the destruction of the nation as indicated in the quote above from Deuteronomy. So part of the motivation for the ban is to put these peoples and their gods out of reach of temptation. As well, having been repeatedly told that they had no innate superiority, they had no reason to look down on any other nation.

We also need to keep in mind the truth of "progressive revelation" and recognize that at this stage in the Story, not all of God's truth is available to those actually taking part in the events recorded. Those who would take the Conquest as some kind of justification for religious war or ethnic cleansing in the name of God need to ask themselves what is at the center of the revelation given in the entire Bible. If they do, they will realize that this episode is the exception rather than the rule. Only a direct and unmistakable revelation could overcome such considerations.

Another thing we need to remember is the character of the God who instigated the ban. When we read the entire Story we are satisfied that he does not act arbitrarily or out of base motives. He is a just and holy God whose judgment is entirely justified. If we cannot ourselves see the justification, then it comes down to this: Should we trust him for what we cannot understand? To ask this, for the believer, surely, is to answer it.

Finally, one of the reasons this ban seems so extreme to us is that we have lost the proper sense of the seriousness of sin and its consequences. The book of Joshua can serve, like our earlier consideration of the sacrificial system,[5] as a healthy antidote to such thinking.

Again, none of this reasoning entirely removes the offence we feel when we ponder the ban. But it does take the edge off somewhat and remind us that, sometimes more than others, "we see through a glass darkly."

Already/Not Yet

If the Conquest is seen, properly, as a time when the Promise is being fulfilled, it must at the same time be acknowledged that it is not a complete fulfillment. In a very real sense the Land is in Israelite possession but many other inhabitants remain all around them and threaten their way of life, even their continued existence. This state of affairs can be described as "already/not yet": simultaneously "already" in possession of the Land, but "not yet" possessing it in full.

At first glance this phrase seems self-contradictory but it nicely manages to catch the human experience of God's salvation. It is lived along the line of the tension between these two realities. It started with Eden, an "already" if ever there was one. That was lost and became almost entirely a "not yet" but with a gathering sense of "already" with Noah being saved, Abraham being called, Joseph saving his family, and finally Moses leading the people out of captivity and to the border of Canaan. All this

---

5. See 152, above.

was done in the midst of all the ambiguities of history and the weaknesses of human nature.

So this time, while we have moved a long way down the line, we are still "not yet" at "already." What this part of the Story has done is reveal this pattern more clearly and whet our appetites: it is easier to believe that there is more "already" to experience.

Therefore Joshua is not the Serpent Crusher, the expected One, after all. But his name ("YHWH is salvation") surely points us in the right direction.

THE STORY

Joshua Gets His Marching Orders (1:1–11)

The long and bitter experience of the Israelites in the wilderness is over and a new era is about to dawn: the Land is in view and is theirs to be taken. The keenly anticipated time of fulfillment has finally arrived. At God's direction a new leader has been commissioned, Joshua son of Nun, already proven in faith and successful in battle. YHWH gives him his instructions:

> Moses my servant is dead. Now therefore arise, go across this Jordan, you and all these people, to the land which I am giving to them, even to the children of Israel. I have given you every place that the sole of your foot will tread on, as I told Moses. From the wilderness and this Lebanon even to the great river, the river Euphrates, all the land of the Hittites, and to the great sea toward the going down of the sun, shall be your border. No man will be able to stand before you all the days of your life. As I was with Moses, so I will be with you. I will not fail you nor forsake you. (1:2–5)

Here is presented a vision of the Land at its most extensive, matching the final dimensions God gave to Abram and confirmed by Moses himself in his final charge to the people.[6] It is also clear that Joshua shares in the authority that Moses enjoyed and has the assurance of YHWH's presence and protection. Moses is dead, but not the Promise. It is about to become reality, but not without a struggle! A lot will be required of the new leader, and so YHWH continues his charge:

> Be strong and courageous; for you shall cause this people to inherit the land which I swore to their fathers to give them. Only be strong and very courageous. Be careful to observe to do according to all the law which Moses my servant commanded you. Don't turn from it to the right hand or to the left, that you may have good success wherever you go. This book of the law shall not depart from your mouth, but you shall meditate on it day and night, that you may observe to do according to all that is written in it; for then you shall make your way prosperous, and then you shall have good success. Haven't I

---

6. Gen 15:18; Deut 1:7, 11:24.

commanded you? Be strong and courageous. Don't be afraid. Don't be dismayed, for Yahweh your God is with you wherever you go. (1:6–9)

If Joshua has a motto it is surely "Be strong and courageous!" It is repeated like a refrain a number of times in these pages and, by and large, Joshua lives up to it. He makes no excuses when God calls him, leaving the impression he is a man of unquestioning faith, superior in this even to Moses who exhibited great reluctance when he was first called. Of course, Joshua has had the advantage of seeing YHWH at work through his eighty-five years or so and has learned to trust him. And to have the direct promise of God to always be with him must have been a great source of strength throughout his many trials. "God is with me" could have been his motto too.

Preparations for Conquest (1:12—12:24)

The first thing the new commander does is enlist the men of the tribes of Reuben and Gad and the half-tribe of Manasseh to join their fellow Israelites in the takeover of the Land on the west side of the Jordan. Moses had indicated to these people that they would inherit territory east of Jordan if they would cross with their fellows to help them and they had agreed to do so.[7] Long ago Jacob had 'adopted' Joseph's two sons, Ephraim and Manasseh, as his own,[8] and now it is they, not "the tribe of Joseph," who are each assigned a section of the Land.

This makes things a bit confusing when we refer to the twelve tribes of Israel. Joseph's two son's descendants are "half-tribes" and each is allotted its own territory. As any map of the division will indicate, the size of their portions shows how favored Ephraim and Manasseh truly are. They later come to Joshua asking for even more territory on the basis of what God had done for them: "we are a numerous people, because Yahweh has blessed us so far?" (17:14b). The legacy of Joseph finally matches his place in the history of the nation with his descendants getting a double portion of the Land.

But that does not bring the total number of portions to thirteen, because the tribe of Levi is to live among the others with cities of their own—but no territory as such. They are the "religious," with general responsibility for the spiritual life of the nation. Thus they do not appear on the maps at all. The Land is divided into twelve tribal areas, but two belong to half-tribes, as we have noted.

Joshua, perhaps drawing on his own experience as a spy, sends only two men into the Land on a reconnaissance mission. They cross the river and sneak into Jericho, a city that stood squarely in Israel's path on the other side. Helped by a prostitute named Rahab, they promise her and her family safety in the coming battle. Upon their return they bring good news to Joshua:

7. See Num 32.
8. See Gen 48.

> Truly Yahweh has delivered all the land into our hands. Moreover, all the inhabitants of the land melt away before us. (2:24)

The next morning they set out to cross the Jordan river. At last.

Roll, Jordan, Roll (3–5)

Joshua orders the tribes to follow the Ark of the Covenant (at a safe distance), telling them that "... tomorrow Yahweh will do wonders among you." (3:5). It is also to be a very public authentication of Joshua's leadership:

> Yahweh said to Joshua, "Today I will begin to magnify you in the sight of all
> Israel, that they may know that as I was with Moses, so I will be with you." (3:7)

Then YHWH does just that by causing the Jordan, in its flood stage at the time, to roll up like the Red Sea did under Moses. The people cross over easily on dry ground, no doubt seeing Joshua in a new light. Twelve large stones are taken from the middle of the river and set up on the western shore as a perpetual memorial to the miraculous event. According to Joshua, YHWH has done this:

> ... that all the peoples of the earth may know that Yahweh's hand is mighty,
> and that you may fear Yahweh your God forever.' (4:24)

This last phrase is Covenantal-type language and it is fitting that those men who had been born in the wilderness are now circumcised and brought under the Covenant. It is clearly a fresh start with YHWH on the other side of the Jordan. He tells Joshua: "Today I have rolled away the reproach of Egypt from you" (5:9). From now on they would be looking forward, not backward.

It is surely not a coincidence that a new year is just beginning. The stones out of the Jordan had been set up on the tenth day of the first month, the day the lamb is taken from the flock in preparation for Passover. And now, on the fourteenth day, they observe that festival for the first time in the Promised Land. The promise inherent in the first Passover has finally been realized. It is entirely appropriate that the Exodus and the entrance should be brought together in this celebration on the west bank of the Jordan. Surely the significance of the occasion is lost on none of the participants.

They now begin to live off of the fruit of the Land. It is an event the writer finds of considerable importance:

> The manna ceased on the next day, after they had eaten of the produce of the
> land. The children of Israel didn't have manna any more, but they ate of the
> fruit of the land of Canaan that year (5:12)

Finally, like Moses before him, Joshua even has a "holy ground" moment to ready him for his first act of liberation.

> When Joshua was by Jericho, he lifted up his eyes and looked, and behold, a man stood in front of him with his sword drawn in his hand. Joshua went to him and said to him, "Are you for us, or for our enemies?"
>
> He said, "No; but I have come now as commander of Yahweh's army."
>
> Joshua fell on his face to the earth, and worshiped, and asked him, "What does my lord say to his servant?"
>
> The prince of Yahweh's army said to Joshua, "Take off your sandals, for the place on which you stand is holy." Joshua did so. (5:13–15)

He awaits his instructions.

To Jericho, and Beyond! (6:1—8:29)

If God's command to confront Pharaoh had seemed an overwhelming challenge to Moses, his orders for Joshua seem even more impossible. He is to have the Ark of the Covenant, accompanied by seven priests, lead his men in a march around the walls of Jericho once every day for six days and then seven times on the seventh day. Then the priests are to blast away on their trumpets and the people are to give a great shout. He is told that this will result in the collapse of the city walls, allowing easy access for his troops (and, no doubt, total immobilization of the enemy!).

But Joshua, unlike his mentor, does not even blink. He follows the instructions word for word and it works! The walls come tumbling down and the army rushes in for the kill. According to Joshua's explicit command, every inhabitant except Rahab and her family is killed and the contents of the city are completely destroyed. Or so it seems.

After the success of Jericho's fall, the Israelites attack the city of Ai, a little further into the Land. Surprisingly, they are easily repulsed by the inhabitants. Their confidence shaken, Joshua complains to YHWH, managing to sound like both the people *and* Moses in the wilderness:

> Alas, Lord Yahweh, why have you brought this people over the Jordan at all, to deliver us into the hand of the Amorites, to cause us to perish? I wish that we had been content and lived beyond the Jordan! Oh, Lord, what shall I say, after Israel has turned their backs before their enemies? For the Canaanites and all the inhabitants of the land will hear of it, and will surround us, and cut off our name from the earth. What will you do for your great name? (7:7–9)

YHWH makes it clear that Israel had been humiliated because someone had taken for themselves some of the items put under the ban at Jericho. As a result, the nation faces a stark choice:

> I will not be with you any more, unless you destroy the devoted things from among you . . . It shall be, that he who is taken with the devoted thing shall be

burned with fire, he and all that he has, because he has transgressed Yahweh's covenant, and because he has done a disgraceful thing in Israel. (7:12b, 15)

In obedience to YHWH, the guilty Achan, along with his entire family and livestock, are rooted out and put to death. Once this taken care of, Ai is easily taken and plundered.

At the Gates (8:30–35)

Once the area around Jericho and Ai is secure, Joshua proceeds to build an altar on nearby Mt. Ebal and there he copies the Ten Commandments onto stones as Moses had commanded. He also carries out the instructions to have half the tribes stand on Mt. Ebal and the other half opposite on Mt. Gerizim while the covenant Curses and Blessings are read out by Joshua. Indeed, he proclaims the entire Law of Moses in what appears to be a covenant renewal ceremony.[9]

What an superlative moment this is! They have arrived in the Land, YHWH has won for them great victories and even greater vistas of Promise lie before them. It is like a pep rally for the football team on homecoming weekend! They know what they have to do, as well as the consequences in the event of failure. But, in the moment, failure is just not an option. On to victory!

Victory!—More or Less (9–11)

As we all know, once the big game actually begins, things don't always go well for the home team. The Gibeonites, for example, motivated by fear, actually managed to trick the Israelites into sparing them. However, they become the servants of Israel and enter into history as the infamous "hewers of wood and drawers of water."[10] Although this act of disobedience seems to have gone unpunished, the author makes a point of the fact that the Israelites "didn't ask counsel from Yahweh's mouth" (9:14) for guidance in the matter. It is one thing to be ignorant, it is another to be willfully ignorant. Through this episode we can see that not all of the nations are eliminated in the Conquest: some continue to coexist with the Israelites in the Land.

Five Amorite kings, alarmed because Gibeon had made peace, then come together against Israel. Belatedly, they discover that their real opponent is YHWH, not the invading Hebrews. When Joshua ambushes them, YHWH puts them to confusion, pummels them with large hailstones and then, in response to Joshua's plea, even causes the sun to stand still so that Israel can wreak total havoc upon them. They are not having a good day! The author is duly impressed:

9. See Deut 27.

10. "Infamous," that is, to us Canadians. The phrase has often been used by Canadians of our economy in relation to that of the United States. It is a treasured part of our national inferiority complex! The biblical references are Josh. 9:21, 23, and 27 (KJV).

> There was no day like that before it or after it, that Yahweh listened to the voice
> of a man; for Yahweh fought for Israel. (10:14)

Such is the fate of the Amorites, that nation whose sins had finally reached their full measure. It is a sobering thought.

The account repeatedly emphasizes the fact that the victories are a result of YHWH's being on Israel's side, even personally fighting on their behalf.[11] Numerous times it is said that God has *given* them the Land and its inhabitants.[12] This does not imply, however, that the nation simply sits back and watches YHWH at work. Israel still has to fight with all its strength, many presumably wounded and dying in the effort.

Turning first to the south and then to the north, they annihilate many more kings and peoples in a sweep of desolation that also sees their cities burned and plundered. Striking a note reminiscent of Pharaoh, the following explanation is given for such consistent local opposition:

> For it was of Yahweh to harden their hearts, to come against Israel in battle,
> that he might utterly destroy them, that they might have no favor, but that he
> might destroy them, as Yahweh commanded Moses. (11:20)

Although the text says at this point and at others that Joshua has taken the entire Land,[13] there in fact remains much to be conquered, especially the coastal plain that continues to be occupied by the Philistines. There is even a suggestion that part of the problem may be technological: the Israelites did well in the hill country but not as well in the lower areas where the enemy had the advantage of using their chariots.[14] But, the main factor, as the account itself stresses, is YHWH's activity or inactivity on their behalf.

Enough of the Land was in their hands to say that "the land had rest from war" (11:23b), enabling them to allot it to the various tribes for their possession. This is another wonderful moment of fulfillment for the entire nation, a moment long anticipated. It is now well over forty years that they had been on the road and now they are "home" at last. But the road stretches all the way back beyond Moses to Jacob, Isaac and Abraham.

> So Yahweh gave to Israel all the land which he swore to give to their fathers.
> They possessed it, and lived in it. Yahweh gave them rest all around, according
> to all that he swore to their fathers. Not a man of all their enemies stood before
> them. Yahweh delivered all their enemies into their hand. Nothing failed of

---

11. Josh 10:14 and 42; 23:3.
12. Cf. 2:9; 10:19; 18:3; 23:3–5.
13. Another case of "Semitic exaggeration"?
14. Cf. 17:16, 18.

any good thing which Yahweh had spoken to the house of Israel. All came to pass. (21:43–45)

This is a remarkable statement, given what we have just been told about the territory still under non-Israelite rule, let alone the more expansive dimensions of the Promise still unclaimed. Perhaps it is another case of "semitic exaggeration"! Certainly, the Land had been conquered in principle, but there is a lot of mopping up left to be done. It is an "already/not yet" experience for Israel. But they can be excused, perhaps, for being so strongly in the "already" moment that they overlook something of the "not yet."

A Slight Altarcation (22)

Enough has been accomplished to enable Joshua to send the Reubenites, the Gadites and the half tribe of Manasseh back to their allotments east of the Jordan River. They have done well, fighting faithfully with their brothers. He blesses them, saying:

> Return with much wealth to your tents, with very much livestock, with silver, with gold, with bronze, with iron, and with very much clothing. Divide the plunder of your enemies with your brothers. (22:8)

Upon returning home, the Transjordan tribes erect a large altar at Gelioth (22:10–34). Their fellow Israelites are alarmed, naturally assuming that sacrifices would take place there instead on the altar in the Tabernacle as prescribed by the Law. Such a travesty would surely bring the wrath of God upon them all. They begin to prepare for war with their fellow Israelites in order to prevent this from happening. But they soon learn that they have apparently been too quick to judge. The Transjordan leaders explain their position:

> The Mighty One, God, Yahweh, the Mighty One, God, Yahweh, he knows; and Israel shall know: if it was in rebellion, or if in trespass against Yahweh (don't save us today), that we have built us an altar to turn away from following Yahweh; or if to offer burnt offering or meal offering, or if to offer sacrifices of peace offerings, let Yahweh himself require it. (22:22–23)

Instead, they explain, this altar has been set up simply to remind them all that the river divides them only in the physical sense because they all worship the same God in the same place:

> Therefore we said, 'Let's now prepare to build ourselves an altar, not for burnt offering, nor for sacrifice; but it will be a witness between us and you, and between our generations after us, that we may perform the service of Yahweh before him with our burnt offerings, with our sacrifices, and with our peace offerings;' that your children may not tell our children in time to come, 'You have no portion in Yahweh.'

> Therefore we said, 'It shall be, when they tell us or our generations this in time to come, that we shall say, "Behold the pattern of Yahweh's altar, which our fathers made, not for burnt offering, nor for sacrifice; but it is a witness between us and you." (22:26–28)

This episode underlines the remarkable unity of the nation, sharing as they do a national identity and fighting together under one leader. However, a certain amount of tension clearly remains between the national and tribal identities.

Joshua's Last Altar Call (23–24)

And so it is that Israel is at rest and Joshua's task is completed. He is about 110 years of age and he can look back with some satisfaction at what has happened under his leadership. Like Moses and the patriarchs before him he delivers a farewell discourse to the nation in which he emphasizes the main thing:

> You have seen all that Yahweh your God has done to all these nations because of you; for it is Yahweh your God who has fought for you. Behold, I have allotted to you these nations that remain, to be an inheritance for your tribes, from the Jordan, with all the nations that I have cut off, even to the great sea toward the going down of the sun. Yahweh your God will thrust them out from before you, and drive them from out of your sight. You shall possess their land, as Yahweh your God spoke to you. (23:3–5)

Here the "already/not yet" tension is obvious. The nations are already "cut off" but not yet "driven out." In fact, Joshua uses his own motto to put the Israelites on notice about their precarious situation:

> Therefore be very courageous to keep and to do all that is written in the book of the law of Moses, that you not turn away from it to the right hand or to the left; that you not come among these nations, these that remain among you; neither make mention of the name of their gods, nor cause to swear by them, neither serve them, nor bow down yourselves to them; but hold fast to Yahweh your God, as you have done to this day. (23:6–8)

Continuing in a passage bristling with this same tension, Joshua asserts once again that YHWH has kept every promise that he made to them! Nevertheless, he adds that disaster is still a real possibility:

> You know in all your hearts and in all your souls that not one thing has failed of all the good things which Yahweh your God spoke concerning you. All have happened to you. Not one thing has failed of it. It shall happen that as all the good things have come on you of which Yahweh your God spoke to you, so Yahweh will bring on you all the evil things, until he has destroyed you from off this good land which Yahweh your God has given you, when you disobey

> the covenant of Yahweh your God, which he commanded you, and go and serve other gods, and bow down yourselves to them. Then Yahweh's anger will be kindled against you, and you will perish quickly from off the good land which he has given to you. (23:14b.–16)

If it is true to say that the people are finally at "rest" and all the Promises have been "fulfilled," it must also be acknowledged that they have not yet arrived at a final settled state. Deadly enemies still remain and the possibility of losing it all is just too real.

In this context Joshua summons all of Israel to Shechem in order that they might be challenged to renew their commitment to follow YHWH. Beginning with Terah (Abraham's father) he recites their history to date and especially how YHWH has not only been with them but has fought for them time and again. Reminding us of Moses once more (Deut 30:19–20), he ends with a stirring call to follow only YHWH:

> Now therefore fear Yahweh, and serve him in sincerity and in truth. Put away the gods which your fathers served beyond the River, in Egypt; and serve Yahweh. If it seems evil to you to serve Yahweh, choose today whom you will serve; whether the gods which your fathers served that were beyond the River, or the gods of the Amorites, in whose land you dwell; but as for me and my house, we will serve Yahweh. (24:14–15)

The people respond as one that of course they will not serve other gods, knowing very well that they owe everything to YHWH. Joshua, sensing some hesitation or perhaps remembering their many previous commitments and failures, boldly challenges their sincerity:

> You can't serve Yahweh, for he is a holy God. He is a jealous God. He will not forgive your disobedience nor your sins. If you forsake Yahweh, and serve foreign gods, then he will turn and do you evil, and consume you, after he has done you good. (24:19b–20)

Again the people promise their obedience and the renewed covenant is marked and duly witnessed.

Joshua's task is finished at last and he passes from the scene. The nation's hopes and dreams have been more or less realized under his leadership. Fittingly, he is buried in his tribal allotment and for his epitaph we read:

> Israel served Yahweh all the days of Joshua, and all the days of the elders who outlived Joshua, and had known all the work of Yahweh, that he had worked for Israel. (24:31)

Although Moses gets most of the press, it can be argued that, as far as redemption itself is concerned, Joshua was the greater man. But he, consistently with his lesser role in revelatory matters, has no prophecy regarding the future. He is still not the One.

And so this great cycle of redemptive history draws to a close. But it has a footnote: we read of the burial of Joseph's restless old bones that had been brought all the way from Egypt. This is done at Shechem where Jacob had settled and from whence Abraham had been shown the full extent of the Promised Land so many years ago. "This dreamer," then, who was stolen from his father's arms by his own brothers and lived his life in exile, can finally rest in peace, with a view of the entire Land before him. Some dreams never die.

IN THE BOSOM OF ABRAHAM

1. The Land/Place

For the first time in its history Israel has come into actual possession of the Promised Land, and this is the story of how it overcomes the nations that currently inhabit the area. Each of the tribes is allotted a portion of the Land in accordance with the command of Moses (remembering that the Levites are scattered throughout the rest and Joseph's portion is divided between his sons Ephraim and Manasseh). This allows the tribes to retain a separate identity and history in line with the blessings pronounced upon them earlier by Jacob/Israel.

Only a fraction of the Promised Land is actually occupied at all, considering that its ultimate dimensions were to stretch from the Euphrates in the east to the Mediterranean Sea in the west and from Lebanon in the north to the desert in the south. Presently they are living in only a small part of this vast territory. There must be more of this Story to come.

As far as the "place" for YHWH is concerned, the tabernacle and its holy of holies continues to be his dwelling during this period. Once the nation is established in the Land, the tabernacle comes to rest at Shiloh, and, as the episode of the "alternative" altar demonstrates, this is regarded by all Israel as the one true place of worship. Indeed, Shiloh seems to begin taking on the sense of being a holy city as a result (Josh. 18:1; 22:19). As the Land is cleared of its pagan occupiers and settled by the children of Israel it too gathers about itself the feeling of being a sacred place. It is YHWH's gift to his people and in which he alone is to be worshipped.

2. Many Descendants

The present portion of the Story reveals little direct indication of this Promise at work. However, it will be recalled that YHWH had told the people that they would occupy the Land in step with their population increase until they were numerous enough to possess it properly.[15] Since the Land is now occupied to a significant degree, it is fair

---

15. Exod 23:29–30; see 135, above.

to assume that some of the required increase has occurred. There are other hints that suggest that the Promise is bearing fruit.

As part of the covenant renewal process at the end of the period, YHWH reminds the people through Joshua that he had given Abraham many descendants.[16] The clear implication is that this applies to the nation at the end of the Conquest as well as to their time in Egypt and in the wilderness. There are certainly no indications that numbers had declined once they had crossed the Jordan.

In fact, the opposite is suggested when the leaders of the tribes of Ephraim and Manasseh come to Joshua and demand more territory. In language echoing to the original Promise to Abraham they point out that they ". . . we are a numerous people, because Yahweh has blessed us so far" (17:14). Joshua has to agree:

> You are a numerous people, and have great power. You shall not have one lot only; but the hill country shall be yours. Although it is a forest, you shall cut it down, and it's farthest extent shall be yours; for you shall drive out the Canaanites, though they have chariots of iron, and though they are strong. (17:17b–18)

Of course the children of Joseph are implying that they have increased more than the other tribes (and so need more territory) but this cannot exclude the likelihood that the others, too, had at least maintained their numbers or grown somewhat themselves. God has blessed them all and his blessing must include the abundance of offspring if it is truly to be counted as a blessing.

Negatively speaking, the Curse that will fall upon all of Israel for disobedience strikes a truly ominous note. They will, Joshua asserts, simply ". . . perish quickly from off the good land" (23:14b, 16). Again we note that the Curse takes the form of "few descendants" or even annihilation. But this possibility seems a long way off during the Conquest.

3. Blessing to All Nations

If Israel had little to do with other nations while in the wilderness, once the Jordan is crossed the opposite holds true. This Land is definitely not desert and has attracted many peoples to live off of its "milk and honey." In confronting them, Israel shows itself mostly as a deadly enemy rather than a blessing. Where has this Promise gone?

It shows itself primarily in those episodes that conform to the pattern we have seen earlier: the Blessing will come to those nations that themselves bless the Israelites. The latter also undergo several experiences that serve to increase our understanding of the nature of this Blessing.

For one thing, we are told that crossing of the Jordan was intended for the express purpose of making the nations sit up and take notice of YHWH:

16. Josh 24:3.

> For Yahweh your God dried up the waters of the Jordan from before you until you had crossed over, as Yahweh your God did to the Red Sea, which he dried up from before us, until we had crossed over, that all the peoples of the earth may know that Yahweh's hand is mighty... (4:23–24)

From this one could conclude that there is a "pre-evangelistic" objective to the Conquest. The Gibeonites seem to get it.

Unlike the other nations, the Gibeonites are impressed with Israel's successes at Jericho and Ai, and recognize the superiority of YHWH their God. Their response is to deceive the Israelites by pretending to come from outside disputed Canaan in order to make a peace treaty. In this they are successful as Israel commits itself to the treaty. Even after discovering the ruse they refuse to break the agreement "... because the princes of the congregation had sworn to (the Gibeonites) by Yahweh, the God of Israel" (9:18). In this fashion, the Gibeonites are saved from destruction.

As instructive as this episode is, the story of the pagan prostitute Rahab has even more to offer, if on a smaller scale. She protects and helps the two Hebrew spies who are sent into the city of Jericho. The account makes it clear that she does so because she, too, has seen how YHWH is with the Israelites and "... I know that Yahweh has given you the land..." (2:9) and that "... Yahweh your God, he is God in heaven above, and on earth beneath" (2:11b). In other words, she comes to believe in response to how Israel is exalted by YHWH. Later, when the city is taken, she is spared and makes her home among the Israelites, along with her entire family.

These stories together may provide us with an illustration of how the nations are to bless Israel and be blessed through her. First of all, they observe Israel, are impressed by her God, and act accordingly. This puts them on the right path. Rahab takes the further step of putting her faith in YHWH, helping his people, and then being incorporated into them. Is this the way in which Israel's original calling at Sinai as a "kingdom of priests," a go-between for YHWH and the nations, will work itself out on a larger scale?[17] Reinforcing this idea is the Law's provision to welcome the (circumcised) foreigner living among them to the celebration of Passover.[18]

Again, the "inner logic" of the Three Promises further reveals itself once we understand that both the Land and Many Descendants, as blessings to Israel, serve the bigger purpose of the Blessing to All Nations. It is the latter Promise that seems to drive the others and is, in a sense, their "superior."

Even the utter destruction of the inhabitants of Canaan (the ban) makes a kind of gruesome sense from this perspective. In order for Israel to be blessed it must be faithful to YHWH; in order to be faithful it must not turn to other gods; in order not to turn to other gods, it must distance itself from pagan influence. Paradoxically, to be

---

17. See 135–36, above.
18. See 135, above.

a light to the nations Israel must remain separate from them. Otherwise it would be swallowed by their darkness.[19]

4. Fruitfulness

Because this account is focused on the details of how the Land was first conquered it does not reveal much about its fruitfulness. At the end of the story it is characterized simply as a "good land" three times, emphasizing its general fertility (23:13, 15 &16). But one fact makes it fair to assume that Fruitfulness is at work not so far beneath the surface: the Israelites have been victorious and YHWH has often allowed them to keep the spoils of war, thereby receiving indirectly the products of the Land.

We have an indication of this a couple of times in reference to the Transjordan tribes. They come to Joshua to demand more territory because they have increased in number and ". . .Yahweh has blessed us so far" (17:14). When they go home to their region after the Conquest Joshua says to them:

> Return with much wealth to your tents, with very much livestock, with silver, with gold, with bronze, with iron, and with very much clothing. Divide the plunder of your enemies with your brothers. (22:8)

And the other tribes also shared in such material gain:

> I gave you a land on which you had not labored, and cities which you didn't build, and you live in them. You eat of vineyards and olive groves which you didn't plant. (24:13)

It is therefore safe to conclude that, possessing the Land "flowing with milk and honey" along with the rich spoils of war the nations had yielded, the children of Israel are at last directly enjoying the benefits of material "Fruitfulness." This is an important dimension of God's blessing and it makes a significant contribution to the sense that the time of fulfillment has arrived.

This feeling is very much strengthened by the repeated use of the term "rest" in this narrative. At the beginning of the Conquest Joshua reminds the people:

> Remember the word which Moses the servant of Yahweh commanded you, saying, 'Yahweh your God gives you rest, and will give you this land. (1:13)

Is this "rest" not an echo of Eden? God had rested after making the world and its creatures, declaring that it was all "very good" (Gen 1:31) and then the Bible zeroes in on Eden and the first couple, indicating what that "rest" was like. Now God's people are entering into rest again as they occupy Canaan, enjoying a taste of paradise as they do. We are surely on the road back again. Maybe even there.

---

19. Perhaps we have here another partial "justification" for the ban to be added to our earlier discussion.

5. Relationship

In this episode the relationship of YHWH and Israel reaches beyond fragile equilibrium to actual harmony. Almost. All is not perfect, but there are no significant moments of tension: at no time does the nation as a whole rebel against the ways of YHWH, at no time does YHWH threaten to destroy it like he did in the wilderness.

The relationship is again a mediated one, this time through Joshua instead of Moses. Early on, YHWH informs Joshua:

> I have given you every place that the sole of your foot will tread on, as I told Moses. . . .. No man will be able to stand before you all the days of your life. As I was with Moses, so I will be with you. I will not fail you nor forsake you.
> (1:3, 5)

Secure in this relationship, Joshua seems to go from strength to strength, leading the people into the Land their fathers had only dreamed about.

Upon crossing the Jordan the entire nation is confirmed in its relationship with YHWH in the great circumcision at Gilgal where "the reproach of Egypt" was "rolled away" from them by YHWH (5:9). They have received a clean slate, a new beginning, with the implication that the problems of the wilderness caused by the constant pull of Egypt on the hearts of their fathers are now put firmly behind them.

Against this background, the sin of Achan in disobeying the ban on Jericho stands out in sharp contrast. It is clear that the whole nation did not disobey and, in fact, only one man had sinned. Nevertheless, ". . . Yahweh's anger burned against the children of Israel" and ". . . transgressed my covenant" (7:1,11). Unless this is dealt with, YHWH makes it clear that "I will not be with you any more" (7:12b). The entire nation is held responsible for the sin of one man even though they knew nothing about it and certainly did not condone it. In fact, as soon as they became aware of what Achan had done the whole nation stoned and burned him, his family and all of his possessions. The sin was thus removed from the nation and the relationship restored with YHWH. Significantly, we hear of no other outright acts of rebellion, even on the individual level in the rest of the story.

The only other misstep was the failure to consult YHWH when the Gibeonites arrived deceptively clothed and provisioned. Because it seemed that they were "from away," the Israelites deemed it appropriate to make a peace treaty with them even though they were, in fact, occupants of the Land. This was against the policy that YHWH had laid out for them and resulted in the Gibeonites being allowed to live among the Israelites but only as servants. We often have to live with our mistakes!

6. Grace/Obedience

The idea that we are saved by grace and yet called to obedience in order to maintain our salvation is much in evidence in this section of the narrative. In fact, it could be argued that it is presented in such sharp relief that it should be imprinted on the corporate memory of God's people for all time!

It is impossible, first of all, to escape the notion that Israel's coming into possession of the Land is a work of God alone. At its very beginning, in a phrase that is characteristic of the narrative, YHWH refers to ". . . the land which I am giving to them, even to the children of Israel" (1:2). No less than seventeen times it is repeated that this land and all that goes with it is a gift from YHWH.

Reinforcing this idea, we see that Joshua is told "Yahweh your God is with you wherever you go" (1:9); "I will drive them out" (13:6); "I will deliver them up all slain before Israel"; "for it is Yahweh your God who has fought for you" (23:3); and more picturesquely: "I sent the hornet before you, which drove them out from before you" (24:12). And lest there be any doubt remaining after all this, we are told:

> For it was of Yahweh to harden their hearts, to come against Israel in battle, that he might utterly destroy them, that they might have no favor, but that he might destroy them, as Yahweh commanded Moses. (11:20)

If we add to these general ascriptions the actual events experienced by the Israelites, the picture is unmistakably clear. The collapse of the walls of Jericho and the sun standing still in the sky both indicate that God was absolutely on the side of the Israelites. The entire Conquest is an act of grace.

At the same time obedience is nonnegotiable. At the beginning of his leadership Joshua is himself challenged to this end:

> Be careful to observe to do according to all the law which Moses my servant commanded you. Don't turn from it to the right hand or to the left, that you may have good success wherever you go. This book of the law shall not depart from your mouth, but you shall meditate on it day and night, that you may observe to do according to all that is written in it; for then you shall make your way prosperous, and then you shall have good success. (Josh. 1:7–8)

When the Transjordan tribes return to their inheritance Joshua delivers this charge:

> Only take diligent heed to do the commandment and the law which Moses the servant of Yahweh commanded you, to love Yahweh your God, to walk in all his ways, to keep his commandments, to hold fast to him, and to serve him with all your heart and with all your soul. (22:5)

The ultimate penalty for walking in disobedience is the subject of Joshua's own farewell discourse:

> It shall happen that as all the good things have come on you of which Yahweh your God spoke to you, so Yahweh will bring on you all the evil things, until he has destroyed you from off this good land which Yahweh your God has given you, when you disobey the covenant of Yahweh your God, which he commanded you, and go and serve other gods, and bow down yourselves to them. Then Yahweh's anger will be kindled against you, and you will perish quickly from off the good land which he has given to you. (23:15–16)

The familiar pattern is thus observed once again: salvation is by grace alone, but obedience is required to remain in that state. This time, however, the people appear to be fulfilling this obligation instead of constantly being inconstant. Perhaps a corner has been turned and this earlier behavior is now behind them for good. Perhaps they had finally circumcised their hearts. Perhaps. One can only hope.

11

Here Come the Judges
An Unsettling Experience

Suggested Reading

Judges; 1 Samuel 1–8; Ruth. Scriptural references are to the book of Judges unless otherwise indicated.

MAJOR DEVELOPMENTS

- After Joshua's death the nation continues with the mopping up phase of the Conquest, but soon a dismal pattern emerges as, in an oft-repeated cycle, they:
    1. turn away from following YHWH (fall into apostasy)
    2. become subject to another nation (as the covenant provided)
    3. cry out to YHWH for help
    4. are given a "judge" to deliver them
    5. defeat their oppressors, usually through miraculous means
    6. enjoy a period when the Land is "at rest"
    7. go back to the first step above and start the cycle all over again
- As this pattern would suggest, there are a large number of judges who come and go from the scene over this period of approximately four hundred years. Notable among them are:
    1. Deborah, who stirred up the Hebrews to military action and sang about the victory

2. Gideon, who, after "putting out a fleece," led a few men to a great triumph over many

3. Samson, who dallied with women and was given physical strength to overcome the Philistines

4. Samuel, the last of the judges, who, after a miraculous birth, is called by YHWH as a young boy in the temple and becomes a great leader who subdues the Philistines

- Toward the end of the time of the judges, some Benjaminites commit a terrible sin and the tribe is almost completely annihilated by their fellow Israelites
- Israel asks for a king such as the other nations have
- David's grandmother, a Moabite woman named Ruth, is incorporated into Israel

PERSPECTIVES

Introduction

After the great advances under Joshua one might expect the next phase to be focused on how Israel follows through and finishes the task of purging the Land. Instead, the wind seems to go right out of the Israelite sails and they settle down to live among their neighbors. This may not be their best move.

Israel Fails to Grade, Again

The continued coexistence of Israel and the Canaanites is, according to YHWH, another period of spiritual testing:

> Because this nation transgressed my covenant which I commanded their fathers, and has not listened to my voice, I also will no longer drive out any of the nations that Joshua left when he died from before them; that by them I may test Israel, to see if they will keep Yahweh's way to walk therein, as their fathers kept it, or not. (2:20–22)

In context this last phrase is most likely a reference to the time of the Conquest, rather than the Exodus, in which they exhibited consistent disobedience. If so, our sense that the time under Joshua was indeed a rare moment of covenantal obedience is confirmed. Now, disobedience rules again. What happens next is entirely predictable: the nation, predisposed to sin, begins to worship the gods of their neighbors. It fails the test as often as it is administered. That is to say, a lot.

Israel Recycles

The beginning of the book of Judges has the angel of YHWH confronting the children of Israel about their gross disobedience in not removing all of the inhabitants from the Land.[1] The angel goes on to say that, although YHWH will not abandon them completely, he will now use their disobedience against them:

> I will not drive them out from before you; but they shall be in your sides, and their gods will be a snare to you. (2:3)

This sets the scene for the whole era. Disobedience once again sets in motion the covenant mechanism, this time in the form of repeatedly becoming subject to the nations. They had successfully escaped slavery in Egypt only to fall into it again. Right in the Promised Land! And for a similar four-hundred year period, too, just in case they didn't get it.

Each time the people cry out in their misery YHWH raises up a deliverer for them and they enjoy a season of restoration only to fall away after a while. This cyclical pattern dominates the entire era of the judges and nicely reflects the fact that Israel is "spinning its wheels" spiritually, going nowhere fast in its relationship with YHWH.

Although two of the judges, Samson and Samuel, get the reader's attention by reason of their miraculous births to barren women, neither goes on to qualify as the expected One, the Serpent Crusher. Both have spectacular careers, but their stories quickly disabuse anybody of the idea that salvation has finally arrived in any permanent sense.

Indeed, the nature of the account, with its many repetitive cycles, serves to distract the reader's attention from any one character, creating a sense that nothing will be resolved during such times. By the end of the last cycle the Israelites are utterly weary of the endless treadmill, longing for some progress, any progress, to be made. And so is the reader.

A King-Sized Appetite

The only solution to the situation the people can see is to approach Samuel, the last of the judges: "Now make us a king to judge us like all the nations." (1 Sam 8:5). Under the judges, leadership has been "charismatic," each new judge chosen and anointed by God individually for the task at hand. The "office" of judge is not usually inherited or automatically endowed on some other person. In fact, there is no provision for succession at all. Typically, this leaves a "leadership gap" in between judges and these inevitably prove to be particularly dangerous for the spiritual health of the nation.

---

1. Again suggesting the reports of a complete occupation in the book of Joshua may have been greatly exaggerated!

This helps us to understand how attractive the concept of a "king" becomes to Israel. The institution of monarchy is designed to fill such leadership gaps by the appropriate son routinely taking over from his father in a regular and smooth succession. No wonder it seemed like a good idea at the time!

With this development Israel begins to transition from the rule of judges to the rule of kings. But, given YHWH's reaction to the idea, it may not be a smooth one:

> Yahweh said to Samuel, "Listen to the voice of the people in all that they tell you; for they have not rejected you, but they have rejected me as the king over them. According to all the works which they have done since the day that I brought them up out of Egypt even to this day, in that they have forsaken me and served other gods, so they also do to you. Now therefore, listen to their voice. However, you shall protest solemnly to them, and shall show them the way of the king who will reign over them." (1 Sam 8:7–9)

No reader can miss the implication of what it would mean to reject YHWH as king: this is clearly not a good move on Israel's part. It may be their last. It certainly marks a significant deterioration in the covenant relationship and creates a sense of dread in the reader for what might lie ahead.

This feeling is offset to some degree by the curious fact that YHWH goes along with their rebellious demand, although clearly unhappy with it:

> Listen to their voice, and make them a king. (1 Sam 8:22a.)

This seems puzzling, to say the least. Even more so when we consider that, in seeking to be like all the other nations Israel is showing its past tendency to imitate its neighbors: this time their form of government rather than the gods they worship. This is another denial of Israel's calling to be a special, separate, and holy people unto YHWH.[2] But, like many children, they want to be like all the other kids in the neighborhood.

Could it be that YHWH's response is an ancient example of tough love? Like an earthly father, is YHWH giving in to them in hopes that it teaches them a necessary lesson, knowing at the same time how painful it will be? Or, even better, will this unfaithful demand for a king somehow be woven into the very fabric of his redemptive purpose? After all, Princess Sarah was promised that kings would be among her descendants.[3]

---

2. In Deut 17:14ff. Moses foresees the advent of the monarchy but he does not include it under the necessary provisions of his Covenant. He only says that this development will occur after the occupation of the Land and he provides an outline of the character to look for in a prospective king while also affirming that Yahweh will do the choosing.

3. See 80, above.

A Woman in Charge

Meanwhile, the assumptions of our own day make it necessary to take a moment to consider the fact that a woman named Deborah is among the judges. We might think that women were automatically excluded from leadership in the ancient patriarchal world, but there she is, front and center. Indeed, the matter-of-fact way in which Deborah is introduced into our narrative actually makes it seem that a woman leading the nation is perfectly acceptable, if not normal. This in itself is remarkable. Is Deborah the exception to the rule or the tip of the iceberg?

Fire and Ice

The period of the judges is more than just a transitional phase between the classical theocracy under Moses/Joshua and the monarchy that follows. Two aspects in particular seem to amplify themes that have already appeared in the biblical narrative but are easily overlooked. Not any more.

In this part of the narrative, the Bible clearly ascribes the successful leadership of YHWH's people to the specific endowment of YHWH's Spirit upon the leader. It had previously implied this in the cases of Moses, the seventy elders, and Joshua[4] but in the case of the judges it is made even more clear.

Our present narrative describes the Spirit of YHWH coming upon the judges Othniel (3:10), Gideon (6:34), Jephthah (11:29), and Samson (13:25; 14:6, 19; 15:14), enabling them to deliver Israel. Although this cannot be characterized as a general outbreak of the Spirit, being limited to the judges themselves, something is certainly beginning to stir.

Secondly, wallowing in disunity and instability, the nation sows the seeds for the possibility of even more serious division in the future. Things get so bad at one point that civil war breaks out between the tribe of Benjamin and the others. This is not the first time we have noted tensions between the tribes but, heretofore, open war has been avoided.[5] Now it erupts with disastrous results for the tribe of Benjamin and eventually the nation as a whole. Although there is a measure of healing, the cracks beneath the surface have been exposed and the nation may be skating into its future on very thin ice.

---

4. See Num 11:25; 27:18; Deut 34:9. See also 165, above. Two other previous cases of the work of the Spirit Fall into slightly different categories than "leadership": Balaam seems to have been turned into a genuine prophet when "the Spirit of God came upon him" (Num 24:2) and the chief craftsman for the original tabernacle was endowed by the Spirit with the necessary skills (Exod 31:3; 35:31).

5. See 180–81, above.

Here Come the Judges

THE STORY

The Pre-Occupation of Israel (1:1—3:6)

While it is true to say that the Israelites occupy the Land under Joshua, it is also true to say that it is, at best, the beginning of a proper occupation. Pockets of Canaanites remain throughout and continue to pose a significant threat. So it is that the book of Judges opens with accounts of YHWH still directing the task of taking over the Land.

The reader is made aware that in order for the Israelites to be successful, YHWH must drive out the nations, but at the same time we are told (explicitly this time) that one of the reasons for their failure is that they lag behind in the technology of war! The enemy possesses iron chariots and so continues to prevail on the plains, leaving the hilly portions to the less well-equipped invaders.[6]

This explanation seems especially curious in light of the many occasions both before and after this moment when such considerations were irrelevant to YHWH. After all, were not the chariots and horsemen of Egypt destroyed in the waters of the Red Sea? Furthermore, the defeats suffered by Israel are repeatedly ascribed to their worshipping the gods of Land instead of breaking down their altars as they were ordered to do.[7] Perhaps YHWH is simply putting more distance between himself and this often rebellious nation. No doubt our puzzlement is yet another indication of the inadequacy of our modern distinction between natural and supernatural causes.

Cycling through Canaan

INTRODUCTION

After the death of Joshua and those who had crossed the Jordan with him, we read that:

> . . . another generation arose after them who didn't know Yahweh, nor the work which he had done for Israel. The children of Israel did that which was evil in Yahweh's sight, and served the Baals. They abandoned Yahweh, the God of their fathers, who brought them out of the land of Egypt, and followed other gods, of the gods of the peoples who were around them, and bowed themselves down to them; and they provoked Yahweh to anger. (2:10–12)

This is clearly intended as a general description of the period, as is the comment that YHWH then turns them over to their enemies; they appeal to him for help and he sends them judges to deliver them. This happens repeatedly and, with only a

---

6. Cf. Judg 1:19.

7. Esp. Baal, the god of fertility and rain, and the goddesses of war and sex, Anath, Asherah, and Astarte.

little special pleading, it is possible to group the subsequent events into seven distinct leadership cycles.

Cycle #1: Othniel (3:7–11)

Not long after the death of Joshua, disobedient Israel becomes subject to the king of Aram, but after eight years of slavery it calls out to YHWH and he raises up Caleb's nephew, Othniel. He succeeds because the Spirit of YHWH comes upon him, enabling him to defeat Aram and to "judge" Israel for forty years of relative peace.[8]

Cycle #2: Ehud (3:11–30)

After Othniel dies the nation slides back into disobedience. This time it is the king of Moab who rules over them and once again the people eventually call out to God for help. He sends Ehud to deliver them and an extended peace of eighty years ensues, during which the Israelites rule over Moab.

Cycle #3: Deborah (4–5)

Some time after Ehud's passing, the nation falls away from YHWH again, resulting in a particularly cruel twenty-year subjection to the Canaanites.[9] Of course, as usual, they cry to YHWH for help. Enter Deborah and her partner in deliverance, Jael, two remarkable women, through whose not-so-gentle ministrations Israel is delivered. Of Deborah, we are told that she is both a prophetess and the leader of Israel (4:4), while all we know about Jael is that she is the wife of Heber the Kenite (4:17).

Deborah informs an Israelite leader named Barak that YHWH wants him to attack the Canaanite general Sisera and that he will be successful. Barak balks at the idea and insists that she accompany the troops. His hesitancy greatly provokes her:

> I will surely go with you. Nevertheless, the journey that you take won't be for your honor; for Yahweh will sell Sisera into a woman's hand. (4:9)

She is not just referring to herself here, because it is Jael who actually kills the enemy leader by enticing the weary Sisera into her tent to rest and then driving a tent peg through his head after he falls asleep! This leads to the eventual submission of the Canaanites and forty years of peace for Israel.

---

8. "Forty" should probably be taken in these descriptions as representing roughly a generation.

9. In the Bible this term seems to refer both generally to all those nations then occupying the Promised Land (Canaan) and, as here, more locally to settlements of a particular people among the others who also lived there. Cf. Thompson, "Canaan, Canaanites," I:701–8.

Cycle #4: Gideon & Co. (6:1—10:5)

The children of Israel once more return to their evil ways, this time coming under the rule of the Midianites. An angel of YHWH appears to Gideon, a young warrior of the tribe of Manasseh. The messenger tells him that YHWH is with him and when Gideon questions this

> Yahweh looked at him, and said, "Go in this your might, and save Israel from the hand of Midian. Haven't I sent you?" (6:14)[10]

In spite of this double assurance of God's assistance, Gideon hesitates and then is told plainly that he will in fact be successful. But this is still not enough for the reluctant warrior, who has the nerve to ask YHWH for a sign "that it is you who talks with me" (6:17). He is granted his wish when fire flares from a rock to consume a food offering. Even though he then makes an attempt at obedience it is becoming clear that this man has a serious problem with trusting God and his Word.

Indeed, even after the Spirit of YHWH comes upon him he still questions and asks for yet another sign. When God complies with his demand to make a fleece wet in the morning while the ground around remains dry, this is still does not satisfy Gideon. Amazingly, he asks that God reverse the process to really, really, really affirm his promise. Even more amazingly, YHWH does so: in the morning the fleece is dry and the ground is wet. Gideon is finally convinced, ready and able to lead the Israelites against their foes.

In order to do so, he assembles an army of thirty-two thousand men, but YHWH tells him this is too many because the Israelites might assume that their own strength delivered them instead of YHWH. All those who are afraid are dismissed, leaving ten thousand. Still too many! Finally, the army is reduced to a mere three hundred soldiers who then soundly rout the Midianites. This progressive downsizing of the army of Israel in the face of a mighty enemy provides a neat counterpoint to Gideon's similar upsizing of his demands for proof of God's promise. His newfound faith must have been severely tested as he saw his army dwindle away to almost nothing. To give him his due, however, he does not waver in the face of such odds.

Even more impressive is his response to the nation when it begs him to become its "ruler" and pass the office on to his offspring:

> I will not rule over you, neither shall my son rule over you. Yahweh shall rule over you. (8:23)

Here, theocracy is clearly affirmed and it may also be inferred that the leadership provided by Gideon and the other judges is fully compatible with this ideal. On the

---

10. Once again, the Bible identifies the visitor as an angel and then calls him YHWH. The most likely explanation for this phenomenon is the identity, in ancient cultures, of the authorized messenger with the one who sent him. A modern example of this would be an ambassador and the country from which he comes.

other hand, there is an implied tension between the rule of a king (which seems to be what the people are, in effect, asking for here) and the rule of God.

Gideon's leadership is less than perfect but the Land enjoys a forty-year peace during his lifetime. Things quickly go off the rails again after his son Abimelech is made king of Shechem and then badly governs Israel for three years after murdering all but one of his seventy brothers! Again the nation is flirting dangerously with monarchy, but Abimelech is followed by Tola and then by Jair, two nonrelatives who each simply "lead" Israel for about twenty years. No kingly pretensions are mentioned again and the situation seems to be settling down.

Cycle #5: Jephthah & Co. (10:8—12:15)

Yet another falling away from the path of obedience leads to eighteen years of serious oppression by the Philistines and the Amorites. When the Israelites cry out for help a new note is added to their lament: this time they admit that they have erred by following the Baals. On previous occasions they had simply appealed to God because of the dire straits in which they found themselves. Now they acknowledge their guilt, but at first YHWH is not impressed and tells them to cry out instead to the other gods they have been serving. It is only when they persist in their repentance and show it by changing their ways that he relents. This time God chooses a proven warrior named Jephthah and endows him with the Spirit to deliver his people over the next six years.

Three minor judges then lead the nation which, soon afterwards, backslides into doing "evil in Yahweh's sight" (13:1) again. This is so serious that it leads to a forty-year period of domination by the Philistines.

Cycle #6: Samson (13–16)

Then, in a now familiar pattern, a mysterious angelic messenger comes to a barren woman promising the birth of a son. Another savior is clearly about to step onto the stage. His name is Samson.

Samson is to be set apart to God from birth (13:5) as a Nazirite, abstaining from wine and all fermented drinks as well as never cutting his hair. As a young man "...Yahweh blessed him. Yahweh's Spirit began to move him..." (13:24–25).

Unfortunately, women begin to stir him as well. They will figure prominently in his many misadventures. First of all, he insists on having a Philistine woman as his wife, and, while this was against the divine prohibition, we are told in an editorial aside that his disobedience nevertheless was part of YHWH's plan to deliver Israel (14:4)! The woman wheedles the answer to a riddle out of him and betrays him to win a bet for her countrymen. Then "Yahweh's Spirit came mightily on him" and he slays thirty men in order to get their clothes to settle the wager (14:19). We are thereby led to conclude that his great might was due to the endowment of the Spirit rather than any natural physical strength. It is hard to imagine Samson as a "ninety-pound weakling," however!

This episode sets in motion a series of events that pit him firmly against the Philistines. When the newlyweds are separated, he tries to visit her but discovers she has been given to another man, a friend of his. In a rage he sends three hundred foxes dragging torches into the Philistine fields, destroying their crops. The enemy, in turn, kills his wife and father-in-law, causing Samson to respond by slaughtering many of their number. This family feud is far from over, however. The Philistines, who are now ruling over the Israelites, lean on the tribe of Judah to hand over Samson, which they do, binding him securely. Once again the Spirit enables Samson to break loose and wreak havoc on his enemy using only the jawbone of a donkey as a weapon.

His successes in his personal war with the Philistines propel him onto the national stage for a twenty-year judgeship over Israel. At one point he visits a prostitute in Gaza and the locals plan to kill him at dawn, but he escapes in the middle of the night by ripping the massive city gates right out of the ground. Toward the end of his tenure as judge, he gets into woman trouble for the last time. Her name? Delilah.

Samson falls hard for her, but she is bribed by the Philistines to make him reveal the secret of his great strength. At first he outwits her attempts to get this out of him, but he is in love and she continues to nag him about it "... until his soul was troubled to death" (16:16). In the end, he tells her everything, just to get her to stop:

> No razor has ever come on my head; for I have been a Nazirite to God from my mother's womb. If I am shaved, then my strength will go from me and I will become weak, and be like any other man. (16:17)

While Samson sleeps she has his head shaved and he wakes up to discover that, along with his hair, both YHWH and his strength have departed. Consequently, the Philistines finally capture him and put out his eyes, making him power a grindstone in a prison. During this time his hair begins to grow back in. When they drag him out of the prison to make fun of him at a great celebration, he prays for renewed strength and, in one last great effort, manages to bring down the great temple of the god Dagon upon everyone in the place, including the Philistine rulers. He himself dies in the rubble, inspiring this epitaph:

> So the dead that he killed at his death were more than those who he killed in his life. (16:30)

Like his entire life, what seems to be mostly a personal story turns out to be of national significance as Israel's enemies suffer many losses, including that of their leadership. From this perspective, the extraordinary working of the Holy Spirit in the rather sordid details of this man's career makes perfect sense.

Furthermore, it is tempting to see the episode as a kind of parable of Israel itself. Set apart for YHWH, under an oath, blessed when faithful to the oath and cursed when the oath is broken, but in the end returning to a state of obedience and final triumph through YHWH's Spirit. But it is a strange triumph that comes through self-sacrificial death. Is there here also an ominous hint of Israel's own destiny?

Cycle #7: Samuel

PART ONE: DESCENT INTO CHAOS (19–21)

Beginning and ending with the suggestive observations that "In those days there was no king in Israel" and "Everyone did that which was right in his own eyes" (17:6 & 21:25), this episode details Israel's chaotic internal affairs. The worship of idols, even by the Levitical priesthood, sinks its venomous fangs ever deeper into Israelite life. It infects especially the tribe of Dan while in the process of seeking and finding a territory of its own in the northern reaches of Canaan, far from the altar of YHWH.

The text then features a story of depravity that reminds the reader of Lot's misadventure so long ago in Sodom.[11] A travelling Levite from Ephraim, along with his concubine and servant, are offered shelter in Benjamite territory, but the house is then surrounded by a local mob demanding that his host hand him over to them to be sexually assaulted. In an attempt at appeasement, the local man offers them his own virgin daughter and the concubine instead, but they refuse. Finally the concubine is surrendered to the crowd, who rape and abuse her so badly that she dies. The Levite takes her body home, cuts it into twelve parts, and sends them as a gruesome message to all the tribes of Israel.

> It was so, that all who saw it said, "Such a deed has not been done or seen from the day that the children of Israel came up out of the land of Egypt to this day! Consider it, take counsel, and speak." (19:30)

Incited by what the Benjamites had done to the woman,[12] the rest of Israel attacks and almost exterminates the offending tribe in a terrible civil war. So extensive is the slaughter that no women are left for the few remaining Benjamite men, leaving the tribe without a way to repopulate itself. Ordinarily they could have taken wives from the other tribes, but the latter had earlier taken a heated oath not to allow their own women to marry a Benjamite, guilty as they were of this horrific crime. Was this tribe, descendants of Jacob's favorite, to be no more?

> The people came to Bethel and sat there until evening before God, and lifted up their voices, and wept severely. They said, "Yahweh, the God of Israel, why has this happened in Israel, that there should be one tribe lacking in Israel today?" (21:2–3)

---

11. Gen 19:1–11.
12. The text passes over the behavior of the Levite and his host.

At this point, they discover a group of Israelites who had decided not to participate in the attack on Benjamin, and who had not taken the oath. For their lack of solidarity these men too, with all their families except four hundred virgin women, are slaughtered. These women are then provided as wives to the surviving Benjamites, thus solving their dilemma. However, the cost in bloodshed among brothers is beyond reckoning. It is surely a low point in the history of Israel. Maybe they do need a king, after all. But not quite yet.

Part Two: The Last Judge (1 Sam 1–8)

At this point the book of Judges comes to a close, but there is still one more judge to come. The thread is picked up in the book of 1 Samuel, as it recounts the circumstances surrounding the birth of Samuel. These once again signal a child that is destined for great things in the Story: YHWH miraculously grants a son to a barren woman who had been taunted by "the other wife" and who, of course, is fertile.

The woman's name is Hannah and, as the story opens, she lays her petition out before YHWH at Shiloh:

> Yahweh of Armies, if you will indeed look at the affliction of your servant and remember me, and not forget your servant, but will give to your servant a boy, then I will give him to Yahweh all the days of his life, and no razor shall come on his head. (1:11)

When her son Samuel is subsequently born she keeps her end of the bargain and delivers him to Eli, the priest at Shiloh, as soon as she can. Eventually YHWH blesses her with five more children to take the place of the one she gave up, three boys and two girls (2:21).

At Shiloh the boy grows up between the corrupt religious practice of the aged Eli's two sons and the silence of God: ". . . Yahweh's word was rare" and "there were not many visions" (3:1). So it is all the more surprising when the boy starts to hear from YHWH and shows every promise of living up to the reader's expectations of him for Israel's future. In fact, he is soon recognized by the entire nation as a "prophet," one who to whom YHWH reveals his word and speaks for him. Subsequently Samuel assumes overall leadership of Israel, combining all three roles of priest, prophet, and judge.

In the meantime, things are going very badly for God's people as we would expect. The Philistines even capture the sacred Ark when Israel dares to take it into battle as a kind of magic charm. The army of Israel is destroyed and Eli's sons are killed. When he hears the news, the old man collapses and dies on the spot. However, possession of the Ark brings tribulation instead of blessing upon the Philistines and, subsequently, they return it to Israel. But even at home its presence proves troubling for a period of some twenty years. Samuel, who has been absent from this part of the story, then leads the nation in a renewal of its commitment to follow only YHWH. Then, in the familiar cyclic pattern, the Philistines are repelled and peace is reestablished.

Samuel grows old and, having seemingly forgotten Eli's experience, appoints his two sons as successor judges. They soon prove themselves unworthy, being very corrupt in their dealings with the people. Things then come to a dramatic head:

> Then all the elders of Israel gathered themselves together and came to Samuel to Ramah. They said to him, "Behold, you are old, and your sons don't walk in your ways. Now make us a king to judge us like all the nations." (8:4–5)

Samuel seems to take this personally and, upset, he turns to YHWH for consolation:

> Yahweh said to Samuel, "Listen to the voice of the people in all that they tell you; for they have not rejected you, but they have rejected me as the king over them. According to all the works which they have done since the day that I brought them up out of Egypt even to this day, in that they have forsaken me and served other gods, so they also do to you. Now therefore, listen to their voice. However, you shall protest solemnly to them, and shall show them the way of the king who will reign over them." (8:7–9)

Even when Samuel catalogues all the abuse kings will impose on them, co-opting their sons for his armies, their daughters for his household, and the best of their harvests and livestock for his table, it has no effect:

> But the people refused to listen to the voice of Samuel; and they said, "No, but we will have a king over us, that we also may be like all the nations; and that our king may judge us, and go out before us, and fight our battles." (8:19–20)

And so the die is cast.

And Now for Something Completely Different (Ruth 1–4)

The story of Ruth, full of romance and faith, stands in gentle contrast to the tumultuous time of the judges in which it is set. Whereas in the book of Judges the Israelites are constantly succumbing to the gods of the nations, here the flow is all in the other direction. It is an account of a foreigner who turns from those gods to the God of Israel and makes a critical contribution to its future glory. It is also a story of how even sin can be turned to a good end and as such it reminds us of Joseph. Are all of the best stories of the Bible (Isaac and Rebecca, Jacob and Rachel, Joseph and his dreams, and now Ruth and Naomi) set outside of the Land?

This one begins during a time of famine in Canaan. An Israelite and his small family migrate southeast of the Dead Sea to Moab where he dies, leaving his wife Naomi and their two sons alone in a foreign land. Against the direct command of YHWH, the sons marry Moabite women and then die themselves, childless. It is not clear if this fate is to be seen as punishment or not, but it leads to a clear step forward in the history of redemption.

When she hears that the famine had eased in Canaan, Naomi decides to return and tries to persuade her daughters-in-law to remain in their own country and among their own people. One agrees, while the other, Ruth, in one of the most beautiful passages in the Bible, expresses undying loyalty to her mother-in-law:

> Don't urge me to leave you, and to return from following you, for where you go, I will go; and where you stay, I will stay. Your people will be my people, and your God my God. Where you die, I will die, and there I will be buried. May Yahweh do so to me, and more also, if anything but death parts you and me. (1:16–17)

What could Naomi do but take Ruth back to the Promised Land with her? There, Ruth soon catches the eye of Naomi's kinsman Boaz, whom she subsequently marries. In due course she presents her husband and her mother-in-law with a new son, named Obed. The narrator is careful to point out that Obed became the grandfather of David, the greatest of all the kings of Israel. So not only is Ruth saved, but she provides Israel with a savior. It is a wonderful story, all the more so as it takes place during the declining days of the judges.

IN THE BOSOM OF ABRAHAM

1. The Land/Place

By the end of the time of the judges, the Israelites have been occupying the Promised Land for about four hundred years. And yet it is still not entirely in their possession, pushing the time of complete fulfillment of this Promise yet further away. Indeed, after the steady stream of victories over the occupants under Joshua things have settled into a discouraging ebb and flow pattern in regard to the Land. Sometimes the nation has the upper hand and the Land has peace, while at others it is under the control of one or other of the nations, especially the Philistines.

While the narrative gives little clue as to exactly what portions of the Land were in the possession of the Israelites, the story of the Danite migration provides some insight. The tribe of Dan had originally been allotted territory in the plain along the coast of the Mediterranean but had been unable to subdue its original inhabitants. Judges 18 relates how they move to a portion of the Land around Mt. Hermon in the north and manage to become among the worse compromisers of their covenantal faith in the process. Forever after, the extent of the Land will be defined by the phrase "from Dan to Beersheba"[13] and the North will take on a reputation for opposition to the unpolluted religion of YHWH more evident in the South.

---

13. Cf. Judg 20:1 (KJV).

While the account indicates that there was some consolidation of the Land during this time, in no way can it be said that it is at any time, in plain fact, wholly in the hands of the Israelites. It remains just beyond their grasp, even while they live in it. There can be little doubt that this makes a significant contribution to the national sense of frustration that expresses itself as a demand for a king.

As to the place where YHWH meets with his people, in the time of the judges we read that "God's house was in Shiloh" (18:31), not far north of Bethel. This is where the tent of meeting was set up under Joshua and it appears to be the primary holy place during this entire period. By the time we get to the time of Samuel the structure at Shiloh is referred to as "Yahweh's *temple*" (1 Sam 1:9) for the first time. This implies a more substantial building than the tabernacle, but we read that, later, in the time of Eli the Ark was housed in a tent (again?) (1 Sam 2:22). The actual nature of the structure at this time is unclear but it still represents a particular place where God dwelt among his people.[14] More precisely, this place was between the cherubim over the Ark of the Covenant (1 Sam4:4), wherever it happened to rest.

2. Many Descendants

Although there is again little direct evidence to go on, this aspect of the Promise seems to ebb and flow along with the rest of Israel's fortunes during this period.

Frequent warfare with the occupants of the Land is bound to include some significant loss of Israelite lives but specific numbers are not mentioned. Curiously, such information can be gathered in reference to two "civil" wars during the period. Here we catch a glimpse of major loss of life, especially when we remember that women and children were not counted.

Judges 12 records a dispute between the clan of Gilead (a major clan in the half-tribe of Manasseh) and the Ephraimites after the latter felt excluded from a victorious campaign conducted by the former. We read that forty-two thousand Ephraimites were killed. As usual, no mention is made of how many from the winning side fell on that occasion. Beyond this, the almost-extermination of the tribe of Benjamin noted earlier points in a similar direction.

The evidence regarding the fulfillment of this Promise is at best ambiguous, pointing once again to the sense that the nation is spinning its wheels under the judges. The Promise of God remains, but there seems to be little progress toward its realization. Indeed, for the conflict with Benjamin the rest of the tribes are apparently able to assemble an army of four hundred thousand, a figure that suggests that Israel as a whole may be just about maintaining its pre-Conquest population.

---

14. The confusion may arise from a later scribal note or "gloss" that became incorporated into the text.

In this context the birth narratives of Samson and Samuel can vividly remind us of the fact that YHWH is indeed willing and able to turn barrenness into fruitfulness for those who are faithful. It is just a matter of timing.

3. Blessing to All Nations

While this narrative yields little that would suggest that this Promise is being realized, it is possible to catch glimpses of how progress in this direction might develop in the future. One arises out of the complex relationships we can see here between Israel and the nations, while another comes from one of the stories that emerge from the period. It seems to shine a more optimistic light on the subject.

This era is generally marked by the intense antagonism between Israel and the various nations that continue to occupy the Land. In fact, much of the time God's people are oppressed or subjugated by their neighbors. Although one could argue that they are then a blessing (as slaves are to masters) this could hardly be considered a fulfillment of the Promise!

Rather, Judges casts this period of conflict as a "test" for the nation to see if they would continue in obedience to the covenant (2:22 & 3:4). The nations provide the means of temptation with their gods and their women. When Israel subsequently derails in its commitment to YHWH, the nations then become the means by which Israel comes under the Curses provided by the covenant mechanism. Their victories are intended to shove God's people back onto the obedience track and that is just what we see happening repeatedly in this period.

From all of this, one again gets the impression that for Israel to become a blessing to the nations, it must paradoxically isolate itself from them and perhaps even destroy some of them. If Israel can finally learn this lesson through this "testing," progress can be made toward the eventual blessing of the nations. In the meantime, it is difficult to see how the Blessing can be operative within the dynamic of this period. It is at this point that the story of Ruth may shed some light.

As noted above, this is a kinder, gentler narrative than that of the book of Judges. Instead of the latter's tales of conflict between the Israelites and the nations, here we have an intimate story of bonding at the levels of family and faith. The pagan Ruth finds herself fully incorporated into Israelite life and blessed with a good marriage and a son to continue the line of his bereft grandmother. There may be a hint here of how Israel will be a Blessing to All Nations in line with its priestly calling. By Israel being a faithful witness like Naomi, it may be that other peoples will believe in YHWH and so come under the covenant, with all its attendant benefits. Only time will tell.

4. Fruitfulness

Does the Land continue to flow with "milk and honey" once we get past the Conquest under Joshua? Again, the evidence is as scarce as it is unclear.

The story of Gideon contains some useful clues:

> ... the Midianites, the Amalekites, and the children of the east came up against them. They encamped against them, and destroyed the increase of the earth, until you come to Gaza. They left no sustenance in Israel, and no sheep, ox, or donkey. For they came up with their livestock and their tents. They came in as locusts for multitude. Both they and their camels were without number; and they came into the land to destroy it. (6:3–5)

It can be concluded from this that even part of the Land is capable of sustaining a large occupying force and perhaps even allowing it to flourish while the invaders are ruining the Israelite portions. This suggests that the Land was still fruitful, in and of itself. It is likely that it is this very quality that at least partly motivates outside nations to invade, or its present occupants to resist the Israelite invasion. This is good land.

This judgment is confirmed by the Danite invasion of the country around Laish in the north. This action is taken because "the land is large; . . .a place where there is no lack of anything that is in the earth" (18:9–10).

On the other hand, it is a famine in the Land that provides the incentive for Elimelech and his family to migrate to Moab in the story of Ruth. Clearly the Land is being subject to serious devastation from both natural and human causes.

One can conclude that the Land, ravaged by war and famine, is not living up to its billing, at least as far as the children of Israel are concerned. It may indeed be still capable of flowing with milk and honey, but they are not enjoying its benefits in any consistent way. Not exactly Eden yet.

5. Relationship

It should come as no surprise to suggest that the relationship of YHWH with his people during the time of the judges conforms to the cyclical nature of the period itself. It is "on-again, off-again" throughout the entire narrative.

A low point in this cycle occurs just before the judgeship of Jephthah when the Israelites were sorely oppressed because of their disobedience (10:6–9). As usual, they cry out to YHWH, but this time he points out how he had listened to them many times before and saved them, but they always slide back into idolatry. YHWH's exasperation is obvious:

> ... you have forsaken me and served other gods. Therefore I will save you no more. Go and cry to the gods which you have chosen. Let them save you in the time of your distress! (10:13–14)

They persist in begging for mercy and he has pity on them because "... his soul was grieved for the misery of Israel" (10:16). In spite of his wavering, YHWH now seems even more committed to this relationship and this is perhaps the main point we are to take from the narrative. It is the same unfathomable commitment which no doubt explains why he gives in to the demand for a king even when it represents their rejection of him as king.

Against this general backdrop the stories of Ruth, Gideon, Samson, and Samuel shine as lights in the darkness. Each one speaks of differing but close relationships with YHWH, showing, in these personal glimpses, that faith was not entirely lacking in the Israelite camp. This is especially true of the women involved: Ruth comes to faith and the mothers of Samson and Samuel selflessly dedicate their sons to YHWH. Could it be that his reluctance to abandon this people is related to the few faithful who remain? Is this the story of Abraham's bargaining over Sodom writ large?

The endowment of the "Spirit of YHWH" upon a number of judges also has implications for YHWH's relationship with his people, as it did in the cases of Moses and company on Sinai.[15] Here again this gift is limited to a few and is directed toward enabling leadership. Although not much more is revealed regarding this divine-human association, a new note of intimacy is introduced in the account of Gideon's endowment with the Spirit. Judges 6:34 literally reads something like "the spirit of YHWH clothed himself with Gideon"! And in another reminder of Abraham (and Moses), Gideon has the temerity to bargain with YHWH over the "fleeces" he puts out.

All of this has the effect of assuring the reader that all is not lost on the "Relationship" front. Unfortunately, at the end of the period, we read that estrangement seems to have set in once more:

> Yahweh's word was rare in those days. There were not many visions, then. (I Sam 3:1)

6. Grace/Obedience

In order to gain a deeper understanding of the biblical relationship between these realities we have been using, as a proposal, the idea that people are "saved by grace" and then "obligated to obey" in order to maintain their salvation. This narrative can be seen as friendly to this formula, but things are not as straightforward as they might seem at first glance.

First of all, it needs to be said that this is a story of grace from beginning to end. As the previous section has indicated, YHWH's forbearance bears little relationship to the obedience of the nation. Again and again, YHWH raises up a judge to deliver the people from their enemies in spite of their proven track record of disobedience simply

---

15. See 194, above.

because they cried out to him. Sometimes he does this by granting the miraculous birth of a son who will grow up to be a savior.

Other indicators of grace are well evident. In the case of Gideon, we are told that YHWH insisted that the Israelite army be reduced to a mere three-hundred men: ". . .lest Israel brag against me, saying, 'My own hand has saved me'" (7:2). In the case of Othniel, Gideon, Jephthah, and Samson, their successes are credited to the endowment of Spirit of YHWH upon them.[16] Even bound to the Philistine temple pillars, Samson experiences grace: he prays to YHWH to "strengthen me, please, only this once," so that he would be able to pull down the pillars in order to destroy all those assembled (16:28).

God is clearly the one who is orchestrating Israel's deliverance step by step and this is grace at work. In the case of the elderly Eli, when things go off course with his own sons he is told by YHWH that they will die as a result of their sins, but all is not lost:

> I will raise up a faithful priest for myself who will do according to that which is in my heart and in my mind. I will build him a sure house. He will walk before my anointed forever. (1 Sam 2:35)

This is seems to be a reference to Samuel, first of all, whose story follows immediately.[17] But in any case, it is clear that grace continues to have priority.

The fact that obedience is necessary in order for the people to stay in a right relationship with YHWH shows itself in the "covenant mechanism" which drives this narrative. It seems to imply that obedience brings a period of rest (the Blessing) while explicitly affirming that disobedience brings the enemies of the Israelites upon them (the Curse). It all hinges on obedience. But it's complicated. This is especially evident in the fact that YHWH saves in each case, not on prior obedience, but merely upon the plea of the people.

It is painfully obvious that during this period Israel has reverted to its wilderness-type behavior after seemingly reaching a more consistent level of obedience under Joshua. The reader had a right to expect that the new generation that entered the Promised Land had finally left behind the waywardness of their forefathers. Now that illusion is shattered for good. Perhaps this explains the introduction of the Spirit of God so dramatically into the narrative at this point, leaving the impression that in order to do things for God, his Spirit is necessary.

This last point coincides with our growing perception of the need of humanity for grace-enabled obedience. Certainly that conclusion has been strongly confirmed by events under the judges. But we have also been given an insight that points to the

---

16. 3:10, 6:34, 11:29, 13:25, 14:19, 15:14.

17. This promise obviously must stretch beyond Samuel, whose house, it turns out, was not "firmly established."

Spirit of God as the source of the spiritual power needed to transform the human heart and obey the commandments of YHWH.

12

Israel Under the Kings (Part One)
The United Kingdom

Suggested Reading

1 Samuel 9–1 Kings 11; 1 Chronicles 10–29 ;2 Chronicles 1–9. Note: The passages from 1 & 2 Chronicles cover the same ground as Samuel and 1 Kings but seem to present a somewhat idealized portrait of David and Solomon, leaving out most negative elements and adding in material from other sources.

MAJOR DEVELOPMENTS

- Samuel anoints Saul as the first king of Israel
- Saul is acclaimed as king by the people
- Saul enjoys early successes against Israel's enemies
- Saul falls into disobedience and YHWH rejects him as king
- Samuel anoints David as the second king of Israel while Saul still reigns
- David kills Goliath and incites Saul's jealousy
- David, on the run from Saul, spares his life on two occasions
- Saul, defeated by the Philistines, commits suicide
- David becomes king, conquers Jerusalem, makes it his capital, and defeats the Philistines
- The Ark is installed in Jerusalem
- YHWH makes a covenant with David, establishing his house forever

- David defeats all of his enemies
- David has an affair with Bathsheba and has her husband murdered when she becomes pregnant
- Nathan confronts David, who repents, but the baby dies
- Bathsheba gives birth to Solomon
- Trouble erupts in David's household and his son Absalom leads a rebellion and is killed
- David makes Solomon king and then dies of old age
- Solomon asks for and receives wisdom from YHWH
- Solomon builds and dedicates the temple
- YHWH confirms the Davidic covenant to Solomon and exhorts him to obedience
- The Queen of Sheba visits Solomon and is duly impressed at the magnificence of his regime
- Solomon takes foreign wives/concubines and through them he falls away from true religion
- An official of Solomon, Jeroboam, leads a rebellion but fails and flees into exile
- Solomon dies after a brilliant (for the most part) reign

PERSPECTIVES

Introduction

With the introduction of the monarchy the Story takes on the character of a royal narrative centered upon the lives of the kings: the course of the entire nation, for good or for evil, is intertwined with that of the king.[1] At the same time, the kings are clearly subject to YHWH, and in this sense theocracy continues as Israel's mode of government (at least in principle).

A Golden Era

The reader has been prepared for the transition to kingly rule, of course, but mostly in a negative sense. After all, YHWH had seen the nation's demand for a king as rejection of himself as king. This could not be good. And then there were those dire predictions of troubles to come as a result of having a king over them.

---

1. Cf. 2 Sam 5:12 and 1 Chr 4:2.

Surprisingly, the opposite proves to be true, at least during this period. In fact, under David's son Solomon, the nation settles in to an unrivalled period of peace and prosperity. It is not stretching the point to suggest that these two reigns together comprise a golden era for the nation of Israel. Running underneath, however, are the continuing fault lines of religious syncretism and tribal division. By the end of Solomon's reign, these subterranean tremors will erupt with altogether tragic consequences for the nation.

The Rise of the Prophet

One of the most intriguing features of this narrative is the increased importance of the prophet in the life of Israel. This prominence stems from a new role for the prophet under the monarchy.

Up until this point, YHWH has been communicating directly with the national leader, whether it be Moses, Joshua, or one of the judges. It may be that in rejecting YHWH as king, the nation is desiring even more of an arm's length relationship with him, to be more independent. For one thing, under a king they would not be as reliant on upon YHWH for the succession and the leadership of the nation. Theocracy is in for an adjustment.

Accordingly, then, the kings are not generally portrayed as being in direct contact with YHWH. Instead, YHWH reveals his word to a prophet who then relays the message to the king. The classic example of this would be Nathan, the court prophet during the reign of David. Over time, as the monarchy reaches beyond David and Solomon into the days of Elijah and Elisha, it becomes clear that it is the prophet with whom we are to identify rather than the king.

Prophets have long been part of the biblical Story: early on, God himself identifies Abraham, Moses, and Aaron as prophets, while the latter pair's sister Miriam (and, later, Deborah the judge) are referred to as a prophetesses.[2] Additionally, the Law of Moses addresses the issue of distinguishing between true and false prophets, making it clear that the fundamental role of the prophet is simply to receive and proclaim the word of God (Deut 18:14–22). While this will, on occasion, involve looking into the future, more usually it is YHWH's perspective on current events that is presented.

However, "prophet" becomes a kind of formal position, or "office," during the monarchy, and it is Samuel who embodies the transition. He is uniquely qualified for this, being a judge, a priest, and a prophet. The combined weight of these roles may be what seems to grant him the right to "authenticate" both Saul and David, the first two kings, by anointing them with oil.[3]

---

2. Gen 20:7; Deut 18:18; Exod 7:1, 15:20; Judg 4:4.

3. Samuel seems to be functioning as the high priest. While he is a Levite and qualifies as a priest, he is not from line of Aaron, from which the high priest must come. The text is silent about this anomaly. Cf. 1 Chr 6:26, 33.

After Samuel, leadership of the nation resides in the separate but intersecting offices of king, prophet, and high priest. It is in this arrangement that the prophet, as the messenger of YHWH, often finds himself having to "speak truth to power" and suffer the consequences.

The advent of "the prophets" as gathered into distinct groups or "schools" during this period is also worth noting.[4] Exactly what these were, or even their role, remain unfortunately obscure, but their very appearance on the scene suggests that we are entering into a time when prophets and prophecy will play a more prominent role in the narrative.

The Davidic Covenant

YHWH's initial opposition to Israel having a king and the failure of Saul as king leaves the reader completely unprepared for what happens next. Instead of adopting an "I-told-you-so" attitude, YHWH makes a wholehearted and permanent commitment to the institution of the monarchy!

But not at first. Saul, after a good start, turns out to be a disaster, confirming the reader's suspicion of kings that was generated by YHWH's own low expectations. Even before Saul has departed the scene, YHWH chooses a man "after his own heart," David, as the second king of Israel (1 Sam 16) and things begin to look up. He has considerable success in defeating his enemies and establishing control of the government and then, inexplicably, YHWH makes him the following promise through Nathan the prophet:

> I have been with you wherever you went, and have cut off all your enemies from before you. I will make you a great name, like the name of the great ones who are in the earth. I will appoint a place for my people Israel, and will plant them, that they may dwell in their own place. . . Moreover Yahweh tells you that Yahweh will make you a house. When your days are fulfilled, and you sleep with your fathers, I will set up your offspring after you, who will proceed out of your body, and I will establish his kingdom. He will build a house for my name, and I will establish the throne of his kingdom forever. I will be his father, and he will be my son. . . .my loving kindness will not depart from him, as I took it from Saul, whom I put away before you. Your house and your kingdom will be made sure forever before you. Your throne will be established forever. (2 Sam 7:9–16)

Neither YHWH nor our text offers an explanation of why YHWH chose the line of David beyond a hint that it may be related to his character. From the perspective of the Story itself, however, such a development is in remarkable continuity with Jacob/Israel's own deathbed promise to his son Judah:

---

4. Cf. 1 Sam 10:5 and 19:20.

> The scepter will not depart from Judah,
> > nor the ruler's staff from between his feet,
> until he comes to whom it belongs.
> > The obedience of the peoples will be to him. (Gen 49:10)

With the choice of David from the tribe of Judah, this promise takes a giant step forward but much still remains unfulfilled.

In addition, it is worth asking whether or not there is something about a king and a kingdom that is best suited to YHWH's ultimate purpose. After all, YHWH has so thoroughly embraced the institution of the monarchy that redemption itself will bear its stamp! Will the Davidic line take on the characteristics of YHWH's own kingship and be transformed into his image? How could it otherwise bear the weight of such lofty expectations?

These questions relate to the ambiguous nature of the promise itself. It is not immediately clear if it contemplates merely the continuance of David's line one after the other forever, or if we are to imagine one particular 'son' who will reign forever. Read in isolation, the promise seems to suggest the former, but read through the prior blessing upon Judah, the latter fits right in. There is even here a suggestion of a significant change in the way the world works or even, perhaps, the divinity of this 'son.' For the time being all of these questions will have to remain open. We appear to be dealing with yet another case of progressive revelation and there is undoubtedly more to come.

Of course, the natural effect of this amazing promise on the reader is to rivet attention on this offspring as the expected One, the Serpent Crusher. The bold certainty of the proclamation narrows the scope of prospects considerably to this one line while its imagery expands one's anticipation of what YHWH has in store for his people. Although the reader may have briefly considered David himself, the great warrior-king, as the One, his or her eye has been raised now to a far more distant horizon. Or at least to his son.

It is important to see how this covenant fits in with those of Abraham and Moses. First of all, these latter seem to continue unabated. From one angle David's covenant simply fits inside them, subject to their authority and furthering their ends. The house of David will be YHWH's instrument in bringing home the blessing.

From another angle, there are strong affinities between the covenants of Abraham and David that suggest that the latter also has a status "over" that of Moses.

Both:

- are personal, between YHWH and a single man[5]
- promise descendants, special sons, which are to come "out of your body"
- come out of the blue

---

5. The Mosaic covenant was between YHWH and the nation. Moses was its mediator, not its subject.

Israel Under the Kings (Part One)

- are unconditional

It is the last of these that seems especially to bind these covenants together, guaranteeing that they will be instrumental in bringing about YHWH's ultimate purpose for Israel. Such certainty means that they will be able to deliver the Promise. The Mosaic covenant has already proven itself an extremely unlikely vehicle to that end, not through any fault of its own but through human inability to adhere to its conditions.

With the Davidic covenant, the Story has obviously reached another critical stage, making it possible to see more clearly the nature of things to come. The course of the nation is forever directed toward an ideal kingdom perpetually ruled by the house of David. Like the rope prairie pioneers strung from the house to the barn to guide them during a winter blizzard, the people of God are now provided with a tangible line anchored in the sure promise of YHWH and stretching all the way to the End. Even when that line disappears into the storm, hanging on will guarantee a safe arrival. The trick, as those pioneers sometimes discovered to their great loss, is to not let go.

We have the following expansion of the covenantal diagram to help us understand the relationship of the various covenants dealt with so far. The Davidic bears the Abrahamic shape because it does not introduce any new understanding of what "salvation" fundamentally looks like. Rather, it clarifies that picture by adding that all the Blessings of the Abrahamic Covenant will come into reality through the agency of a Davidic king and an eternal kingdom. It is drawn with solid lines because it is unconditional as well, if on a smaller "scale."

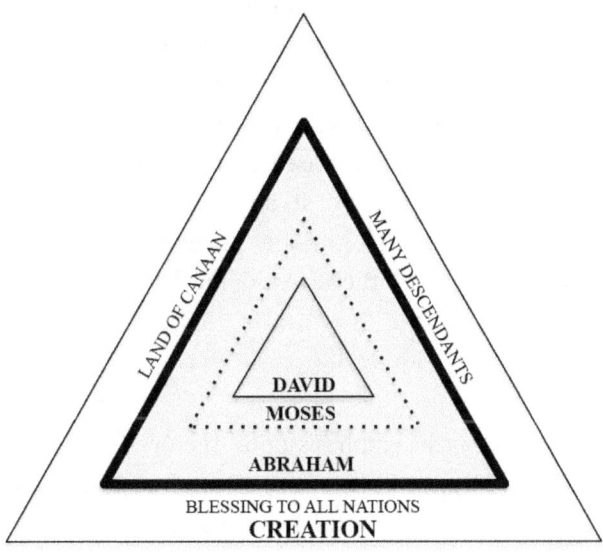

**Covenantal Diagram 4
Abraham-David**

The Death and Resurrection of the Beloved Son, Yet Again

It has been suggested in previous chapters that it is possible to detect this motif in the narratives concerning Seth, Isaac, Joseph, and the Exodus (where Israel itself is the son in question).[6] Now it seems to appear once again in connection with the covenant YHWH makes with David.

As we have seen above, David is promised a "son" who will build the temple and whose line will endure forever upon the throne of Israel. For our present purpose it is interesting that that this man will be God's Beloved Son as well:

> I will be his father, and he will be my son. If he commits iniquity, I will chasten him with the rod of men, and with the stripes of the children of men; but my loving kindness will not depart from him, as I took it from Saul, whom I put away before you. (2 Sam 7:14–15)

When a son is born to Bathsheba, the woman involved in David's great sin, we read the following remarkable account:

> She bore a son, and he called his name Solomon. Yahweh loved him; and he sent by the hand of Nathan the prophet, and he named him Jedidiah... [*loved by YHWH*]. (2 Sam 12:24–25)

The story goes out of its way to emphasize Jedediah/Solomon's special status as a son loved by YHWH, a status not shared even by his illustrious father.

The implication seems to be that Solomon will always be the recipient of YHWH's love in spite of doing wrong. At the end of his life we read that because of his disobedience his kingdom will be shattered. And yet the dazzling promise of a "kingdom forever" to the son of David remains hovering over the narrative.

We can only assume that this promised blessing will somehow arise from the ashes of the mess Solomon has made of it, and, in so doing, the Beloved Son will somehow be resurrected.[7] And with him any hopes for the Serpent Crusher that were aroused and then dashed with the advent of the first "son of David" to be king.

The Temple of Solomon

While the narrative places great emphasis upon the events leading up to and surrounding Solomon's building of the awe-inspiring temple, its completion does not involve any significant change in the way Israel worships. However, it does lead to the elevation of Jerusalem in the life of the nation.

Ever since the time of Moses, for about five hundred years the worship of Israel has been focused upon the tabernacle. It was there that the priesthood conducted the

---

6. See 78, 91, 115, above.
7. Cf. Levenson, *Death and Resurrection*, 29–30.

various rituals and sacrifices called for by the Law. More importantly, it was the place where, in some profound sense, YHWH himself dwelled in the holy of holies along with the Ark of the Covenant.

The tabernacle is by definition a portable structure, what we would call a tent. It went through the wilderness and into the Promised Land with the children of Israel. It appears that the tabernacle took up residence in, among other possible locations, Shiloh, Nob, Gibeon, and eventually Jerusalem itself in the time of David and Solomon.[8] In other words, Israel has had no one final geographical location for its national shrine.

With the building of the temple, however, portability obviously becomes a thing of the past. From now on Jerusalem, having been recently established as the capital city by David himself, also becomes the permanent worship center of the nation. The place where God dwells is at rest. Subsequently Jerusalem becomes routinely seen as "the holy city" and even the "city of God."[9] Eventually these designations take on an even deeper resonance as "Zion," the transcendent focus of hope in the age to come.[10]

But Will God Really Dwell on Earth?

Solomon's prayer of dedication offers a sophisticated understanding what it means for YHWH to dwell in this temple:

> But will God in very deed dwell on the earth? Behold, heaven and the heaven of heavens can't contain you; how much less this house that I have built! Yet have respect for the prayer of your servant, and for his supplication, Yahweh my God, to listen to the cry and to the prayer which your servant prays before you today; that your eyes may be open toward this house night and day, even toward the place of which you have said, 'My name shall be there;' to listen to the prayer which your servant prays toward this place. Listen to the supplication of your servant, and of your people Israel, when they pray toward this place. Yes, hear in heaven, your dwelling place; and when you hear, forgive. (1 Kgs 8:27–30)

YHWH dwells in heaven *and* in the holy of holies, the focus of his presence on earth.

Here we can see that the "both/and" characteristic of Hebrew thought and language reflects the character of their God: he is beyond human understanding and cannot be confined within the limitations of human language and thought. And yet he has revealed to human understanding true aspects of who he is and what he expects of his creatures.

---

8. Josh 18:1; 1 Sam 21:1; 1 Chr 16:39; 2 Sam 6:17; 1 Kgs 8:4.
9. Cf. Neh 11:1; Ps 87:3.
10. Cf. Ps 87.

The same can be said of all those spiritual realities that comprise his religion: true things can be said of them but it must not be imagined that such words can encompass their whole meaning. Speaking of words, it would also do well to note Solomon's emphasis on prayer, suggesting once more that sacrifice, what we might think is the primary function of a temple, is only part of what this building is all about.

Fire! (Again)

As we shall see, this narrative continues a pattern noted in the last chapter. Both Saul and David (but not Solomon, explicitly) are said to be endowed powerfully with the Spirit when they are anointed as king. This enables them to lead the people of YHWH and assures them of his divine blessing and help. The case of Saul, from whom the Spirit is taken and upon whom an evil spirit is placed when he turns away from YHWH, is particularly instructive. But the work of the Spirit, in an overt sense at least, remains confined to the lives of these two important leaders in this part of the Story.

THE STORY

Saul is Made King (1 Sam 9–11)

This chapter of salvation history begins with the selection of Saul as the first king of Israel. While the demand for a king represents a rejection of YHWH as king, the text also makes it clear that YHWH remains at the center of their national life. Far from turning his back, YHWH guides Samuel to the man of his choice:

> Tomorrow about this time I will send you a man out of the land of Benjamin, and you shall anoint him to be prince over my people Israel. He will save my people out of the hand of the Philistines; for I have looked upon my people, because their cry has come to me. (9:17)

Shortly Samuel anoints Saul, son of Kish, with oil (making him a "messiah," or "anointed one") and the Spirit of YHWH comes upon the young man in such a powerful way that he is "turned into another man" (10:6). The whole assembly of Israel then acknowledges him as their king, but some still manage to grumble against the choice.[11] The new king will have his work cut out for him and Saul wisely begins his reign by acting to consolidate his position. After subduing the Ammonites he is reaffirmed as king by all the people at Gilgal in the midst of great celebration.

---

11. 1 Sam 9 and 10.

Samuel Retreats and Then Charges

During the festivities, the elderly Samuel takes the opportunity to step back publicly from his role as judge. As he does so, like many leaders before him, he delivers a final charge to the people. He recites their somewhat spotty history with YHWH since the days of Moses and ends by reminding them that they have desired a king "when Yahweh your God was your king" (12:12). YHWH has now given them their king but if they obey the Law things will still go well with them.

After a great storm of thunder and rain is called forth by the old man, the people "greatly feared Yahweh and Samuel" (12:18). They acknowledge their sin in asking for a king and Samuel once more exhorts them to covenant faithfulness and promises to pray for them and to teach them "the good and the right way" (12:23). He ends on this sobering note:

> But if you keep doing evil, you will be consumed, both you and your king.. (12:25)

There is no record of what the people said in response but the context makes it clear that they are in a contrite mood and, it is safe to assume, renew their commitment to the covenant. Nevertheless, the recital of their past failures and their present mistake in asking for a king hang over them like a cloud from the storm they have just witnessed. A prudent reader might well head for shelter.

Saul: A Mixed Blessing (1 Sam 13–15)

It is not surprising when, before long, Saul gets himself into serious trouble with YHWH. Facing down some Philistines he grows impatient with the slow-arriving Samuel to offer sacrifice and proceeds himself in an attempt to win YHWH's favor. Not only is this against the Law because Saul was not qualified to be a priest, but also it goes against Samuel's direct command.[12] The judgment upon him proclaimed by Samuel is severe indeed:

> You have done foolishly. You have not kept the commandment of Yahweh your God, which he commanded you; for now Yahweh would have established your kingdom on Israel forever. But now your kingdom will not continue. Yahweh has sought for himself a man after his own heart, and Yahweh has appointed him to be prince over his people, because you have not kept that which Yahweh commanded you. (13:13–14)

Talk about a missed opportunity! An eternal kingdom! Guaranteed! Who knew this was YHWH's intent for Saul, let alone Israel itself? Perhaps he would have behaved differently if he had known what was at stake. While this sentence might seem

---

12. Deut 12:5–14; 1 Sam 10:8.

all out of proportion to the crime (as it may have been with Moses), Saul's disobedience here lays bare an inclination to disobedience that is simply unacceptable in a leader of God's people. What YHWH is looking for is, instead, "a man after his own heart" and Saul does not qualify. But the good news is that apparently someone else does! The reader once again begins to lean forward in anticipation.

In spite of this pronouncement, Israel's armies enjoy considerable success against the Philistines along the coastal plain under the leadership of Saul and his son Jonathan. Indeed, many of their enemies are subdued and kept at bay, even if not being totally defeated. It is clear that YHWH has not abandoned them (yet). On a number of occasions Saul shows himself not bereft of godly intentions, but when he fails to enforce the ban YHWH had placed on the Amalekites and allows the troops to keep some of the best plunder for themselves, things come to a head. Saul tries to excuse their actions as the pious acquisition of animals to be sacrificed to YHWH, but Samuel will have none of that:

> Has Yahweh as great delight in burnt offerings and sacrifices, as in obeying Yahweh's voice? Behold, to obey is better than sacrifice, and to listen than the fat of rams. For rebellion is as the sin of witchcraft, and stubbornness is as idolatry and teraphim. (15:22–23)

This echoes Israel's earlier rejection of YHWH as king and drives home the warnings that had been given at that time. It also signifies for Saul a point of no return because, in spite of his apparent repentance, he has lost the kingdom forever:

> Yahweh has torn the kingdom of Israel from you today, and has given it to a neighbor of yours who is better than you. (15:28)

From this point on Saul is on his own: Samuel, his conduit to YHWH, leaves him for good.[13] We are even told that the same goes for the Spirit of God with which Saul had been endowed after his anointing. As if this was not bad enough, God sends an evil spirit to torment him (16:14). It is obvious that Saul's day is done.

The Last Shall Be First: David Selected as Messiah (1 Sam 16:1–13)

Already hinted at twice now, a star is beginning to rise, this time over Bethlehem. No sooner does Samuel depart from Saul for the last time than YHWH sends him to anoint the son of Jesse the Bethlehemite he has chosen to be the next king. Unfortunately, he fails to tell Samuel which of Jesse's eight sons it is. One by one the assembled sons are brought forward but none receive YHWH's assent, although several look the part of a king.

At this point YHWH reveals what is important to him:

---

13. Except, perhaps, in a posthumous appearance recorded in 1 Sam 28.

> I don't see as man sees. For man looks at the outward appearance, but Yahweh looks at the heart. (I Sam 16:7b)

It is the quality of the inner person that impresses the Almighty, nothing else: it is what he seeks in humanity above all. This accords well with our developing understanding that it is precisely the heart that is in need of renovation before obedience will ever be forthcoming in the human race.

Finally, Samuel asks if there are any other sons and is told about the youngest, whom his father had not even considered as a possibility, leaving him in the fields to tend the sheep. It turns out that he is the one God has chosen: David. When Samuel anoints him with oil the Israelites have another "messiah" or "anointed one." And, as happened to Saul before him, ". . .Yahweh's Spirit came mightily on David from that day forward" (16:13). He is not yet king, however, but only king-in-waiting. Saul, already informed that the kingdom was going to a better man, continues to rule. The potential for deadly conflict is pointedly clear.

David Increases and Saul Decreases

David and Goliath (1 Sam 16:14—17:58)

The relationship between the contenders starts off well enough: David is summoned to play his harp in order to help soothe the king, who is now troubled by the evil spirit mentioned earlier. Saul is so pleased with the young man that he asks Jesse to allow him to remain in royal service as one of Saul's armor-bearers. Although his father apparently agrees, David still has to return home to tend the sheep from time to time.

It was on one of these occasions that Jesse sends him with supplies for his three oldest brothers, now serving as soldiers in the army of Israel. He discovers the troops facing the Philistines, each army encamped on a hillside with a valley between them. The Israelites are cowering in fear because the enemy has put forward a champion, a giant of a man named Goliath, and he has dared them to send out their own champion for a winner-take-all contest. No one has had the courage to respond in spite of Saul's promise of his daughter as wife to the successful warrior.

David, showing his Godward heart for the first time, exclaims:

> For who is this uncircumcised Philistine, that he should defy the armies of the living God? (17:26)

For David it is simple. It is his God against the gods of the Philistines and it isn't even a fair fight. The story builds itself on this faith as it recounts how he offers himself (or, really, YHWH) as Israel's champion. Even though he is only a boy, his willingness to take on the giant comes to Saul's attention, but David distains even the king's help. Daring to face Goliath armed only with his shepherd's sling, he even has the audacity to taunt the giant to his face:

> Today, Yahweh will deliver you into my hand. I will strike you and take your head from off you. I will give the dead bodies of the army of the Philistines today to the birds of the sky and to the wild animals of the earth, that all the earth may know that there is a God in Israel, and that all this assembly may know that Yahweh doesn't save with sword and spear; for the battle is Yahweh's, and he will give you into our hand. (17:46-47)

Miraculously, he kills Goliath with a single stone and Israel enjoys a great victory. Saul is so impressed that he immediately appoints David to his staff. The king's son, Jonathan, becomes his close friend, while he himself rises quickly through the ranks, making quite a reputation as a military leader in the process.

Cat and Mouse Begins (1 Sam 18:1—25:1)

Saul is thereby stirred to intense jealousy and the two begin a deadly game of cat and mouse. Tension mounts when Saul personally tries to murder David with a javelin, but misses. Saul, then changes tactics by offering his daughter Michal to David as a wife, only with a catch: David has to present the king with a hundred enemy foreskins! Naturally Saul is hoping that David will be killed by the Philistines when he tries to obtain the stated bride-price. Instead, David presents him with *two* hundred of the grisly trophies. Saul not only loses his daughter, he loses his mind as he descends even deeper into jealousy and paranoia. He attempts once again to kill David, but is prevented by the Spirit of God.

David is now on the run, hiding out in caves and forests from the rampaging Saul, who even kills some priests who have aided the elusive shepherd. On one occasion, needing to relieve himself, Saul actually enters the cave where his prey is hiding. Faced with a golden opportunity, David is unable to bring himself to kill "Yahweh's anointed" (24:5). When Saul exits the cave and returns to his troops, David calls out to him, telling the king how he had not killed him when he had the chance and that this proved that his loyalty should not be questioned.

Saul's response finally seems to bring an end to his animosity to David, even an acceptance of his own destiny:

> . . .may Yahweh reward you good for that which you have done to me today. Now, behold, I know that you will surely be king, and that the kingdom of Israel will be established in your hand. Swear now therefore to me by Yahweh, that you will not cut off my offspring after me, and that you will not destroy my name out of my father's house. (24:19b-22)

At this point in the story Samuel finally succumbs to old age and all Israel gathers to bury him at his home in Ramah. From the day of his dedication to YHWH as a boy he has served faithfully: as prophet, priest, and judge. His only major misstep was appointing his wayward sons to be his successors. It was this mistake that had precipitated the demand for a king and brought an end to the period of the judges.

Cat and Mouse Continues (1 Sam 25:2–2 Sam 1:21)

Saul soon reverts to form. He renews his determination to get rid of David by chasing him out of the Land altogether. In flight, David again passes up a clear chance to kill the king and once again Saul seems to give up the chase. For over a year the cagy young messiah finds shelter among the Philistines, even earning the trust of one of their king's sons. Over and over his integrity and trustworthiness are demonstrated in stark contrast to character of Saul, which continues to deteriorate.

When the Philistines decide to attack Israel, a terrified Saul, realizing he needs divine help, finds he cannot contact YHWH by any of the usual means. Desperation driving him to break the Law, he consults a witch and commands her to bring up Samuel from the dead in order to ask him what he should do. The witch cries out in fear when Samuel actually appears, suggesting this is not what she was expecting. In any event, Samuel has only bad news for Saul: he and his sons will die in the battle and the kingdom will be given to David. Saul realizes his end is near.

In the ensuing battle at Mount Gilboa, Israel is routed and Saul is mortally wounded by archers after three of his sons have fallen. Realizing that all is lost, consumed to the point of madness by jealousy and rejection, he falls on his own sword and dies. It is a sad end to a promising beginning.

When David learns the news he does not rejoice as we might expect. It is YHWH's anointed who is dead and so, too, is his son Jonathan, David's faithful ally and friend. His grief for both is very real and he composes a lament that repeats the line "How the mighty have fallen" three times,[14] expressing both his great sorrow and his strength of character in honoring the God-appointed office of a man who had been out to destroy him.

Mouse Triumphant (2 Sam 2–5)

Immediately after Saul's death, however, only the tribe of Judah accepts David as their king. The next few years are marked by civil war because the other tribes largely remain loyal to the remnants of the house of Saul. The latter's son Ish-Bosheth is installed as a rival king over the northern tribes by Abner, the commander of Saul's army. It seems that it is Abner who has the heart for this fight and, when Ish-Bosheth and he have a falling-out, he conspires to betray the king by arranging for David to take over the entire nation and bring the mess to an end.

---

14. 2 Sam 1:19, 25, 27.

Meanwhile, David's own general, Joab, not trusting Abner (who had killed his brother in battle), murders him, much to David's dismay. When Ish-Bosheth is also murdered by some men thinking they were doing David a favor, he is enraged and has them killed. With these developments the wind has finally been taken out of the sails of rebellion and all Israel accepts David as king.

In consolidating his control of the Land, he captures Jerusalem and makes it his capital, building a palace there for his ever-expanding circle of wives, concubines, and children. Last but not least, David soundly routs an attacking Philistine army, giving the Land a real measure of peace.

YHWH Promises David a Forever House (2 Sam 7/1 Chr 17)

Turning his attention to matters of religion, David arranges for the Ark of the Covenant to be returned from Kiriath-Jearim, where it has been for some time. It is brought on a cart to Jerusalem in celebratory procession. During the journey, an attendant reaches out to steady the cart when the oxen stumble and is struck down by God because of his irreverent act (2 Sam 6:7). Logically concluding that it was dangerous to have the Ark too close, the king orders that it be left outside of Jerusalem. However, when he sees that it brings blessing to the man who keeps it, he decides to bring it all the way into the city and places it in the tabernacle.

But it occurs to David that there is still something wrong with this picture. Here he is, settled in a grand palace, while the Ark of God, and in some sense God himself, remains in a mere tent. He consults Nathan, who appears to be chief among the prophets on his staff, and he gets the green light to rectify the situation in any way he sees fit. What instinctively appears to be the right thing to do, however, is not part of YHWH's plan. That very night Nathan receives a divine message for David: not only will his name be great and the land prosperous, but YHWH will build David a house instead of the other way round!

> Yahweh tells you that Yahweh will make you a house... Your house and your kingdom will be made sure forever before you. Your throne will be established forever. (2 Sam 7:11b, 16)

Although the narrative has taken pains to show David as a man of exemplary character, this personal covenant[15] goes well beyond any sense of having been deserved. David's own response indicates that he is simply blown away:

> Who am I, Lord Yahweh, and what is my house, that you have brought me this far? This was yet a small thing in your eyes, Lord Yahweh; but you have spoken also of your servant's house for a great while to come; and this among men, Lord Yahweh! (2 Sam 7:18–19)

---

15. Not called a 'covenant' here, but cf. 2 Sam 23:5; 2 Chr 7:18 and 21:7.

After all the ambiguity over the introduction of kings to rule Israel, the reader is blown away too. For here YHWH himself embraces the institution "forever"! Before this moment the narrative has stressed the nation's rejection of YHWH as king, even though he subsequently guided the selection of Saul. And how can all this be squared with YHWH's previous warnings of kingly dominance? The very fact that these questions are ignored suggests the Story has moved on to another stage altogether. But they linger with the reader, creating a premonition that all might not be well.

David's Troubled Reign (2 Sam 8–24/1 Kgs 1:1—2:12/1 Chr 18–29)

Blood on His Hands

Part of YHWH's promise to David at this time was "rest from all your enemies"[16], but David's relationship with the nations surrounding Israel continues to be one of ongoing war and conquest for much of his reign. So much so that one begins to suspect that this promise is more for his descendants than for him personally. In fact, one of the reasons YHWH gives for not allowing him to build the temple is the amount of blood he has shed (1 Chr 22:8). On the other hand, by the time of his death he has established the borders of the kingdom and conquered almost all his enemies. His son Solomon inherits a Land that is at rest, but David has spent himself in the effort to make it happen.[17]

David and Bathsheba

Troubling David even more than his enemies was his own moral failure. 2 Sam 11–12 tells the story, one of those omitted by the chronicler[18] in his account. Israel is at war, again, but it is Joab who is in the field leading the troops while David remains behind in Jerusalem. There, he succumbs to his lust for the beautiful Bathsheba, the wife of one of his soldiers. He takes her to his bed, she becomes pregnant, and in an effort to cover up his sin, he has her innocent and loyal husband murdered.

When Nathan the prophet dramatically fingers him for the crime, David instantly recognizes that he has sinned terribly against YHWH. Amazingly, Nathan abruptly informs him that this great sin has simply been "put away" by YHWH (12:13). Many a reader will note that he also avoids the death penalty prescribed by the Law.[19] However, the son born of the affair is struck ill by YHWH and soon dies, in spite of David's pleas. David accepts this as just punishment for his sin and is somewhat consoled when Bathsheba gives birth to another son who is named Solomon.

---

16. 2 Sam 7:11.
17. Cf. 1 Kgs 5:3 and 1 Chr 22:9.
18. This is the term many scholars give to the person or persons who compiled 1 and 2 Chronicles.
19. See previous discussions of this issue, 145–46, 152, above.

Sons of Anarchy: Absalom and Adonijah

But trouble continues. Indeed, from this point on things begin to go seriously off the rails for David. Perhaps it is ironic that it is more sexual intrigue within his family that sets his son Absalom in motion towards open rebellion. He cunningly gathers so much support that David and his followers are actually forced to flee temporarily from Jerusalem. However, Absalom is killed in battle by Joab and the rebellion fizzles out. But David is filled with grief for a son again, this time a son who had become an enemy:

> My son Absalom! My son, my son Absalom! I wish I had died for you, Absalom, my son, my son! (2 Sam 18:33)

Toward the end of David's long life another son, Adonijah, is filled with ambition and proclaims his intention to take over as king. Most of David's sons and even his old general, Joab, side with the young man, as does Abiathar (one of the chief priests), and they proclaim him king. The other chief priest, Zadok, remains loyal to David. Again, division and chaos threaten the kingdom, but then the chosen son comes to the fore.

The True Successor is Anointed

At Nathan's urging, Bathsheba reminds her husband that he had promised the throne to *her* son Solomon. In response David commands his officials to anoint Solomon as his heir to the throne:

> So Zadok the priest, Nathan the prophet, Benaiah the son of Jehoiada, and the Cherethites and the Pelethites went down and had Solomon ride on king David's mule, and brought him to Gihon. Zadok the priest took the horn of oil from the Tent, and anointed Solomon. They blew the trumpet; and all the people said, "Long live king Solomon!" All the people came up after him, and the people piped with pipes, and rejoiced with great joy, so that the earth shook with their sound. (1 Kgs 1:39–40)

Gihon was an important spring just outside the eastern walls of Jerusalem. And so it is that the first anointed "son of David" rides a borrowed mule into Jerusalem to the wild acclaim of all the people and there ascends his throne. Eventually he has both Adonijah and Joab executed while Abiathar the priest is banished, removing all opposition.

The King is Dead; Long Live the King (1 Kgs 2:1–10)

Following this, David breaths his last, having reigned forty tumultuous years. His son Solomon, appropriately, is the recipient of *his* farewell "charge":

> I am going the way of all the earth. You be strong therefore, and show yourself a man; and keep the instruction of Yahweh your God, to walk in his ways, to keep his statutes, his commandments, his ordinances, and his testimonies, according to that which is written in the law of Moses, that you may prosper in all that you do, and wherever you turn yourself. Then Yahweh may establish his word which he spoke concerning me, saying, 'If your children are careful of their way, to walk before me in truth with all their heart and with all their soul, there shall not fail you,' he said, 'a man on the throne of Israel. (1 Kgs 2:2–4)

A complex and even humble man, David was also renowned as a poet, "the sweet psalmist of Israel" (2 Sam 23:1). Above all, he walked with integrity before his God, but not without the occasional stumble. In the end, he got the job done: Solomon would do well to heed his last words.

Solomon Wisely Asks for Wisdom (1 Kgs 3/1 Chr 1)

Not long into Solomon's reign YHWH appears to him in a dream and asks what he would like to have. This is an extraordinary encounter and opportunity. The young king, perhaps overwhelmed by his responsibilities and the high standard his father had set, makes a surprising request:

> I am just a little child. I don't know how to go out or come in. Your servant is among your people which you have chosen, a great people, that can't be numbered or counted for multitude. Give your servant therefore an understanding heart to judge your people, that I may discern between good and evil; for who is able to judge this great people of yours? (1 Kgs 3:7b-9)

YHWH is pleased with this response:

> Because you have asked this thing, and have not asked for yourself long life, nor have you asked for riches for yourself, nor have you asked for the life of your enemies, but have asked for yourself understanding to discern justice; behold, I have done according to your word. Behold, I have given you a wise and understanding heart; so that there has been no one like you before you, and after you none will arise like you. I have also given you that which you have not asked, both riches and honor, so that there will not be any among the kings like you for all your days. If you will walk in my ways, to keep my statutes and my commandments, as your father David walked, then I will lengthen your days. (1 Kgs 3:11–14)

What extravagant promises: wisdom, riches, honor, and even, possibly, a long life to enjoy it all! And it all comes true! At its height, Solomon's kingdom extends from the Euphrates to the Egyptian border, while his people multiply both numerically and in wealth. His wisdom is legendary, with many of the surrounding nations sending delegations to listen to his judgments and see for themselves what he has accomplished. It is unlikely that there will ever be anyone greater than Solomon.

The House That Solomon Built (1 Kgs 5–9/2 Chr 2:1—6:10)

Solomon remembers YHWH's promise to David that his son would be the one to build him a house and he dedicates himself to this great undertaking. Using only the finest materials and craftsmen he proceeds to build Israel's first temple, a spectacular place of worship. Its fundamental structure is based on the tabernacle but it is imbued with a kind of holy extravagance, following the detailed instructions given by David himself (1 Chr 28).

In an amazing feat of craftsmanship, its walls are constructed out of stone blocks fully dressed at the quarry so that no iron tool is heard at the site itself. The inner walls are lined with cedar from Lebanon and then overlaid with pure gold. Gold is everywhere: ceilings, floors, carvings, and altar! It takes seven years and astronomical sums to complete. David had previously accumulated over 3,700 tons of gold, 37,000 tons of silver, plus vast amounts of bronze and iron. No doubt Solomon added yet more! It is altogether awe inspiring.

As this place intended for sacrifice is being constructed, however, YHWH appears to Solomon to remind him, as he did Saul (1 Sam 15:22–23), that it is *obedience* that he is looking for most of all:

> Concerning this house which you are building, if you will walk in my statutes, and execute my ordinances, and keep all my commandments to walk in them; then I will establish my word with you, which I spoke to David your father. I will dwell among the children of Israel, and will not forsake my people Israel. (1 Kgs 6:12–13)

While there is no hint of any divine displeasure at the extravagance of the building, this message is no doubt intended to encourage Solomon to keep things in perspective. On the occasion of the dedication of the building YHWH demonstrates his overall approval by "moving in," appearing in a magnificent cloud and filling the new temple with his glory, much as he did with the tabernacle (Exod 40:4–38).

Solomon is very conscious that a high point in Israel's pilgrimage has been reached:

> Blessed be Yahweh, who has given rest to his people Israel, according to all that he promised. There has not failed one word of all his good promise, which he promised by Moses his servant. (1 Kgs 8:56)

It just doesn't get any better than this. They have finally arrived.

A Bridge Too Far (1 Kgs 11:1–13)

Up to this point in the story of Saul, David, and Solomon, there has been no report of widespread idolatry continuing among the people of Israel. This is remarkable, given their history, but perhaps it is due in part to the fact that the account has been focused more on the activities of the kings than on the nation as a whole. Ironically, just after describing the dedication of the temple and exulting over the glories of Solomon's reign, the text returns to this recurring nightmare.[20]

It seems that in order to secure his kingdom, Solomon, against YHWH's command to his people (Exod 34:16), takes for himself seven hundred foreign wives. Of royal birth, they are part and parcel of the alliances he has forged with Israel's neighbors. But it is a bridge too far: in the end they turn his heart to their own gods and away from YHWH. It turns out to be his undoing:

> Because this is done by you, and you have not kept my covenant and my statutes, which I have commanded you, I will surely tear the kingdom from you, and will give it to your servant. (1 Kgs 11:11)

Camelot, sadly, has only existed for one brief shining moment. What a way for it to end! All is not lost, however:

> Nevertheless, I will not do it in your days, for David your father's sake; but I will tear it out of your son's hand. However I will not tear away all the kingdom; but I will give one tribe to your son, for David my servant's sake, and for Jerusalem's sake which I have chosen. (1 Kgs 11:12-13)

The covenant with David holds, if only by a thread. Although this word speaks of terrible trauma ahead for Israel, it will not be fatal. More importantly, YHWH remains faithful and has not abandoned his people. But Solomon's time is up. Mercifully there is no record of his reaction to what YHWH had to say.

It is at this point that we first read of YHWH raising up adversaries against Solomon. The last and most important of these is Jeroboam, one of his own officials from the half-tribe of Ephraim. YHWH entices him to rebellion by promising him the kingship over all of Israel except for "one tribe" that will stay under the rule of the house of David. His first attempt at rebellion fails and he escapes down into Egypt until Solomon dies. It is very plain, however, that this is not over.

Solomon passes away after forty years of mostly blessed rule. It is simply recorded that he dies, and perhaps that is all we need to know. While this man, known universally for his wisdom, does not pass it on in a farewell discourse to his successor, he does bequeath his famous Proverbs and the Song of Songs to the ages.

---

20. Again, the chronicler is silent about this blotch on Solomon's career.

IN THE BOSOM OF ABRAHAM

Introduction

This period of the united kingdom is characterized by significant fulfillment of the Promises made to Abraham. David is quite explicit about this:

> Remember his covenant forever,
>   the word which he commanded to a thousand generations,
>   the covenant which he made with Abraham,
>   his oath to Isaac.
> He confirmed it to Jacob for a statute,
>   and to Israel for an everlasting covenant,
> saying, "I will give you the land of Canaan,
>   The lot of your inheritance... (1Chr 16:15)

Furthermore, the kingdom of Solomon especially is a high-water mark in the entire Story. Solomon, like his father before him, believes that the people of Israel have entered into the time of fulfillment:

> Blessed be Yahweh, who has given rest to his people Israel, according to all that he promised. There has not failed one word of all his good promise, which he promised by Moses his servant.[21] (I Kgs 8:56)

The discussions in this section will examine this claim. Even if we come to share Solomon's view, we cannot forget the little cloud that is forming on the horizon at the end of his reign. The problem with high-water marks is that they are only visible once the water has receded to its normal level.

1. The Land/Place

As far as the Land is concerned, it becomes, at last, the settled possession of the Israelite nation. Not only that, but in Solomon's reign it stretched far beyond Canaan to include all of territory that YHWH had eventually promised to Abraham: all the way from the Egyptian border in the west to the Euphrates River in the east.[22]

As the period opens, the Land is still disputed territory and the reigns of Saul and David are marked by almost continuous warfare with the occupying and neighboring nations. Ultimately David is successful in a way that even Joshua might envy. We have to go all the way back to the early days of the Conquest to locate a time when the people enjoyed anywhere near such consistent success over their enemies.

---

21. Although he refers specifically to the Promises given through Moses, we have already seen that these originate with Abraham. See 130–31, above.

22. Gen 15:18–19. Cf. Van Gemeren, *Progress of Redemption*, 233.

The long struggle seems to have come finally to an end and it looks for a while like Solomon is in fact that "offspring" of David of whom YHWH declared "I will be his father and he will be my son" and whose kingdom will be established forever (2 Sam 7:11–16). By the end of his reign, however, it seems such hopes are misplaced, as Solomon falters badly. What the implications of this are for the Land are yet to be seen, but we have noted YHWH's ominous reference to having the kingdom torn away from him.

Finally, the full possession of the Land heightens the sense of it being a special "place" for YHWH and his people. The same intensification is observed when the temple is constructed in Jerusalem and the glory of YHWH descends upon it. It is the most holy "place" of all, infusing the entire city with the divine Presence.[23]

2. Many Descendants

Toward the end of his reign David takes it upon himself to conduct a census of the fighting men of Israel. It reveals that there are about 1.5 million men at arms available to the king.[24] From this is it may be inferred that there has been some significant population growth since the Exodus. The subsequent long period of incessant warfare under Joshua, the judges, and Saul has failed to negate this Promise.

A rather more limited count of part of the army and tribal chiefs includes the following note:

> But David didn't take the number of them from twenty years old and under, because Yahweh had said he would increase Israel like the stars of the sky. (1 Chr 27:23)

This seems to be a clear reference to the Abrahamic Covenant, even using "covenantal language" to underline the connection. One possible meaning of the passage is that David is confident that YHWH had indeed fulfilled his Promise. At the same time, he does take a census and is rebuked by YHWH for his trouble!

The other covenantal metaphor for many descendants is used by a man named Hushai when giving Absalom some advice, referring to Israel being "as the sand that is by the sea for multitude" (2 Sam 17:11). Solomon holds that the kingdom he has inherited is "a great people, that can't be numbered or counted for multitude" (1 Kgs 3:8) and of his own day we read that the nation is "numerous as the sand which is by the sea in multitude" (1 Kgs 4:20).

---

23. If ancient Jewish tradition is correct, it is also the same place where Abraham was called to sacrifice Isaac his son. It was named Moriah, "God will provide," a fitting motto for this whole period as Israel finally comes into its own.

24. Cf. 2 Sam 24:9 and 1 Chr 20:5. There are slight differences in the accounts.

These references strongly affirm that the Israelites have become quite numerous during this period and even at the time this is recognized as a fulfillment of the Promise to Abraham.

3. Blessing to All Nations

It is under David that the nations immediately surrounding Israel are conquered and thereby brought into his sphere. At the end of his life David ponders the fact that YHWH had "kept me to be the head of the nations. A people whom I have not known will serve me" (2 Sam 22:44). To the extent that these peoples are subject to his benevolent rule, they would enjoy the considerable blessing that goes with it as well.

This possibility is not directly remarked upon by our text, but our conclusion is strengthened by the fact that there is also no mention of the nations being abused by Israel. Still, it is an argument from silence and must remain largely speculative. What we do find here, however, is an understanding that the grateful exaltation of YHWH by his people, particularly in the newly constructed temple, will draw the nations into the worship of their God.

We get a taste of this idea in the psalm that David wrote to celebrate the return of the Ark to Jerusalem. His call to worship soars spectacularly beyond Israel to include the whole earth:

> Oh give thanks to Yahweh.
>   Call on his name.
>   Make what he has done known among the peoples.
>
> Sing to Yahweh, all the earth!
>   Display his salvation from day to day.
> Declare his glory among the nations,
>   and his marvelous works among all the peoples.
>
> Ascribe to Yahweh, you relatives of the peoples,
>   ascribe to Yahweh glory and strength!
> Ascribe to Yahweh the glory due to his name.
>   Bring an offering, and come before him.
>   Worship Yahweh in holy array.
> Tremble before him, all the earth.
>   The world also is established that it can't be moved.
> Let the heavens be glad,
>   and let the earth rejoice!
>
> Let the heavens rejoice, let the earth be glad;
>   let them say among the nations, "YHWH reigns!" (1 Chr 16:8, 23-24, 28-31)

No small vision here! The nations are included in the Blessing and the overall context would suggest the path, or what we have called the "inner logic," that it will take: YHWH's blessing/salvation of David > the blessing/salvation of Israel > the recognition of YHWH as God by the nations > the worship of YHWH by the nations > the blessing of the nations. Israel, by being blessed, becomes the means by which the nations themselves become blessed, so fulfilling her role as a kingdom of priests and a holy nation.[25]

Given the expansive scope of this vision, the following section of Solomon's prayer of dedication for the temple does not come as a total shock:

> Moreover concerning the foreigner, who is not of your people Israel, when he comes out of a far country for your name's sake (for they shall hear of your great name, and of your mighty hand, and of your outstretched arm); when he comes and prays toward this house; hear in heaven, your dwelling place, and do according to all that the foreigner calls to you for; that all the peoples of the earth may know your name, to fear you, as do your people Israel, and that they may know that this house which I have built is called by your name. (1 Kgs 8:41–43)

Here is further confirmation that the Blessing to All Nations is to be, in fact, their being brought into relationship with YHWH through Israel's witness in the world. YHWH has chosen to work through Israel (and its temple) to include the nations in his salvation.

Although this is relegated to the future, a taste of it is enjoyed by those nations that are touched by the fabulous reign of Solomon. For an example we can look to the Queen of Sheba in southern Arabia and what she has to say to him:

> It was a true report that I heard in my own land of your acts, and of your wisdom. However I didn't believe the words until I came and my eyes had seen it. Behold, not even half was told me! Your wisdom and prosperity exceed the fame which I heard. Happy are your men, happy are these your servants, who stand continually before you, who hear your wisdom. Blessed is Yahweh your God, who delighted in you, to set you on the throne of Israel. Because Yahweh loved Israel forever, therefore he made you king, to do justice and righteousness. (1 Kgs 10:6–9)

She is blessed and perhaps her nation is as well, as it seems that the visit results in a trade agreement between the monarchs. And she is not alone:

> So king Solomon exceeded all the kings of the earth in riches and in wisdom. All the earth sought the presence of Solomon, to hear his wisdom, which God had put in his heart. (1 Kgs 10:23–24)

The eyes of the nations, indeed, of "all the earth," are smiling upon a blessed Israel and her God. As a result the Blessings are beginning to flow more powerfully in their direction.

---

25. Exod 19:6 See esp. discussion, 135–36, above.

4. Fruitfulness

During this era we hear of famine only once, lasting for three years during David's reign.

Otherwise, the Land seems to persist in its natural fruitfulness and, when David surveys all the precious material he had accumulated for the temple, he is humbled by YHWH's provision and provides posterity with a valuable perspective upon material blessings:

> But who am I, and what is my people, that we should be able to offer so willingly as this? For all things come from you, and we have given you of your own. For we are strangers before you, and foreigners, as all our fathers were. Our days on the earth are as a shadow, and there is no remaining. Yahweh our God, all this store that we have prepared to build you a house for your holy name comes from your hand, and is all your own. (1 Chr 29:14–16)

While David's possessions are certainly impressive, they pale in significance beside those of his son:

> Solomon's provision for one day was thirty cors of fine flour, sixty measures of meal, ten head of fat cattle, twenty head of cattle out of the pastures, and one hundred sheep, in addition to deer, and gazelles, and roebucks, and fattened fowl. Judah and Israel lived safely, every man under his vine and under his fig tree, from Dan even to Beersheba, all the days of Solomon. (1 Kgs 4:20, 22–23, 25)

If we add to this the lengthy accounts of Solomon's staggering wealth we cannot escape the impression of a Land that was fairly bursting at the seams with bounty of every description. Here is part of just one report:

> Moreover the king made a great throne of ivory, and overlaid it with the finest gold. Twelve lions stood there on the one side and on the other on the six steps. Nothing like it was made in any kingdom. All king Solomon's drinking vessels were of gold, and all the vessels of the House of the Forest of Lebanon were of pure gold. None were of silver, because it was considered of little value in the days of Solomon. For the king had a fleet of Tarshish at sea with Hiram's fleet. Once every three years the fleet of Tarshish came, bringing gold, silver, ivory, apes, and peacocks. So king Solomon exceeded all the kings of the earth in riches and in wisdom. (1 Kgs 10:18, 20–23)

Can there be any doubt that the Land sustaining all this was itself exceedingly fruitful, so much so that it is bound to remind the reader of Eden? Indeed, we have already noted Solomon's characterization of this period as "rest," linking it to the very Sabbath rest of God and thus, again, to Eden.

This connection may have been reinforced through the general decoration of the temple that some scholars find suggestive of the garden of Eden[26]:

> He carved all the walls of the house around with carved figures of cherubim, palm trees, and open flowers, inside and outside. (1 Kgs 6:29)

It does not take a lot of imagination to see how an Israelite would feel, surrounded by such imagery: it was like stepping back through the guarded gates of paradise itself.

What a time this must have been! The Promises are all at hand. All you have to do is reach out and help yourself.

5. Relationship

Remarkably, after what we have seen in most previous eras, there is little mention of general apostasy or disobedience among the people, boding well for their relationship with YHWH. However, it must be kept in mind that the narrative is narrowly focused on the three kings themselves. Here we can discern an initial positive relationship with God that is followed by an increasingly negative one.

In Saul's case this pattern plays out in his own lifespan. Initially he seeks YHWH, but then he turns away to a medium and generally fails to consult YHWH, not even inquiring of him before the Ark (1 Chr 13:3). In the end we read that he is rejected for this and dies because "of Yahweh's word, which he didn't keep" (1 Chr 10:13).

Regarding David and Solomon, the same pattern is also apparent if we consider their combined reigns, being together the high point of the royal narrative, as a single unit. It starts with David, who, in spite of several serious lapses, follows YHWH faithfully throughout his own life.[27] His relationship with YHWH is symbolized by his bringing back the Ark to center stage in Jerusalem.

Solomon starts off on an extraordinarily high note as well, taking over where his father left off and building a permanent house for the Ark. When Solomon dedicates the new temple, God's awesome Presence comes down to remain among his people. If the décor is to remind them of Eden, it would also remind them of the unbroken fellowship with their God that Eden represents and which they are enjoying once again in this place. The relationship is at an all-time high at this point. YHWH seems to have fully entered into the national life of Israel.

But, unfortunately, the story does not end there. Just when everything seems to be headed in the right direction, it all falls apart. As he grows older, Solomon, in spite of all his wisdom and the blessings he has enjoyed, begins to worship the gods brought into his palace by the foreign wives he has taken. Naturally this angers YHWH, who punishes him by "tearing away" the greater part of the nation from his descendants. The relationship is broken. And so the pattern continues on its weary way.

---

26. Cf. *NIV Study Bible*, 482.
27. Cf. 1 Kgs 11:6.

6. Grace/Obedience

As YHWH sets out the terms of his relationship with each of these kings we can observe how the "saved by grace/obligated to obey" theme shows itself in this segment of the history of redemption. It must be kept in mind that we are dealing with different covenants and the interplay between them can be quite subtle. Grace is what brings David into this "new" covenant but it is disobedience to the *Mosaic* covenant that threatens its course.

The story of Saul, which could be seen as YHWH's first movement toward the Davidic covenant, conforms to this pattern. Just the fact that YHWH, given his own reluctance, involves himself in Saul's selection as king is evidence of grace at work (if that is not a theological contradiction!). The story makes it clear that Saul was YHWH's choice, even changing him into a "another man" by an endowment of the Spirit for the task ahead. This is grace "in the beginning" for sure. After what appears to be an excellent start, however, cracks begin to occur in Saul and he ends up being thoroughly rejected because of his many disobediences. In fact, his whole line of succession is rejected.

In his farewell address Samuel shows he understands how this works. He starts on a positive note, charging the people to serve YHWH faithfully, because he is faithful:

> For Yahweh will not forsake his people for his great name's sake, because it has pleased Yahweh to make you a people for himself. (1 Sam 12:22)

At the same time he stresses the need for obedience if they themselves are to be part of this great future:

> Only fear Yahweh, and serve him in truth with all your heart; for consider what great things he has done for you. But if you keep doing evil, you will be consumed, both you and your king. (1 Sam 12:24–25)

As usual, there is some considerable tension in these statements: how can the nation be both "not forsaken" and "consumed"? Some of our difficulty is no doubt created by our modern preoccupation with the individual as opposed to the corporate. It is fairly clear that Samuel is saying that the present generation might indeed be destroyed but that the nation itself would somehow continue. This is exactly what happened during the forty years of wandering in the desert. You will never catch YHWH simply winking at disobedience. There is a price to pay. Just ask David.

A careful reading of what happens with David and Solomon may also help us to understand how this tension might be resolved. We begin by noting that David is so unlikely a candidate for king that his father doesn't even consider him a possible choice. But he is not completely without merit as the narrative emphasizes that YHWH chooses him because of his inner qualities. If the choice of David is not a matter of grace alone, the opposite is true of the covenant that YHWH establishes with him: even disobedience cannot dissolve it:

> . . .Yahweh will make you a house. When your days are fulfilled, and you sleep with your fathers, I will set up your offspring after you. . . If he commits iniquity, I will chasten him with the rod of men, and with the stripes of the children of men; but my loving kindness will not depart from him. . .Your house and your kingdom will be made sure forever before you. Your throne will be established forever. (excerpts taken from 2 Sam 7:11–16)

From this it seems that disobedience will result in some kind of punishment but it will not negate the Promise itself: it will endure regardless.

However, just to make things more complicated, in his charge to Solomon, David himself seems to interpret this Promise in a conditional sense:

> . . .keep the instruction of Yahweh your God, to walk in his ways, . . . Then Yahweh may establish his word which he spoke concerning me, saying, 'If your children are careful of their way, to walk before me in truth with all their heart and with all their soul, there shall not fail you,' he said, 'a man on the throne of Israel.' (1 Kgs 2:3–4)[28]

The same perspective is seen in YHWH's word to Solomon:

> . . . if you will walk in my statutes, and execute my ordinances, and keep all my commandments to walk in them; then I will establish my word with you, which I spoke to David your father. I will dwell among the children of Israel, and will not forsake my people Israel. (1 Kgs 6:12–13)

While both of these warnings could be taken to mean only that *Solomon's* line would be disinherited and that the succession would shift to the line of another "son of David," YHWH then expands on this promise after the temple is dedicated:

> But if you turn away from following me, you or your children, . . .but go and serve other gods, and worship them; then I will cut off Israel out of the land which I have given them; and I will cast this house, which I have made holy for my name, out of my sight; and Israel will be a proverb and a byword among all peoples. (1 Kgs 9:6–7)

This seems even more like the Promise to David could come to naught. But, again, the penalty for disobedience is not total annihilation by YHWH, but banishment from the Land and a rejection of the temple as the place of his Presence. The nation will continue to exist but as a kind of negative example for the nations. This may leave open the possibility that a day of restoration might come.

Finally, Solomon presents us with an actual case of serious disobedience and it is instructive simply to observe how the covenant works in practice:

---

28. Cf. Ps 132:11–12, which also stresses the conditionality of the Davidic covenant.

> Therefore Yahweh said to Solomon, "Because this is done by you, and you have not kept my covenant and my statutes, which I have commanded you, I will surely tear the kingdom from you, and will give it to your servant. Nevertheless, I will not do it in your days, for David your father's sake; but I will tear it out of your son's hand. However I will not tear away all the kingdom; but I will give one tribe to your son, for David my servant's sake, and for Jerusalem's sake which I have chosen." (1 Kgs 11:11–13)

Although terrible consequences are incurred, Solomon's disobedience does not negate the covenant. Instead, it seems underwritten by YHWH's own choice of both David and Jerusalem. However, he tells Jeroboam that it is also due to David's keeping of the divine Law (1 Kgs 11:34). He then says that he is not bringing Solomon's line to a complete end:

> . . . that David my servant may have a lamp always before me in Jerusalem, the city which I have chosen for myself to put my name there. (1 Kgs 11:36)

Once again, as we have noted in connection with Abraham, one man's obedience seems to outweigh the disobedience of the generations that follow.[29]

The reader is simply left to wonder how all this fits together. How can a promise depend on obedience and at the same time be guaranteed? Is this another of those Hebrew "both/and" situations? And for how long and for how many can one man's obedience suffice? However we might seek to resolve these tensions, it is clear that grace and obedience are not so much polarities as they are somehow fellow travelers.

A further clue as to how this relationship might work may be discerned in the way this narrative continues a theme that began with the story of Noah. There it was made clear that the real cause of disobedience lies in the evil human heart and that a cleaned-up environment did not offer a cure. What is really needed is a changed heart.[30]

The call of Abraham and the provision of the Law of Moses can be seen as movements toward this end. The former sets forth absolutely that blessing will come and the latter seems to provide the means by which it does so. Instructed to love YHWH with all their heart and to have the Law in their hearts, the Israelites seem to be provided with the tools to get the job done. In fact, the wilderness experience was designed:

> . . .that he might humble you, to test you, to know what was in your heart, whether you would keep his commandments or not. (Deut 8:2)

Unfortunately, they not only failed that test but every subsequent one as well. Even with the provision of the Law and the Land the heart still has clearly not yet been

---

29. See 107, above.
30. See 54, above.

renovated. Moses himself knew this and looked forward to a day in which YHWH would "circumcise the hearts" of Israel, enabling them, finally, to keep the Law.[31]

David may represent an interesting exception to the rule.[32] YHWH looks "at the heart" of the young man and is pleased that he finds "a man after his own heart."[33] This is what he has been looking for all along. But his son Solomon, in spite of a great beginning, demonstrates that he has not inherited his father's heart:

> When Solomon was old, his wives turned away his heart after other gods; and his heart was not perfect with Yahweh his God, as the heart of David his father was. (1 Kings 11:4)

And so we are back to square one. It has become clear that a long obedience can only arise out of a heart that is changed from its sinful orientation. It is also clear that this change can only come from YHWH himself. At the height of his wisdom Solomon asks of YHWH:

> ...that he may incline our hearts to him, to walk in all his ways, and to keep his commandments, and his statutes, and his ordinances, which he commanded our fathers.. (1 Kgs 8:58)

By the end of Solomon's reign the Story has already begun its descent into the depressing era of the divided kingdom and the reader is left wondering when (or if) YHWH will answer this plea.

We are, however, put further on notice in this section that the Spirit of God will have something to do with this needed change of heart. Saul was endowed with the Spirit upon being anointed king and he became able to do the job. Although he was not fully obedient as a result, when the Spirit was removed from him he fell completely away from following YHWH. David was also powerfully endowed by the Spirit at his anointing. Perhaps because he already had a heart after God, this was enough to keep him from falling or bring him back when he did.

For our present purposes, however, it simply needs to be observed that if disobedience arises from our evil heart and only God can provide a changed heart, then, in the end, our obedience is in God's hands and a matter of grace. From this perspective it could be argued that they are two sides of the same coin. Heads or tails, we win.

---

31. See 132, above.
32. And perhaps also Joseph: see 106, above.
33. 1 Sam 16:7 and 13:14, respectively.

13

Israel Under the Kings (Part Two)
The "House" of Jeroboam

Suggested Reading

Portions of 1 Kings 12–2 Kings 17; Hosea; Amos; Jonah. Note: The two books of Kings use interweaving segments to tell the stories of Israel and Judah after they became separate nations. For purposes of this chapter those segments dealing with "Israel" only should be read, as referenced in the captions of "The Story" sections below. This can most easily be done by scanning the text and using a highlighter to mark the Northern portions before reading.

MAJOR DEVELOPMENTS

- Jeroboam reigns twenty-two years after he rebels against Solomon's son Rehoboam and takes the ten Northern tribes out of the union, becoming the first king of "Israel" as distinct from "Judah"

- Jeroboam also takes the Northern tribes further away from YHWH, setting the standard for his successors at a very low level

- After Jeroboam's son Nadab reigns only two years, Baasha (twenty-four years) seizes the throne and destroys all of Jeroboam's family

- Baasha's son Elah reigns only two years when Zimri seizes the throne and destroys all of Baasha's family and is in turn killed immediately by Omri (twelve years), who becomes the new king and makes Samaria the capital

- Omri's son Ahab reigns twenty-two years and builds a temple for Baal in Samaria

Israel Under the Kings (Part Two)

- Elijah appears and announces a YHWH-induced drought brought on by the king's great evils
- Elijah retreats to the wilderness, is cared for by a widow, and then restores her son to life
- Elijah demonstrates the clear superiority of YHWH over Baal before the nation on Mt. Carmel
- Queen Jezebel seeks to kill Elijah who flees to the wilderness where he has an encounter with YHWH on Mt. Horeb (Sinai)
- Ahab dies in battle and his son Ahaziah (one year) succeeds him and continues along the same wayward path
- Ahaziah dies sonless and his successor is another relative, Joram (twelve years)
- Elisha becomes Elijah's successor after the latter is taken up into heaven in a whirlwind
- Through miracles and successful predictions Elisha establishes himself as a "man of God," consulted by kings in times of crisis
- Jehu (twenty-eight years) assassinates Joram in a bloody coup in which Jezebel is killed, along with all the royal house and the remaining prophets of Baal
- Jehu, his son Jehoahaz (seventeen years), and grandson Jehoash (sixteen years) all fail to follow YHWH
- Elisha dies with no successor
- Amos and Hosea proclaim their messages of warning and hope
- Jehoash is followed by his son Jeroboam II (forty-one years) and then, after a very brief reign the latter's son Zechariah is murdered by Shallum who is himself almost immediately killed
- Menahem (ten years) is the new king who bribes the invading Assyrian emperor in order to spare the nation
- Pekah (twenty years) takes the throne after murdering Menahem's son Pekahiah (two years) and then invades Judah with some success
- Assyria invades Israel again, resulting in serious loss of people and territory
- Pekah loses his life to Hoshea (nine years) in yet another coup
- Assyria invades for the final time, utterly defeating the nation and scattering most of its inhabitants throughout its vast empire
- "Israel" is no more

PERSPECTIVES

Introduction

The united kingdom of Israel is unraveling even as Solomon descends to his grave. His son Rehoboam immediately blunders his way into reigniting the failed rebellion of Jeroboam. As a result, only the two southern tribes of Judah and Benjamin remain loyal to David's line while the rest form a separate kingdom under Jeroboam.

It is a critical moment in the life of Israel: from this point on it is a divided nation, the North retaining the name "Israel" and the South becoming "Judah." In 1 & 2 Kings their stories are told in a complicated overlapping narrative with each new king in one "half" dated in relation to the rule of the king in the other.[1] The account then goes back and forth between the two nations, making it extremely difficult to follow.

While confusing for the reader, this way of telling the story does make the point that the nation, while divided politically, is still one people. This consciousness is maintained in the biblical narrative even after the northern kingdom of Israel actually ceases to exist.

For the sake of clarity, this chapter will for the most part tell the story of "Israel" in isolation from that of Judah. The next chapter will reverse the process, recounting only what happens to the Southern kingdom. In this way their respective stories form parts two and three of the Israelite experience of kingly rule.

Prophets Up, Royalties Down

Focusing on the story of the Northern tribes reveals how the role of "prophet" grows into its classical form during this period. While political/military/religious leadership certainly remains firmly in the hands of the monarchy, Israel is still a theocracy, under the ultimate rule of YHWH.

Partly because her kings in this period were often extremely sinful, the focus of the Story turns away from the kings toward the prophets who emerge as YHWH's action heroes, often called to confront a wayward monarch. Indeed, long sections of the narrative are given over to their adventures, especially those of Elijah and Elisha. Serving as the conscience of the nation, the prophets have direct contact with YHWH while the kings do not, usually having to consult these holy men in order to know the will of YHWH. It is often an uneasy relationship, to put it mildly, and things get complicated as a result.

---

1. This starts at 1 Kgs 15:1 and continues until the Fall of the North recounted in 2 Kgs 17.

Covenant Mechanics

In this period the role of prophet is taken to the next level: they become full-fledged "covenant prosecutors," proclaiming the specific details of YHWH's case against the nation. They also pronounce the "sentence" that can be expected unless national repentance is forthcoming. Both "case" and "sentence" are defined in terms of the Law of Moses, calling the nation back to covenant faithfulness. In this sense, in contrast to their image as wild men on the fringe of society, they are quite conservative.

In fact, they are simply working within the "covenant mechanism" we have discussed earlier.[2] Under the terms of the Mosaic covenant, obedience would result in Blessings while disobedience would result in Curses. As we have also noted, YHWH exercises considerable forbearance with his wayward flock and this renders the "mechanism" somewhat less mechanical than the name implies! The Curses do not rain down immediately upon them as we might expect. YHWH proves himself a patient and merciful God, not rushing to condemn, but extending every opportunity for repentance. But eventually he does act in judgment, as the following lament sadly bears witness:

> Yet Yahweh testified to Israel, and to Judah, by every prophet, and every seer, saying, "Turn from your evil ways, and keep my commandments and my statutes, according to all the law which I commanded your fathers, and which I sent to you by my servants the prophets." Notwithstanding, they would not listen, but hardened their neck, like the neck of their fathers, who didn't believe in Yahweh their God. They rejected his statutes, and his covenant that he made with their fathers, and his testimonies which he testified to them; and they followed vanity, and became vain... (2 Kgs 17:13–15a [my emphasis])

That last phrase would be a fitting epitaph to inscribe on the nation's tombstone and a fair warning to all who come after.

But is a tombstone really necessary? It certainly is for now. At the end of this period the covenant between YHWH and the people of the Northern kingdom lies utterly shattered. The nation has been vomited out of the Land as Moses himself had warned (Lev 18:28; 20:22). Amos and Hosea, however, both speak of life beyond the death of exile. In so doing they explicitly cling to another covenant that could not be broken: YHWH had established David's house forever (Hosea 3:5; Amos 9:11). Their hope of an eventual return to a renewed Land is rooted in this promise, a promise that is in turn connected to the primary Covenant made with Abraham, as we have seen.[3] These continue in effect, even and especially in these miserable circumstances.[4]

---

2. See 129–30, above
3. See 214–15, above.
4. Cf. 2 Kgs 13:23.

Amos and Hosea are also among the first of what are called the "literary prophets." Earlier prophets (e.g., Elijah and Elisha) have both their activities and their messages recorded entirely within a larger historical narrative (1 and 2 Kings). The literary prophets tend to appear only briefly, if at all, in the narrative portions of the Bible, but their messages were written down and gathered into the books that bear their names. These contain clues that allow us to locate a prophet's approximate place in the Story, and this, in turn, enables us to obtain his divinely inspired perspective on the events of the period.

A Curse on Jeroboam's "House"

The narrative focuses, first of all, on an unrelenting series of seriously wayward kings who lead this part of the nation to its ultimate demise. It is a depressing tale that begins and ends, in a way, with their first king, Jeroboam.

As the instrument of YHWH's punishment upon the wrongdoing of Solomon, Jeroboam does not thereby automatically qualify as "righteous." Indeed, YHWH charges the new king with doing "evil above all who were before you" (1 Kgs 14:9). This is not to be taken as an exaggeration because the punishment is equally extreme. Not only will his entire line be exterminated, but also "Israel" itself will eventually be removed from the Land and scattered to the wind. In no uncertain terms he is informed that this disaster is a result of the sins (idolatry, especially) into which he leads the nation.[5]

Like the sound of a church bell slowly tolling at a funeral, this judgment hangs like a pall over the nation. It rings out for no less than fifteen of Jeroboam's nineteen successors. Here, for example, is how it sounded for Omri:

> For he walked in all the way of Jeroboam the son of Nebat, and in his sins with which he made Israel to sin, to provoke Yahweh, the God of Israel, to anger with their vanities. (1 Kgs 16:26)

It becomes evident that this story should not be read as if "Israel," starting with Jeroboam, enters into a downward spiral of increasing sin until YHWH is finally provoked to act. Rather, her first king's excessive sin plunges the nation directly into the abyss, from which none of the subsequent kings are able to escape. Only YHWH's forbearance restrains immediate destruction in each reign. It is the story of the Fall, all over again. And the result is the same: removal from the garden.

> . . .and Jeroboam drove Israel from following Yahweh, and made them sin a great sin. The children of Israel walked in all the sins of Jeroboam which he did; they didn't depart from them until Yahweh removed Israel out of his

---

5. Cf. 1 Kgs 14:14–16, fitting the pattern of "as goes the king, so goes the nation."

sight, as he said by all his servants the prophets. So Israel was carried away out of their own land to Assyria to this day. (2 Kgs 17:21–23)

That is why this chapter is entitled "The 'House' of Jeroboam." Of all the kings of Israel, only one was Jeroboam's actual physical descendent. However, in taking care to "relate" the other kings of Israel to his apostasy, the narrator invites us to understand that they all shared his spiritual DNA and, in that sense, belong to the same royal "house" from its miserable beginning to its miserable end.

The Elijah/Elisha Cycle (1 Kgs 17:1–2 Kgs 13:21)

The second prominent feature of the account of the Northern kingdom is its central focus on the prophet Elijah and his successor, Elisha. Whereas the narrative is generally about the various kings with only incidental reference to a prophet, the reverse is true in this section. The camera has moved from the kings to zoom in on prophets for a relatively brief period. It is part of the same Story, but up close and personal with these men of God, while royal matters recede somewhat into the background.

Elijah is introduced during the reign of Ahab and his queen, the wicked Jezebel, and he immediately becomes the story's central character. An outsider who possesses a confrontational style, Elijah's recorded career is mostly set in the wilderness and he is depicted as wearing a distinctive garment of hair cinched with a leather belt. He is YHWH's champion in an age when God's people were largely given over to the worship of Baal and other idols. His message amounts to a constant call to repent, to change their behavior. However, the king and the nation continue in their wicked ways in spite of his exertions. Although he is ultimately unable to stem the tide of covenant unfaithfulness, his activities prepare the way for Elisha, his somewhat more successful apprentice.

Elisha asks Elijah for and receives a double portion of the spirit that had rested upon his mentor. It has been noted that in fact Elisha performs some twenty miracles as opposed to Elijah's ten. Of course, some of this may be due to the fact that the successor has a much longer career, spanning about fifty-two years, compared to the older prophet's twenty. The text also makes it clear that Elisha is essentially carrying on Elijah's ministry and in that sense he remains in the shadow of his master.

It is during Elisha's time that the worship of Baal (but not all idolatry) is temporarily eradicated, but he seems to have had little to do with this accomplishment. Indeed, Baal is just not on his agenda. Instead, he mostly acts as a divinely appointed political/military consultant and his many miracles serve to provide him with the necessary credentials for this role.

"A Prophet Like Me?"

It will be recalled that Moses had promised that YHWH would someday raise up a "prophet like me,"[6] an expectation that has not yet been fulfilled so far in the Story. It is interesting that a number of parallels can be drawn between Moses and Elijah, suggesting that Elijah might be the One. These would include:

- A sense that they alone remain faithful in an apostate nation
- Personal encounters with YHWH on Mt. Sinai/Horeb with fire and earthquakes in which their calls are confirmed
- Ringing calls for the nation to make up its mind and follow YHWH
- Spectacular demonstrations of YHWH's superiority over the gods of the nations
- Forty years/days in the wilderness upon being pursued by unconvinced royalty (Pharaoh/Ahab)
- Passing the mantle to a favored protégé who arguably has more success
- Failing to turn the nation around from disobedience and idolatry
- Parting the waters (Red Sea/Jordan) to cross on dry ground
- End of lives are unique and directly involve YHWH

At the very least these similarities invite us to compare Elijah favorably with Moses, even to consider him as the long-expected Serpent Crusher. Certainly he and Elisha are the only possible candidates in this otherwise depressing narrative, but it must be remembered that they themselves defer to Moses (or the Law). In the end, their triumphs prove only temporary and partial at best: the serpent still has the nation wrapped firmly in his coils.

Nevertheless, the master and the apprentice both have amazing careers, while, as befitting his status in the Story, Elijah enjoys a most spectacular departure from this world. Transported to heaven in a whirlwind and chariot of fire, no less, he remains permanently lodged in the imagination of the faithful, head and shoulders above many of the other Old Testament characters.

A "House" Built Upon the Sand

With Elisha's passing, the story of the Northern kings and their general unfaithfulness to YHWH resumes its monotonous downbeat. Altogether in the North, of its twenty monarchs, seven are assassinated, the perpetrator then attempting to establish his own dynasty. As a result, "Israel" never really develops a royal house and the sense of legitimacy that goes with it. The throne is available to the strongest contender from

---

6. Deut 18:15: cf. 34:10. See earlier discussion, 147, above.

among the people. To say that all of this contributes to a sense of underlying instability would be a serious understatement.

It could not last. By the reign of Hoshea, Israel is under the thumb of Assyria and when its emperor discovers that Israel's king is conspiring with the king of Egypt and refusing to pay tribute, the writing is on the wall. The end comes when the capital, Samaria, is attacked and falls to the Assyrians. In accordance with Assyrian policy, most of the people are deported and scattered throughout the far reaches of the empire while other conquered peoples are brought in to replace them in the Land. The desired effect is to destroy any continuing sense of national identity in order to ensure that the conquered peoples would never rise again against imperial rule.

Those Israelites who remain intermarry with the importees and create the people that would become the "Samaritans" of the New Testament. They develop a religion based on the five books of Moses and eventually build a temple at Mt. Gerizim in opposition to the one at Jerusalem. In doing so, were they were claiming for themselves the Blessings for obedience that were proclaimed from those same slopes when the Israelites entered the Promised Land under Joshua?[7]

The Ten Lost Tribes?

These events have led to the development of a number of legends regarding what happened to the so-called "ten lost tribes" of Northern Israel. Intriguing though many of these speculations may be, they are also mutually contradictory. Besides, in reality, these tribes never did totally vanish into thin air with the Assyrian deportations.

It is true that as a political entity the Northern tribes ceased to exist at this time. However, there is evidence that, out of loyalty to the house of David, some of their members had already ended up in Judah shortly after Solomon's death.[8] Many others appear to have come to the South as refugees to escape the Assyrian invasion.[9] Later, during the reign of Josiah of Judah, it is mentioned that money was received for the repair of the temple from "the people of Manasseh, Ephraim and the entire remnant of Israel."[10]

St. Luke also mentions that Anna the prophetess, who recognized the infant Jesus as Messiah, was from the tribe of Asher.[11] So seven hundred years after its fall, there were Israelites who could still trace their identity to the Northern tribes. Their DNA no doubt continues to live on in modern Jews and their history may still await its final chapter.

---

7. .Deut 27:12–13; Josh. 8:30–33. See also 178, above.
8. 2 Chr 11:13–17 and 15:9.
9. Cf. Burke, "Anthropological."
10. 2 Chr 34:9.
11. Luke 2:36.

THE STORY

Going to the Dogs (One): Jeroboam–Omri (1 Kgs 12:1—14:20; 15:25—16:27)

After his successful rebellion against Solomon's son Rehoboam, Jeroboam quickly institutes idolatrous religious practices in his new Northern kingdom by setting up golden calves in Bethel and Dan as alternatives to the worship of YHWH in Jerusalem. This proves such an affront to YHWH that he sends a prophet named Ahijah to the king with a terrifying pronouncement:

> ...[you] have done evil above all who were before you, and have gone and made for yourself other gods, molten images, to provoke me to anger, and have cast me behind your back; therefore, behold, I will bring evil on the house of Jeroboam, and will cut off from Jeroboam everyone who urinates on a wall, he who is shut up and he who is left at large in Israel, and will utterly sweep away the house of Jeroboam, as a man sweeps away dung, until it is all gone. The dogs will eat he who belongs to Jeroboam who dies in the city; and the birds of the sky will eat he who dies in the field: for Yahweh has spoken it. (1 Kgs 14:9–11)

YHWH may have spoken, but Jeroboam is clearly not listening: he continues his defiant ways for his entire reign of twenty-two years. When he dies, apparently of natural causes, we have a forbidding sense of unfinished business between YHWH and his house.

Although no specifics are given about his reign, Jeroboam's son Nadab lasts only two years before he and all of Jeroboam's family are killed by a usurper named Baasha. The text is silent about the dogs and the birds, but the reader's imagination can fill in the blanks.

Baasha's twenty-six-year reign is marked by apostasy and continual war with Judah. The prophet Jehu is sent to him with a familiar message:

> Because I exalted you out of the dust, and made you prince over my people Israel, and you have walked in the way of Jeroboam, and have made my people Israel to sin, to provoke me to anger with their sins; behold, I will utterly sweep away Baasha and his house; and I will make your house like the house of Jeroboam the son of Nebat. The dogs will eat Baasha's descendants who die in the city; and he who dies of his in the field, the birds of the sky will eat. (1 Kgs 16:2–4)

He, too, seems to come to a natural end and is buried in the usual fashion. However, after reigning only two years, his son Elah is assassinated by one of his officials named Zimri. The latter exterminates Baasha's remaining family just as Baasha himself had done to the house of Jeroboam. Again, it doesn't take much imagination to hear the snarling of dogs.

Zimri, in turn, lasts only seven days in office before dying in a battle with the vengeful Omri, who had been Elah's army chief. Omri takes the throne for the next seven years during which he establishes the city of Samaria as the capital. Subsequently, the Northern kingdom is sometimes called "Samaria."

Going to the Dogs (Two): Elijah vs. Ahab and Jezebel (1 Kgs 17:1–22:40, 2 Kgs 22:51–52; 2 Kgs 1:1–2:14)

Israel Baals on YHWH

Omri's son Ahab bears the dubious distinction of sinking even lower than Jeroboam! This takes some doing, but he manages it by marrying the daughter of a pagan king and beginning to worship Baal, even building a temple for him right in Samaria. This god is chief among the old deities of Canaan and now his worship is conducted right in the very heart of Israel. Baal supposedly controls rain and fertility and, in an environment that has few natural sources of water and uncertain rainfall, such a god must be appeased, even to the extent of child sacrifice.[12]

Elijah Pronounces a Drought

Such is the context for the adventures of the prophet Elijah. Originally from the northern Transjordan area of Gilead, he abruptly appears in the text to confront the apostate Ahab:

> As Yahweh, the God of Israel, lives, before whom I stand, there shall not be dew nor rain these years, but according to my word. (1 Kgs 17:1)

By demonstrating that he, not Baal, controls the rain, YHWH is essentially reasserting his claim to be Israel's God. Just as the plagues of Egypt were proclaiming YHWH's superiority over the gods of Egypt, this drought is sending the same message to the Israelites and King Ahab regarding the gods of Canaan.

Elijah Brings Life

Sent by YHWH into the wilderness for the duration of the famine, Elijah is fed by ravens and drinks from a brook until the water supply dries up. After that, he arranges to stay with a widow by providing her with a miraculous supply of flour and oil that does not run out until it starts to rain again. When her son unexpectedly dies, Elijah appeals to YHWH for the child:

> Yahweh listened to the voice of Elijah; and the soul of the child came into him again, and he revived. Elijah took the child, and brought him down out

---

12. See Cundall, "Baal," I:431–33.

of the room into the house, and delivered him to his mother; and Elijah said, "Behold, your son lives." (1 Kgs 17:22–23)

It is difficult to read this text without thinking of the utter contrast between deities: Baal demands the death of children, but YHWH restores them to life.

The Hour of Decision

After three years of drought it is time to bring things to a head. YHWH instructs Elijah to go to the king once more:

> When Ahab saw Elijah, Ahab said to him, "Is that you, you troubler of Israel?" He answered, "I have not troubled Israel; but you, and your father's house, in that you have forsaken Yahweh's commandments, and you have followed the Baals. Now therefore send, and gather to me all Israel to Mount Carmel, and four hundred fifty of the prophets of Baal, and four hundred of the prophets of the Asherah, who eat at Jezebel's table." (1 Kgs 18:17–19)

What follows sharply brings to mind Moses calling upon the Israelites, about to enter the Promised Land, to "choose life" (Deut 30:19–20):

> Elijah came near to all the people, and said, "How long will you waver between the two sides? If Yahweh is God, follow him; but if Baal, then follow him."
> The people didn't say a word. (1 Kgs 18:21)

This noncommittal response is a truly worrying contrast to their ancestors' immediate commitment to follow YHWH.

All Fired Up

Elijah then sets up a test to determine whether it is YHWH or Baal who is truly God: the deity who lights a sacrificial fire solely at the invocation of his prophet will prove himself. A very colorful account then follows, in which the impotency of Baal is dramatically exposed. His prophets are unable to start the fire in spite of appealing to him in most theatrical fashion. Audaciously, Elijah then soaks the altar of YHWH with water and implores him before the assembled masses:

> "Yahweh, the God of Abraham, of Isaac, and of Israel, let it be known today that you are God in Israel, and that I am your servant, and that I have done all these things at your word. Hear me, Yahweh, hear me, that this people may know that you, Yahweh, are God, and that you have turned their heart back again."
> Then Yahweh's fire fell, and consumed the burnt offering, the wood, the stones, and the dust, and licked up the water that was in the trench. (1 Kgs 18:36–38)

This awesome display results in a serious return to YHWH and leads to what appears to be a rooting out of Baalism in the Northern kingdom. Elijah has all of Baal's prophets immediately destroyed and one would think that would be enough to seal the deal. However, a little later, during the time of Elisha, another terrible purge is again necessary. What we have here is "covenant renewal lite." As usual.

Encountering YHWH in the Wilderness

Meanwhile, after the fire consumes the waterlogged altar it finally begins to rain, ending the drought and confirming once again the superior power of YHWH over Baal. Jezebel, seeing her god humiliated and his prophets killed, turns her malevolent gaze towards the now fearful Elijah. Once again he escapes into the wilderness where, suffering from a bout of depression, an angel provides him both spiritual and bodily refreshment. Strengthened, he travels forty days and forty nights until he reaches Horeb, the mountain of God and there retreats into a cave.

There, hidden in the rock, YHWH finds him and asks him what he is doing there. Elijah replies:

> I have been very jealous for Yahweh, the God of Armies; for the children of Israel have forsaken your covenant, thrown down your altars, and killed your prophets with the sword. I, even I only, am left; and they seek my life, to take it away. (1 Kgs 19:10)

In spite of an unmistakable note of self-pity in this answer, YHWH "appears" to Elijah in a "still small voice" (1 Kgs 19:12) following a mighty wind and a shattering earthquake. Elijah is instructed to anoint three men for office: Hazael as king of Aram, Jehu as king of Israel, and Elisha as his own successor prophet. He is assured of the utter destruction of Ahab and his house at the hands of these men.

It is also revealed to him that he is not alone in his devotion to YHWH: seven thousand faithful remain in Israel. While this number may have been of some comfort to Elijah in his loneliness, as a tiny fraction of the total population it is a stark measure of how far Israel had sunk into the worship of Baal. And this so soon after the triumph on Mt. Carmel! Shortly after this Elijah encounters Elisha plowing with the family oxen and, throwing his mantle over the younger man, he takes him on as his protégé. Maybe things will take a turn for the better.

Ahab's Last Days

Meanwhile Ben-Haddad, the king of Aram (Syria/Damascus), attacks Israel in two successive years and is defeated by YHWH and the army of Israel on each occasion. However, an anonymous prophet tells Ahab that he will die and Israel will be defeated because he let Ben-Haddad go free after capturing him.

Ahab then murders a man named Naboth in order to confiscate his vineyard. Elijah enters the picture again to condemn him for doing such a wicked thing:

> 'Yahweh says, "In the place where dogs licked the blood of Naboth, dogs will lick your blood, even yours." (1 Kgs 21:19)

And also concerning his wife and all who were his, YHWH utters the same sentence:

> The dogs will eat Jezebel by the rampart of Jezreel. The dogs will eat he who dies of Ahab in the city; and the birds of the sky will eat he who dies in the field. (1 Kgs 21:23–24)

All this finally gets through to Ahab and he humbles himself before YHWH, delaying the predicted disaster for an entire generation.

After three years of peace, Ahab incites Jehoshaphat, the king of Judah, to join him in attacking Ben-Haddad in order to regain the city of Ramoth Gilead that was in the territory of Manasseh across the Jordan. In spite of a gloomy prediction by a faithful prophet named Macaiah, the two armies attack Aram and are routed by the enemy. But not before Ahab himself is mortally wounded by one of their archers.

So dies the king. His body is brought to Samaria and buried there, while his bloody chariot is washed at a pool in Samaria (where the prostitutes bathed). There the dogs lick up his blood, as the word of YHWH had declared.

That same word had condemned his family as well and when his son Ahaziah takes the throne the reader has an expectancy of impending judgment. This is amplified when we are informed that the new king reestablishes Baal worship, provoking YHWH to anger. Upon injuring himself seriously in a fall, Ahaziah attempts to consult the pagan god Baal-Zebub, but Elijah intervenes and tells him that he is not going to recover. He subsequently dies and, having no sons, the throne passes to his brother Joram. Jezebel still lives, but you can hear the dogs beginning to howl again.

Chariot of Fire/Cloak of Succession

In the meantime, we have the account of the amazing last moments of Elijah's earthly life. His departure is as much unprecedented as it is dazzling. Even Moses's mysterious burial by YHWH himself absolutely pales in comparison.

The story also emphasizes the continuity between Elijah's ministry and that of Elisha, who stubbornly refuses to leave his master's side until the end. The two prophets reach the Jordan and, after Elijah strikes it with the same cloak he had thrown over Elisha earlier, they cross over on dry ground. The drama heightens:

> When they had gone over, Elijah said to Elisha, "Ask what I shall do for you, before I am taken from you."

Elisha said, "Please let a double portion of your spirit be on me."[13]

He said, "You have asked a hard thing. If you see me when I am taken from you, it will be so for you; but if not, it will not be so."

As they continued on and talked, behold, a chariot of fire and horses of fire separated them, and Elijah went up by a whirlwind into heaven. Elisha saw it, and he cried, "My father, my father, the chariots of Israel and its horsemen!"

He saw him no more. Then he took hold of his own clothes, and tore them in two pieces. He also took up Elijah's mantle that fell from him, and went back, and stood by the bank of the Jordan. He took Elijah's mantle that fell from him, and struck the waters, and said, "Where is Yahweh, the God of Elijah?" When he also had struck the waters, they were divided apart, and Elisha went over. (2 Kgs 2:9–14)

The mantle had fallen upon a worthy successor.

Going to the Dogs (Three): Elisha and the End of Jezebel (2 Kgs 2:15—10:27)

As expected, Elisha becomes the new "head prophet" in Israel. While a number of his deeds may resemble those of his mentor, from the get-go he comes across as more aggressive, never suffering from self-pity or depression. His role as a kind of military advisor to the king of Israel is highlighted and this too sets him apart from Elijah.

He seems to excel in performing miracles that both meet some immediate need and also establish his credentials as a true "man of God":

- In response to a plea from a fellow prophet's widow he miraculously provides her with enough oil to live on and pay her way out of debt (cf. Elijah and the widow's unfailing oil and flour)
- At Shunem he assures a childless woman of a son and then raises him to life later (cf. Elijah's raising the son of the widow of Zarephath)
- At a meeting of the prophets he restores some stew to make it edible
- He multiplies some loaves in order to feed one hundred men and has some left over
- He is instrumental in the healing of Naaman, the leprous commander of the army of Aram (this story, one of the best in the Bible, is beautifully told in 2 Kgs 5)
- When a prophet's borrowed axhead falls into the Jordan, Elisha simply makes it float to the surface

---

13. This should not necessarily be taken as meaning that Elisha desired to have twice as much of Elijah's spiritual power. Rather, it probably refers to the "double portion" of the eldest son as prescribed in the Law (Deut 21:17). As such he would "carry on (Elijah's) name and work." Wiseman, *1 and 2 Kings*, 195.

Elisha's predictions come true again and again, sometimes overlapping with the fulfillment of Elijah's prophecies as they work themselves out. YHWH is unmistakably (still) in control of the course of history.

Joram, the second of Ahab's sons to be king, is now ruling the Northern kingdom. In order to quash a rebellion by his vassal Moab (east of the southern Dead Sea) he allies himself with Edom (even further south) and Judah. When the army runs out of water Elisha is consulted with the result that abundant water is miraculously provided and Moab is devastated.

Later, Elisha's advice to the king of Israel is so effective against Aram (Syria) in the north that its ruler is convinced he must have a spy in his midst. As one of his officers tells him:

> No, my lord, O king; but Elisha, the prophet who is in Israel, tells the king of Israel the words that you speak in your bedroom. (2 Kgs 6:12)

And when Elisha's servant shakes in fear at the superior number of enemy troops, the prophet appeals to YHWH:

> "Yahweh, please open his eyes, that he may see." Yahweh opened the young man's eyes; and he saw: and behold, the mountain was full of horses and chariots of fire around Elisha. (2 Kgs 6:16–17)

This is reminiscent of God telling Elijah there were still seven thousand faithful in Israel. On this occasion, Elisha calls upon YHWH to intervene and the Arameans, are blinded and captured (surely an irony, given the servant's experience).

After a few more such adventures, Elisha arranges for Jehu to be anointed king while Joram is still on the throne. In this he is completing the task set for Elijah some time earlier.[14] Jehu personally kills Joram along with Ahaziah, king of Judah, who is with him, and then has Jezebel, who had survived all this time, thrown to her death from a window in the wall of Jezreel. The dogs are there, impatiently waiting to devour her flesh even before she lands.

Jehu has all seventy sons of the house of Ahab murdered and then himself kills any offspring who are left over. It is a total bloodbath that is only finished when all of the ministers of Baal who remain in the land are also slaughtered. So ends what Elijah had begun on Mount Carmel and the circle is now complete. But it is filled to the brim with blood.

End of an Era (2 Kgs 10:28–36; 13:1–25)

All is not well as it seems the ghost of Jeroboam continues to haunt the Land:

---

14. Cf. 1 Kgs 19:16.

> Jehu destroyed Baal out of Israel. However, Jehu didn't depart from the sins of Jeroboam the son of Nebat, with which he made Israel to sin, the golden calves that were in Bethel and that were in Dan. But Jehu took no heed to walk in the law of Yahweh, the God of Israel, with all his heart. (2 Kgs 10:28–29; 31)

YHWH promises Jehu, however, that because he had carried out his will in regard to the house of Ahab, his dynasty will last four generations. His son Jehoahaz succeeds him and, while he does evil he also seeks and receives YHWH's favor when Aram is once again causing problems. This fails to change the basic waywardness of the king, however, and even worse, his son Jehoash follows in his father's footsteps.

At this point Elisha becomes seriously ill and dies. It is worth noting that Elisha's passing is entirely unremarkable: there is no sensational departure, no chariot, no whirlwind, and, sadly, no successor. But after he dies a dead person revives after coming into contact with his bones, as if Elisha has to get in the last word: "See, I too was a man of God."

And it is true: even in the shadow of the great Elijah, Elisha comes across as a major figure in his own right. Together the two men were a powerful tag team, wrestling with hydra-headed forces of evil. Unfortunately, the tide of idolatry has continued to rise in spite of their best efforts.

The Good News According to Amos (Amos)

With the passing of Elijah and Elisha from the scene, the narrative of the Northern kingdom reverts to its almost exclusive focus on the activities of the kings. But this does not mean that prophets were inactive during this period. During the reign of Jeroboam II, Amos and Hosea proclaim their messages, as recorded in the separate books now bearing their names. These writings offer glimpses of YHWH's perspective on the dramatic events of Israel's final years.[15]

If Elijah and Elisha focused their attention on the kings and their fostering of idolatry in the Land, Amos confronts the nation as a whole for its gross abandonment of the moral aspects of the Law even while maintaining the ceremonial ones. Proper religious observance, it is clear, does not meet the demands of the Almighty:

> I hate, I despise your feasts,
>   and I can't stand your solemn assemblies.
> Yes, though you offer me your burnt offerings and meal offerings,
>   I will not accept them;
>   neither will I regard the peace offerings of your fat animals.
> Take away from me the noise of your songs!

---

15. Jonah is another prophet who appears incidentally in this narrative. His story, of course, is told in the book of Jonah, but it is focused upon what happens when God calls him to preach repentance to Nineveh, the capital of the rising power of Assyria, and thus contributes little to our understanding of this period in Israel itself.

> I will not listen to the music of your harps.
> But let justice roll on like rivers,
>   and righteousness like a mighty stream. (Amos 5:21–24)

Lifting his eyes beyond the immediate issues of the day, Amos sees the big picture: the habitual ethical waywardness of both Israel and the nations is going to result in a great and terrible "day of YHWH" from which there will be no escape.[16] YHWH has held up the famous "plumb line" (probably to be understood as the Law) to Israel and found her to be well out of true (7:7–8). At the same time, the prophet proclaims that this coming "Day" will also be part of an amazing restoration of Israel to the Land, itself transformed, as the Davidic "house" rises again:

> On that day I will raise up the tent of David who is fallen, and close up its breaches, and I will raise up its ruins, and I will build it as in the days of old;
>
> > I will bring my people Israel back from captivity,
> >   and they will rebuild the ruined cities, and inhabit them;
> >   and they will plant vineyards, and drink wine from them.
> > They shall also make gardens,
> >   and eat their fruit.
> > I will plant them on their land,
> >   and they will no more be plucked up out of their land which I have given them... (9:11, 14–15)

Good news! It is true that terrible things lie ahead because of disobedience to the Law, but that is not the end of the Story. Instead, YHWH will be faithful to his Promises in the End.

The Good News According to Hosea (Hosea)

Active about the same time as Amos, Hosea sees the same situation through a different lens: his own marriage to a prostitute. YHWH's relationship with Israel is likened to that of a faithful man who has a wayward wife. Hosea is instructed to love her anyway in order to show God's steadfast love for Israel in spite of her utter disregard of the covenant entered into at Mt. Sinai. But, as we have previously noted, "you don't have to keep a promise to be a Promise Keeper."[17] Although a terrible "Day" of punishment of the nation is foreseen (1:5; 10:15), after a period of exile from YHWH and the Land there will be reconciliation and restoration under a Davidic king:

> For the children of Israel shall live many days without king, and without prince, and without sacrifice, and without sacred stone, and without ephod or idols. Afterward the children of Israel shall return, and seek Yahweh their

---

16. See esp. 5:18–27.
17. See 107, above.

God, and David their king, and shall come with trembling to Yahweh and to his blessings in the last days. (3:4–5)

Hosea also describes a future covenant that YHWH will make with Israel that will extend even to the animal kingdom while peace and safety reign supreme in a fruitful Land.

> In that day I will make a covenant for them with the animals of the field,
>   and with the birds of the sky,
>   and with the creeping things of the ground.
> I will break the bow, the sword, and the battle out of the land,
>   and will make them lie down safely.
> I will betroth you to me forever.
>   Yes, I will betroth you to me in righteousness, in justice, in loving kindness, and in compassion. (2:18–19)

Using the language of covenant, YHWH says:

> I will sow her to me in the earth;
>   and I will have mercy on her who had not obtained mercy;
>   and I will tell those who were not my people, 'You are my people;'
>   and they will say, 'My God! (2:23)

It will be noted that Hosea, like Amos, uses "that day" or "the day" to signify both the moment of judgment and the moment of final redemption that is in store for Israel.

There is considerable fluidity in the imagery of this prophet. The future seems to hold out complete annihilation of the Northern kingdom in one pronouncement while in another proclaiming its eventual revival. Another confusing element is the intertwined fates of Israel in the north and Judah in the south. It seems odd for Hosea (and Amos) to be addressing the restoration of the Northern tribes in terms of the coming of a Davidic king! The implicit assumption is that there will be an eventual reunion of the separated brethren. Amazing good news again!

Hosea's vision of Israel as an adulterous wife makes the enormity of national faithlessness something that could be felt by every Israelite. At the same time, it offers extraordinary insight into YHWH as a God of steadfast love who suffers real pain as a result of his people's sin.

Both Amos and Hosea provide a scathing indictment of Israel and, while pressing home the absolute certainty of coming judgment, also hold out the promise of eventual restoration. They offer glimpses of YHWH's long-term strategy for the winning of the war and thus become the bearers of good news. Such visions soar well beyond the "here and now," marking a significant departure from the messages of Elijah and Elisha who were mostly engaged in hand-to-hand combat at the front line of national disobedience.

Bad to the Bones: (2 Kgs 14:23–29; 15:8–31; 17:1–41)

Against this widened background we can pick up the thread of the royal narrative with the reign of Jeroboam II, who followed Jehoash in about 781 BC. It is perhaps a measure of the depths to which Israel has sunk that any king would name his son after the nation's greatest apostate! In any event, Jeroboam II lives down to his name and leads the nation away from YHWH. Nevertheless, YHWH takes pity on the beleaguered nation and uses this king to deliver them during a long reign of forty-one years. YHWH does this, we are told, only because he has not actually said that he would "blot out the name of Israel from under the sky" (2 Kgs 14:27).

Jeroboam II's son Zechariah is on the throne for only six months, which is five months longer than his assassin Shallum lasts before he himself suffers the same fate. Menahem is the new ruler and during his ten-year reign Israel is invaded for the first time by Tiglath-Pileser (or Pul), the emperor of Assyria. Menahem wisely offers him a large bribe and he withdraws his troops. Pekahiah then succeeds his father Menahem but is murdered by one of his officers, Pekah, within two years. This is not a pretty story.

Pekah survives twenty years and at one point has considerable success in a war with Judah, capturing a large number of noncombatants and a great deal of plunder. On the way home, his triumphant army has the wind taken from its sails by a prophet named Oded:

> Behold, because Yahweh, the God of your fathers, was angry with Judah, he has delivered them into your hand, and you have slain them in a rage which has reached up to heaven. Now you intend to degrade the children of Judah and Jerusalem as male and female slaves for yourselves. Aren't there even with you trespasses of your own against Yahweh your God? Now hear me therefore, and send back the captives that you have taken captive from your brothers, for the fierce wrath of Yahweh is on you. (2 Chr 28:9–11)

Remarkably, the soldiers comply, no doubt avoiding a catastrophe for Israel. Pekah, however, is perfectly capable of providing one himself by failing to defeat Tiglath-Pileser when he invades again. This time the result is the loss of significant Northern territory and the deportation of many inhabitants, leading to yet another bloody coup, led by Hoshea.

Upon becoming king, Hoshea attempts to ally himself with Egypt while refusing to pay tribute to the king of Assyria. A bad move. In fact, it is Israel's last move. Ever. The great northern army of Assyria invades the whole country this time, capturing its capital of Samaria and scattering the population into various parts of their empire, like bones over a forsaken battlefield. Mercifully, no word is given of Hoshea's own fate.

The "house" of Jeroboam has finally run its wicked course and the history of the Northern tribes as a separate nation has come to a bitter end. It is game over. It is 721 BC.

Israel Under the Kings (Part Two)

IN THE BOSOM OF ABRAHAM

Introduction

No surprises here: most, if not all, of our indicators point away from this part of the Story having much do with the fulfillment of God's great Promises. Indeed, the Northern kingdom of Israel, having let go of the line of David, immediately loses its way and stumbles out into the gathering storm never to be seen again. It seems we can expect little from this particular "false start," but we must remember that YHWH has a way of bringing things back from the dead—maybe even Israel. After all, this nation still shares the DNA of the "Beloved Son."

1. The Land/Place

In this period the Land loses its integrity as a single entity. Each side of the divide suffers a loss and sees itself deprived of its rightful inheritance. The rupture between Israel and Judah does not necessarily negate this Promise by itself as the total territory remains the possession of the children of Abraham. However, it sets in motion a dangerous in-house rivalry for domination: a divided Land is simply an anomaly and neither kingdom can rest easy until the situation is resolved. Add to this the old reality that "united we stand, divided we fall." Can either smaller nation resist the much greater powers that surround them?

In the North, the Land is further reduced in size after the trauma of the division. We read that because of Israel's sins "Yahweh began to cut away parts of Israel" (2 Kgs 10:32). This has an ominous ring to it and although there was some temporary regaining of territory, eventually the Northern kingdom loses all of its land to the Assyrians.

But, as we are learning, "never say never" is a good rule to follow when dealing with a God like YHWH. Indeed, both Amos and Hosea proclaim the good news that although the Land will indeed be lost through a great judgment upon the nation, an eventual return to a permanent and glorious reoccupation will follow. Exactly how this would take place remains unspecified but is anyone caught up the nation's terrible death agony really paying attention?

Even before the end Israel has undoubtedly lost much of her sense of "place" when the kingdoms were first divided. Both Jerusalem (the city of God) and the temple (the house of God) are left behind in Judah. It is unlikely that the new capital of Samaria and the worship centers at Dan and Bethel will have completely filled the holes left behind in the wounded psyche of the people.

2. Many Descendants

This Promise, too, is in deep, deep, recession. It would be hard to believe the North would be able even to maintain its population during its bloody and tumultuous history. In addition, many die during the devastating war with Assyria and eventually, as the survivors are assimilated into the populations of the far-flung empire, it becomes practically meaningless to continue to think of them as a part of Israel. The same would apply to those remaining and intermarrying with imported foreigners. For all intents and purposes the Israelite population of the Northern kingdom is reduced to zero. As far as the Story is concerned, they almost disappear from view altogether. Almost.

Hosea uses distinctive covenantal language to describe an amazing future reversal of fortune:

> Yet the number of the children of Israel will be as the sand of the sea which can't be measured or counted; (Hosea 1:10a)

For now this remains a distant hope, relegated completely to the realm of promise. Nothing new about that: perhaps Abraham is smiling through his tears.

3. Blessing to All Nations

In this script the nations mostly serve as YHWH's agents to punish Israel and, as such, they could be said to be enjoying the blessing of military victory and territorial expansion as the flip side of Israel's demise. But, of course, this is not the kind of blessing in view under this Promise, i.e., a blessing that comes to those nations that bless Israel.

A more covenantal understanding of how the nations would be blessed through Abraham's descendants is hinted at in the stories of the prophets of this era. As we have in other periods, in them we can see in miniature what will eventually be realized in full.

There is Elijah, who is fed by the widow of Zarephath. This is between Tyre and Sidon along the Mediterranean coast, making her a Gentile. Having saved the prophet, she and her son are in turn saved from famine by the prophet. Not only that, she sees her son raised from the dead!

There is also Jonah, whom YHWH sends to preach repentance to the great Assyrian city of Nineveh. And it responded positively! Indeed, we actually read that the Ninevites believed God (Jonah 3:5) and as a result enjoy the blessing of divine compassion. The fact that the Assyrians are Israel's most dangerous enemies in this period surely gives added significance to this episode and hints strongly at even their inclusion in YHWH's redemption. The walls continue a-tumblin' down.

While Jonah is sent like a foreign missionary into the Gentile world, the story of how Naaman comes to be healed of his leprosy represents a more typical Old

Testament understanding of the way the Blessing would come to the nations. In fact, it can be seen as a kind of parable of the process.

In spite of his affliction, Naaman is a commander in the army of Aram or Syria (as opposed to Assyria) who has conducted raids into Israel. On one of them he captures a young girl who becomes servant to his wife. Referring to Elisha, she informs him that there is a prophet in Israel who could cure him. He decides to go and is healed in due course. As a result of this miracle he comes to believe in YHWH as the one true God:

> See now, I know that there is no God in all the earth, but in Israel. (2 Kgs 5:15)

So here we have the pattern: Gentiles entering into the Blessing through the faithful witness of Israel among the nations and even coming to worship her God. A kingdom of priests, yes, but also evangelists.

As for the future, Amos sees the day when Israel is finally restored and the "nations who are called by my name" (9:12) are incorporated within its jurisdiction. Again we have a reference to an eventual inclusion of the Gentiles in the Blessing,[18] and even a hint that they may be incorporated into Israel. We have already noted this process at work earlier in the stories of Rahab and Ruth and so it comes as no real surprise to see it here too. Not to mention that Jacob himself had been promised that a "community of nations" would come from him.[19]

These indicators are, of course, no more than hints and shadows, seemingly insubstantial against the reality of imminent threat and actual disaster. For now, these same nations are hell-bent on unleashing holocaust upon Israel. They are part of the problem, not part of the final solution. At least not yet.

4. Fruitfulness

It is likely that during this era of internal and external warfare the Land itself would not escape unscathed. Invasions, tribute payments, sieges, and destruction seem to form the general background to the story. Adding to this impression is the fact that the text yields little or no evidence of any kind of abundance.

On at least two occasions YHWH himself brings about serious droughts upon the Land, three years long in Elijah's day and seven in Elisha's. These should probably be taken, in part, as the prescribed divine response to national apostasy, as laid out in the provisions of the Sinai covenant.[20] In stark contrast, YHWH works through these prophets to provide miraculously abundant food for two needy widows who exhibit faith in him. It is clear who controls the fruitfulness of the Land.

---

18. Motyer makes this point persuasively in *Message of Amos*, 201–5.
19. See 104, above.
20. Cf. Deut 28:18, 23–24.

A similar picture emerges from Amos and Hosea. Part of the former's indictment against Israel reads as follows:

> "I also have given you cleanness of teeth in all your cities,
>   and lack of bread in every town;
>   yet you haven't returned to me," says Yahweh..."I struck you with blight
> and mildew many times in your gardens and your vineyards;
>   and the swarming locusts have devoured your fig trees and your olive trees;
>   yet you haven't returned to me," says Yahweh. (Amos 4:6,9)

In contrast, as we have seen, both prophets describe the good news of Israel's ultimate restoration in terms of an abundant and productive Land.

As an indication of how Israel is doing in terms of the Abrahamic covenant Blessings, "Fruitfulness" is relegated almost completely to the future. At the moment it can only register as the faintest of possibilities, the elusive scent of a childhood garden long forgotten.

5. Relationship

In general terms this period is marked by a deteriorating relationship between YHWH and Israel. As we have noted earlier in this chapter, the very rise of the prophets seems to have been at least partially necessitated by the fact that YHWH was alienated from the kings, no longer dealing directly with them as he had with previous leaders.

Led by the kings, the people were turning away to serve other gods. This, along with an accompanying moral decline, was bound to have a negative impact on their relationship with YHWH. At the end of this depressing tale, 2 Kings states no less than three times that because of Israel's sin they have been removed not just from the Land, but even from YHWH's "sight" (2 Kgs 17:18, 20, 23). It is difficult not to see the connection between this disaster and the expulsion of Adam and Eve from the garden of Eden. It is déjà vu all over again.

The same conclusion is reached in the messages of Amos and Hosea. The latter, having viewed the relationship of YHWH and Israel through the lens of his marriage, is told to name his second child by Gomer, his prostitute-wife:

> Call his name Lo-Ammi; for you are not my people, and I will not be yours.
> (Hos. 1:9)

This, of course, is a dark and forbidding negative image of the fundamental relationship God had entered into with this people under Moses.[21]

However, as usual with the prophets, this is not the last word. In the next breath YHWH says:

---

21. Exod 6:7; Lev 26:12.

> . . .it will come to pass that, in the place where it was said to them, 'You are not my people,' they will be called 'sons of the living God.' (Hos. 1:10; cf. 2:23)

Later, Hosea is instructed to take back his unfaithful wife as an explicit enactment of God's attitude to Israel:

> Go again, love a woman loved by another, and an adulteress, even as Yahweh loves the children of Israel, though they turn to other gods . . . (Hos. 3:1)

Herein lies the clue to YHWH's relationship with Israel. He loves her with an everlasting love. He just does. Although she is severely punished, even to the vanishing point, Israel will someday undergo a glorious restoration that includes the renewal of the covenant relationship with YHWH:

> But I am Yahweh your God from the land of Egypt.
>   I will yet again make you dwell in tents,
>   as in the days of the solemn feast. (Hos 12:9)

But for now, the wayward "wife" has been forced to leave home at the hand of the husband she has provoked into jealous anger. However, knowing the One who has married her, she has ample reason to hope for an eventual reconciliation if she can show that she is truly committed to this relationship. That's a big "if," as we know.

6. Grace/Obedience

How does the story of the Northern kingdom fit the formula that we are "saved by grace" and "called to obedience" in order to maintain that salvation? Because the emphasis in this part of the biblical narrative is clearly on what happens in the event of persistent disobedience, it can offer insight into the subtle interplay between grace and works presented in the Bible.

First of all, the fact of being a saved people is a given. Essentially this means that they are rescued out of Egypt by the power of YHWH and enter into a special covenant relationship with him at Sinai simply because he had chosen them in their father Abraham. YHWH continues, even when angry, to refer to the people of Israel as "my people"[22] and himself as "your God"[23] (with the one exception noted immediately above from Hosea). It is because of this underlying relationship that covenant unfaithfulness cuts so deeply and can be compared to adultery in a marriage. Some of this sense is captured by Amos:

> I have only chosen you of all the families of the earth.
>   Therefore I will punish you for all of your sins. (Amos 3:2)

---

22. Cf. Amos 9:10.
23. Cf. Hos 14:1.

Punishment, yes. But our question might rather be about the possibility of God turning his back on them altogether. Is he not irrevocably committed to this people? Even as the nation is staggering toward its end they are granted a reprieve:

> But Yahweh was gracious to them, and had compassion on them, and had respect for them, because of his covenant with Abraham, Isaac, and Jacob, and would not destroy them, and he didn't cast them from his presence as yet. (2 Kgs 13:23)

Here is grace surely being stretched right up to the breaking point. However, the tension continues to increase and ultimately wholesale destruction does take place.

While this may look like the End, it is not. The promise of ultimate restoration remains at the center of the prophetic word. Does this mean that obedience is then not required for the covenant Blessings to be given, that it doesn't matter in the long run?

It would be dangerous to resolve the tension by simply answering in the affirmative, no matter how tempting. Look at what happened to Israel: it underwent intensive suffering and many died terrible deaths. The whole nation was destroyed. That YHWH would someday reconstitute it is scant comfort to those who were caught up in the destruction, who suffered grievously under the covenant Curse. There are real consequences: obedience does matter. On the other hand, perhaps, at the end of the day we can say that grace matters more.

Again, part of our bewilderment stems from our reading this narrative through the lens of our extremely individualistic culture. It is very difficult for us to fully comprehend the more corporate focus of the biblical narrative. The promise of national restoration is much more meaningful to the ancient Israelites than it is to us. This fact adds substantial weight to the evident priority of grace.

On a related matter, Elijah's plea to YHWH on Mt. Carmel affirms afresh that what is ultimately needed is a transformation of the heart:

> Hear me, Yahweh, hear me, that this people may know that you, Yahweh, are
> God, and that you have turned their heart back again. (1 Kgs 18:37)

Unfortunately, this prayer remains unanswered in our narrative. Perhaps the lesson is once again that great demonstrations of YHWH's power result in only a temporary change of heart. Something even deeper, something more permanent, is needed. In this context, it may be significant that there is no reference to the Spirit of God in this section of the narrative.

14

Israel Under the Kings (Part Three)
The "House" of David

Suggested Reading

1 Kings 12–2 Kings 25; 2 Chronicles 10–36; Jeremiah 21, 22, 26–30, 34, 36–44, 52. Note: For purposes of this chapter only those portions of 1 & 2 Kings dealing with "Judah" should be read, as referenced in the captions of *The Story* sections below. If the reader has already used a highlighter to mark the Northern portions before reading chapter 13, the unmarked passages can now be easily read. 2 Chronicles concerns itself only with Judah and has its own point of view, adding in extra material from other sources besides the books of 1 & 2 Kings. The readings from Jeremiah provide further insight into the events surrounding the last days of Judah.

MAJOR DEVELOPMENTS

Note: All of the kings of Judah succeed their fathers except for three of the last four, who are all sons of Josiah and brothers to each other. In that last generation the succession goes sideways but still remains in the line of David.

- Rehoboam, son of Solomon, inherits the kingdom for seventeen years but foolishly provokes the ten Northern tribes into leaving, with only Judah and Benjamin remaining loyal to the house of David
- When king and people provoke YHWH through covenant disobedience, Egypt attacks and the palace and temple are sacked for the first time
- The somewhat more positive reigns of Abijah (three years) and Asa (forty-one years) follow in direct succession, but the latter leads the nation into an

inconclusive war with Israel

- His son Jehoshaphat (twenty-five years), a religious and social reformer, seeks to encourage covenant obedience by having the Law taught throughout the Land. His efforts raise the nation to significant heights, earning him riches and esteem.

- Jehoram (forty-one years) does not follow in his father's footsteps, leading Judah astray and dying after being afflicted by YHWH

- Ahaziah dies after just one year of rule and then his mother Athaliah (seven years) murders what she thinks is the entire royal house and takes over herself

- After a few years her evil reign causes a rebellion in which her young grandson Joash is made king under Jehoiada the priest

- Joash (forty years) begins well, but as soon as he is on his own he goes so far astray that he is assassinated by his own people

- Amaziah (twenty-nine years) starts in a godly direction but ignores advice from YHWH's prophet and attacks Israel, is defeated, and then is murdered after the temple and the city are sacked again

- Blessings for obedience mark the reigns of Uzziah (fifty-two years) and his son Jotham (sixteen years), although the former is afflicted with leprosy as a result of proudly acting as a priest contrary to the provisions of the Law

- Ahaz (sixteen years) proceeds to turn his back on YHWH in favor of the gods of the nations, even incorporating them into Judah's worship, provoking YHWH to anger, but no specific disaster overtakes him

- With Hezekiah (twenty-nine years) the nation has yet another reversal of course as the king leads a serious revival of true religion, capped by a memorable celebration of the Passover

- At this point, Jerusalem is threatened by Sennacherib, but YHWH provides a great deliverance from the Assyrian horde

- Hezekiah sows the seeds of Judah's ultimate demise when he flaunts his wealth in the face of Babylon, negating all the good he had done

- Manasseh (fifty-five years) pushes the pendulum so far back into wickedness that the text identifies his reign as the point of no return for Judah in spite of the king's late conversion to the ways of YHWH

- Amon is such a bad king that he is assassinated by members of his own administration after only two years of rule

- Josiah (thirty-one years), although it is too late, makes a last-ditch effort to win YHWH's approval through another religious reformation, this time sparked by discovery of "the Book of the Covenant" and resulting in the meticulous observation of the Passover by the entire nation

- Against the word of God, Josiah rushes to intercept an Egyptian army and is killed in battle while his son Jehoahaz is immediately deported to Egypt and his wayward brother Jehoiakim (eleven years) is installed instead
- Jehoiachin, son of Jehoiakim, lasts only three months before the rising power of Babylon attacks and plunders Jerusalem, carting off the king and other members of the ruling class
- Zedekiah (eleven years), the third son of Josiah to be king, actually tries to rebel after nine years under Babylonian rule. Jerusalem is laid siege and falls, the temple and palace are destroyed, and most of the people are exiled to Babylon, including Zedekiah, while all his sons are executed
- The prophet Jeremiah has been trying in vain to persuade the people and the last of their kings to accept the inevitable victory of Babylon
- Babylon appoints a man named Gedaliah as governor but he is killed by rebels and his followers flee to Egypt taking Jeremiah with them

PERSPECTIVES

Introduction

In turning our attention from the Northern to the Southern kingdom we encounter both similarities and differences. While the tribes of the South do not break away from the chosen line of David, they cannot claim any similar loyalty to YHWH their God. At the same time, under the leadership of some of their more faithful kings their story is marked by periods of covenant renewal that were unknown in the North. At the end of the day, however, disobedience rules, and as a result Judah, too, suffers defeat, ruin, and exile.

The Bible presents this story in an even more complicated way than it does that of the Northern kingdom because, in addition to the intertwined narrative of 1 and 2 Kings, we have the witness of 2 Chronicles 10ff. The stated portions of Jeremiah also shed up-close and personal light on Judah in her last days as experienced by the prophet.

Mirror Image Prophets

The last point above leads to a further observation: the two prominent Northern prophets, Elijah and Elisha, as we have seen, produced no writings of their own and yet are the subject of lengthy portions in the historical narrative (1 & 2 Kings). Just the opposite is true in the South: the two greatest prophets, Isaiah and Jeremiah, each produce lengthy books but receive relatively little attention in the historical narrative

(2 Kings, 1 & 2 Chronicles). This is one of a number of suggestions that the story of the South may be, in some important ways, a kind of mirror image to that of the North.

While miracles vividly marked the ministries of Elijah and Elisha, they are almost entirely absent in the somewhat later activities of Isaiah and Jeremiah. The ministries of these Judean prophets mark the beginning (Isaiah) and the end (Jeremiah) of the nation's life after the fall of Samaria. While they may lack in miracles, the fact that their prophecies inevitably come true provides them with all the "street cred" they need.

As Judah's story unfolds, the focus of the prophets is moving somewhat further away from active engagement with the leadership of the nation. Their role as covenant prosecutors, however, still necessitates occasional confrontation and they are even consulted for advice from time to time. But they mostly function as outsiders, who, instead of enjoying the office of "prophetic consultant" and leading the "school" of prophets, are routinely opposed by both. Indeed, they even begin to focus their attention outside of Judah itself, daring to address the surrounding nations with dire messages of YHWH's impending judgment.

For Future Considerations

Although we are limiting our scope to the narrative sections of the Bible, as we saw in the North the prophetic writings provide insight into YHWH's perspective on what is taking place. Adding their own distinctive flavor, they help us discern the temper of these turbulent times and for this reason alone deserve our attention.

In addition, as with Hosea and Amos, the Southern prophets paint a picture of the future redemption awaiting Israel, a redemption that ultimately envelops the whole of creation. In this they provide a detailed and vibrant depiction of what amounts to a history-yet-to-come. As such, it forms an integral part of the Story (its final chapter) and is therefore subject to our analysis in the usual categories. The next chapter will attempt to do this and, indeed, its Major Developments section presents a broad outline of that "history-yet-to-come." For the purposes of this chapter, the Southern prophets will enter the picture only as their pronouncements are relevant to current events.

David: The Gold Standard

The impression that what happens in Judah is the "mirror image" of Israel's experience is reinforced when we turn to the account of the historical events itself.

It will be remembered that the story of the North was marked by a constant refrain in which the performances of the Northern kings were likened to that of Jeroboam, their first king, the baddest of the bad. Similarly, in the South, another refrain alerts us to the fact that David is the one against whom the kings of Judah are to be judged. Unlike Jeroboam, however, David is seen as the ideal king to whom his successors only fitfully measure up. His son Solomon receives both positive and negative assessments, while five later kings are commended and three are condemned. Typical of the latter is this pronouncement on Ahaz who reigned almost 250 years after David:

> Ahaz was twenty years old when he began to reign, and he reigned sixteen years in Jerusalem. He didn't do that which was right in Yahweh his God's eyes, like David his father. (2 Kgs 16:2)

While the North was under the malignant spiritual covering of Jeroboam so the South is blessed because of David. This is true more in the early years of the kingdom than in the later ones. The very fact that Judah is allowed to continue as a separate nation, we are told explicitly, is on account of David.[1] Judah and Jerusalem both escape Assyrian exile for the same reason.[2] But this stockpile of spiritual capital seems to be entirely used up by the time the nation is exiled to Babylon and an end comes to the Davidic kingdom.

Jezebel's Revenge: The Exception That Proves the Rule

Roughly midway in the life of the Southern kingdom, King Ahaziah dies prematurely and his mother Athaliah usurps the throne of Judah for six years. She is the daughter of King Ahab of Israel in the North, who, with his queen Jezebel, had been Elijah's nemesis.[3] Viperlike, this wicked woman slithers into the royal nest of David and attempts to destroy all of Judah's royal family, including her own grandchildren! She was probably thinking to supplant it with members of her own Northern dynasty and thereby bring Judah under its rule.

However, her one-year-old grandson Joash is hidden by his aunt Jehosheba and survives the general slaughter in much the way the infant Moses did so many years earlier. And so the line of David continues against all odds. Jehoiada the priest acts as a serpent crusher by successfully leading a rebellion against Athaliah and having her killed. He then installs Joash as king, bringing an end to a unique interruption in the line of Davidic kings.

This episode fits a long-established pattern of unlikely rescues, demonstrating once again that God has a way of dealing with such "ends" to his promises (cf. Noah in the Flood and Joseph in Egypt). It isn't over till it's over. *YHWH's promise to David has not been broken in spite of the most terrible threats.* This is something for the nation to take to heart in while in Babylonian exile.

---

1. Cf. 1 Kgs 11:12–13, 32, 34.
2. 2 Kgs 8:19; 19:34; 20:6.
3. While it is not entirely certain that Jezebel was Athaliah's mother, with Ahab being her father the remarks here concerning the family heritage apply in any event.

A Cracked Mirror

If Judah was a perfect mirror image of Israel we would expect all its kings to be good. But here the mirror is cracked: as we have noted, only some measure up to the gold standard of David. Furthermore, like David before them, their faithfulness is not enough to stem the rising tide of idolatry and injustice. Against this general background three Southern kings, Jehoshaphat, Hezekiah, and Josiah, stand out for their attempts to hold the line. But they do not succeed. Once on the loose, the serpent seems impossible to corner.

No Sin Left Behind: Manasseh

Unfortunately, by the reign of Manasseh, between Hezekiah and Josiah, the patience of YHWH has been tried one too many times. The nation's deep current of disobedience has finally managed to exhaust even his vast reserves:

> . . . Yahweh didn't turn from the fierceness of his great wrath, with which his anger burned against Judah, because of all the provocation with which Manasseh had provoked him. Yahweh said, "I will also remove Judah out of my sight, as I have removed Israel, and I will cast off this city which I have chosen, even Jerusalem, and the house of which I said, 'My name shall be there.'" (2 Kgs 23:26–27)

From this it appears that Manasseh's reign is the fatal tipping point in YHWH's relationship with Judah, and so even a final reform under Josiah is not enough to avert disaster. Rather than a conclusive return to YHWH, it is merely the last in a depressing series of failed efforts. The doom of the nation is sealed.

But why is Manasseh singled out as the one who has gone too far? He certainly excels at evil: he worships the stars, sacrifices his own son in the fire and places pagan images in the temple, among other things. The authors of both 2 Kings and Chronicles seem to imply that it is the last of these that finally went too far while 2 Kings also adds that:

> . . . he filled Jerusalem with innocent blood, and Yahweh would not pardon. (24:4)

In the end both accounts agree that:

> Manasseh seduced them to do that which is evil more than the nations did whom Yahweh destroyed before the children of Israel. (2 Kgs 21:9/2 Chr 33:9)

The author of 2 Kings follows through on this mention of the Conquest by specifically referring to the sin of the Amorites:

> Because Manasseh king of Judah has done these abominations, and has done wickedly above all that the Amorites did, who were before him, and has also made Judah to sin with his idols; (2 Kgs 21:11)

YHWH had told Abraham that the Conquest would be delayed until the sin of the Amorites was "complete"[4] and they had apparently reached that stage by the time Joshua carried out YHWH's judgment upon them. The allusion here at this point strongly suggests that the sin of Judah is now more than "complete," even worse than the nations at the time of the Conquest. In the bitterest of ironies, Judah itself has come under the ban. It is the end of a long, long descent into judgment:

> . . . because they have done that which is evil in my sight, and have provoked me to anger, since the day their fathers came out of Egypt, even to this day. (2 Kgs 21:15)

The reader rightly hesitates to turn the page.

The Final Curtain

The last dramatic scenes of Judah's existence, like those of Israel, are played out on the wider stage of ANE history. From this perspective the fate of the nation is determined by its relationships with the more powerful nations of the day.

When the Assyrians have finished with Samaria in the North they naturally turn their attention to Jerusalem. In the face of this, Hezekiah, a zealous religious reformer, realizes that he is helpless to deliver the city and he appeals to YHWH. Miraculously, the enemy is destroyed and the Assyrian king sent packing.

In the meantime, Assyria itself is beginning to succumb to the power of Babylon, the new empire on the block, and allies itself with Egypt to hold them off. Judah is caught in the middle as usual, trying to pick a winner with which to side. Manasseh is exiled to Babylon for a time when it is still under Assyrian rule. Later, Josiah gambles and attacks Egypt as it makes its way to assist the Assyrians against Babylon. He loses both the battle and his life. Within twenty years Judah succumbs to the armies of Babylon for good. The nation is essentially reduced to only a few miserable exiles living in the awe-inspiring capital of their conquerors.

It looks like YHWH really has finally abandoned them. However, the narrative makes it plain that Judah is not in the hands of the nations but in the hands of YHWH, even now. As noted above, the prophets of the time hold up pictures of a golden era that awaits the remnant of Israel on the other side of this judgment. The history of Israel has repeatedly demonstrated that YHWH does not need great human resources to work out his saving purposes. A "few" will do. Perhaps even One is enough.

---

4. Gen 15:16. Also, see 171–72, above.

It is worth noting that the pattern discerned here conforms nicely to one we have had occasion to note at several points along our journey: the death and resurrection of the Beloved Son.[5] Again, Israel is the Beloved Son in question and "his" continuation on the other side of this grave is not a possibility which can be ignored.

What's It All About, Really?

At this point it is important to be reminded of what Moses told this people concerning YHWH's purpose in redeeming them from Egypt so long ago:

> Did a people ever hear the voice of God speaking out of the middle of the fire, as you have heard, and live? Or has God tried to go and take a nation for himself from among another nation, by trials, by signs, by wonders, by war, by a mighty hand, by an outstretched arm, and by great terrors, according to all that Yahweh your God did for you in Egypt before your eyes? It was shown to you so that you might know that Yahweh is God. There is no one else besides him. (Deut 4:33–35)

It now seems clear that this is an extremely hard lesson to learn and an easy one to forget. In the North, Israel fails repeatedly and eventually is expelled. In the South, the failures end up overwhelming the successes. This is the great tragedy at the center of this Story: Israel, both North and South, has proven unable to be faithful to YHWH. Furthermore, one despairs for humanity itself because "to know that YHWH is God" was to be Israel's legacy for the nations.[6] And now, sadly, that nation has died leaving them nothing at all in the will.

A Wrench in the Covenant Mechanism?

One would imagine that after seeing what had happened to their Northern cousins, the kings and people of Judah would have been well motivated to ensure covenant obedience in their own territory. Instead, like moths to a flame, they continue to be drawn into the idolatrous practices of the surrounding nations, with devastating consequences.

For the reader there is another unsettling implication of this part of the Story. It confirms our earlier suspicion that the path that Moses set before the chosen people has itself proved to be just too steep for *any* human beings to negotiate.[7] The sordid events recorded in this chapter expose even further the unwelcome truth that no one can consistently measure up to the righteousness demanded by this holy God. Again,

---

5. See 78, 103, 115, 216 above.

6. Cf. Josh 4:24; 1 Sam 17:46; 1 Kgs 8:60; Ps 100:3; Isa 37:20; Jer. 24:7; Ezek. 39:22; Joel 2:27. Many of these have to do with the nations coming to know YHWH through his redeeming of Israel.

7. See 133, above.

we see that this brings the Law itself into question as the means by which Promises to Abraham were to be realized. Its "covenant mechanism" of Blessings and Curses has been hopelessly jammed by humanity's overwhelming inclination to disobedience.

THE STORY

Rehoboam Drops the Ball (1 Kgs 14:21–31; 2 Chr 11–12)

In the wake of Solomon's death, his son Rehoboam, the new king, is presented with a golden opportunity to keep Jeroboam and his Northern followers onside. An assembly of all the tribes tells him that they will serve him gladly if he will lighten the load his father had put upon them. The elders of the nation reveal a remarkably enlightened understanding of the role of a leader of God's people:

> If you will be a servant to this people today, and will serve them, and answer them with good words, then they will be your servants forever. (1 Kgs 12:7)

These words seem wise enough to be one of Solomon's own proverbs. But Rehoboam is not his father and rather than acting wisely, he does the opposite. Scorning the advice of the elders, the young king instead consults his own peer group and then tells the nation:

> My father made your yoke heavy, but I will add to your yoke. My father chastised you with whips, but I will chastise you with scorpions. (1 Kgs 12:14)

Can we not hear the echo of Pharaoh's tyrannical response to Moses's request to "let my people go"?[8] Perhaps the people do as well: the ten Northern tribes rebel and follow Jeroboam out of the union. The rest, as they say, is history.

Only two of the tribes, Judah and Benjamin, stay loyal to Rehoboam, but they immediately prostitute themselves before the gods of the nations. When King Shishak of Egypt attacks, the prophet Shemaiah has an ominous message for the king:

> Yahweh says, 'You have forsaken me, therefore I have also left you in the hand of Shishak.' (2 Chr 12:5b)

Shishak imposes a humiliating defeat upon Judah, ransacking both the royal palace and Solomon's great temple. Stripped of its gold, the latter loses much of its luster, literally and figuratively. This disaster seems to get Rehoboam's attention for a time, but he falls far short of covenant obedience in a reign marked by continual warfare with Jeroboam and the Northern tribes. He is ultimately unsuccessful in trying to regain the whole kingdom for himself. Things are off to a bad start.

---

8. See Exod 5:6–9.

Abijah and Asa: Mixed Blessings (1 Kgs 15:1–24; 2 Chr 13–16)

In the eighteenth year of his kingship Rehoboam dies of natural causes and his son Abijah takes over for the next three years, following in his father's sinful ways. Nevertheless, YHWH gives him twenty-two sons and sixteen daughters and makes Jerusalem strong, all out of his regard for David (1 Kgs 15:4). His troops even soundly defeat Jeroboam, regaining some of Israel's southernmost territory because "they relied on Yahweh, the God of their fathers" (2 Chr 13:18–21).

Abijah's son Asa comes to the throne next, generally doing "that which was good and right in Yahweh his God's eyes;" (2 Chr 14:2). His long rule of thirty-nine years is marked by twenty years of peace, the direct result of a mid-reign religious revival that includes a renewal of the covenant:

> They swore to Yahweh with a loud voice, with shouting, with trumpets, and with cornets. All Judah rejoiced at the oath, for they had sworn with all their heart, and sought him with their whole desire; and he was found by them. Then Yahweh gave them rest all around. (2 Chr 15:14–15)

Then follows a period of conflict with Israel that proves to be Asa's undoing. Instead of trusting in YHWH, he bribes Ben-Hadad, the king of Damascus, to break his treaty with Israel and attack it from the north. Although some territory from Israel is recovered, Hanani the seer tells Asa that his lack of trust will condemn the rest of his reign to continuous warfare. This same attitude leads to his death not long after when he relies only on his physicians when faced with his final illness (2 Chr 16:1–14). At best he gets mixed reviews.

Jumping Jehoshaphat (1 Kgs 22:1–50; 2 Chr 17–20)

The narrative makes it clear that Asa's son Jehoshaphat encourages his nation to make a great leap forward in their obedience to YHWH. Jehoshaphat is cited for his faithfulness on many occasions and as a result he is blessed with great wealth and honor (2 Chr 17:5).

This is in spite of the fact that he fails to eliminate the "high places" where people are worshipping instead of at the temple.[9] These ancient sites are generally associated with foreign gods and this makes them off-limits for the worship of YHWH. Some are being used for that purpose while others remain as outright pagan worship centers. In both cases allegiance to the one true God is being compromised by their continued use.

Early in his reign, when asked by Ahab of Israel to attack the Syrians, Jehoshaphat insists upon consulting a true man of God before they go to battle and then he ignores his advice and assists Ahab anyway. Later on, perhaps having learned his lesson, he

---

9. This is mentioned in both 1 Kgs 22:43 and 2 Chr 20:33.

prays in humility to YHWH when the nation is threatened by the Moabites and the Ammonites:

> Our God, will you not judge them? For we have no might against this great company that comes against us. We don't know what to do, but our eyes are on you. (2 Chr 20:12)

It is surely significant that he addresses YHWH directly and not through a prophet as has been the pattern with other recent kings of both Judah and Israel. The relationship is personal, although in this case the Spirit of God answers through a Levite in the assembly (2 Chr 20:14–17). He is told simply to have his army take up battle positions and watch. The enemy then turns upon itself while Judah enjoys a great victory and there is so much plunder it takes them three days to gather it all.

Jehoshaphat is also an ambitious religious and social reformer. As his reign begins he sends officials, along with religious scholars, throughout the land, and they take with them "the book of Yahweh's law" (2 Chr 17:9). He appoints judges in every city and admonishes them to be just and impartial. In Jerusalem he uses some of the Levites and elders there for a similar purpose, "for the judgment of Yahweh, and for controversies," and to "do this in the fear of Yahweh, faithfully, and with a perfect heart." (2 Chr 19:8–9). Above all, they are to warn the people not to sin against YHWH.

Through this enlightened and ambitious program it is clearly his intent to jumpstart the entire nation on the road to covenant obedience. And it seems to work: his administration is a high point in Judah's history, building as it does on the efforts of his father Asa. Especially in his early years, he measures up to the gold standard, walking "in the ways of his father David" (2 Chr 17:3).

Bad Blood Begins: Jehoram (2 Kgs 8:16–29; 2 Chr 21)

Jehoram, son of Jehoshaphat, seems determined to reverse his father's progress. He had married Athaliah, a daughter of Ahab and Jezebel, the evil rulers of Israel who had given Elijah such a hard time. His father had probably arranged the marriage in order to ally himself with that regime. Whatever his motives were, the kingdom of Judah was infected with the unfortunate DNA of the Northern dynasty of the day and it pays the price over the next several generations. It starts when Jehoram comes to the throne himself and he shows that he is more in tune with his father-in-law than his father by murdering all his brothers!

> He walked in the way of the kings of Israel, as did Ahab's house; for he had Ahab's daughter as his wife. He did that which was evil in Yahweh's sight. (2 Chr 21:6)

This is one of those places where one might expect a frustrated YHWH to execute terrible judgment upon Judah. Not so, however:

> However Yahweh would not destroy David's house, because of the covenant that he had made with David, and as he promised to give a lamp to him and to his children always. (2 Chr 21:7)

This does not mean that Jehoram is not held to account. Indeed, he gets a letter from the famous Northern prophet Elijah informing him that because he has led the people of Judah away from YHWH he will be struck with a lingering, painful, and ultimately fatal illness.[10] In addition, all of his sons except the youngest are killed by Judah's enemies.

Bad Blood: Ahaziah (2 Kgs 8:25—29:29; 11:1–16; 2 Chr 22–23)

The survivor is twenty-two year old Ahaziah, named after his mother's brother, Ahab's successor in the North. Taking after his mother's side of the family, he allies himself with Joram the king of Israel, against the Aramaeans. After only a year in power he travels to visit Samaria at the very moment when God finally brings about a terrible end to Joram and the whole house of Ahab. Ahaziah also dies, caught up in the holocaust.

Bad Blood Forever: Athaliah (2 Kgs 11)

As we noted earlier, Ahaziah's mother Athaliah, true to family form, steps into Judah's power vacuum with a real vengeance, her reign amounting to a near-death experience for David's line. Of Judah's royal family, only her infant grandson Joash escapes her murderous attention.

Athaliah has been the problem for far too long. After six years of her disastrous rule, Jehoiada the priest organizes an uprising during which Athaliah has a *real* death experience!

Bad Blood Returns: Joash (2 Kgs 12; 2 Chr 24)

Jehoiada leads the people in covenant renewal and they proclaim the seven-year-old Joash as the legitimate king while Jehoiada continues as his mentor/regent. The worship of Baal is again exterminated from the kingdom.

The book of 2 Chronicles makes it clear that as long as Joash is under the tutelage of Jehoiada he does what is right in the eyes of YHWH. In fact, he undertakes a major repair of the temple because it had been abused and desecrated by the sons of

---

10. 2 Chr 21:12–15, thus making Elijah into something of a literary prophet after all.

Athaliah. When Jehoiada dies at the incredible age of 130 he is buried with the kings in Jerusalem because he has done so much good for the kingdom, especially in his role as regent.

But as soon as the old priest dies things begin to fall apart. Joash gathers about him a cadre of poor advisors and sets Judah once more on the road to apostasy. YHWH sends prophets and even speaks through Zechariah the priest, son of the king's late mentor. It is all to no avail. Once again we hear the usual sentence:

> Why do you disobey Yahweh's commandments, so that you can't prosper?
> Because you have forsaken Yahweh, he has also forsaken you. (2 Chr 24:20b)

For standing up to the king, Zechariah is stoned to death in the temple courtyard.

Not long after this travesty, a small army of Aramaeans attacks, executing judgment upon Judah. Joash himself is wounded and then is put to death by his own officials for the murder of Zechariah. He had been in power for forty years but fittingly, he is not buried with the kings where Jehoiada had been laid to rest. If this were Israel we might well expect the leader of the officials to take the throne. Instead, Joash's son Amaziah is crowned and succeeds him in the normal fashion. The lamp of David still refuses to go out.

A Duel in the Sun: Amaziah (2 Kgs 15; 2 Chr 25)

In an all too familiar scene, Amaziah's first move is to execute those who had conspired to kill his father. Wisely, he spares their sons as the Law required. Reigning for twenty-nine years, he generally does what was right in the eyes of YHWH. However, he fails to eliminate the "high places" associated with idolatry and where people continue to worship.

After a decisive victory over the Edomites, Amaziah foolishly begins to follow their gods, and this leads to his own defeat. In spite of being warned by a prophet not to do so, he issues a challenge to Jehoash, king of Israel: "Come! Let's look one another in the face" (2 Chr 25:17). They confront each other at Beth Shemesh ("The House of the Sun") and the showdown proves to be his undoing: soundly defeated, he is later captured by Jehoash. In the process, the wall of Jerusalem is broken down and the temple is looted once again.

Although Amaziah outlives Jehoash by fifteen years, in the end, like his father, he falls victim to a conspiracy and is murdered. And his son (Uzziah/Azariah) follows him on the throne, put there, we are told, by "All the people of Judah"[11]. The Davidic succession is maintained in spite of murder and mayhem all around. Bad blood, indeed.

---

11. 2 Chr 26:1. The exact role of "the people" in this process remains obscure, but that they had a role at all is significant. Cf. 1 Kgs 12:20; 2 Kgs 14:21, 21:24; 1 Chr 11:3; 2 Chr 22:1, 33:25, 36:1.

Blessing Upon Blessing: Uzziah and Jotham (2 Kgs 15:1–7, 32–38; 2 Chr 26–27)

Repeating yet another pattern, Uzziah starts out well enough by generally doing what was right, excepting that he too fails to do away with the high places. His reign is generally successful both militarily and economically:

> Moreover Uzziah built towers in Jerusalem at the corner gate, at the valley gate, and at the turning of the wall, and fortified them. He built towers in the wilderness, and dug out many cisterns, for he had much livestock; in the lowland also, and in the plain. He had farmers and vineyard keepers in the mountains and in the fruitful fields, for he loved farming. Moreover Uzziah had an army of fighting men . . . His fame spread far and wide, for he was greatly helped until he became powerful. (2 Chr 26:9–11, 15c)

It is not going too far to suggest that we find something of David and Solomon's glory reflected here. And, as with them, it does not last. In fact, like both his illustrious predecessors, Uzziah has a lapse that casts a terrible shadow over his future:

> But when he was strong, his heart was lifted up, so that he did corruptly, and he trespassed against Yahweh his God; for he went into Yahweh's temple to burn incense on the altar of incense. (2 Chr 26:16)

This contravention of the Law (he was not a priest) leads to his being afflicted with leprosy, and his son Jotham ruling as regent until his death in the same year that Isaiah saw YHWH, high and lifted up (Isa 6:1). Jotham, too, proves to be a faithful king (except for those troubling high places, again) and the blessings continue unabated during his own sixteen-year rule. But things change when his son Ahaz ascends the throne.

The Darkest Hour?: Ahaz (2 Kgs 16; 2 Chr 28)

Ahaz is so unfaithful to YHWH that both Kings and Chronicles put him in the same league as the kings of Israel! Like them he worships pagan gods and even sacrifices his sons to them in the fire. Losing conflicts with Aram/Syria and Israel he actually loots the temple and the palace himself for a bribe to pay to the king of Assyria. It seems to work because the latter attacks Damascus instead, temporarily providing some relief.

Ahaz continues to paganize Judah, thinking that the superiority of his enemies is because their gods are more powerful than YHWH. Both he and the nation suffer as a result. In the meantime, Israel falls to the Assyrians and ceases to exist as a nation. Six years after, Ahaz himself passes away. While Judah's prospects appear to be very bleak indeed, what happens next proves the old saying that "it is darkest just before dawn." It also disproves another: "like father, like son."

A True Son of David: Hezekiah (2 Kgs 18–20; 2 Chr 29–32)

Day and night would be a good way of describing the difference between Hezekiah and his father. His first act is to remove all of the pagan abominations from the temple and reboot the sacrificial system, the neglect of which had angered YHWH and made Judah and Jerusalem "to be an astonishment, and a hissing, as you see with your eyes" (2 Chr 29:8b). It takes the Levites sixteen whole days to purify the temple complex before it is ready for its proper use.

Hezekiah immediately leads the people in worship, beginning with a series of sacrifices designed as sin offerings for the king, the temple, and the people. These are followed by more sacrifices, accompanied this time by praise songs in tune with David's words and instrumentation. Finally, the people bring yet more sacrifices as thank offerings, fellowshipping, and rejoicing together in their renewed state of covenant obedience.[12]

The king then sends out a Passover invitation to all his subjects, as well as all those Israelites remaining in the North after the recent Assyrian deportation. To them he presents the event as one last chance to be the instruments of redemption for their nation:

> For if you turn again to Yahweh, your brothers and your children will find compassion before those who led them captive, and will come again into this land, because Yahweh your God is gracious and merciful, and will not turn away his face from you, if you return to him. (2 Chr 30:9)

Although some from the North, especially from the tribes of Asher, Manasseh, and Zebulun, "humbled themselves, and came to Jerusalem" (2 Chr 30:11), the invitation is largely ignored. Fortunately, Judah itself responds with universal enthusiasm and the Passover is celebrated with those who do come down from the former territory of Israel. We read simply that Yahweh ". . . listened to Hezekiah, and healed the people" (2 Chr 30:20). It is a high point almost unparalleled in the nation's history:

> So there was great joy in Jerusalem; for since the time of Solomon the son of David king of Israel there was nothing like this in Jerusalem. Then the Levitical priests arose and blessed the people. Their voice was heard, and their prayer came up to his holy habitation, even to heaven. (2 Chr 30:26–27)

The record leaves little doubt that this is a revival of true religion among all the people.

According to the chronicler, this heady experience is followed directly by a great crisis: Sennacherib the king of Assyria invades the Land. At first Hezekiah attempts to hold him off by acknowledging his sovereignty and paying him tribute garnered from

---

12. I have benefitted here from the analysis of 2 Chr 29 offered by Selman, "2 Chronicles," 488–92.

the treasuries of the temple and the palace. He also prepares Jerusalem for a siege and he is wise to do so: Sennacherib continues to press down from the north.

Hezekiah then assumes the role of David against this new Goliath, and, echoing the shepherd of Israel, reaches back to the charge of Joshua for inspiration:

> "Be strong and courageous. Don't be afraid or dismayed because of the king of Assyria, nor for all the multitude who is with him; for there is a greater one with us than with him. An arm of flesh is with him, but Yahweh our God is with us to help us and to fight our battles." The people rested themselves on the words of Hezekiah king of Judah. (2 Chr 32:7-8)

The Assyrian leader then sends officers to deliver a threat to the city. Like Goliath, in the emperor's name they loudly taunt the people of Judah, exulting in their overwhelming military superiority. They also convey Sennacherib's daring challenge to YHWH himself:

> Who was there among all the gods of those nations which my fathers utterly destroyed, that could deliver his people out of my hand, that your God should be able to deliver you out of my hand? Now therefore don't let Hezekiah deceive you, nor persuade you in this way. Don't believe him, for no god of any nation or kingdom was able to deliver his people out of my hand, and out of the hand of my fathers. How much less will your God deliver you out of my hand? (2 Chr 32:14-15)

Shaken, Hezekiah consults with Isaiah the prophet who promises deliverance and, indeed, Sennacherib withdraws again. However, hearing that the king of Egypt is marching against him, he sends another threatening message to Hezekiah, urging him to abandon his trust in YHWH: The latter, still believing in his God, famously spreads out the emperor's letter before YHWH and appeals for divine intervention:

> Incline your ear, Yahweh, and hear. Open your eyes, Yahweh, and see. Hear the words of Sennacherib, which he has sent to defy the living God. Truly, Yahweh, the kings of Assyria have laid waste the nations and their lands, and have cast their gods into the fire; for they were no gods, but the work of men's hands, wood and stone. Therefore they have destroyed them. Now therefore, Yahweh our God, save us, I beg you, out of his hand, that all the kingdoms of the earth may know that you, Yahweh, are God alone. (2 Kings 19:16-19)

Isaiah, who appears in the historical narrative only during Hezekiah's reign, delivers YHWH's answer, promising the fall of this arrogant pagan and complete deliverance for Jerusalem. In a way it could even be said that it is David who slays this giant too:

> For I will defend this city to save it, for my own sake, and for my servant David's sake. (2 Kgs 19:34)

This is the same reason given, again through Isaiah, when YHWH later heals Hezekiah of a fatal disease even though the king had appealed on the grounds of his own faithfulness. Once again it is made clear that it is only because of the Davidic covenant that Judah and its kings are being preserved.

In the meantime, immediately after Isaiah's assurance of deliverance "Yahweh's angel" (2 Kgs 19:35) destroys a hundred and eighty-five thousand Assyrian troops and Sennacherib judiciously withdraws from the Land. Upon arriving home in Nineveh he is murdered by two of his own sons. It is almost a relief to see that this kind of behavior is not limited to Israel and Judah! It just seems to be the way of the world.

After he had recovered from his illness, Hezekiah does a foolish thing: he boastfully shows all of his considerable wealth to messengers from the court of Babylon, a power that is now beginning to challenge Assyria. In so sinning he squanders all of his efforts to be a godly king. Isaiah's final pronouncement to him is that Babylon will end up carrying away not only all of this treasure but also some of his own descendants. Hezekiah's own last recorded thoughts were simply of relief that he would not live to see that day. Pride truly cometh before a fall.

Brink Dancing: Manasseh and Amon (2 Kgs 21; 2 Chr 33)

Hezekiah's all too human inconsistencies might help explain the terrible start to the reign of his son Manasseh. Of course, the fact that he is only twelve no doubt has something to do with it. As we have already noted in *Perspectives* above,[13] this king's long and terminally wayward fifty-five year reign marks a fatal turn in the narrative, bringing with it the distinct likelihood of exile.

Indeed, Manasseh himself tastes exile in Babylon (still under Assyrian control) as a direct result of his unfaithfulness. This causes him to humble himself before YHWH, who relents and brings him back home to his throne, likely near the end of his reign. Once there he begins a campaign of religious reform.

Earlier we noted a pattern of kings in Judah beginning well and then ending badly: Joash, Amaziah, Uzziah, and lastly, Hezekiah. With Manasseh we see the reverse: a king who starts badly and ends well. In so doing he seems to bring the nation back from the brink. But again, as we have already noted, with his reign Judah has passed the point of no return.

If Manasseh hesitated on the edge of the abyss, his son Amon, on the throne for only two years, shows no such wisdom. He lurches his way to the very precipice in his efforts to follow in his father's original footsteps. His unwillingness to humble himself may explain the fact that he is assassinated by some of his officials and replaced by his son Josiah, only eight years old, but a king of a different color altogether.

---

13. See 270–71, above.

Covenant Renewal Late: Josiah (2 Kgs 22:1—23:30; 2 Chr 34-35)

In spite of coming to the throne when still a boy, Josiah's thirty-one year reign appears to be the last overhanging branch for the nation to grasp before it is swept away by the flood:

> He did that which was right in Yahweh's eyes, and walked in all the way of David his father, and didn't turn away to the right hand or to the left. (2 Kgs 22:2)

This is high praise indeed, being compared favorably to Judah's gold standard. And it gets better:

> There was no king like him before him, who turned to Yahweh with all his heart, and with all his soul, and with all his might, according to all the law of Moses; and there was none like him who arose after him. (2 Kgs 23:25)

As goes the king, so goes the nation. When "the Book of the Covenant"[14] is discovered during a renovation of the temple, Josiah tears his robes, recognizing immediately that the nation has been causing divine anger with its habitual disobedience. Worried, he quickly consults Huldah the prophetess[15], who informs him that Judah is indeed going to suffer the Curses laid out in the book. Echoing Isaiah's word to Hezekiah, she then relays YHWH's judgment:

> '...because your heart was tender, and you humbled yourself before Yahweh, when you heard what I spoke against this place, and against its inhabitants, that they should become a desolation and a curse, and have torn your clothes, and wept before me; I also have heard you,' says Yahweh. 'Therefore behold, I will gather you to your fathers, and you will be gathered to your grave in peace. Your eyes will not see all the evil which I will bring on this place.' (2 Kgs 22:19-20)

Josiah, perhaps seeing that YHWH responded to his own repentance, still seems to think that the nation has a chance if it too will turn back to YHWH—and, given their history, who can blame him? He leads a renewal of the covenant during which "all the people, both small and great" pledge to keep all of YHWY'S "commandments, his testimonies, and his statutes" (2 Kgs 23:2-3), as he himself had done. Furthermore, he expands his earlier efforts to rid the Land of all pagan places of worship (even including those in what used to be Israel[16]) with a thoroughgoing extermination not only of idolatrous priests, but of mediums and spiritists as well.

---

14. Or "Book of the Law." Both are used in 2 Kings and 2 Chronicles. Many scholars believe this book is related to the book of Deuteronomy, but the precise nature of that relationship remains obscure.

15. The fact that she is a woman seems unremarkable to the authors of 2 Kings and 2 Chronicles. Selman, "2 Chronicles," 533, cites Miriam (Exod 15:20), Deborah (Judg 4:4), and Anna (Luke 2:36) as other female prophets in the Bible.

16. It seems that Josiah was able (in the temporary absence of Assyrian resistance) to expand his

The king then orders a celebration of Passover according to the regulations in the newly discovered book. According to both accounts of this momentous event, the whole nation had not celebrated the Passover with such care and enthusiasm since the days of the judges. Judah seems to be coming into line with the book, but apparently it is covenant renewal late, way too late.

The Assyrian empire is now gasping its last and its southern portions are coming under the new power of Babylon. Continuing the Egyptian policy of supporting Assyria against Babylon, Pharaoh Neco II rushes up the coast past Judah to help his old ally. For reasons that remain unclear, Josiah and his army head to intercept them at Megiddo, a town not far from Elijah's Mount Carmel. In the ensuing battle an enemy arrow fatally strikes Josiah in his chariot.

According to the chronicler, his death is a direct result of ignoring a warning from God spoken by Pharaoh Neco, of all people. Here is raw irony: the pious reformer fails to obey YHWH's word and so he dies in exactly the same way as the wicked Ahab, his mirror-image in the North. The prophet Jeremiah, entering the narrative for the first time at this point, composes laments for Josiah that are eventually incorporated into the liturgy of Israel. For now, defeated Judah remains a vassal of Egypt.

The Death of a Nation: Jehoahaz, Jehoiakim, Jehoiachin, Zedekiah (2 Kgs 23:31—25:30; 2 Chr 36; Jer 21, 22, 26–30, 34, 36–44, 52)

Josiah's wayward son Jehoahaz lasts only three months before Neco deposes him and takes him to Egypt, where he dies just as Jeremiah had earlier predicted (22:11–12). With Judah now thoroughly under Egypt's thumb, Neco appoints Jehoiakim, another of Josiah's sons, as "ruler." Although he pays tribute to his Egyptian masters, he soon proves to be as unfaithful to them as he is to YHWH.

When Egyptian power in the region then comes under assault from Babylon, Jehoiakim sees an opportunity: he switches sides and becomes vassal to Nebuchadnezzar, the king of Babylon. But then he changes his mind again and rebels, perhaps hoping for Egyptian help by playing one superpower against the other. It is a very dangerous game to play.

Even at this late stage YHWH tries one more time, saying to Jeremiah:

> Take a scroll of a book, and write in it all the words that I have spoken to you against Israel, and against Judah, and against all the nations, from the day I spoke to you, from the days of Josiah, even to this day. It may be that the house of Judah will hear all the evil which I intend to do to them; that they may each return from his evil way; that I may forgive their iniquity and their sin. (Jer 36:2–3)

---

territory into what used to belong to the Kingdom of Israel. Cf. Thompson, *Book of Jeremiah*, 18–19.

When the scroll is read to the king, he shreds it and tosses the fragments into the fire with contempt. In so doing he unwittingly prefigures the fate of his nation.

Nebuchadnezzar orders an invasion of Judah just as Jehoiakim dies[17] and is replaced by his eighteen-year-old son Jehoiachin. The latter's three-month reign is marked by covenant disobedience as well. Under Nebuchadnezzar's pressing attack Jehoiachin's forces are defeated on 15/16 March, 597 BC[18] and he is deported to Babylon along with the queen mother, other officials, and considerable plunder. Jeremiah's predicted epitaph for Jehoiachin has come true:

> Record this man as childless,
>   a man who will not prosper in his days;
> for no more will a man of his offspring prosper,
>   sitting on David's throne,
>   and ruling in Judah. (Jer 22:30)

The spoils sent back to Babylon include articles plundered from the temple, but the temple itself and the city of Jerusalem are spared. Nebuchadnezzar then names Zedekiah, Jehoiachin's uncle, as king, making him the third son of Josiah to take the throne of David.

As a puppet king Zedekiah is in a precarious position to begin with, but what is he thinking when, after nine years on the throne, he openly rebels against Babylon, by now the unquestioned superpower in the region? Perhaps he thought YHWH would surely back him up, but the chronicler's assessment of the low spiritual condition of the king and the nation suggests such hopes would surely be in vain:

> . . .he stiffened his neck, and hardened his heart against turning to Yahweh, the God of Israel. Moreover, all the chiefs of the priests, and the people, trespassed very greatly after all the abominations of the nations; and they polluted Yahweh's house which he had made holy in Jerusalem. (2 Chr 36:13b–14)

While 2 Kings and 2 Chronicles give an overview of the ensuing events, the book of Jeremiah takes us right inside the royal court and allows us to listen in on the debates within the king's inner circle (chapters 32–38). It turns out that Jeremiah is a key player in the drama unfolding as Nebuchadnezzar's forces invade again and systematically eliminate the fortified cities of Judah. Closing in on Jerusalem, they finally subject it to a devastating two-year siege.

Although Zedekiah himself seems to hold Jeremiah in high regard, the prophet is suspected of treason by many in the administration because he consistently advises against resisting the Babylonians. It is not the enemy's military superiority that

---

17. According to Jeremiah's prediction (22:18–19) he would suffer a humiliating death in Jerusalem and not be mourned by the people. However, 2 Chr 36:6 suggests (but does not state explicitly) that Jehoiakim was taken into Babylonian captivity.

18. Thompson, *Book of Jeremiah*, 24. Scholars are able to date this event from the records kept by the Babylonians.

informs his opinion, however, but the divine insight that Babylon is actually YHWH's instrument of final judgment upon disobedient Judah! For this inconvenient truth he is imprisoned or kept under guard for much of the siege. Jeremiah's sense of futility merely reflects that of the Almighty himself:

> Yahweh, the God of their fathers, sent to them by his messengers, rising up early and sending, because he had compassion on his people, and on his dwelling place; but they mocked the messengers of God, and despised his words, and scoffed at his prophets, until Yahweh's wrath arose against his people, until there was no remedy. (2 Chr 36:15–16)

It is clear that the nation is now in free-fall and will soon be shattered on the jagged rocks of God's approaching judgment. Again, the book of Jeremiah provides an intimate account of the action at this critical moment (52:1–9a): the food in the city runs out just as the enemy breaches the walls and comes swarming in upon the starving population. Zedekiah, along with his family and some of his troops, manages to escape briefly out onto the plains of Jericho but is captured there. It is a black day in July, 587 BC.

It gets even blacker for Zedekiah, both literally and figuratively. The last thing he sees before his captors put out his eyes is the execution of his sons. He is then shackled and carted off to captivity in Babylon. Like his vision, his line is extinguished forever. The holy city of Jerusalem is sacked and burned along with the palace and the great temple of Solomon. It all lies in utter ruin. As for the survivors, all but a few of the poor, left to tend the fields, are taken to Babylon as well.

One of Zedekiah's officials, a man named Gedaliah, is appointed governor (no more kings) and although Jeremiah rallies to his side, he is soon assassinated by some Jewish hotheads (Jer 40–44). Fearing repercussions from Babylon, the remainder of Gedaliah's administration flees to Egypt against the word of YHWH given through Jeremiah. They take the unwilling prophet with them and there he continues with his futile ministry.

Unbelievably, these exiles fall once again into idolatry, having failed to learn the lesson of their nation's demise. Jeremiah prophesies that they will suffer Egypt's own terrible fate at the hands of its enemies and be extinguished, but they refuse to listen. It is the same message he has been preaching for forty years and getting the same response. Fittingly, it is also his last recorded message. We hear no more of him. No wonder he is called "the weeping prophet"!

Although Jeremiah appears to have died a frustrated man, the book that bears his name ends with a glimmer of hope borrowed from the end of 2 Kings.[19] It is a report from Babylon twenty-five years after the destruction of Jerusalem and concerns

---

19. 2 Kgs 25:27–30. Wiseman, *1 and 2 Kings*, 317, observes, that Jews of the diaspora "reckoned years by Jehoiachin's captivity." An end to one era and a beginning to another.

Jehoiachin, grandson of Josiah and nephew of Zedekiah, apparently the only surviving member of Judah's royal family and arguably the true successor to the throne of David:

> [The king of Babylon] lifted up the head of Jehoiachin king of Judah, and released him fom prison. He spoke kindly to him, and set his throne above the throne of the kings who were with him in Babylon, and changed his prison garments. Jehoiachin ate bread before him continually all the days of his life. For his allowance, there was a continual allowance given him by the king of Babylon, every day a portion until the day of his death, all the days of his life. (52:31–34)

Not to be outdone, the chronicler ends his work on a positive note as well by skipping ahead seventy years after the deportation to cite a decree of Cyrus, the future king of Persia:

> Yahweh, the God of heaven, has given all the kingdoms of the earth to me; and he has commanded me to build him a house in Jerusalem, which is in Judah. Whoever there is among you of all his people, Yahweh his God be with him, and let him go up. (2 Chr 36:23)

From these postscripts the reader understands that, in spite of the disaster that has overtaken Judah, the lamp of David still flickers and the ancient promise of return remains in play. Hope springs eternal for YHWH's chosen people.

IN THE BOSOM OF ABRAHAM

Introduction

Since the heady days of Solomon the tide has been steadily going out, exposing the rotting timbers of the good ship "Judah," caught up on the rocks of faithless indifference. The glories of that famous king soon evaporated and too few other "sons of David" came close to measuring up to the lofty expectations created through YHWH's covenant with their "father." Once again we lift our eyes to the far horizon for any hope for the nation.

In the foreground, as we watch the traumatized exiles marched toward Babylon, we are not surprised to see that each of the Promises of the Covenant with Abraham seem to have come to a bitter end. In the next chapter we shall discover, however, that they find spectacular new life in the visions of the same prophets who had repeatedly tried to warn the children of Israel of the coming disaster. But who ever listens to them?

Israel Under the Kings (Part Three)

1. The Land/Place

Abraham's descendants have so identified themselves with this Promise that it has become an integral part of their self-understanding as a people. After all, they have been living in it now for over five hundred years, a period twice as long as the United States has existed. The loss of Judah's territory at the time of the exile, coming on top of the eradication of Israel in the North, shakes the nation to its very core. The whole of the expansive territory that was promised to them is now in the possession of their victors. This Promise seems only to mock them with every painful step toward Babylon and captivity.

Judah starts its existence in possession of less than half of the united kingdom of David/Solomon and just a fraction of the Land that YHWH had sworn to Abraham. The division of the Promised Land threatens its integrity as much in the South as in the North. Nevertheless, during Judah's existence there are a few moments when it looks like it might be rooted in the Land left to it. For example, King Asa, early on in Judah's existence, exhorts the nation as follows:

> "Let's build these cities, and make walls around them, with towers, gates, and bars. The land is yet before us, because we have sought Yahweh our God. We have sought him, and he has given us rest on every side." So they built and prospered. (2 Chr 14:7)

And it is true that under Josiah's benevolent rule toward the end, even some of what had belonged to Israel was taken over, but this proved to be only temporary.

In the end, Judah is unable to keep Babylon at bay by either diplomatic or military means. All its territory is lost and to a significant degree devastated by terrible waves of fighting and pillaging, leading to one of the saddest verses in the Old Testament:

> So Judah went into captivity, away from her land. (2 Kgs 25:21b)

Even in this darkness, however, it is possible to see a silver lining even after it is all over. As the chronicler puts it, the seventy-year exile could be seen as a time of renewal:

> . . .until the land had enjoyed its Sabbaths. As long as it lay desolate, it kept Sabbath, to fulfill seventy years. (2 Chr 36:21)

Of course, this is only visible from a later perspective. But the fact that it is included at this point in the narrative signals to the reader that this Story is not over after all. A greater purpose is deeply hidden in this disaster, one unimaginable, perhaps, to the devastated exiles. If they had not turned a deaf ear to their prophets who glimpsed this purpose they may have been comforted.

The sense of "Place" during this period only seems to intensify after the division of the Land. The sacred sites of Jerusalem and the temple remain in the territory of Judah and one gets the impression that the establishment of Northern counterparts causes Southerners to rally around them all the more. In fact, Jeremiah rails at some length against those who even regard the temple as a kind of lucky charm to ward off defeat by pagan armies (Jer 7). The fact that many Northerners also still consider these as the only legitimate sacred places deepened such sensibilities. The terrible destruction of both the city and the temple marks nothing less than the end of their world. No "place" to go anymore. It is already gone.

2. Many Descendants

The biblical record suggests that for most of its existence Judah is able to field large numbers of fighting men when called upon to do so. Indeed, during the reign of Jehoshaphat these total over one million. An army of this size, of course, indicates a much larger general population from which it is drawn. This fact alone may contribute to the false sense of security that seems to have possess the people. Such numbers are a sign of YHWH's blessing, after all. Aren't they?

Such attitudes, however, prove horribly illusory. With the unmitigated disaster of the Babylonian triumph goes a serious and almost fatal decline in population. Although absolute numbers are unavailable, two images from the biblical account make this absolutely clear.

The first of these comes from the prophet Ezekiel writing about the fall of Jerusalem from the perspective of the exile. To represent the people of the city he is told to shave his head and divide the fallen hair into thirds:

> A third part you shall burn in the fire in the middle of the city, when the days of the siege are fulfilled. You shall take a third part, and strike with the sword around it. A third part you shall scatter to the wind, and I will draw out a sword after them. You shall take of it a few in number, and bind them in the folds of your robe... (Ezek 5:2–3)

It is difficult to imagine a more vivid image of how few survivors remained.

The second image used in this period is that of the "remnant." While not quite as stark, it conveys the same impression of a devastating loss of population. In common language a "remnant" is the small bit of cloth still left of the bolt after all the rest has been measured out and used. It is too small to be used for making anything. In the Bible, the term was first used by Joseph when he makes himself known to his estranged brothers after they come down to Egypt to beg him for help:

> God sent me before you to preserve for you a remnant in the earth, and to save you alive by a great deliverance. (Gen 45:7)

Of course, the *idea* of remnant goes back much further, at least to Noah and Moses and their families. In all these cases YHWH is using or planning to use just a few remaining people to further his plan of salvation. Even just One.

The word is dramatically re-injected back into the biblical bloodstream by Isaiah and Jeremiah, who use it to describe those few who survive the destruction of Judah. Like Joseph, they see it in positive terms, as a vehicle of redemption:

> I will gather the remnant of my flock out of all the countries where I have driven them, and will bring them again to their folds; and they will be fruitful and multiply. (Jer 23:3)

But, looking around at their horribly depleted ranks, it couldn't seem much like redemption. The nation might be hanging by a thread, but it feels much more like a rope.

3. Blessing to All Nations

During this period Judah is constantly involved with other nations but it is only rarely that these are blessed by the association. As the final days of Judah gradually unravel, the only "blessing" seems to be what the nations (especially Babylon) can obtain through either the receipt of tribute or the looting of the great city of Jerusalem with its palaces and temple.

The prophets of Judah make it clear that the nations that have been involved in Judah's fall are actually under a curse. Isaiah and Jeremiah have long sections that denounce these countries one after the other in the most terrifying terms.[20] Jeremiah, whose appointment by YHWH is specifically to be "a prophet to the nations" (Jer 1:5), saves his best vitriol for Babylon itself:

> Babylon will become heaps,
>   a dwelling place for jackals,
>   an astonishment, and a hissing,
>   without inhabitant. (Jer 51:37)

This fate awaits even though, as all the prophets know very well, Judah's enemies have actually been serving as YHWH's agents![21] This, however, does not absolve them of acting out of wickedness, bloodlust, greed, and pride.[22]

Judah, instead of acting faithfully and attracting the nations to the worship of YHWH, does the opposite. Speaking through Jeremiah to the small group of refugees who had fled down into Egypt, YHWH asks them why they continue in the idolatrous ways of the people of Judah:

> ...that you may be cut off, and that you may be a curse and a reproach among all the nations of the earth... (Jer 44:8b)

---

20. See Isa 13–23; Jer 24–51.

21. On three occasions Jeremiah quotes YHWH's own characterization of Nebuchadnezzar, king of Babylon, as "my servant" (25:9; 27:6; 43:10).

22. Cf. Isa 10:2.

Rather than gathering the nations into the worship of YHWH, Judah was pushing them further away from the one true God. Isaiah even sees a time when the people of Judah will look back at this period and berate themselves because:

> We have not worked any deliverance in the earth; neither have the inhabitants of the world fallen. (Isa 26:18)

Perhaps many are hoping for YHWH to give them victory against all odds one more time as a way of establishing YHWH's reality before the nations. Hezekiah certainly sees this possibility when he prays in the face of Sennacherib's invasion:

> Now therefore, Yahweh our God, save us, I beg you, out of his hand, that all the kingdoms of the earth may know that you, Yahweh, are God alone. (2 Kgs 19:19)

Although they are delivered at that time, the nations are not impressed enough to change their minds. We have seen hints that this would only come when consistent covenant obedience, appropriate to a "kingdom of priests," brought in the Blessing: that (and that alone) would get the attention of the nations.

All this is not to deny that there are certainly passing moments in Judah's life when she is "lifted up" among the nations. Under Jehoshaphat the nation is at peace because all the nations recognized that YHWH has been fighting for him. Uzziah's fame spreads far and wide and Hezekiah as well is "was exalted in the sight of all nations" (2 Chr 32:23). But as for blessings being extended to these peoples, even at these moments, there is no hint. In the end, according to the prophets, the nations are under a dark cloud of impending doom, sinners in the hands of an angry God.

4. Fruitfulness

As we might have expected, given the wars and rumors of wars in this period, the Land is eventually devastated to the point of desolation. It is not just lost to Judah: it is destroyed, unable to produce its usual harvests for *anyone* trying to live off of it. Isaiah looks ahead and sees such a time coming:

> It will happen in that day that every place where there were a thousand vines at a thousand silver shekels, shall be for briers and thorns... All the hills that were cultivated with the hoe, you shall not come there for fear of briers and thorns; but it shall be for the sending out of oxen, and for sheep to tread on. (Isa 7:23–25)

If the references to "briers and thorns" reminds us of the curse on the earth, Jeremiah even sees the situation in terms that suggest the state of the *pre*-created earth, when chaos ruled:

> I saw the earth, and, behold, it was waste and void, and the heavens, and they had no light... I saw, and behold, there was no man, and all the birds of the sky had fled. I saw, and behold, the fruitful field was a wilderness, and all its cities were broken down at the presence of Yahweh, before his fierce anger. (Jer 4:23, 25–26)

Paradise has indeed been lost. Eden is no more. It's almost as if it never was.[23]

Against this picture are a few brief glimpses of fruitfulness during the reigns of the more faithful kings.[24] Even within an overall pattern of disobedience, the "covenant mechanism" of Blessings for obedience is still at work to some degree. Jehoshaphat, for example, has great wealth, partly as a result of tribute from surrounding nations.[25] And Hezekiah grows very rich, having:

> ...also storehouses for the increase of grain, new wine, and oil; and stalls for all kinds of animals, and flocks in folds. Moreover he provided for himself cities, and possessions of flocks and herds in abundance; for God had given him abundant possessions. (2 Chr 32:28–29)

Memories of these times only make the devastation and loss of the Land all the more painful.

5. Relationship

The new and decisive factor in discerning the state of YHWH's bond with Judah is the destruction of Jerusalem and especially the temple. Here is the city of God, gone. Here is the very dwelling place of the Most High on earth, gone. Here is the one place where God and man meet together, gone. Nothing could speak more graphically of YHWH's absence from their midst. Gone, gone, and gone.

This is the only word that adequately describes Judah's relationship with YHWH at the end. The overall thrust of the narrative makes this abundantly clear: YHWH is finally unwilling to associate himself at all with this rebellious crowd. They have been weighed in the balances and found wanting.

YHWH's efforts to establish a nation that would "know" him seem to have ended in utter failure. Although the text indicates that the final straw was Manasseh's reign[26], Israel ("he who struggles with God") has lived up to its name right from the time of

---

23. This connection is strengthened in observing that the phrases in the Hebrew Bible translated "formless and empty" and "there were no people" are used only here and in Gen 1:2 and 2:5 respectively. Dempster, *Dominion and Dynasty*, 163.

24. Cf. 278, above, re: Uzziah.

25. Cf. 2 Chr 17:10–13.

26. 2 Kgs 24:4

the Exodus.[27] In spite of the reforming efforts of Hezekiah and Josiah, disobedience continues to be the norm.

While it is true that YHWH, speaking through the prophets of the day, commonly refers to Judah (and Israel) as "my people," this should not be taken to mean that they are still on good terms, given what we have seen above. The phrase really only affirms their historic relationship and YHWH's enduring claim upon them, not their actually experiencing such a relationship. To be "the people of God" is hardly a guarantee of his constant blessing or grounds for boasting!

Fittingly, the writer of 2 Kings expresses YHWH's final judgment upon Judah in words that bring to mind what happened to Adam and Eve:

> For through the anger of Yahweh, this happened in Jerusalem and Judah, until he had cast them out from his presence. (2 Kgs 24:20)

They were gone. The Land which once bristled with Edenic promise and where YHWH was pleased to dwell has been laid waste: instead of paradise regained, it is paradise lost. Again. The road back to Eden has been washed away by a torrent of disobedience. Gone, gone, and gone, indeed.

6. Grace/Obedience

The narrative of this period is dominated by Judah's obstinate and persistent slide into ever-increasing covenant disobedience. Even the fact that there were a number of righteous kings and moments of covenant renewal is not enough to prevent this rush to judgment. Judah has entered the "end game," the point at which she has acquired such a weight of disobedience as to disqualify her from her status as "saved." The theoretical possibility of this happening, often threatened, has turned into a terrible reality and the frightening Curses of the "covenant mechanism" have been unleashed. The nation, chosen by YHWH in Abraham and saved by YHWH through Moses has lost its land, its population and its capability of being a blessing to anyone, least of all to the nations. It seems to be a straightforward case of "saved by grace, maintained by obedience" gone bad.

Of course, things are not quite that simple. On three occasions YHWH's promise to David is given as the reason why the nation is spared disaster.[28] Here we see grace at work, overwhelming the mandated effects of rank disobedience and providing us with more complexity to consider. Furthermore, when compared to the many changes of dynasty in the North, the very survival of the line of David in such turbulent times must be considered an amazing sign of grace. It endures in spite of two coups, two child-kings, Jehoram (who kills all his brothers), and his wife Athaliah (who murders all but one of her son's sons and rules herself). Even in its last terrible days, as long as

---

27. See 122, above.
28. 1 Kgs 15:4; 2 Kgs 8:19 and 19:34

there is a king in Judah, it is a son of David who occupies the throne. And as a sign of hope we are told that still the line persists in exile. It is a line that will hold through the worst blizzard. Grace, squandered, trampled upon and despised, is again poised to triumph in the End. Somehow.

15

Morning Star of New Creation
The Prophetic Vision

Suggested Reading

Isaiah and Jeremiah

PREAMBLE

Due to the nature of the material under consideration, this chapter only partially conforms to the format we have been using so far. The "Major Developments" section, given the notorious difficulties with chronology in prophecy, will present only a rough sequential outline of the events foreseen by the prophets. Because the Bible does not present these in a narrative form, *The Story* section is omitted altogether and replaced with "The Prophetic Vision." The "Perspectives" and "In the Bosom of Abraham" sections will function as close to normally as possible.

MAJOR DEVELOPMENTS

- The Day of YHWH arrives
- Judgment upon Judah
- Judgment upon the nations
- Restoration of Israel/Judah to the Land
- Leadership of Suffering Servant/Davidic King
- The New Covenant is instituted

- Israel is exalted before the nations
- The nations come to worship YHWH
- New Creation
- Land restored to Israel/Judah (expands to whole earth)
- Many Descendants expands to include the entire population of the world
- Blessing comes to All Nations (incorporated into Israel under YHWH)
- Fruitfulness abounds in the Land (and the whole earth)
- Relationship with YHWH is made perfect through outpouring of the Spirit
- Grace overwhelms obedience as newly renovated hearts enable YHWH's people to do his will

PERSPECTIVES

More of the Same

As noted in the last chapter, as the Story progresses the literary prophets come more fully on stage. In the North, Elijah and Elisha are the undoubted heroes of the narrative, but they left no independent writings of their own. Perhaps this is because their calling was simply to address the specific immediate situation. It is when we encounter the written works of Amos and Hosea that horizon broadens and we learn of the coming of a great judgment that is to be followed by great blessing on the nation as a whole.

These two Northern prophets begin to outline a picture of Samaria's future that includes the destruction of the Land and its restoration, the exile of the people and their permanent return, and even hints of a new creation, a new covenant, and the ultimate rule of a Davidic king.[1] This is evidently the End to which all of salvation history has been moving. Often scholars refer to this as the "eschaton," and its study is known as "eschatology," after the Greek word for "last."

The Southern prophets (represented here primarily by Isaiah and Jeremiah[2]) share the vision of their Northern colleagues. They, too, see judgment and then restoration in store for YHWH's people and use some of the same concepts in describing it, but of course expand the picture to include Judah. And they just keep on expanding it until it encompasses the whole cosmos.

---

1. See 256, above.

2. Obadiah seems to set early in Judah's life, while Joel and Nahum are difficult to place chronologically.

More Than More of the Same

Although the Northern prophet Amos begins with a fiery blast towards six of Israel's immediate neighbors, the Southerners add to both the number of doomed nations and the detail of the coming destruction. It becomes such a dominant theme that the reader is bound to wonder why these nations are subject to such terrible judgment when they are merely acting as YHWH's instruments of punishing Israel and Judah. According to Isaiah it is because they act out of pride and do not acknowledge the true source of their victory:

> Therefore it will happen that when the Lord has performed his whole work on Mount Zion and on Jerusalem, I will punish the fruit of the willful proud heart of the king of Assyria, and the insolence of his arrogant looks. Should an ax brag against him who chops with it? Should a saw exalt itself above him who saws with it? As if a rod should lift those who lift it up, or as if a staff should lift up someone who is not wood. (Isa 10:12 & 15)

Once again we find ourselves at the perplexing intersection of God's will and human responsibility, of divine sovereignty and human freedom, and unable to see where the one ends and the other begins. But here, at least, we are given reason to believe that YHWH's judgment is not arbitrary.

But Judah's prophets do not just multiply the number of the nations who are subject to judgment. They go on to envisage the inclusion of these same nations in the coming restoration! And, as if this is not startling enough, their vision stretches out to encompass the renewal and even the renovation of the entire creation. Talk about an expansive vision! In fact, ordinary human language is stretched to the breaking point in trying to describe such extraordinary events.

Reaching for their palettes, in broad impressionistic strokes these artists of the word fill in the previous Northern sketch with a riot of shades and shapes, coloring well outside the lines. Up close it seems all tumult and confusion, but if we pull back a little to gain perspective, a clearer picture begins to emerge.

"Prophecy" as a Literary Genre

We need to keep in mind that we are dealing with a type of literature that demands a unique interpretive approach. If we read prophecy in a simple, straightforward manner, we soon realize that we must be on the wrong track, if not the wrong train. We are clearly faced with a text that is struggling to portray things beyond normal human experience and therefore must be taken as figurative to a significant degree. In such circumstances it is unwise to seek a great deal of precision. We must be satisfied with the general picture that emerges rather than try to determine the exact meaning of every detail.

An important element of prophecy is what might be called its unstable focus: the prophet often seems to be using a camera whose unstable autofocus is unable to settle itself on just one object. Isaiah speaks of Israel as YHWH's "servant" in chapter 49 and then of another "servant" (Isaiah?) who will bring Israel back to YHWH. Chapter 53 displays a similar elasticity with the term. And, in chapter 7 when YHWH gives Ahaz the sign of an "Immanuel" to be born of a virgin and who will deliver Jerusalem from a contemporary enemy, the vision then seems to expand to a scene of universal judgment.

Similarly, the message often appears to be jumping from the present to the past to the future with no clear boundary between them. The book of Jeremiah, for instance, while following a rough chronological order overall, jumps around seemingly at random within that order. For example, chapter 21 is about King Zedekiah, while chapter 26 takes place during the earlier reign of King Jehoiakim.

The fact that their writings often seem jumbled chronologically[3] and thematically seems to reflect the reality of the crisis-ridden and chaotic times in which these prophets were active. Nahum artfully portrays this general sense of disorder and tumult in describing Nineveh's fate:

> Woe to the bloody city! It is all full of lies and robbery. The prey doesn't depart. The noise of the whip, the noise of the rattling of wheels, prancing horses, and bounding chariots, the horseman mounting, and the flashing sword, the glittering spear, and a multitude of slain, and a great heap of corpses, and there is no end of the bodies. They stumble on their bodies... (Nah 3:1–3)

While the WEB translates this passage into prose, it is very much like poetry. It conveys much beyond mere description. Indeed, the oracles of the prophets are often given in poetic form, in part because this genre is able to convey something of a reality beyond ordinary description. Because of this, poetry too has its own set of interpretive rules, and this gives us another reason to be less dogmatic in our conclusions. Again, let the interpreter beware! This chapter will therefore attempt to analyze only the broadest brush strokes of these enigmatic men of God.

It should be noted that a few of the prophet Joel's pronouncements will be included in spite of the fact that it is uncertain as to whether he was working in the North or in the South. However, he does seem to throw some light on our attempt to understand the overall message of the prophets. If he is from the North, he speaks with a decided Southern accent.

A New Covenant

Because it bears so directly on how the Story hangs together, this element of the prophetic picture demands our attention in this section. It should also be noted that,

---

3. Some of this may be attributed to later editors of their material, but the conclusion still holds.

due to the fact that "covenant" is Biblespeak for "relationship," this discussion is also relevant to the "Relationship" section below. Our particular question here has to do with how the "new" covenant is related to the "old" covenant.

A future covenant is mentioned in passing by both Amos and Hosea, and, while Isaiah refers to the coming of an everlasting "covenant of peace" (Isa 54:10[4]), it is Jeremiah who uses the term "new covenant" and fills in its features (Jer 31:31–34; 32:38–41). The first of these to note is that this new covenant will be with both Israel *and* Judah:

> Behold, the days come," says Yahweh,
>   "that I will make a new covenant with the house of Israel,
>   and with the house of Judah." (Jer 31:31)

As the next verse indicates, the new covenant is "new" specifically in relation to the Mosaic covenant.

> ". . .not according to the covenant that I made with their fathers in the day
> that I took them by the hand to bring them out of the land of Egypt;
>   which covenant of mine they broke,
>   although I was a husband to them," says Yahweh. (Jer 31:32)

While this text seems to indicate that the "new" is meant simply to *replace* the "old," which lies "broken," Jeremiah goes on to provide more details that suggest a more nuanced distinction is necessary:

> "But this is the covenant that I will make with the house of Israel after those days,"
>   says Yahweh:
> "I will put my law in their inward parts,
>   and I will write it in their heart.
> I will be their God,
>   and they shall be my people.
> They will no longer each teach his neighbor,
>   and every man teach his brother, saying, 'Know Yahweh;'
> for they will all know me,
>   from their least to their greatest," says Yahweh:
> "for I will forgive their iniquity,
>   and I will remember their sin no more." (Jer 31:33–34)

> "Then they will be my people, and I will be their God. I will give them one heart and one way, that they may fear me forever, for their good, and the good of their children after them. I will make an everlasting covenant with them, that I will not turn away from following them, to do them good. I will put my fear in their hearts, that they may not depart from me. Yes, I will rejoice over

---

4. Cf. Isa 55:3; 59:21, and 61:8.

them to do them good, and I will plant them in this land assuredly with my whole heart and with my whole soul." (Jer 32:38–41)

These passages together provide fuller context for a proper understanding of "new" covenant. What becomes clear is that it's uniqueness lies primarily in the amazing provision of a changed heart and mind which guarantee that the Mosaic covenant will never again be broken.

As we have seen again and again in humanity an inability to obey the laws of God because of a fault in the "heart." Now, as exile looms in the days of Jeremiah, YHWH himself expresses the same disturbing conclusion. Desperation and bewilderment mark his words:

> The heart is deceitful above all things
>   and it is exceedingly corrupt.
> Who can know it? (Jer 17:9)

By this point in the Story it could not be more clear: *the heart of the matter is a matter of the heart.* In order to be in a lasting Relationship with YHWH, humankind needs nothing less than a complete inner transformation.

While the narrative has often expressed or implied the need for this change,[5] the coming eschaton will be the time to "name it and claim it." In that day, the law will be followed perfectly by a people whose hearts are entirely in tune with the ways of YHWH. The "new" covenant then transcends the problematic question of conditionality that was so central to the Mosaic covenant. Disobedience will not be part of the equation anymore.

> I will give them a heart to know me, that I am Yahweh. They will be my people, and I will be their God; for they will return to me with their whole heart. (Jer 24:7; cf. Isa 59:2)

In effect, this suggests that the "new covenant" is perhaps best regarded as the Mosaic covenant raised to "unconditional" status alongside those of Abraham and David. In the process, all of the elements related to its former conditionality, such as the covenant mechanism and both the ceremonial law and the civil law,[6] fall away. After all, these were in place to deal with the results of human sin: without the latter, they become unnecessary. Once the moral law is being obeyed perfectly from the heart, there won't be any need for incentives to avoid sin, any sacrifice to atone for it, or any disputes needing settlement!

However, in reference to the ceremonial law, it must be cautioned that there are a few verses in the prophets that refer to sacrifice taking place in the coming age. It is uncertain how these are to be taken and some may certainly be symbolic references to

---

5. Cf., 239, above.

6. Indeed, this is where these rather artificial and limited categories prove themselves most helpful.

other matters.[7] As for the civil law, there is even less evidence in the prophets for its continuing validity into the eschaton.

It should be noted, as well, that the "new" covenant, by virtue of its provision of a changed heart for each person, represents a shift away from a corporate and mediated relationship with YHWH to a more individual and personal relationship with him. We have noted how the people needed, because of their sin, to keep YHWH at arm's length under the Mosaic covenant.[8] In the eschaton, sin will no longer pose a barrier to the relationship.

The unconditional covenants with Abraham and David continue unabated into the eschaton as promised. Indeed, as this chapter will demonstrate, the End is the fulfillment of the provisions of both of these covenants and is, in this sense at least, in direct continuity with them.

In summary, the new covenant is not completely new as far as its moral code is concerned, but is radically new in the way *that code is realized*. Partly this is due to what is implied in the above quotations: YHWH's rule will be both direct and fully effective. All this suggests that what is coming will be both continuous *and* discontinuous with what went on before. In this respect it fits perfectly into the general sense of the kind of changes that will take place as the new age is ushered in.

THE PROPHETIC VISION

A Covenantal Choir

One element of the prophetic message is crystal clear: the reason for God's judgment is covenant disobedience. On this they all agree. Indeed, it is not hard to imagine these men gathered together on the slopes of Mt. Gerezim, shaking their fists as they repeat the same terrible Curses Moses ordered to be pronounced from that position as the nation first entered the Promised Land. It had chosen death over life. The time has finally come for those Curses to wreak their final havoc.

> For I didn't speak to your fathers or command them in the day that I brought them out of the land of Egypt concerning burnt offerings or sacrifices; but this thing I commanded them, saying, 'Listen to my voice, and I will be your God, and you shall be my people. Walk in all the way that I command you, that it may be well with you.' But they didn't listen or turn their ear, but walked in their own counsels and in the stubbornness of their evil heart, and went backward, and not forward... You shall tell them, 'This is the nation that has not listened to Yahweh their God's voice, nor received instruction. Truth has perished, and is cut off from their mouth.' Cut off your hair, and throw it away,

---

7. Cf. Isa 56:7b; 60:7 and 66:20–21.
8. See 114, above.

> and take up a lamentation on the bare heights; for Yahweh has rejected and
> forsaken the generation of his wrath. (Jer 7:22–4; 27–9)

That is it in a nutshell. And the essential disobedience of the nation could be packed into two words: idolatry and injustice. Both are assaulted repeatedly by the prophets.

These men are simply working within the "covenant mechanism" as prosecuting attorneys, bringing forward YHWH's case against his people and announcing that he is going to execute the prescribed judgment upon them. In both North and South, they are the arch-conservatives of their day, calling the nation back to its primary commitment. At the same time, their call also makes it clear that YHWH is in no rush to judgment but still desires only the best for the nation he loves and has chosen:

> Yet even now," says Yahweh, "turn to me with all your heart,
>   and with fasting, and with weeping, and with mourning."
> Tear your heart, and not your garments,
>   and turn to Yahweh, your God;
>   for he is gracious and merciful,
>   slow to anger, and abundant in loving kindness,
>   and relents from sending calamity.
> Who knows? He may turn and relent,
>   and leave a blessing behind him. . . (Joel 2:12–14a)

However, Judah's prophets are not just making an appeal to return to the foundations of the past. They are also busy painting startling pictures of the amazing future YHWH has in store after the "covenant mechanism" had rained down its final devastation upon the nation. While it is important to allow each prophet to present his particular vision on its own terms, in the following pages we will outline certain commonalities and general patterns among them. For the most part these conform remarkably to Moses's own forecast of the future Blessings:

> It shall happen, when all these things have come on you, the blessing and the curse, which I have set before you, and you shall call them to mind among all the nations where Yahweh your God has driven you, and return to Yahweh your God and obey his voice according to all that I command you today, you and your children, with all your heart and with all your soul, that then Yahweh your God will release you from captivity, have compassion on you, and will return and gather you from all the peoples where Yahweh your God has scattered you. If your outcasts are in the uttermost parts of the heavens, from there Yahweh your God will gather you, and from there he will bring you back. Yahweh your God will bring you into the land which your fathers possessed, and you will possess it. He will do you good, and increase your numbers more than your fathers. Yahweh your God will circumcise your heart, and the heart of your offspring, to love Yahweh your God with all your heart

and with all your soul, that you may live. Yahweh your God will put all these curses on your enemies and on those who hate you, who persecuted you. You shall return and obey Yahweh's voice, and do all his commandments which I command you today. (Deut 30:1–8)

Like their Northern counterparts, these prophets are adhering strictly to the Mosaic covenant. Even their visions of the future that strike us as so wildly innovative are rooted in Moses, simply (!) erecting a more elaborate structure upon the foundation already laid down by him. They remain covenant men, a choir all singing from the same hymnbook, but not afraid to improvise on occasion or add a descant or two. It is always possible to discern the tune they are using, even if elements of the harmony sometimes remains elusive.

Imagine the various episodes of redemptive history as the nightly services of an evangelistic crusade, YHWH's great "mission to the world." The following analysis presents the themes of the prophetic vision in the form of the "hymns" chosen for its climactic final service. The reader is invited to envision an all-stops-pulled celebration in a magnificent cathedral filled to capacity. The choir and the ministers stream in during the first hymn, the processional, and then, in singing the gradual, the congregation prepares for the proclamation of the good news. In response to the word, the offertory is sung and, finally, the entire congregation, led by the choir and ministers, goes out into the world rejoicing to the music and words of the recessional.

Given the occasion, and that it is the choir of the prophets that is selecting the hymns, it seems natural that these compositions celebrate the main components of the coming eschaton one after the other in approximate order of occurrence. How these "hymns" arise directly out of the Mosaic covenant will be noted by indicating the corresponding passages from Deuteronomy 30 in brackets.

But it is not just simply the Mosaic covenant that provides the prophetic music because Moses was himself working within the Covenant with Abraham.[9] Therefore it comes as no surprise when we see the choir also elaborating upon Abraham. For example, we have had occasion to note YHWH's pronouncement to Abraham, "I will bless those who bless you, and I will curse him who treats you with contempt" (Gen 12:3), and how this has been working itself out in the subsequent story of his descendants.[10] We can see this principle behind the content of the first and last "hymns" of the prophets as outlined below.

By the time they get to that last hymn the choir is in full Abrahamic voice as they put their remarkable vision into words to match the music of YHWH's final redemption. In fact, that last hymn is entitled *In the Bosom of Abraham*, and it will come as no surprise that it has six familiar verses. Because of its importance it will be dealt with in its own section at the end of this chapter. Not all hymns are the same length, and

---

9. See 132–33, above.

10. See 72–3, 104–5, 163, above.

the last, our recessional, has to allow time for *everyone* to join in the parade out of the great cathedral and into the beckoning future.

Hymns for the Final Service

Processional: A Judgment Upon the Nations (Cf. Deut 30:7)

As Judah's final days begin to unfold in all their horror, the focus of her prophets widens with increased intensity upon "all the nations." They begin to address the nations directly and it is not with words of comfort, as we have already noted.[11] At least, not at first.

Jeremiah dedicates six chapters to this subject, saving his longest rant for Babylon itself and its future desolation and abandonment (51:62–64). Isaiah has a long segment condemning one nation after the other (13–23). Later, he summarizes his message:

> Come near, you nations, to hear!
>   Listen, you peoples.
>   Let the earth and all it contains hear,
>   the world, and everything that comes from it.
> For Yahweh is enraged against all the nations,
>   and angry with all their armies.
> He has utterly destroyed them.
>   He has given them over for slaughter. (Isa 34:1–2)

Zephaniah has a lesser amount dedicated to the same topic while Nahum's entire message is directed at the foreign city of Nineveh. The fact that the fate of the nations is bound up with that of Israel has now become fully apparent. But wasn't it a blessing that was promised to them through Abraham? True, but this is just the opening hymn: the service isn't over yet.

Gradual: The Awesome Day of YHWH

The Southern prophets, like those in the North,[12] characteristically use the phrases "the day of YHWH" or "that day" to describe the moment in time when YHWH finally acts in judgment on Judah and on the nations. Here, for instance, is Isaiah referring to "the house of Jacob":

> For there will be a day of Yahweh of Armies for all that is proud and arrogant,
>   and for all that is lifted up;

---

11. See 296, above.
12. Amos 5:18–20; Hos 1:5.

> and it shall be brought low:
> Men shall go into the caves of the rocks,
> > and into the holes of the earth,
> > from before the terror of Yahweh,
> > and from the glory of his majesty,
> > when he arises to shake the earth mightily. (Isa 2:12, 19)

It is perhaps no accident that the language in this pronouncement seems to extend beyond the immediate circumstances of pending exile to encompass something that is more universal in scope. For the same phrases are used of the terrible judgment that will fall on the nations when their time comes. Here is Isaiah again, on mighty Babylon's fate:

> Behold, the day of Yahweh comes, cruel, with wrath and fierce anger; to make the land a desolation, and to destroy its sinners out of it. For the stars of the sky and its constellations will not give their light. The sun will be darkened in its going out, and the moon will not cause its light to shine. (Isa 13:9–10)

There seems to be something in Southern "prophetspeak" that finds it difficult to confine itself to the normal experience of disaster and reaches out to what we might call more "end of the world" language involving the entire cosmos.

To prove their use of terms even more elastic, the "day" concept is also used of the moment when YHWH ushers in his redemption, again for both Judah and the nations! Conforming to the use of Amos and Hosea,[13] Isaiah says:

> It will happen in that day that his burden will depart from off your shoulder, and his yoke from off your neck, and the yoke shall be destroyed because of the anointing oil. (10:27)

And what is true of Israel is also true of the nations:

> It shall happen in the latter days, that the mountain of Yahweh's house shall be established on the top of the mountains,
> > and shall be raised above the hills;
> > and all nations shall flow to it. (Isa 2:2)

This confirms Amos and Hosea's similar use of the "day of YHWH," proving itself to be a double-sided concept, serving as the portal between judgment and redemption.

Offertory: The Suffering Servant-King

On a number of occasions the prophets proclaim that YHWH would work through a key man in bringing about his coming redemption. At first, because different titles

---

13. Cf. Amos 9:11–15; Hos 2:16.

and functions are given in different passages, it might be assumed that a variety of different men would be YHWH's agents.

However, there are persuasive reasons to conclude that we are rather presented with one person who assumes different identities in order to undertake various redemptive roles. For one thing, there is the nature of the prophetic portrayals themselves. Each time such a character is referred to, he alone is the central actor bringing about the expected redemption. Indeed, there is never any allusion that there will be more than one important person who will be acting on YHWH's behalf. Furthermore, in Isaiah 9:6–7, quoted below, a single figure is given a variety of titles/roles, confirming that we are likely being presented with one individual who can be described in a number of ways.

The very form of the overall biblical narrative also creates an expectation that there is "only the One." Every other act of salvation has come through a single man specifically called to be YHWH's agent: Adam, Noah, Abraham, Jacob, Joseph, Moses, Joshua, judges, Samuel, David/Solomon, a king, a prophet. And usually each is presented as a possible candidate to be the expected One, the "Serpent Crusher." The biblically-shaped mind comes to understand that when YHWH acts for us, he does so through a single human instrument of his own choosing. For him not to do so in the end would be an anomaly to say the least.

For these reasons, we will proceed on the assumption that the different portrayals of a central eschatological figure in the prophets refer to the same individual. Like a good secret agent, he may be able to assume a number of identities as circumstances dictate. Two of them deserve our special attention.

1. A Davidic King

It would be difficult not to connect these visions of the eschaton with the everlasting and glorious kingdom that YHWH had promised to David for one of his descendants.[14] Among the prophets, it is Isaiah and Jeremiah who emphasize this identity but with the concurrence of the Northern prophets as well. Somewhat enigmatically, YHWH says through Amos:

> In that day I will raise up the tent of David who is fallen, and close up its breaches, and I will raise up its ruins, and I will build it as in the days of old; (9:11)

And, oddly, Hosea suggests that David himself somehow will return:

> Afterward the children of Israel shall return, and seek Yahweh their God, and David their king, and shall come with trembling to Yahweh and to his blessings in the last days. (3:5)

---

14. See 213–15, above.

Isaiah and Jeremiah both use the image of a fresh "branch" or "shoot" that springs forth from the "tree" of David so viciously chopped down by the Babylonians when they put an end to the monarchy:

> In those days and at that time,
>   I will cause a Branch of righteousness to grow up to David.
>   He will execute justice and righteousness in the land. (Jer 33:15)

> A shoot will come out of the stock of Jesse,
>   and a branch out of his roots will bear fruit. (Isa 11:1)

These passages appear to be expressions of the same reality: the agent of YHWH's coming redemption will come from the line of David, to even "be" David and reign as king over Israel. And, as Israel expands to include the nations, this King will find himself ruler of the whole earth:

> Behold, I have given him for a witness to the peoples,
>   a leader and commander to the peoples.
> Behold, you shall call a nation that you don't know;
>   and a nation that didn't know you shall run to you,
>   because of Yahweh your God,
>   and for the Holy One of Israel;
>   for he has glorified you. (Isa 55:4–5; cf. 11:10)

The birth of such a King will naturally be cause for intense celebration:

> For a child is born to us. A son is given to us; and the government will be on his shoulders. His name will be called Wonderful Counselor, Mighty God, Everlasting Father, Prince of Peace. Of the increase of his government and of peace there shall be no end, on David's throne, and on his kingdom, to establish it, and to uphold it with justice and with righteousness from that time on, even forever. The zeal of Yahweh of Armies will perform this. (Isa 9:6–7)

In this passage we can find four other titles/identities for the agent: Wonderful Counselor; Mighty God; Everlasting Father; Prince of Peace. Of course, anyone familiar with the British royal family will not be surprised by this multiplicity of names/titles/functions in connection with a king.[15] Isaiah elsewhere refers to "Immanuel" ("God with us") on three occasions[16] and it would appear that this could also be another of the agent's personas or titles. However, the context is somewhat more ambiguous, making such a link a bit tenuous. In any event, we clearly have a number of identities for YHWH's secret agent.

There is one other important feature of the agent's identity as Davidic King: he will be specially endowed with the Spirit of YHWH:

---

15. Queen Elizabeth II has at least twenty-seven titles.
16. Isa 7:14 and 8:8 (cf. 8:10).

> Yahweh's Spirit will rest on him:
>> the spirit of wisdom and understanding,
>> the spirit of counsel and might,
>> the spirit of knowledge and of the fear of Yahweh.
> 3 His delight will be in the fear of Yahweh.
> He will not judge by the sight of his eyes,
>> neither decide by the hearing of his ears; (Isa 11:2–3)

This description is bound to remind the reader of Solomon, the first "son of David," but at the same time it reaches well beyond him to the deepest yearnings of humanity for a better world. One greater than Solomon is here.

2. The Suffering Servant

The second major persona assumed by YHWH's agent is that of "servant." Confined to the writings of Isaiah (42:1–9; 49:1–6; 50:4–9; 52:13—53:12), this designation signifies a role exactly opposite to that which we usually associate with a king. Even more jarring is the fact that the agent is portrayed not just as a servant, but as a *suffering* servant:

> He was oppressed,
>> yet when he was afflicted he didn't open his mouth.
> As a lamb that is led to the slaughter,
>> and as a sheep that before its shearers is silent,
>> so he didn't open his mouth...
>
> Yet it pleased Yahweh to bruise him.
>> He has caused him to suffer. (Isa 53:7, 10a)

He appears as an unobtrusive, humble, and compassionate character who suffers rejection, shame, wounding, and death. Through these experiences he somehow brings salvation to Israel and light to the nations. The identity of the Servant is complicated by the fact that in one short passage he is identified both *as* Israel and someone whose mission is *to* Israel (Isa 49:3–6)!

Recombinant DNA?: A Suffering Servant-King

At first these two identities seem completely distinct from each other, if not mutually exclusive altogether. However, the Story has already provided us with a few precedents that offer some hint about how their respective DNAs might ultimately be spliced together.

In fact, the narrative has already linked the concepts of "servant" and "king." It begins to point in this direction when YHWH occasionally refers to a leader who serves him faithfully as "my servant." The expression is first used of Abraham,[17] and then of Moses.[18] Eventually it is used of David himself: in fact, out of twenty-five usages of this term, he is the subject of thirteen of them. So it is David who comes to embody this characterization in his role as the king of Israel. He is the first servant-king in this sense of the word and it should not come as any great surprise that God's coming agent, as Davidic King, should then be cast in the same mold.

But, of course, the sense used here is not fully reflective of the prophetic use of the term "servant," which has a distinct suggestion of deep humility about it. The elders of Israel perhaps come closer to this meaning in their advice to Solomon's son Rehoboam:

> If you will be a servant to this people today, and will serve them, and answer them with good words, then they will be your servants forever. (1 Kgs 12:7)

Using this verse as a lens, it becomes apparent that the concept of a servant-king expresses the ideal of how a good king would conduct himself in regard to his subjects. He is to serve *them,* rather than the other way around.

However, the prophetic Servant is not just a humble servant of YHWH and the people: he undergoes abject humiliation and suffering. We need to reach back further, to the very Beginning, in order to find any hint that God's agent of redemption will endure anything like this.

As we have noted, the first pages of the Bible, in pointing to a coming Serpent Crusher, create an expectation that naturally turns the reader's attention to each of the possible candidates that subsequently appear in the text. A truly attentive reader will have noticed that in the original promise the Serpent Crusher is to suffer significantly in his victory over the serpent. His heel will be struck or even crushed. It is this truth that now finds expression in the person of YHWH's coming agent as portrayed by the prophets.[19] Here is the Serpent Crusher at last, stricken but victorious, Servant but King.

But the Servant is not just to suffer. He is to die! And, of all things, to die as a substitutionary and atoning sacrifice:

> Surely he has borne our sickness
>   and carried our suffering;
> yet we considered him plagued,
>   struck by God, and afflicted.
> But he was pierced for our transgressions.
>   He was crushed for our iniquities.
> The punishment that brought our peace was on him;

---

17. Gen 26:24
18. Num 12:6, 7; 14:24; and Josh 1:2, 7.
19. Coralie Losier, one of my former students, drew this connection to my attention. She is obviously more attentive than I!

> and by his wounds we are healed.
> All we like sheep have gone astray.
>> Everyone has turned to his own way;
>> and Yahweh has laid on him the iniquity of us all...
> Yet it pleased Yahweh to bruise him.
>> He has caused him to suffer.
> When you make his soul an offering for sin,
>> ...yet he bore the sins of many
>> and made intercession for the transgressors. (Isa 53:4–6, 10a, 12b)

What can we make of this? The only explicit precedent in Scripture for such language is found in the sacrificial system. The Servant assumes the role of the sacrificial animal and bears the sin of "all." This is a profound conceptual leap, to say the least! It may, however, provide an answer to a question that we raised earlier about the sacrificial system in that it offered atonement only for "accidental" sins: What, then, is the (greater) sacrifice for serious sins?[20] Is the atoning death of the Servant to be seen as the answer to this question?

And just to complicate things a bit further, there is another way in which the death of the Servant arises out of the Story so far. To see this, we must remember that the Servant seems to sometimes be identified as Israel itself. From this perspective his suffering and death is the suffering and death of the *nation*. This would fit with the wider vision of the prophets that the nations would come to worship the God of Israel after observing its "death" through devastation and exile being followed by a glorious exaltation and vindication. This also coincides with the prominent role of the Servant in the salvation of the nations:

> It is too light a thing that you should be my servant to raise up the tribes of Jacob,
>> and to restore the preserved of Israel.
> I will also give you as a light to the nations,
>> that you may be my salvation to the end of the earth. (Isa 49:6; cf. 42:4)

All this will come about after the Servant has been humiliated and then exalted:

> Behold, my servant will deal wisely.
>> He will be exalted and lifted up,
>> and will be very high.
> Just as many were astonished at you—
>> his appearance was marred more than any man, and his form more than the sons of men—
> so he will cleanse many nations.
>> Kings will shut their mouths at him; (Isa 52:13–15a)

---

20. See 145–46. above.

If the Servant is taken as Israel, then, the prophetic vision might well be put together something like this: God's Beloved Son and Servant, Israel, will undergo an experience of terrible suffering and an humiliating death followed by a glorious resurrection to an entirely new and wonderful mode of existence into which the observant nations are then drawn. In the "Blessing to All Nations" section of this chapter we will come back to how this scenario corresponds nicely with the prophetic expectation of Israel's role in reference to the nations.[21]

In spite of this, we still need to be somewhat tentative in our conclusions, as usual. For one thing, it is difficult to imagine much of a connection between this understanding of the Suffering Servant with the expected Davidic King unless, to triangulate, the latter also takes on the identity of Israel! While this may seem an unlikely possibility, it needs to be said that there are intriguing parallels between the fate of the Davidic King and that of the nation: both are exalted by YHWH, get the attention of the nations, and come to rule over them. Are they one and the same?

This last overlap again suggests a continuing convergence of titles and roles upon a single individual. Indeed, we have been able to trace some of this: servant and king; suffering and YHWH's agent of redemption; the Servant's death and the "missing" sacrifice for serious sins; the suffering, death, and resurrection of the Servant (as Israel); David and Israel.

On the other hand, we are faced with such variety and complexity that it is extremely difficult to imagine how all these identities could be combined into anything like a coherent personality. From this point of view such an occurrence would be nothing short of miraculous.

But, of course, our choir has no problem with the miraculous! Organist: all stops out please for the final hymn.

RECESSIONAL: IN THE BOSOM OF ABRAHAM

Introduction

For the prophets, the "day of YHWH" becomes a tsunami, gathering up everything and every nation in its devastating sweep. But like the Flood of old, it also cleanses and renews the whole earth. In truth, as we have been learning all along, YHWH's acts of salvation are always double-sided, bringing both judgment upon sin for the sinner and salvation for the redeemed.[22]

Having encompassed the whole of creation, the prophetic vision then stretches out to an everlasting age, the last stage of the journey, not only for Israel/Judah but also for all of humanity. It represents nothing less than full and final redemption. Like every other phase of salvation history, it too is shaped primarily by the Covenant that

---

21. See 311-13, below.
22. See 54, 121, 302 above.

YHWH made with Abraham. What follows will demonstrate how the entire prophetic picture of the eschaton can be understood in the same six categories we have employed at the end of each of the previous chapters. Hence the six verses of this hymn. It turns out that we have been humming the tune all along.

Verse 1. The Land/Place (Cf. Deut 30:2–5)

The prophets consistently hold out the promise that the exile will come to an end and the nation will return to the Land. This theme is especially prominent in Isaiah and Jeremiah. The latter, like Hosea in the North, goes even further:

> In those days the house of Judah will walk with the house of Israel, and they will come together out of the land of the north to the land that I gave for an inheritance to your fathers. (Jer 3:18; cf. Hos 1:11)

The expected return is to include Israel as well as Judah in spite of the fact that the North has been scattered throughout the old Assyrian empire for some 130 years: that is, the nation will once again be whole. It sounds like these events are to happen simultaneously, but we should remember that prophecy is notoriously slippery about the timing of future events.

On the other hand, Jeremiah, unlike the other prophets, goes so far as to predict the actual length of Judah's exile:

> For Yahweh says, "After seventy years are accomplished for Babylon, I will visit you and perform my good word toward you, in causing you to return to this place. (29:10)

But again, caution is necessary: seventy is a rounded figure employing the symbolic number seven, making a literal interpretation doubly risky. Whatever the precise timing may be, it is clear that the whole people of God will be fully restored to the Land of Promise. This is absolutely central to the prophetic vision and to the hope of Israel.

Jerusalem and the temple are specifically included in the overall vision of restoration:

> They shall bring all your brothers out of all the nations for an offering to Yahweh, on horses, in chariots, in litters, on mules, and on camels, to my holy mountain Jerusalem, says Yahweh, as the children of Israel bring their offering in a clean vessel into Yahweh's house. (Isa 66:20)

> But be glad and rejoice forever in that which I create;
>   for, behold, I create Jerusalem to be a delight,
>   and her people a joy.
> I will rejoice in Jerusalem,
>   and delight in my people;

and the voice of weeping and the voice of crying
> will be heard in her no more. (Isa 65:18–19)

Of course, both city and temple are also vital to the sense of Place that we have been tracing throughout our study, and here they are again, in the End, even more glorious than ever.

But there is still more, much more. Isaiah sees that "the Land" cannot possibly be contained even within the generous boundaries of YHWH's original Promise to Abraham. Only a whole new earth, a whole New Creation, will do:

> For, behold, I create new heavens and a new earth;
> and the former things will not be remembered,
> nor come into mind. (Isa 65:17)

As the prophet contemplates the new Jerusalem that is part of this scenario, the scene before him bursts out into full and glorious Technicolor:

> ...behold, I will set your stones in beautiful colors,
> and lay your foundations with sapphires.
> I will make your pinnacles of rubies,
> your gates of sparkling jewels,
> and all your walls of precious stones. (Isa 54:11b–12)

> ...but you will call your walls Salvation,
> and your gates Praise.
> The sun will be no more your light by day;
> nor will the brightness of the moon give light to you,
> but Yahweh will be your everlasting light,
> and your God will be your glory.
> Your sun will not go down any more,
> nor will your moon withdraw itself;
> for Yahweh will be your everlasting light,
> and the days of your mourning will end.
> Then your people will all be righteous.
> They will inherit the land forever... (Isa 60:18b–21a)

> The wolf and the lamb will feed together.
> The lion will eat straw like the ox.
> Dust will be the serpent's food.
> They will not hurt nor destroy in all my holy mountain... (Isa 65:25)

This kind of language signals a reality well beyond our present experience of the world. The serpent feeding on dust and the vegetarian beasts connect this vision to the original Eden, as does the absence of sin in the people. But the final state will move beyond creation to an eternal day without need of sun or moon, basking in the light of YHWH's Presence. And this "day" will be a day of rest:

> My people will live in a peaceful habitation,
>> in safe dwellings,
>> and in quiet resting places. (Isa 32:18[23])

This rest is undoubtedly not only due to the transformed physical environment but also to a transformed humanity, no longer "on probation" but living in a state of full and perpetual obedience. This is the unmistakable implication of being righteous forever: another "Fall" is out of the question. The world as we know it, full of sin and corruption and disorder, is fully and permanently transformed.[24] These allusions strongly confirm that we are not just "back to Eden" but "back to Eden+++."

Verse 2. Many Descendants (Cf. Deut 30:5, 9)

In the last chapter we noted the use of the term "remnant" to depict the small number who went into exile in Babylon and this is indeed the starting place for the prophetic expectations.[25] For them, these folk are in fact those who are left in the ark and from whom a new world would, in part, be populated:

> A remnant will return, even the remnant of Jacob, to the mighty God. For though your people, Israel, are like the sand of the sea, only a remnant of them will return. (Isa 10:21–22a)

> I will gather the remnant of my flock out of all the countries where I have driven them, and will bring them again to their folds; and they will be fruitful and multiply. (Jer 23:3)

> The little one will become a thousand,
>> and the small one a strong nation. (Isa 60:22)

But even though "Many Descendants" is definitely in the blessed future of God's people, there are even greater dimensions to this Promise as we shall soon see in the next section.

Verse 3. Blessing to All Nations

As we have observed on a number of occasions, this Promise has been relegated to the back burner during much of Israel's history, perhaps even forgotten at times. But here,

---

23. Cf. 32:18; Jer 50:34.
24. Rendtorf reminds us that this vision remains rooted in a "this worldly" perspective:
    > Even when there is talk of a "new heaven" and a "new earth," expectations remain within the realm of the conceivable, even if sometimes they brush against its borders. But in particular there is as yet no idea of a world "beyond" and of an "eternity" that is fundamentally different from "time."
    >
    > *Canonical Hebrew Bible*, 690.
25. See 288–89, above.

in the mouths of the prophets, it enjoys an astounding last-minute comeback. It is all the more amazing because the nations are villains in most of these visions and the last thing the reader expects is to see them here, included in the Blessing that awaits Israel. But that is exactly what happens.

A rough outline of how this will work is also part of the picture:

> At that time I will bring you in, and at that time I will gather you; for I will give you honor and praise among all the peoples of the earth, when I restore your fortunes before your eyes, says Yahweh. (Zeph 3:20)

> Arise, shine; for your light has come,
>   and Yahweh's glory has risen on you.
> For, behold, darkness will cover the earth,
>   and thick darkness the peoples;
> but Yahweh will arise on you,
>   and his glory shall be seen on you.
> Nations will come to your light,
>   and kings to the brightness of your rising. (Isa 60:1–3[26])

Israel will be exalted, the nations will be drawn to YHWH, and then actually be incorporated into the salvation YHWH has brought to Israel! They will put their faith in the one true God and come to worship him. Perhaps Zephaniah again puts it best:

> For then I will purify the lips of the peoples, that they may all call on Yahweh's name, to serve him shoulder to shoulder. From beyond the rivers of Cush, my worshipers, even the daughter of my dispersed people, will bring my offering. (3:9–10)

Even the gates of the (clearly rebuilt[27]) temple will be open wide to the nations:

> "I will bring these to my holy mountain,
>   and make them joyful in my house of prayer.
> Their burnt offerings and their sacrifices will be accepted on my altar;
>   for my house will be called a house of prayer for all peoples."
> The Lord Yahweh, who gathers the outcasts of Israel, says,
>   "I will yet gather others to him,
>   in addition to his own who are gathered." (Isa 56:7–8)

All this is further confirmation of what it meant for Israel to be a "kingdom of priests," as the vocation into which she was called at Mt. Sinai snaps sharply into focus in the eschaton. As we have noted, Isaiah even suggests that the nation's failure to take this calling seriously is one of the reasons for the exile in the first place.[28] But, "on that Day," Israel will finally come into its own, the people exhorting one another:

---

26. Cf. 55:5 and 25:8; Jer 16:19–21.
27. Cf. Isa 44:28.
28. See 290, above.

In that day you will say, "Give thanks to Yahweh! Call on his name! Declare his doings among the peoples! Proclaim that his name is exalted! Sing to Yahweh, for he has done excellent things! Let this be known in all the earth! (Isa 12:4–5; cf. 55:4)

Israel has a Story to tell to the nations:

"You are my witnesses," says Yahweh,
  "With my servant whom I have chosen;" (Isa 43:10)

Directly alluding to Israel's calling, the prophet Isaiah says:

But you will be called Yahweh's priests.
  Men will call you the servants of our God.
You will eat the wealth of the nations.
  You will boast in their glory. (Isa 61:6; cf. 49:5–6)

In summary, the Blessing to All Nations will apparently go something like this: Israel comes back from exile, is exalted above all other principalities and powers, and draws all humanity unto herself and to YHWH her God, who has so obviously bestowed this great salvation upon her. This is the fullest expression yet of the "death and resurrection of the beloved son" theme we have been encountering throughout this Story.[29]

The Least Shall Be Greatest

Now that the eschatological vision of the Three Promises is more or less in place, it becomes possible to see more clearly what we have been calling their "inner logic." In previous discussions we have noted that the Blessing to All Nations, although the last and the least of the Promises in the overall narrative, now shows signs of actually being the first and the greatest.[30] With the full character of the Promises now before us we can see that this is, in fact, the case.

In the eschaton the Promises of Land and Many Descendants are themselves universalized by the Blessing to All Nations. It does this by incorporating all the nations into the company of the redeemed, automatically creating Many Descendants beyond all imagination.[31] And the Land, as the indispensable living space for such unlimited numbers, expands to a glorious New Creation in order to accommodate them all. The third Promise, as the ultimate object of YHWH's redemptive purpose, turns out to be the spring from which the other Promises naturally flow.

---

29. See 77–78, 91, 115, 216, above.
30. See 37, 65–66, 136–37, 184, 230, above.
31. This further implies that the definition of a "descendant of Abraham" will also have to expand well beyond mere DNA. For further discussion, see 316, below.

It is for this reason that the base of the triangle in all of our covenantal diagrams has been the Blessing to All Nations in its various forms. The following, incorporating the prophetic vision as New Creation (Eden +++), is the last in the series.

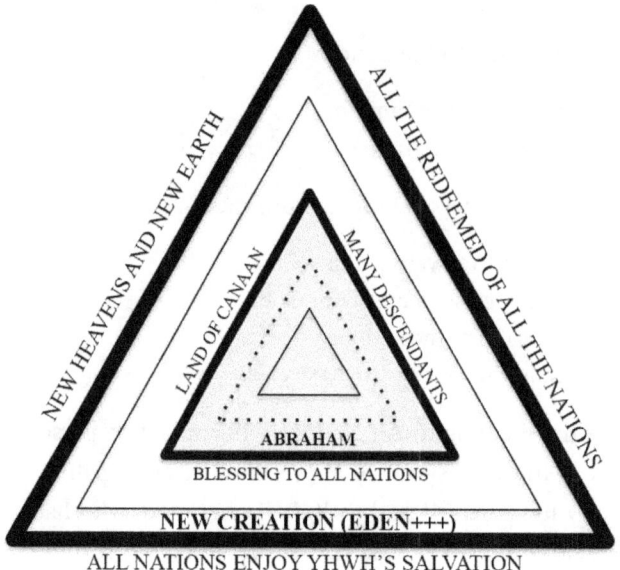

**Covenantal Diagram 5
Abraham–New Creation**

The New Creation, as the fullest expression of the Three Promises, encompasses the whole plan of YHWH's redemption. Its bold outline suggests that this, the final goal of God's great purposes, provides the fundamental pattern for all that has preceded it, including the Covenant with Abraham.

Verse 4. Fruitfulness (Cf. Deut 30:5,9):

If we are amazed at Israel's exaltation and the inclusion of the nations, it may be hard to believe that "we ain't seen nothin' yet!" For when the prophets speak of the coming fruitfulness of the Land their inspired imaginations really begin to soar. Words almost fail them. Almost.

A number of passages affirm that the coming time of blessedness will feature a Land restored to incredible fruitfulness. We start with Jeremiah:

> "Yet again there will be in this place, which is waste, without man and without animal, and in all its cities, a habitation of shepherds causing their flocks to lie down. In the cities of the hill country, in the cities of the lowland, in the cities of the South, in the land of Benjamin, in the places around Jerusalem, and in the cities of Judah, the flocks will again pass under the hands of him who counts them," says Yahweh. (Jer 33:12–13)

Enabling this flourishing of humans and livestock will be a divine renewal of the underlying environment:

> I will open rivers on the bare heights,
>   and springs in the middle of the valleys.
>   I will make the wilderness a pool of water,
>   and the dry land springs of water.
> I will put cedar, acacia, myrtle, and oil trees in the wilderness.
>   I will set cypress trees, pine, and box trees together in the desert; (Isa 41:18–19)

While this is conventional enough in its conception, there is more. The future state of the Land is just too productive to be contained within such ordinary imagery. It requires another mode altogether:

> It will happen in that day,
>   that the mountains will drop down sweet wine,
>   the hills will flow with milk,
>   all the brooks of Judah will flow with waters,
>   and a fountain will flow out from Yahweh's house,
>   and will water the valley of Shittim. (Joel 3:18)

Amos even talks of such extreme fruitfulness that those who plow, those who reap and those who process, will not be able to keep up with each other:

> Behold, the days come," says Yahweh,
>   "that the plowman shall overtake the reaper,
>   and the one treading grapes him who sows seed;
>   and sweet wine will drip from the mountains,
>   and flow from the hills. (Amos 9:13)

We are not in Kansas anymore! We are, in fact, in Paradise:

> For Yahweh has comforted Zion.
>   He has comforted all her waste places,
>   and has made her wilderness like Eden,
>   and her desert like the garden of Yahweh.
> Joy and gladness will be found in them,
>   thanksgiving, and the voice of melody. (Isa 51:3)

This is the goal that the Story has been reaching for all along: the Return to Eden. But as we have been coming to understand, Eden, conceived as a limited geographical space, cannot contain it. A whole New Creation is required. Eden, too, is universalized in the eschaton.[32]

---

32. Perhaps it was so "in the beginning" as well, Eden then being taken as symbolic of the whole earth. Indeed, it may be possible to speak of the latter being "in Eden" in the same sense that all the

While the first Flood failed to usher in a new creation, this time it is a deluge of another kind. The destructive events that mark the first phase of the eschaton will last:

> ...until the Spirit is poured on us from on high,
> and the wilderness becomes a fruitful field,
> and the fruitful field is considered a forest. (Isa 32:15)

The coming age will be characterized by the extraordinary abundant presence of the Spirit of God. The Relationship section following below will provide an opportunity to explore this a bit further. For now, we note that the Spirit comes bearing fruit, the fruit of the new earth.

Verse 5. Relationship (Deut 30:6,9)

INTRODUCTION

A restored divine-human Relationship, the inner aspect of Eden, is part and parcel of the prophetic vision as well. Indeed, it is arguably the most important characteristic of the eschaton. However, some aspects of the latter deal with Relationship more directly than others. We begin with those.

The Rebuilt Temple

The tabernacle/temple has always both symbolized and actualized YHWH's presence among his people. Its loss at the time of the exile is no accident and neither is its restoration in the eschaton. The nation has returned and YHWH has returned with it, the relationship restored. It is not just restored, however—it is enhanced. The tensions previously created by the Presence of YHWH in the midst of sinful humanity have been dissolved.

All Nations Present and Accounted For

Secondly, the inclusion of the nations in eschatological salvation provides dramatic evidence that the estrangement between YHWH and humanity has finally been overcome. In the eschaton, *all* of Adam's descendants are eligible for this restored Relationship with the one true God. Those who were on the outside are now on the inside: in principle the circle now encompasses all of humanity again, as it did "in the Beginning," "in Adam."

This does not necessarily imply that all people who have ever lived will be "saved." There are too many passages indicating the destruction of the wicked to jump to such a conclusion. But the *scope* of YHWH's salvation will extend to all people in all places,

---

nations are "in Adam."

no longer restricted to the people of Israel. The Story, so far, at least, has largely been silent on the whole matter of the ultimate fate of those, righteous and unrighteous, who die before the eschaton.

Universal Peace with God

The prophets also depict the coming age as creation totally at peace. When we see the wolf and the lamb eat together we know we have peace in the natural world! At the human level previous animosities fade into a new and transcending brotherhood as all the nations come together at last. Isaiah captures the flavor nicely:

> Many peoples shall go and say,
>   "Come, let's go up to the mountain of Yahweh,
>   to the house of the God of Jacob;
>   and he will teach us of his ways,
>   and we will walk in his paths."
> For the law shall go out of Zion,
>   and Yahweh's word from Jerusalem.
>
> He will judge between the nations,
>   and will decide concerning many peoples.
>   They shall beat their swords into plowshares,
>   and their spears into pruning hooks.
> Nation shall not lift up sword against nation,
>   neither shall they learn war any more. (Isa 2:3–4[33])

It is to this general sense of universal harmony that Isaiah seems to be referring when emphasizing the permanent status of this environment and a "covenant of peace":

> For the mountains may depart,
>   and the hills be removed;
> but my loving kindness will not depart from you,
>   and my covenant of peace will not be removed. . . (Isa 54:10)

It is clear that the restored relationship of Israel/humanity with YHWH will spill over into the life of nations as well as the elements of creation.

The Spirit is Poured Out

We have already quoted Isaiah to the effect that YHWH's agent of change in the natural environment of the eschaton will be his Spirit. The divine Spirit will also be bestowed upon humanity as well, with wonderful spiritual effect. Up until this point in the Story

---

33. Cf. Mic 4:3; Hos 2:18b.

the activity of the Spirit of God in the lives of persons has been infrequent, of limited duration, and mostly for the leadership of YHWH's people. In the eschaton things will be radically different. It will be the quintessential "age of the Spirit":

> It will happen afterward, that I will pour out my Spirit on all flesh;
>   and your sons and your daughters will prophesy.
>   Your old men will dream dreams.
>   Your young men will see visions.
> And also on the servants and on the handmaids in those days,
>   I will pour out my Spirit. (Joel 2:28–29[34])

No doubt Moses expressed a longing for this Day when, after seeing how the Spirit had affected some of his advisors, he exclaimed:

> I wish that all Yahweh's people were prophets, that Yahweh would put his Spirit on them! (Num 11:29)

Such a Day is now fully in view.

It should also be recalled that when the Spirit of YHWH had come upon Saul, the first king of Israel, he had been "turned into another man" (1 Sam 10:6). This implies that the Spirit is God's likely instrument to renovate the human heart. And, as we have also seen, the bestowal of a new heart forever inclined toward the ways of God is the primary distinguishing characteristic of the new covenant in the eschaton.[35] It can be no coincidence that the latter will also be the age of the Spirit.

For the purposes of this section we note that this unprecedented endowment of the Spirit is another way of affirming the intimacy of humanity's relationship with YHWH in the eschaton. It all fits together: to have his Spirit is in some sense to have YHWH close, in the renovated heart. This is clearly something that goes further than a mere *restoration* of the divine-human relationship to the creation of a new and better one altogether. With the eschaton, we again move beyond Eden.

The Fatherhood of God

The eschaton will be the time in which YHWH fully realizes his fatherly desire in terms of his relationship with Israel:

> But I said, 'How I desire to put you among the children, and give you a pleasant land, a goodly heritage of the armies of the nations!' and I said, 'You shall call me "My Father," and shall not turn away from following me.' (Jer 3:19)

Of course, YHWH has regarded them as such all along:

> When Israel was a child, then I loved him,

---

34. Cf. Isa 44:3.
35. See 299–300, above.

and called my son out of Egypt. (Hos 11:1[36])

When a sinful Israel presumes upon this relationship as God's son, however, YHWH is not moved:

> Will you not from this time cry to me, 'My Father, you are the guide of my youth!'? 'Will he retain his anger forever? Will he keep it to the end?' Behold, you have spoken and have done evil things, and have had your way." (Jer 3:4-5[37])

YHWH has been looking for his people to act like a true son: that is, a son who actually obeys his Father. In the eschaton, this will finally be true of Israel, fitted with new hearts and filled with the Spirit. In the End, the prodigal son will be welcomed home, given the best robe, and honored in an everlasting celebration with his whole family.

Verse 6. Grace/Obedience (Deut 30:1–2; 6–8)

The prophets' constant beating of the "covenant obedience" drum did not work and the nation staggered off into exile. These seers voice little hope that this terrible experience will finally be enough to stimulate the people to obedience. Given what we have been discussing in this chapter, perhaps it is unremarkable that the prophets seem to understand that the promised return and the dramatic arrival of the eschaton are based simply upon YHWH's word and sovereign act. The following passage from Micah is typical:

> Be in pain, and labor to give birth, daughter of Zion,
>   like a woman in travail;
>   for now you will go out of the city,
>   and will dwell in the field,
>   and will come even to Babylon.
> There you will be rescued.
>   There Yahweh will redeem you from the hand of your enemies. (4:10)

Isaiah even suggests that this will be accomplished in spite of a lack of response:

> For Jacob my servant's sake,
>   and Israel my chosen,
> I have called you by your name.
>   I have given you a title,
>   though you have not known me.
>   I am Yahweh, and there is no one else.
>   Besides me, there is no God.

---

36. Cf. Exod 4:22–23.
37. Cf. Hos. 1:10 and Jer 31:9c.

> I will strengthen you,
> > though you have not known me,
> > that they may know from the rising of the sun,
> > > and from the west,
> > that there is no one besides me.
> > > I am Yahweh, and there is no one else. (45:5–6)

This strong emphasis on YHWH's initiative brings to mind his own description of the Exodus:

> You have seen what I did to the Egyptians, and how I bore you on eagles' wings, and brought you to myself. (Exod 19:4)

The reason given for YHWH's eschatological salvation by Micah parallels that given for saving Israel in the days of Moses: YHWH is only being faithful to his Promise to Abraham.

> You will give truth to Jacob,
> > and mercy to Abraham,
> > > as you have sworn to our fathers from the days of old. (7:20[38])

The great and final salvation of the eschaton is then an act of pure grace. Not only that, but it initiates a state of grace which will prevail forever. Whereas the Israelites in Moses's day were saved by God's act as well, they were called to maintain that status by obedience to the Law. We have seen this pattern "from the beginning." And we have seen it end in failure again and again until finally it exhausts itself in the smoking ruins of Jerusalem.

It is true that the passage from Deuteronomy 30 referenced at the beginning of this section seems to imply that the people need to return to YHWH as a condition for returning to the Land. We see a similar pattern in verses like the following from Jeremiah:

> "In those days, and in that time," says Yahweh,
> > "the children of Israel will come,
> > > they and the children of Judah together;
> > they will go on their way weeping,
> > > and will seek Yahweh their God... (50:4)

A close reading, however, reveals only that these two "returns" happen in sequence: the second is not necessarily dependent on the first and it could well be that the experience of God's grace brings forth repentance.

In the eschaton the people of God are still saved by grace and called to obedience. But, as we have seen, there is now a major difference: they will have been given new hearts and the Spirit, empowering perfect and constant obedience. In other words,

---

38. Cf. Exod 2:24 and 32:13.

their obedience will be grace-enabled, of the Spirit, and not of their own strength. We saw earlier how this was hinted at in the time of the judges.[39]

The truth that "good works" are begun, continued, and ended in YHWH has been glimpsed throughout the narrative. It runs underneath the stories of the Exodus led by Moses and the Conquest in Joshua's time. In both it is made clear that the victories of Israel were at the hand of God.[40] It is graphically illustrated by the story of Samson, whose strength comes through an endowment of the Spirit.[41] The psalmist famously and beautifully expresses this juxtaposition of "works" and grace:

> Unless Yahweh builds the house,
>   they who build it labor in vain.
> Unless Yahweh watches over the city,
>   the watchman guards it in vain. (127:1)

And Isaiah neatly captures the same idea:

> Yahweh, you will ordain peace for us,
>   for you have also done all our work for us. (26:12)

Obedience is not ours to offer to YHWH: *it is, in the end, what he offers to us.* The prophetic revelation brings this truth fully to light because in the eschaton it will shine in all its brilliance. In terms of our testing formulation, yes, salvation is a matter of grace, but so too is the obedience with which it is to be maintained. We can now see that the grace-obedience tension we have observed repeatedly finds its final resolution in the eschaton where works are swallowed up in grace.

Conclusion

In this chapter we have been struggling to comprehend a staggering act of inspired imagination in the vision of Judah's prophets. They lay before us the picture of a single nation dead in exile raised by resurrection into a vast transnational community. Living in a transformed creation under the one true God, it will be ruled by his agent/regent, the Son of David, as Servant-King. All this is nothing short of breathtaking! No doubt such an expansive vision would come as an utter shock to Abraham and all his descendants. Certainly the casual reader of the Bible, inattentive to the markers along the way, would wonder from whence all this had come.

However, to those following the Story as outlined in this book it should come as no surprise at all. Chapter 2 discussed the way in which the Promises to Abraham are to be found already embedded in the Creation:

---

39. See 208–9, above.
40. Cf. Josh 23:5.
41. Judg 13–16.

... the various elements of the Promises to Abraham actually reflect what God intended for the entire human race "in the beginning." In Abraham the universal is made particular...[42]

The Covenant with Abraham has universalizing implications built right into it, brought forward from the Creation and extending now to the New Creation. From this perspective, it only seems natural to find the Promises have been both developed and transformed in this direction. Indeed, one of them, the Blessing to All Nations, is obviously "universal" right from the start. And if, as we have been suggesting[43], Israel's priestly calling is to be the conduit of this Blessing and the other two Promises are auxiliaries to that end, they, too, move naturally toward the universal. This tiny seed just keeps on growing into such a tree that all the birds of the air find a home in its branches.

This is the final verse of our hymn's unending note. YHWH's "Mission to the World" has come to an end—but that "end" is a state of perpetual blessedness for the myriads who find themselves among the redeemed. Heaven's gate is truly open wide.

The following diagram attempts to put the eschaton as envisaged by the prophets into the entire sweep of the Story so far. In this way it can more easily be seen how it shares the basic Abrahamic structure of God's unfolding salvation while at the same time transforming its familiar categories. In this multidimensional overview it is possible to gain a fuller sense of how these categories relate to one another and contribute to the fundamental unity of the Story.

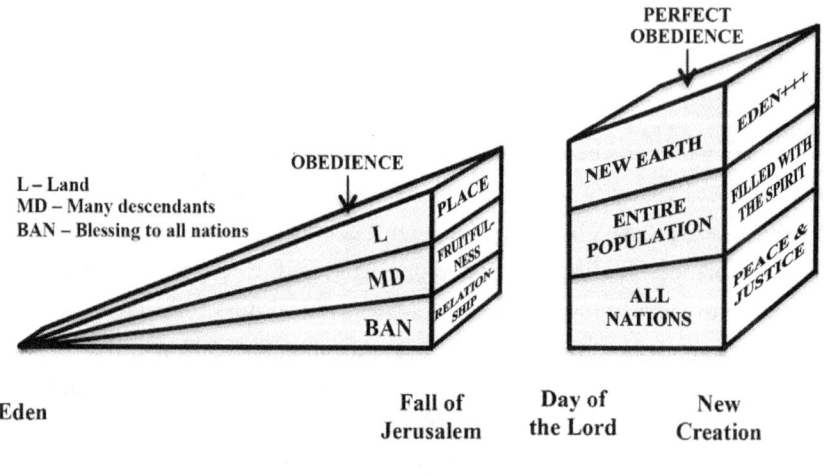

The Story So Far

---

42. See 35, above. See also Covenantal Diagrams 1 and 2, 35, 37, above.
43. See 315–16, above.

16

Conclusion

Introduction

This chapter will summarize the contents of chapters 2–15 in order to distill the essence of what we have been discovering.

Part A will bring together the successive segments of "The Story," centering on the Serpent Crusher theme we have been following in "Perspectives." Originating very early in the biblical account, this expectation of a coming One is surely the instinctive focus of anyone reading the Bible "for the first time, again." Following its lead also provides us with a natural series of connecting links that can serve to weave the biblical narrative into a continuous whole. For the sake of remaining attentive to this theme, different segment headings than those of our chapter titles will be necessary, even though the basic content of the Story is the same.

Part B will apply a similar summarizing process to the "In the Bosom of Abraham" sections. Each of the six categories will be tracked through the various chapters in a condensed form and then reviewed in order to gain a clearer understanding of how it develops within the Story.

Part C will bring together all this information in order to provide a preliminary conclusion regarding the central proposal of this book.

PART A—THE STORY, SO FAR . . .

Eden: Given and Taken Away

The opening chapters of Genesis set the trajectory for this Story, introducing the main characters and setting out the problem to be resolved. God created the heavens and the earth as a life-support system for the man and the woman and their offspring, the entire human race. Placed in a wonderful garden, they enjoyed intimate fellowship with the creator on the condition of obedience to his word. Succumbing to temptation by the serpent, they disobeyed and were exiled from Eden into a world now subject to death.

A Serpent Crusher to Come

But YHWH God had promised that from the offspring of the woman one would appear who would crush the serpent while being himself stricken. The reader inevitably begins to anticipate this confrontation, looking for this One to appear, destroy the serpent, and reopen the gate to Eden.

A Line is Drawn

Adam and Eve died before seeing the promise fulfilled. It could have been different, or so it seemed at one point. Their son Abel seemed like he might be the One, but he was murdered by Cain, his jealous brother. When Eve gave birth to another son, Seth, she saw him as a replacement for Abel and, as the text turned to focus primarily on his line of descendants, the reader naturally assumed that they would produce the Serpent Crusher.

Narrowing the Line Down to One

However, the world was instead engulfed in sin and it seemed that God silently stood by for generations, allowing humankind to sink further and further into its grip. When God did finally act, however, it was to destroy the bulk of humanity and start all over again with a faithful descendant of Seth by the name of Noah. He and his family were the only humans that were saved from a vast destructive flood, emerging from the ark for a fresh start in a new world. Was he the Serpent Crusher? Unfortunately, an altered environment did not result in what had clearly been needed: a reformation of the human heart. Noah's offspring, too, fell into godless living while the Creator once more seemed to step back and merely observe. Noah was not the expected One after all, and he, too, died short of the Promise. The serpent had slipped unmolested from the ark.

A Promising Line

YHWH broke his second long silence when he spoke to Abram, another descendant of Seth. He promised him the possession of the Land of Canaan, Many Descendants, and that through him would come a Blessing to all Nations. Upon reflection, these Promises contain echoes of Eden itself, and the reader cannot but look to Abram as *the* seed of the woman, the One who would crush the serpent. However, the very nature of the Promises deflected attention away from him and toward his descendants. He became the first Promise Keeper instead.

Extending the Line

Abraham's circumstances, especially the barrenness of his wife Sarah, seemed at first to invalidate the Promises but, as YHWH dramatically stepped in to take control of the action it became clear that, along with Sarah's womb, the road back to Eden was being opened. Focus was soon directed to their son Isaac as the One but it became plain that his role was to be only the second link in a chain of Promise Keepers that would eventually lead to the One. His miraculous nativity, as well, served to guarantee all of the covenant Promises.

YHWH continued to overcome obstacles in every generation of Abraham's family line: the barrenness of his daughter-in-law Rebekah, the gullibility of his son Isaac, the guile of his grandson Jacob and the treachery of his great-grandsons in selling Joseph, their father's Beloved Son, into slavery in Egypt. When Joseph, who was considered dead by his father, was found alive in Egypt and ended up rescuing the rest of his family, it was clear that God was still in charge, bending even evil to his own good purpose. But all of these died well short of the Promise. While none of them was the expected One, at least it had become clear that the redemptive line had been extended through the generations of this single family.

A Royal Line Within the Line

These developments alone heightened the reader's anticipation, but there was more. At the end of Jacob/Israel's life he blessed the two sons of Joseph, Ephraim and Manasseh, indicating that they would each become a great nation. On his deathbed he then blessed *all* of his sons and prophesied over them. Two stood out above the rest: Joseph was called the prince among his brothers with great blessings upon him, while Judah's line was singled out for perpetual leadership "until he comes to whom (the scepter) belongs" (Gen 49:10)—a person who would even rule over the nations!

The specific promissory nature of Judah's blessing served to direct the reader's attention to his line for the ultimate good of the entire world. Combined with an unmistakable hint of sovereign rule, it also brought the Edenic promise of the Serpent Crusher to mind. Was the "seed of the woman," then, to be this ruler from the house of Judah who will destroy the serpent and command the obedience of the nations? Surely such a person would be the One.

Moses Begins to Crush the Serpent?

After the death of Joseph we encountered God's third great silence, during which his beloved "son," Israel, became entombed in Egyptian slavery. By now the reader may have been getting the clue that such silences are preludes to important redemptive activity rather than indications that God does not care. He or she may also remember that YHWH had predicted just such an enslavement long ago to Abraham, along with deliverance from its grasp. Would the beloved "son" now experience such a "resurrection"? The reader leant forward in anticipation.

Sure enough, YHWH appeared to Moses, charging him with the responsibility of leading the people out of bondage and back to the Promised Land. Moses's miraculous deliverance as an infant had already disposed the reader to wonder if he was the One, but there were huge barriers in the way of Moses's success. Besides the obvious one of slavery to a powerful nation there was the problem that no one seemed to know just who this "YHWH" was. This included Moses, the people, and especially Pharaoh, a kind of god himself. Why should they pay any attention to him? In spite of these difficulties, YHWH, as he had with the patriarchs, found a way.

He unleashed a series of ten terrible plagues upon the Egyptians that served the double purpose of revealing who he was to all concerned and convincing Pharaoh to "let my people go." The last plague was the angel of death, sent across the land to destroy every firstborn son. Because they obeyed instructions to sacrifice a lamb or a goat, the Israelites alone were passed over by the angel, turning a terrible judgment into a wonderful salvation. Pharaoh finally let the people go. It was a fresh beginning for them as a nation: a new era had clearly dawned and they were instructed to celebrate the Passover and New Year at this time. So far, so good.

The nation escaped into the wilderness but immediately complained bitterly about the lack of water and food. Instead of abandoning this ungrateful and unbelieving rabble, YHWH graciously provided what it needed. Again and again he showed himself to be full of loving kindness and mercy in the face of their unwillingness to trust and follow him.

At Mt. Sinai they entered into a solemn covenant with YHWH, promising to obey the Law given through Moses in the expectation that doing so would lead to the fulfillment of the ancient Promises to Abraham. In effect, the entire nation became the Promise Keeper, a role that the individual patriarchs had borne so long ago. A system of Blessings for obedience and Curses for disobedience were included as a "covenant mechanism" to keep them on the straight and narrow.

Everything needed for success was in place and Moses was looking more and more like the One. After all, at his command Aaron's staff had changed into a serpent and swallowed the staffs of the Egyptian magicians and he even formed a brass serpent to bring healing to the people! He obviously had power over serpents!

Conclusion

Living With YHWH

But it was not to be. A careful reader would have noticed that Moses was from the tribe of Levi, not Judah, the ruler-producing tribe according to Jacob's blessing. Furthermore, it was soon apparent that serpents survive quite well in the desert: the Israelites repeatedly showed themselves incapable of the obedience called for by the covenant. This put everything at risk.

Fortunately, the newly-minted Law, by providing a system of sacrifice designed to atone for "accidental" sins, made it at least possible for YHWH to continue to dwell in the midst of such a people. This must be considered a real advance in the history of salvation. But another question was left hanging when it came to more serious sins. These were often forgiven as well, in spite of the fact that the Law called for the death penalty. The basis of such generous forgiveness remained unclear: certainly no "greater" sacrifice for these sins was mentioned, no substitute provided. YHWH simply seemed to be reacting to Moses's mediating appeals to his own forgiving nature or his commitment to his Promise. But what about that missing sacrifice?

The repeated disobedience of the Israelites caused Moses to despair, but at the same time it was revealed to him that, in spite of coming under the Curses, they would in the end return to YHWH and enjoy the Blessings. At that point, God would circumcise their hearts to ensure that they follow him wholeheartedly. Here, at last, the necessary reformation of the heart suggested by the "failure" of the Flood came into view. It seems that the Law itself, holy as it was, awesome as it was, did not have the power to do this.

Is the deliverance from bondage and the giving of the Law then to be seen as another dead end? YHWH himself characterized it as a "test" and surely the only fair mark for Israel is an "F." The Story was moved towards its goal through all these momentous revelations and experiences but they did not lead to success. They did, however, have the powerful effect of revealing YHWH's fundamental disposition towards Israel to be one of patient love and forbearance. Again and again he was willing to start all over with them, and this suggested that there was still hope for sinful humanity.

The heritage of Moses is without parallel: YHWH had poured out a whole body of revelation through him, the foundation for one of the world's great religions. Their intimate relationship firmly established the ideal for God's rule over his people. In a moment of extreme provocation, YHWH even threatened to destroy all the other Israelites and start over with Moses. The latter stood without question head and shoulders above his contemporaries, but he, too, died short of the Promise. Literally. He certainly gave the serpent a run for his money, but he was not the One, after all. In fact, he himself pointed to another "prophet" yet to come.

One Greater Than Moses?

Joshua, Moses's successor, continued to follow his mentor's path, fully grasping the truth embodied in his name: "YHWH is salvation." It fell to him to lead the nation into the Promised Land and establish it there. A key part of this was the imposition of the "ban" upon the nations and most of their possessions: they were utterly destroyed as a judgment upon their extreme sinfulness. Even in the face of such a graphic object lesson, some of the children of Israel wavered, but, by and large, most followed Joshua faithfully and the nation did not rebel as it had under Moses.

Was Joshua then a greater leader than Moses? Although he enjoyed a close relationship with YHWH, he certainly never received the kind of revelations that made his predecessor justifiably famous. It is true that under him the nation finally came into the Promised Land but at no point was it really completely conquered. It was an already/not yet kind of possession: in the light of their wanderings in the desert it was a giant step forward, but it was far from a done deal. As a descendant of Ephraim, Joshua was an inheritor of Jacob/Israel's special blessing, but his family DNA also excluded him from the promise to Judah of a great ruler. So, in the end, Joshua, too, dies short of the Promise: he was not the One. The serpent was able to breathe a sigh of relief.

One, One After the Other?

Joshua did not have an appointed successor but YHWH himself raised up a series of judges on an "as needed" basis. Repeatedly, the nation went through a dismal cycle: a) covenant unfaithfulness; b) subjection to the nations; c) crying out to YHWH; d) provision of a savior/judge; and then back to a) again. The covenant mechanism was hard at work but Israel did not seem to be learning from its mistakes. In fact, things deteriorated to the point where the nation even fell into a short-lived period of civil war.

In spite of the explicit endowment of God's Spirit upon some of the judges, only a couple of them even came close to being considered the One in the eyes of the reader. None were clearly from the line of Judah, cutting them off from the promise of a ruler from that tribe. As well, the Promises to Abraham continued to be largely unrealized. It is no wonder that the people began to demand a king to get them out of this quagmire. YHWH's recognition that they were really rejecting him as their king, though, sounded truly ominous. Was the nation now thoroughly caught in the coils of the serpent?

Conclusion

Judah's Scepter Rises

Samuel, the last and perhaps the greatest of the judges, was also a transitional character in the sense that he anointed Saul as the first king of Israel. Although at this point the Story essentially turned into a royal narrative, it was made clear that YHWH was not going to speak directly to kings as he had to previous leaders. He kept them at a bit of a distance, instead raising up a whole class of prophets to receive and communicate his word. Gradually, when the Story later moved beyond David and Solomon, the prophets became the heroes rather than the kings. The latter, indeed, more often than not showed themselves as villains.

After a good start, the first king, Saul, proved to be a disaster when he turned away from following YHWH. Naturally he expected one of his sons to follow him onto the throne, but David, a youth from the tribe of Judah, was anointed king by Samuel following YHWH's direction. This set in motion a period of conflict between Saul and David until the former passed away. Through military means David extended the borders of the Land close to those outlined in the original Promise to Abraham. Although he had some succession problems of his own, by and large his long reign formed the foundation for a time of peace and prosperity.

Just as David seemed to be an excellent candidate for the expected Serpent Crusher, attention was suddenly deflected away from him toward the future by an unexpected promise from YHWH. He told David that he would establish the throne of his offspring forever and that the nation would someday enter a wonderful state of everlasting peace. Because David was of the tribe of Judah, the reader would naturally connect this Promise to Jacob's ancient blessing upon his son Judah, seeming to forecast that a mighty ruler would come from his tribe and rule over the nations. The serpent was beginning to coil.

Many of these expectations seemed to be realized when Solomon, son of David, followed him on the throne. He asked for and received great wisdom from YHWH, who granted him peace and prosperity as well. Even the nations were paying attention to him. David had been told that the coming son would build the temple and when Solomon undertook this task, the reader was sure that the time of fulfillment had finally arrived. The temple housed the very Presence of God on earth and when it was dedicated he manifested himself in truly awesome fashion. The time of his wandering was over: YHWH was home at last.

Unfortunately, the great promise of Solomon's reign dissipated after he began to take foreign wives and then following their gods. By the time of his death, the nation had descended into instability and division. Solomon's son Rehoboam did not inherit a shred of his wisdom, precipitating a rebellion led by an official named Jeroboam. Indeed, the ten Northern tribes all departed and became the separate nation of "Israel" with Jeroboam as its first king, while the two tribes of "Judah" remained under the rule of the house of David. While these "nations" sometimes fought and sometimes made up, each followed its own course to a similar destiny. The serpent relaxed again.

Prophets in a Nest of Vipers

Jeroboam proved to be a king so wicked that the subsequent kings of Israel seemed to share his wayward DNA in spite of the fact that, after his son, none were actually related to him. They were his spiritual offspring, however, as, one after the other fell into the "sins of Jeroboam." Short-lived dynasties came and went in an atmosphere of assassination, instability, and idolatry, while the prophets came into their own as covenant prosecutors. It was their role to try to hold king and nation accountable to the Law while warning of its heavy penalties for disobedience.

With the exploits of Elijah and Elisha, especially, the idea of the prophet as hero comes into its own. For a while it seemed that one or both of these wonderworkers might be the "prophet like me" of whom Moses had spoken, but this was not to be the case. The tide of disobedience continued to rise in spite of their best efforts and they pass from the scene. Amos and Hosea, among the first of the literary prophets, warned the Northern tribes that persisting in covenant disobedience would result in exile from the Land. At the same time they held out hope that this would not be the last word.

Worse came to worst and Israel was indeed conquered by the Assyrians from the northeast in 721 BC. Following their normal policy, they scattered the survivors across their great empire, ensuring that any remaining nationalist sentiments would never rise again. The "ten lost tribes" were not completely gone, however, as many among them had migrated South and some evidently remained in the North even after the defeat. While Israel's sun may have been setting, the serpent enjoyed its meager warmth.

Judah's Scepter Falls

If Israel was made in the image of Jeroboam, Judah bore the likeness of David. All of her kings were his descendants as YHWH had promised, and a number of them were generally faithful and presided over periods of genuine covenant renewal. But none proved able to crush the serpent: even the best were unable to reverse the nation's overall slide into disobedience. The reign of Manasseh marked the point of no return, even though Judah still had one hundred years left to run its full course.

During this time Judah was hearing from a number of prophets who, like some of their counterparts in the North, served notice that continued waywardness would soon lead to the implementation of the Curses under the Mosaic covenant. These coming disasters were portrayed in the starkest possible terms and with a note of utter finality. While a number of these men appeared sporadically in the narrative record, their main legacy, unlike the Northern prophets, was the body of writing they left to the ages.

Not surprisingly, in the end the nation covered its ears and refused to listen to its prophets. Over and over again it had demonstrated an unwillingness, and perhaps an inability, to conduct itself according to the Law of God. YHWH had chosen it out of all the nations so that at least one nation would come to know him and be a kingdom of priests through whom salvation would come to the rest of humanity. Judah, like Israel, had utterly failed in this calling.

In a series of devastating invasions culminating in 587 BC, the Babylonians, having triumphed over the Assyrians, completely devastated the Land, the city, and the temple. The pitiful survivors, including remnants of the royal family, were deported en masse to Babylon, leaving only a wasteland behind. Jeremiah may have wept, but the serpent shed not a tear.

A Morning Star is Born

But wait. There is more to this story: as all the furies of hell were breaking over the nation, the prophets saw a better day coming. Incongruously, it came into view through the acrid smoke of the holocaust: after judgment had been executed upon both the people (and the nations that punished them), Israel, both North and South, would be restored and enter an everlasting golden age. What seemed like the end, amazingly, was not the end after all, but a new Beginning. And what a Beginning! It was a new day: the Day of YHWH!

Pointing to a wonderful fulfillment of the Covenant with Abraham, the prophets saw God's people streaming back to the Land while their numbers exploded. And the nations were blessed by being brought into relationship with YHWH and incorporated into Israel! A new covenant would be established, marked by an outpouring of the Spirit on all flesh. Human hearts would finally be conformed to the ways of God revealed to Moses. Universal peace would break out and the Land itself would become exceedingly fruitful, transforming the whole earth into a new Eden, even a New Creation.

The prophets also described a coming agent through whom all of these unparalleled blessings would take place. In their writings, this man seemed to draw to himself all the various expectations of Israel and then some. On the one hand, he appeared as the triumphant Davidic King, while on the other, as the Suffering Servant. As contradictory as these personae appear to be, they conform to the profile of the "Serpent Crusher," revealed to Eve so long ago, who was bruised in his victory. In this vision, the One had made his strongest appearance yet, stepping out for a moment from behind a curtain of repeated disappointments. Although he still remained hard to see clearly, it was enough eventually to rekindle lost hope in God's people and give the serpent reason to worry.

What can we say? In spite of the repeated and now terminal disobedience of the nation, YHWH does not, in the end, turn away from them. In so doing he proves once and for all that "you don't have to keep a promise to be a Promise Keeper."[1] He continues to work through this people, enfolding them in an indestructible embrace and, through them all of humanity and the creation itself. Of course, we should have been expecting this: the same pattern repeated itself again and again throughout the Story. Just when it looked like YHWH was going to destroy his handiwork, he sent a savior. In doing so he is only being true to his own Promise to Eve and all the Eves[2] to follow. Now the serpent has no place to hide.

In the prophetic vision we have reached ahead to the End of the Story. It is all before us but at the same time it is out of reach, postponed to the future. Is it only a mirage? For those on the slow agonizing trek across the long miles to Babylon, there is only the experience of loss and the pain of exile. Will YHWH's Beloved Son really come back from the dead?

PART B—IN THE BOSOM OF ABRAHAM, SO FAR . . .

1. The Land

The Land began its journey as the whole world. Humans, having been created out of it, shared a deep bond with the earth and it was granted to them as their "possession" and "dominion" in order to provide them with the necessities of life. They were at home in it. They were especially at home in the garden of Eden where the fruitful qualities of the earth were concentrated into a cornucopia of delights.

Human disobedience resulted in expulsion from the garden and a curse upon the rest of the earth. The latter became resistant to efforts to render it fruitful, and humans became somewhat alienated from the environment that had been created specifically for them.

Continued human wickedness resulted in the flood of the whole earth in an act of judgment. A righteous man, Noah, along with his family, was provided with the ark as a safe place in the midst of chaotic destruction. They emerged into a cleansed earth to start all over again in an environment that had been altered to some extent to become essentially the world we now inhabit.

However, humans continued to demonstrate their impulse to exalt themselves over their Creator by attempting to build the tower of Babel. For this prideful enterprise they concentrated themselves in one area, but YHWH scattered them throughout the earth. In doing so he affirmed that its entirety was their domain, at least in principle.

---

1. See 107, above.
2. That this happens to be my family name is entirely coincidental!

Conclusion

YHWH then called Abraham and promised to give him a large portion of the earth for his inheritance. It was a fertile Land that called to mind the wonders of Eden. Although he lived in the Land and it was blessed by his presence, with the exception of a family burial plot, he never possessed any of it. For him it remained only a Promise.

For the next three generations the descendants of Abraham also lived in the Land, more or less, but did not possess it either. However, Jacob/Israel encountered YHWH at a site he called Bethel, "the house of God," because of the presence of YHWH there. At this point the Land began to take on a more sacred character. Then, during a time of famine, Israel's family had to leave the Land behind and go down to Egypt where they settled. They were saved from starvation but seemed further away than ever from enjoying the Land as their possession.

After four hundred years Egypt had become more like a prison than an ark, but YHWH pried the bars open and started them on their way back to the Land under Moses. Noah had emerged into a changed earth whereas as the children of Israel emerged from Egypt into a changed way of life. On Mt. Sinai they encountered YHWH and received the Law, its provisions laying out the godly living needed to sustain their presence in the Land once they had gotten there. YHWH's "place" became the holy of holies inside the tabernacle placed in their midst.

Many of the provisions of the Law beyond the Ten Commandments themselves were also tied to the Land. Of that first generation to leave Egypt, however, only twelve spies actually entered it, the rest being excluded because they were so disobedient. Instead, they wandered in the wilderness for forty years before a new generation could approach its borders. In the meantime, a sense of holy place was maintained with the golden cherubim over the Ark of the Covenant, an ever-present reminder of the cherubim that guarded the entrance to Eden.

The period of the Conquest was all about the Land. For the first time this Promise turned into possession, at least to some extent. This seems to reflect the nation's relative obedience to the Law of YHWH. However, the nation only occupied pockets of the Land and its borders fell far short of the fullness of the Promise. The tabernacle took up residence in Shiloh, which then became the national worship center and holy place. The Land was on its way to becoming the "Holy" Land.

Israel, while still occupying the Land to a significant degree in the period after Joshua, never really got to settle down to enjoy it. The era was marked by conflict with the local peoples who repeatedly gained the upper hand when Israel fell into disobedience. At these points the nation would appeal to YHWH who responded by sending a series of judges to deliver them. Although the tabernacle remained in Shiloh, the coming and going of the Spirit in the narrative more accurately reflected the sense of God's place among the people.

Through the military leadership of David, the second king of Israel, the Land finally came into full possession of the nation. In fact, its borders were expanded to coincide roughly with those of the original Promise to Abraham. This time of fulfillment was extended into the reign of his son Solomon who enjoyed peace throughout the realm. Under his leadership the temple was built and through it Jerusalem became seen as the place of YHWH's dwelling on earth.

After Solomon, the Land was divided between Israel in the north and Judah in the south. This development seriously impaired the sense of "the Land" on both sides of the border, but for about two hundred years it was at least all still in the possession of the children of Abraham. In the North disaster eventually struck when the Assyrians invaded, defeated the nation and scattered its inhabitants throughout their empire. Well over half of the Land was thus lost to Abraham. By that time the sense of sacred place in the North had already been seriously diluted, having been cut off from Jerusalem and the temple. The establishment of syncretistic worship centers at Dan and Bethel only added insult to this injury.

With the loss of Israel, the Land shrunk down to just Judah's smaller territory. This lasted only for about 130 years until Judah itself was conquered by Babylon and most of the survivors deported to that city. The Land was not only wrenched away, it was devastated and in every way it was lost. Even so, the chronicler refers to the disaster as the Land's "Sabbath," signaling hope for future restoration. With the loss of the North, the sense of place in the South may have intensified because of the retention of Jerusalem and the temple but both were eventually destroyed and there was no more Place for YHWH among the people.

The restoration and renewal of the Land was a prominent feature of the prophetic vision of the eschaton. Both Israel and Judah would return, reunited and whole again. At the same time the nations would be incorporated into Israel and a New Creation provided for them all. In this way the Land would become the whole earth, as it was in the very Beginning. While the temple was to be rebuilt in a new Jerusalem intensifying the sense of place, it would also diffuse somewhat as the Spirit was poured out on all people, enriching the consciousness of the Presence everywhere.

Summary

- The Land's first appearance was as the earth itself, which provided human beings, who themselves were made from it, with the necessities of life.

- The garden of Eden, as an intensification of these attributes, became the embodiment of the Land, but after the expulsion from the garden the focus shifted back to the whole earth, now itself under the curse..

- The great Flood was a judgment designed to destroy sinful humanity and cleanse the earth/Land, but sin remained in the human heart.

- God then promised Abraham that an Eden-like Land centered in Canaan would belong to his descendants.

Conclusion

- This Promise lay dormant for many generations until YHWH led the Israelites out of Egypt and into the Promised Land.

- However they did not actually possess the entire Land until the reigns of David and Solomon.

- After them, Israel began a long slide toward dissolution and loss of the Land, in the North first and then in the South.

- Their prophets proclaimed that they would nevertheless return to a wonderfully transformed Land, the dimensions of which would expand to encompass nothing less than a whole New Creation.

With this integrated picture of the Land now before us it is possible to observe that it exhibits an intriguing symmetry. The Land begins as the Creation and then narrows down to Eden as a kind of microcosm of the whole, which is then lost. It re-emerges as Canaan, a kind of new Eden, which expands into the New Creation in the eschaton. While Eden is the barred portal to the original Creation, Canaan becomes the open portal to the New Creation. The following can serve as a visual representation of this symmetry:

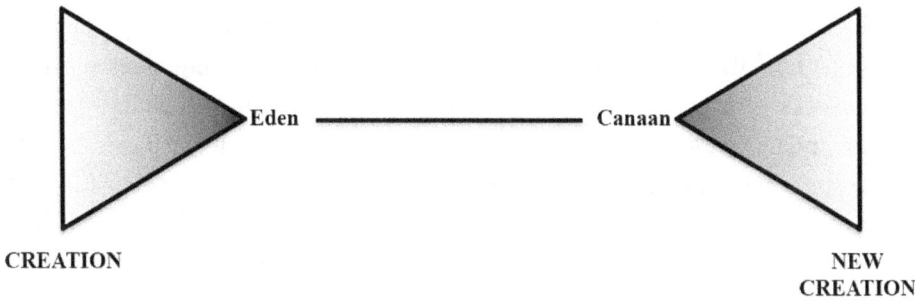

Eden and Canaan

While we have noted that the narrative only hints at Canaan's relationship with Eden,[3] the functional symmetry now visible tends to verify a significant connection. The way back to Eden begins in Ur of the Chaldees, leads between Mounts Ebal and Gerezim and is marked by a cairn of twelve stones on the west bank of the Jordan that are "there to this day" (Josh 4:9b). But that is just the beginning, just a glimpse of greater things to come. A whole new world, in fact.

Conclusion

The Land is a major player in this narrative. It is always in view, always a major factor, even if, in times of exile, it is so only as "lost" and Promise, always dominating the imagination of God's people even then. As such, it surely qualifies as a fundamental

---

3. Cf., 72, above.

structural element binding the Story together from Beginning to End. Its relative degree of possession provides us with an important gauge of how close we are to that End.

2. Many Descendants

A major part of the original Mandate given to Adam and Eve, along with the creatures, was to "be fruitful and increase in number." Many Descendants was thereby built in to the nature of creation from the Beginning. As a God-given mandate it included a strong implication that the Creator would bless humanity's progress towards filling the earth.

This Promise was not mentioned explicitly at the time of the Fall but it is very relevant to the curse upon the woman. Childbirth, the means by which it would be fulfilled, was now more difficult (and dangerous?) than it was. Womankind now faced a harder road in fulfilling the Creation Mandate, a task made even more difficult for the man by the earth's reduced fruitfulness. But it is not the vast increase of Eve's children that will bring salvation. Only One of them will.

The story of Noah and the Flood began with a great increase in the number of humans, but this alone did not mark a blessed time of fulfillment. The problem was that wickedness also increased, to the point of demanding God's judgment. It came in the form of destroying all but one small family and starting all over again with them: Noah's mandate was the same as Adam's, to "be fruitful and increase in number." Except for some environmental tweaks, humanity was back to square one but still in the game.

God then narrowed his attention to one man, Abraham, whose descendants would themselves enjoy a limitless increase in number. Guaranteed. And this in spite of the fact that his wife was barren and past child-bearing age. At first, Abraham's experience was all Promise and no fulfillment, in spite of his best efforts.

As Abraham's story unfolded, eventually Isaac was born, the true son of Promise. Just one. But that was enough to keep things moving toward complete fulfillment, repeatedly confirmed by divine word. Isaac almost died when Abraham obeyed YHWH's command to sacrifice him. But he was delivered at the last minute, providing further assurance that the Promise would not fail, in spite of any and all threats.

In the generations immediately following Abraham, barren wives again did not present a final obstacle to this Promise. Isaac had only two sons, but in the next generation the Promise began to gain traction as twelve sons were born to Jacob, creating a household of seventy by the time this era came to a close. The Promise was affirmed six times in the course of this narrative and began to show slow but discernable progress toward fulfillment.

While in Egypt for over four hundred years the children of Abraham became a great multitude whose very numbers threatened their nervous hosts. As in the days of

Noah, growth by itself did not a blessing make, but there is no denying that this Promise was being fulfilled to a significant degree. However, it was not enough: according to YHWH himself they would have to increase still more in order to properly occupy the Land. One, Moses, was called to lead them there.

On their wilderness journey Moses took a census on two occasions and they showed a population of about 600,000 men. Moses took this as a fulfillment of the Promise by describing them "as numerous as stars in the sky." Even though a generation died in the wilderness, they did so in the normal course of life, not affecting the natural rate of growth. Twice YHWH was so angry at their disobedience that he wanted to destroy them all and start again with just Moses. The latter talked him out of it, and the Promise burned bright once more.

The time of the Conquest under Joshua yields little indication regarding numbers but what evidence there is suggests that it, too, was a time of fulfillment. When just two tribes were called "a numerous people" in need of more land, we could see this Promise at work. It would also be reasonable to deduce from this that the entire nation probably enjoyed some increase in population living in such a fruitful Land.

Under the judges there is again little direct evidence of the size of the population. The impression is given that it ebbed and flowed with the fortunes of the nation. One of the tribes was almost wiped out altogether and this must be counted as a setback for this Promise. Significantly, at the end of the period Samuel was born to a barren woman, yet another reminder of YHWH's ability to keep his Promise in spite of circumstances to the contrary.

After the monarchy was established, David counted his fighting men and discovered he had 1 1/2 million of them. This represented serious population increase since the time of the Conquest. On several occasions the narrative recites the size of the nation in the covenantal language of "sand on the seashore." They clearly saw themselves in a time of significant movement towards fulfillment, and so they were.

At first the division of Israel after the death of Solomon would not have had a direct effect on the number of inhabitants but it led to a time of conflict and instability, especially in the North. While it is reasonable to assume that this resulted in some loss of population during its existence, there is sparse evidence one way or the other. The fact that Hosea held out the covenant Promise so vividly also suggests a context in which the nation was losing population. However, there is no need to read between the lines when Israel fell to the Assyrians: ten tribes, approximately 80 percent of the population, were gone from the Land, and many others were dead. The rest, with the exception of a few left behind, were scattered to the winds and effectively gone from history. It was the Curse being fulfilled, not the Blessing.

Judah in the South seemed to continue as a populous region for most of its existence. Eventually it too was conquered and devastated, leading to a precipitous decline in numbers. They were under the Curse as well, cut down to a tiny remnant in exile. But their prophets assured them this was more than the Promise needed to persist.

The prophetic vision proclaimed that Israel and Judah would be reunited and undergo an incredible population explosion in the coming eschaton. This was the time when, once and for all, this Promise to Abraham would finally be fulfilled beyond all reasonable expectation. But even that was just scratching the surface: the idea that all the nations would actually be incorporated into Israel took this Promise to a whole new level.

Summary

- Humans, simply put, were created to multiply.
- The Fall, through difficult childbirth and a cursed earth, had a negative effect on this goal.
- As humans began to increase, however, wickedness also increased, to the point where they suffered the terrible judgment of the Flood. Being reduced to just eight persons, they had to begin all over again. But now they had meat to eat.
- Within a few generations the narrative lost interest in the progress of humankind as a whole toward this goal in order to focus exclusively on Abraham and his descendants. They, like the entire species, like a wheel within the wheel, were to multiply: in fact, it was guaranteed by covenant Promise.
- Abraham's offspring, after a slow start, found themselves very numerous some four hundred years later but at the same time suffering in Egyptian captivity.
- They escaped into the wilderness and began to experience modest increase a bit later during the Conquest.
- In the time of the judges it seems that there were no advances in population.
- The kingdom of David/Solomon enjoyed significant increase in population, after which a long decline set in.
- Eventually, the fall of the North and then the South brought about a precipitous loss of population.
- With the Promise teetering on the brink, the prophets proclaimed a Day in which Abraham's children would finally enjoy the huge increase they were promised, bolstered beyond measure as all the nations would somehow be incorporated.

As with the Land, this Promise enjoys a curious relationship with the Creation itself. Through both Adam and Abraham offspring are to "increase and multiply." The prophetic vision of the incorporation of the nations into Israel brings the Mandate and the Promise together in the End. The following diagram seeks to express this relationship in a visual form:

CONCLUSION

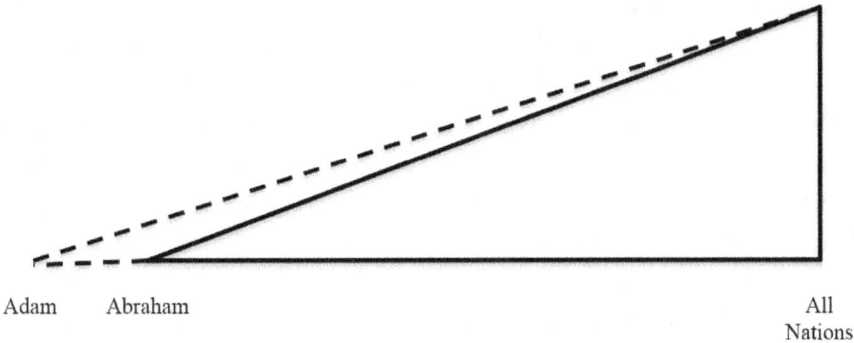

Adam   Abraham   All Nations

All Nations "in Adam" and "in Abraham"

Are the Mandate and the Promise two sides of the same coin, different paths to the same destination? Or is the Promise, like a surrogate mother for the Creation, carrying the embryonic Mandate in order to ensure its safe delivery in the New Creation?

Conclusion

The Promise of Many Descendants was in play from the Beginning, first of all in Creation itself and then in the story of Abraham's family. Both when it seemed to be in jeopardy in the time of the Patriarchs and later as exile loomed, it was explicitly reaffirmed. One way or the other it was always in view. Its road was not straight or smooth but it did continue to gather momentum until the fall of the nation brought it into serious question. There can be no doubt that it too qualifies as an essential part of the Story, visible at all the major intersections. See it, and you can judge where you are on the way.

3. Blessing to All Nations

The fact that God commanded Adam and Eve to "increase in number and fill the earth" makes it plain that all of their offspring were, in principle, included in the original blessing of the Creation. In receiving this amazing life-support system, the first couple represented all who would follow and, by extension, all the families, clans, tribes and nations into which they eventually might form themselves. For Adam and Eve, the nations being "in them," the Blessing was a present reality; for the nations to come from them, it was a reality-in-waiting.

The same association applied to the Curse: out from Adam and Eve to all their descendants and, eventually, to all of the nations. Indeed, it could be argued that the plurality of nations developed, in part, out of the alienation generated through the Fall. It is not hard to imagine that if there had been no sin, there would only be one nation, under God.

By the time of the great Flood, nations had not yet come into existence but the destruction of almost all humankind resulted in their stillbirth in any event. All humanity was saved "in Noah," and as such, participated in the renewal of the Creation Mandate and its blessings. But human sin persisted and continued its destructive path until the tower of Babel raised its ultimate challenge to the Creator. The result was yet further scattering and division, sowing the seeds for the eventual emergence of "nations." In fact, it is at just this point that they are first mentioned in the narrative. Probably not a coincidence.

Although Blessing to All Nations became an explicit Promise for the first time in the Covenant with Abraham, that is all it was, promise. Of course, by definition there is always a gap between a promise and its fulfillment. At the same time, no sooner was the Promise given than its underlying principle began to work: YHWH blessed those representatives of the nations who blessed Abraham and cursed those who cursed him.

While YHWH reaffirmed this Promise at least twice, Abraham still failed to experience much significant fulfillment, seeing it only in his personal relationships with people who were not of his own group. And even then it took the form of just hints and shadows in the background of the Story.

This same pattern of explicit promise but marginal realization continued in the early account of the patriarchs. Laban was certainly blessed through Jacob his son-in-law, but after treating him badly, sees him leave in the end. This Promise started to gain real traction for the first time when Joseph saved Egypt from a terrible famine and became its wise administrator. Finally, at least one of the nations was blessed through a descendant of Abraham.

It did not last. Over a long time the Egyptians came to see the children of Israel as a threat and enslaved them: a cruel parody of the Blessing if ever there was one. But this abuse activated the Curse imbedded in the principle and the Egyptians paid a terrible price for what they did to God's people. The Blessing had little positive expression in this phase, but it was not entirely absent. The inclusion of foreigners in the Passover suggests an openness to the nations while the calling of Israel as a "kingdom of priests" (probably as the mediator between YHWH and the nations) suggests that the Blessing will bring the nations into right relationship with YHWH.

The post-Sinai wanderings of Israel, being in the wilderness, did not bring them into significant contact, positive or negative, with other nations. It was only as they made their final approach to the Land that this Promise began to operate again, at least in the negative sense, bringing disaster on those nations that opposed Israel's advance. Other than this there is little evidence for fulfillment in this phase of the Story.

Once Israel crossed into the Land, this Promise was in play as the people confronted the nations already there. It was seen on a personal scale in the story of Rahab and on a somewhat larger one with the Gibeonites. These episodes confirm that the Blessing includes coming to believe in YHWH as God through his blessings upon

CONCLUSION

Israel and, in the case of Rahab, hint at incorporation into the nation. Israel's ability to fulfill this priestly role depended on her remaining aloof from the religions of the nations while being in their midst, a difficult balancing act as it turns out.

During the period of the judges the same pattern was evident in the story of Ruth which wonderfully confirmed that the Blessing involves a giving up of false gods and a turning to the one true God of Israel. Other than that episode, however, this period of cyclical conflict between Israel and the nations was understandably marked by a general lack of progress towards the fulfillment of this Promise.

The conflict with the nations intensified under the kings, coming to an end only when David had finally defeated Israel's enemies. After becoming his subjects they seemed generally to benefit from his benevolent rule. Both David and Solomon explicitly recognized that part of the temple's function would be to attract the nations to the worship of YHWH. This, too, can be interpreted as the way in which Israel would be a kingdom of priests among the nations. "Blessing to All Nations" was beginning to enjoy some solid fulfillment at last as peace settled upon the Land. When we read of the coming of the queen of Sheba to Solomon and "the whole world" seeking his wisdom, we can see that the Blessing was spreading far beyond Israel's immediate neighbors.

As the Northern kingdom spiraled downward into oblivion, we were presented with two interpersonal stories suggesting blessing to the nations through Israel: the widow of Zarephath who fed Elijah and survived a famine and Naaman the Syrian who was healed by YHWH. The latter, it will be remembered, came to faith through the witness of his Israelite servant girl and the ministrations of Elisha. On a larger scale, Nineveh avoided judgment by responding to the preaching of Jonah while another prophet, Amos, hinted at the incorporation of the nations into Israel itself! In spite of Israel's deteriorating situation, significant signs of this Promise seemed to be showing themselves.

Ironically, it is difficult to say the same for the occasionally more faithful Southern kingdom. Indeed, this Blessing, if present at all, was very elusive: most of the nations surrounding Judah saw her as an object of scorn. Indeed, Isaiah depicted this period as one in which Judah had failed in her mission to the nations, no doubt due to her deep undercurrent of disobedience.

While the actual experience of Judah at her demise was dominated by the overwhelming power and malevolence of the nations, her prophets were sounding a another note altogether. They saw a future in which these same nations would not only turn to YHWH when Israel was vindicated, but also would become part of the covenant people themselves and enjoy all the blessings of a New Creation. This confirms the gathering sense that this would indeed be the way in which Israel's calling as a "kingdom of priests" would be fulfilled. At her lowest moment, then, Israel was provided with her loftiest vision. Of course, it was all still just Promise. But what a Promise!

In the Bosom of Abraham

Summary

- When Adam and Eve were blessed, so also, in principle, were the nations that would come from them.

- Unfortunately, the same process applied to the Curse in the Fall and so the Blessing upon the nations was compromised. You can see the gap begin to open up between reality and the Promise as the population of the earth degenerated into increasing wickedness.

- The Flood represented only judgment upon them, not blessing, but, in principle again, the Blessing would come to all who were "in" Noah. But it seems to have gotten lost in humanity's rush to reach for heaven themselves at Babel and they were scattered as a result.

- When the Promise became explicit in God's word to Abraham, it immediately began to work itself out in small but nevertheless discernable ways as foreigners who blessed him were blessed

- It really gained momentum when his great-grandson Joseph saved the whole land of Egypt in a time of famine.

- But this nation eventually enslaved the children of Israel and came under a curse because they had treated Abraham's descendants badly. This was how the blessing worked.

- The same thing happened to the nations that opposed Israel as she approached the Land and then began to occupy it.

- On a smaller but instructive scale, the Gibeonites were at least partially blessed when they acknowledged the power of YHWH and at least one Canaanite and her family was actually incorporated into Israel for acting upon that same truth.

- During the David/Solomon period at least some of the nations found themselves blessed under their generally benevolent rule and when the temple was built, it was made clear that it would be a means by which the worship of YHWH would come to the nations.

- Even after the nation divided and the North went its errant way, a number of indications continued to show that this Promise was at work, at least in the lives of some individuals.

- It was not so in the South, particularly when Judah was finally overwhelmed by Babylon, most of her citizens sent into exile and she herself became a laughingstock instead of a blessing.

- Ironically, her prophets left them with a vision of the End that depicted all the nations turning to a restored Israel and her God in a New Creation, blessed at last.

Conclusion

This Promise, too, was embedded in the original Creation and in the renewed creation after the Flood and only became explicit in the Covenant with Abraham. He experienced it almost entirely as promise, not present reality. From there it was reaffirmed through Isaac and Jacob and began to show some real substance in Joseph's career. Then, in its positive sense, it mostly went underground until it finally broke surface under David/Solomon, only to almost disappear again for the balance of the nation's existence. While there are certainly traces of it at work during this period, at the terrible finale it forms a surprisingly prominent role in the prophetic vision of the eschaton.

Therefore, it is present throughout the Story, emphatically so with Abraham and in the prophetic vision and with lesser but important appearances in between working on the same underlying principles. Although it is somewhat less in evidence than the first two Promises, there is easily enough to qualify it as an essential structural component of the Story so far. The fact that it gives definition to Israel's sacred calling and purpose as a "kingdom of priests" also serves to underline its importance. However, there is one more consideration to take into account when passing judgment on this Promise.

A Logical Ending

All three Promises have confirmed that they are YHWH's instrument for the restoration of humanity and creation to their original condition and then some. Land and Many Descendants have not been able to confine themselves to Israel as a land or as a people, expanding instead to embrace all the children of Eve and the whole of the environment that was theirs to enjoy. And, of course, Blessing to All Nations is universalistic by nature. In the End the Promises all fully realize what was inherent in the Beginning and so provide a road "back to Eden."

As they relate to one another, the Promises seemed to be dominated by the narrative focus on the Land with a secondary emphasis on Many Descendants. Blessing to All Nations at first played only the role of a bit player compared to the other two, appearing only in "hints and shadows" throughout most of the Story. Our discussions of the "inner logic" of the Promises, however, suggested a more prominent role.

Starting from Israel's calling as a "kingdom of priests and a holy nation" it became increasingly apparent that the last Promise was in fact the first, in the sense that it was both the goal of the others and the key to unlock their connections with each other. This only becomes fully clear in the prophetic vision of the eschaton in which all the nations are incorporated into Israel, causing Many Descendants to multiply exponentially and Land expand to a new earth as their indispensable living space. This one Promise actually generates the others.

The process of incorporation of the nations exhibits another aspect of the inner logic of the Promises. Based on YHWH's assurance that he would "bless those who bless you," it becomes clear that Israel was to incarnate and exhibit a restored relationship with God in such manner that the nations would notice the way the Land and the people were so obviously blessed with extreme fruitfulness, turn to their God themselves, and be restored and added to the family of Abraham. This is the fullest definition of the "blessing" in Blessing to All Nations.

There are moments in Israel's history in which this dynamic peaks through an otherwise gloomy scene: the spies and Rahab; Naomi and Ruth; Solomon and the temple; the servant girl and Naaman. Although Israel was God's "Beloved Son," its failure to obey eventually results in its "death" in utter defeat and exile. The prophets proclaim, however, that YHWH will resurrect the nation so gloriously that it will finally be enabled to fulfill its basic calling. The first two Promises will have fulfilled their functions as was suggested earlier: "When a blessed Land is occupied by a blessed (flourishing) Nation all the nations will then be blessed."[4] The "inner logic" works itself out at the last.

God's overall purpose is to bless humanity as a whole and the threefold Promise to Abraham both reveals an understanding of what that blessing will involve and provides the means to that end.

4. Fruitfulness

The earth was created to be fruitful. Its vegetation was repeatedly characterized as seed-bearing to emphasize its fruit-bearing nature, and, among its animal life, sea dwellers and birds were specifically given the same Mandate as the humans to "be fruitful and increase in number." It is just the way things are supposed to be.

The thorns and thistles introduced after the Fall suggest that the general fruitfulness of creation was diminished to some degree, but certainly not eliminated. The earth would now need to be "worked" by the man in order to better yield what fruit it does bear.

After the Flood the animals in the ark were enjoined to "be fruitful and increase in number" upon the earth. Presumably, whatever was required for this to happen, like plants for food for the animals, would increase in proportion. However, it may be that in the long run, the fact that animals have become human food will become a drag on their multiplication.

The narrative of the first part of Abraham's adventures abounds with references to the great abundance of his flocks and herds and general wealth, even when he escaped a famine in Canaan by going down to Egypt. The recovered Land, when he got back, is explicitly said to be "like the garden of YHWH" it is so fruitful.

---

4. See 136, above.

CONCLUSION

This same basic situation seems to have prevailed in Abraham's later years. Abimelech, a king in the Land, gave him much silver and livestock at one point and we read on a number of occasions that he was blessed with great material wealth. Fruitfulness in terms of possessions marked his entire life.

As far as Isaac and Jacob are concerned, they too were rich men, mostly manifest in "flocks and herds" which, in turn, tells us the Land itself must have produced abundantly for them to eat. Prosperity also followed Joseph to Egypt where he became the Pharaoh's administrator. Negatively, we read of another great famine in Canaan, this time sending Israel and his eleven other sons down to Egypt. Even in hard times, the blessings of YHWH do not fail.

Fruitfulness even marks the Exodus, where, in spite of many years of slavery, the children of Israel depart with huge "flocks and herds." In addition, they plundered the Egyptians as they left. The Land they were going to was "flowing with milk and honey," a "good" Land, exceedingly fruitful but they now were out in the desert. Even there, however, they enjoyed the benefits of YHWH's provision of manna and quails when they had, presumably, soon used up all their animals. Even the barren desert became fruitful under the hand of YHWH.

After Sinai the Israelites continued to eat the manna (and, presumably, the quail) all the way throughout the desert. It was not until they approached the Land and defeated the Midianites that they again acquired great spoils of war. During this period they also had a taste of the fruitfulness of the Land when the spies brought back some of its legendary produce. YHWH promises them several times that the Land would richly blossom under their occupation.

The Land began to live up to its "good" name when Joshua took Israel across the Jordan. They benefited greatly from the spoils of war and in this way indirectly enjoyed the fruitfulness of the Land. The description of them being "at rest" may call to mind the lost pleasures of Eden but they were not there yet.

In the time of the judges, while there are suggestions that the Land was still basically fruitful, we read of a number of serious famines. The overall impression is that Israel had scant time to enjoy any fruitfulness of the Land in a period of so many wars and invasions. It was a time of un-rest. Certainly no character emerges who is obviously blessed of YHWH in terms of material wealth.

As we get into the story of David and Solomon we encounter a dramatic change. Both reigns, especially that of the latter, were marked by an exceedingly fruitful Land and unprecedented wealth. All this was particularly on exhibit in the richly adorned temple and in the impressive descriptions of royal life. It was an extraordinary time of material blessing.

The history of the Northern kingdom was marked by conflict and drought. The text contains no indications of abundance at all. We do read of two faithful widows who were provided for in times of extreme scarcity. The prophets of the era explained such conditions as judgment from YHWH while promising a wonderful abundance in the coming restoration of the nation.

The Southern kingdom did enjoy some periods of fruitfulness, particularly under a few of their more faithful kings. However, its history was also marked by frequent wars, and, in the end, the complete devastation of the Land during the final invasions of the Babylonians.

The prophets of Judah, expanding the vision of their Northern colleagues, spoke of the eschatological restoration of the Land in Eden-like language, but that proved inadequate. They went on to describe a stunning New Creation in which the entire earth would be utterly transformed into a fruitful paradise. Before that, however, it would suffer through a time of terrible judgment- "the Day of YHWH."

Summary

- The original Creation was the very picture of fruitfulness, but this was marred to a significant degree in the Fall.
- The Flood, while it was terribly destructive, nevertheless led to a renewed Mandate for the flourishing of all forms of life.
- When the Story narrowed down to Abraham, the theme of fruitfulness is prominent again in reference to both the Land and his possessions.
- The same can be said of Isaac and Jacob and, in the latter's time, even a famine was overcome by his son Joseph's wise use of Egypt's prior fruitfulness.
- Although they fell into slavery, the children of Israel still prospered in the fruitful land of Goshen
- Their time in the wilderness was sustained by YHWH's bountiful provision and by promises of plenty once they possessed the Land.
- Under Joshua they began, finally, to enjoy the fruitfulness of the Land itself, not to mention the confiscated wealth of its defeated inhabitants.
- Fruitfulness seems to have been curtailed somewhat during the long struggle under the judges.
- When the Land was secured later under David, its natural fruitfulness came to the surface, reaching a climax in the glory days of Solomon and the building of the richly decorated temple.
- With the breaking up of the nation, the Northern kingdom entered into a life of deprivation, it would seem, while their prophets promised a much better future.
- Judah experienced at least a few moments of prosperity but eventually suffered the loss of everything, including the Land, when defeated by Babylon.

- As this was happening, their prophets spoke of a coming restoration of their fortunes that was so intense that they expressed it as a new heaven and a new earth.

Conclusion

Fruitfulness, while not exactly a Promise in the explicit sense, is best seen as kind of auxiliary to Land and Many Descendants (which, in turn, are functions of Blessing to All Nations). It is God's unmistakable intention for the whole of his creation. The Land's fruitfulness is related to its role of supporting an increasing population as well. It seemed to be fruitful in and of itself, but this could be, and often was, negated through covenant disobedience. In terms of prosperity, it was often granted to those who were either Promise Keepers in the sense the patriarchs were, or in the sense of being faithful, like Hezekiah was. Under Solomon, Fruitfulness had reached its highest point and then fell to its lowest with the Babylonian conquest, but the prophets saw that it would be intensified and expanded beyond measure in the coming eschaton.

In all of these manifestations, Fruitfulness showed itself one of the supporting elements of the structure holding the narrative together, constantly providing another measurement of its progress toward the goal.

5. Relationship

The first account of Creation (the big picture) portrayed human beings as the climax and goal of God's creative activity. Given all of the earth to rule, the man and the woman were drawn into a kind of junior partnership with the Almighty. As male and female they were made in his image, and, in the zoomed-in second account, given the institution of marriage in which that image was more fully realized. They were spoken to at length, assigned responsibilities and put in a position of trust. All this suggests a significant relationship was being established, one in which there was as yet no hint of disharmony.

In the account of the Fall, the nature of the relationship previously established was further revealed by the sense of intimacy now broken. Easy two-way conversation seemed a normal part of the relationship, but it became filled with tension because of the shame and fear brought on by disobedience. However, YHWH promised that the source of temptation, the serpent, would eventually be overcome, and, presumably, this new alienation along with it.

Once released into the world, disobedience seemed only to gather momentum, eventually threatening to bring the whole relationship to an end with the total destruction of corrupted humankind. The relationship persisted, however, through righteous Noah and his family, and even though they emerged into a "new" earth, it retained its "fallen" form. The incident at the tower of Babel emphatically proved that fact and even suggested the possibility that matters had deteriorated to the point of no return once again.

Instead of lashing out in judgment as we might have expected, YHWH called Abram out of Ur and began to work out a plan of blessing for all nations through this one man. His story was all about his relationship with YHWH. Initiated entirely by the latter, at its center stood the great Covenant, given and then confirmed. YHWH spoke to him and directed his steps, remaining with him wherever he went. Relationship had stepped to center stage.

It stayed there throughout Abraham's entire lifetime. So intimate was the relationship, in fact, that Abraham even dared to bargain with YHWH over the fate of Sodom. Through his repeated confirmations of the Covenant, YHWH committed himself irrevocably to Abraham and his descendants. Abraham was the "friend of God."

On a number of occasions YHWH reminded the patriarchs immediately following Abraham that "I am with you," pretty well summarizing the relationship during this era. He was actively involved in their story, bending it to his covenantal purpose in each generation. Relationship reached its climax when Jacob/Israel "struggled with God" in what seemed to be a physical sense, but, amazingly, came out the winner! It is difficult to overstate the implication: here a man was not only in relationship with YHWH, he was actually "won" over him. Very strange. Very wonderful.

The Exodus story began with the children of Israel having fallen out of relationship with YHWH. Then Moses was called to renew the affiliation and lead them back to the Promised Land. In this process they became YHWH's people and he became their God. They encountered each other dramatically at Sinai where the nation committed itself to a covenant demanding obedience in order to remain in good standing with him. The first four Commandments spelled out Israel's fundamental responsibilities to YHWH while the last six dealt with interhuman relationships. The Israelites also received instructions for the Tabernacle in their midst, in which the Presence would continue to dwell. During this period, the relationship with YHWH moves from personal to corporate, although it is still mediated through a special personal relationship with one man, Moses.

Repeated disobedience in the wilderness strained the new relationship to the breaking point but a faithful Moses intervened. The people remained obstinate in their disobedience and so were sentenced to wander the desert for forty years, an entire generation forbidden to enter the Promised Land. Meanwhile, Moses's personal walk with YHWH seemed only to deepen, at one point negotiating with him like Abraham, and at another enjoying an awesomely direct theophany. In the end, however, even Moses was disobedient enough to join those who were excluded from the Land.

The relationship between YHWH and his people finally began to improve somewhat as they entered the Land under the leadership of Joshua. No national crisis of obedience marred the record, although, interestingly, the disobedience of just one

Conclusion

man brought the whole nation to the brink of judgment. As for Joshua himself, he remained faithful, living under YHWH's reassuring promise: "I will never leave you or forsake you." Talk about relationship! Unlike Moses, Joshua never falters and so becomes a model leader/mediator/savior.

Under the judges the national pattern reverted back to that of the Exodus with its repeated lapses in national obedience and subsequent judgments. It was another wilderness experience, only this time in the Land. Reflecting the history of the period, the nation had an on-again, off-again relationship with YHWH with no discernable upward or downward trend. Although the Spirit of YHWH came upon a number of the judges, only Gideon and Samuel seemed to enjoy any kind of ongoing personal relationship with God.

During the era of the united kingdom, the narrative was so focused on the kings that there was scant evidence of the corporate relationship of the nation with YHWH (the assumption being that it simply followed the king). The first king of Israel, Saul, began on a good footing with YHWH, even endowed with his Spirit. But, falling into disobedience, he eventually forfeited this relationship and suffered rejection as a result. David followed a different trajectory, remaining close to YHWH his whole life, although the relationship was mediated to a degree through Nathan the prophet. When his son Solomon dedicated the new Temple, YHWH's relationship with the nation reached its highest point to date, embracing both king and people as his Presence filled the place. Although Solomon subsequently turned to other gods, YHWH continued to honor the covenant he had made with David and did not abandon his people.

After the kingdom was divided, the North (Israel) experienced a deteriorating relationship with YHWH. The kings exhibited little evidence of knowing God, in contrast to the prophets Elijah and Elisha. In fact, the prophets became the only ones exhibiting a personal relationship with YHWH, but even at a very low point seven thousand Israelites still were faithful. Using the nation of Assyria, however, YHWH removed the nation from his Presence, while Hosea and Amos continued to insist that YHWH had not ceased to love them and would restore them some day.

While the kings of Judah tended to be somewhat more faithful than those of Israel, the downward spiral away from YHWH continued past the point of no return during their watch. In spite of repeated attempts at reformation, the nation was also removed from YHWH's Presence and banished to exile in Babylon. The destruction of both the Temple and the city symbolized the end of the relationship: YHWH didn't live there anymore.

For the prophets of Judah there was clearly more to come. Like their Northern colleagues, they saw a wonderful restoration of the nation's relationship with YHWH. It would be symbolized by a new temple that would be the center of worship, not just for Israel but for all the nations as well. At this point the relationship of YHWH to his people would go beyond mere restoration to a surprising expansion and deepening.

In the Bosom of Abraham

In the eschaton, all humanity would enjoy a harmonious relationship with God, as a number of its specific features indicate: universal peace; the new covenant; the pouring out of the Spirit on all flesh; the fatherhood of God; inclusion of all nations into Israel.

Summary

- The Story began with God and his creatures enjoying an harmonious relationship that was disrupted by human disobedience. As a result, the humans were cast from his Presence in the garden.

- Wickedness increased throughout the world, necessitating the terrible judgment of the Flood upon all but one good man, Noah, through whose family the relationship was kept alive.

- Their descendants wickedly went their own way, but YHWH chose one, Abraham, and committed himself to him and his offspring, announcing that through them the nations, too, would be blessed.

- Confirming this Covenant several times to Abraham and to his immediate successors, Isaac, Jacob and Joseph, YHWH clearly walked with them.

- After the passing of the patriarchs YHWH appeared to have abandoned their descendants as they fell into slavery in Egypt. Under Moses, however, YHWH reestablished the relationship at the corporate level by means of a covenant with the nation at Mt. Sinai.

- The people failed to keep their end of the bargain, straining the bond almost to the breaking point. But, thanks in part to his relationship with Moses, YHWH did not turn his back on them.

- YHWH led them into the Promised Land under Joshua where the relationship generally seems to have stabilized.

- It deteriorated significantly under the Judges in a cyclic on-again, off-again pattern.

- With the advent of kingly rule things started to change for the better, reaching a peak with David/Solomon and the building of the temple in Jerusalem. YHWH was with them, committing himself especially to David and his descendants forever.

- After the kingdom was divided into North and South, Israel and Judah, it was largely the prophets who maintained the relationship with YHWH as both parts of the nation fell into such disobedience as to be removed altogether from the divine Presence.

- In the darkest hour the prophets announced that in the eschaton, on the other side of judgment, all would not only be restored, but enriched. YHWH would again be at one, not only with the children of Israel, but also with all his creatures.

Conclusion

Human beings were made for relationship with God and with one another. However, they soon fell out with their creator (and one another) who then made repeated attempts to bring them back. When terrible judgment did not work, he chose Abraham and his people as his instrument for blessing the entire world. For the first four generations the relationship was personal, one patriarch after the other, and then it petered out altogether while the nation itself fell into slavery. The covenant through Moses reestablished the connection at the corporate level, but the people struggled to obey right through to the time of the kings. Under David/Solomon the relationship reached its highest point, symbolized by the building of the temple. Because of disobedience, both North and South eventually experienced a complete alienation from YHWH but he still did not abandon them altogether. He continued faithful to his Promises to Abraham and David, comforting the nation with a vision of the End in which they would be fully restored to him and their calling would be fulfilled when all the nations would be brought into the relationship.

At the beginning of this exercise it was noted that, because it is an Edenic quality, tracing Relationship through the Story would provide us with another marker of our progress toward the End.[5] Now that we have done so, Relationship certainly qualifies among the mix of structural elements in the Story, providing another sense of where we are along the way.

6. Grace/Obedience

Introduction

It will be recalled that in this section we have been attempting to answer the following question: *How does this segment of the Story reflect the notion that we are saved by grace and maintained in that salvation by our obedience?* While this inquiry may have seemed a somewhat academic question at the beginning, pursuing it has actually thrown considerable light on the complex relationship of grace to works. As such, it comes close to the heart of how "salvation," the substance of the Promises, actually works. This comes sharply into focus in relation to a question that arises out of the Story and impresses itself strikingly upon the reader: How, given the demonstrated human inability to follow the ways of YHWH, is redemption even possible? Can

---

5. See 8–9, 17, above.

obedience even be part of the equation at all? And, yet, as we noted in the Introduction, calls to obedience permeate both Old and New Testaments.[6]

By now it will be recognized that these questions bear on the age-old problem of the relationship between divine sovereignty and human free will that has come up repeatedly in the Story. Has our exploration of grace/obedience helped us at all in our understanding of *this* issue?

With these questions in mind, we now turn to an overview of our findings.

The account of Creation, placing the humans in the garden under the condition of not eating of one of the trees conforms perfectly to the formulation that we are saved by grace and maintained by works.

The story of the Fall conforms generally as well. Disobedience led to the loss of paradise and alienation from the Creator. The question then became one of restoration, with the assumption being, perhaps, that humanity would be given a second chance to obey.

Through the story of Noah our formula was put on edge as we became fully aware that obedience to God is both an absolute requirement and an unlikely possibility. We saw disobedience multiply and bring about a devastating judgment upon all except one "righteous" man and his family. Through him humanity was given that second chance but it didn't lead to the rule of obedience either. Indeed, the way the Flood story both opens and closes with an observation of humanity's pervasive wickedness leaves the powerful sense that obedience may well be impossible without a fundamental change to the human heart.

The "out of the blue" call of Abram represents another powerful infusion of grace into the Story. The overwhelming impression is that YHWH was acting on his own initiative and would bring about his salvation regardless. Nevertheless, in at least partial conformity to our hypothesis, Abram followed YHWH's directions because he trusted in him. It is the latter action that rendered him "righteous," however, not the obedience, and this suggests that faith has priority over works. While Abram was portrayed as an upright man, we understand that, at the end of the day, YHWH himself was responsible for his continued standing within the Covenant.

YHWH continued his initiative toward redemption in spite of the skepticism of Abraham and Sarah regarding the Promise that she would bear a child. In this narrative there was the appearance of an obligation to walk blameless in order to receive the promised blessings. In context, however, this was eclipsed by the absolute divine assurances that they would eventually materialize. Period. But then, paradoxically, it was the spectacular obedience of Abraham on Mt. Moriah that seemed to seal the deal and drain any remaining contingency from the Promises! Has the need for obedience in order to maintain one's salvation then been reduced to the vanishing point?

The Promise Keepers of the next three generations, Isaac, Jacob/Israel, and Joseph (as one of the twelve), do not owe their success to their exemplary character but

---

6. See 18, above.

to YHWH's faithfulness to the Covenant he had made with Abraham. However, this fidelity seems to be related to the latter's definitive act of obedience on Moriah as well. One could even say that Abraham's obedience became grace to his descendants: Jacob/Israel, the most important of them, was portrayed as blessed in spite of his many defects of character. Grace dominates in these generations, but obedience remains stubbornly part of the equation, even if it is difficult to determine its precise role. It may be dying the death of a thousand qualifications.

On its surface, at least, the story of the Exodus conforms beautifully to our formulation. The text is quite explicit that, in responding to the need of the children of Israel, YHWH was keeping the Covenant he had made with Abraham some five hundred years earlier. The avalanche of grace was still roaring down Moriah. The children of Israel were saved by the hand of YHWH and brought to the foot of Sinai. Unlike the patriarchs, there they entered into a covenant that explicitly demanded obedience to the Law in order to remain "saved." They were even placed under the "covenant mechanism" to encourage obedience and discourage disobedience. Saved by grace, maintained by obedience: as clear as day. However, these waters were muddied by a suggestion that, given the predisposition of humanity to sin, obedience may only be forthcoming if it was grace-enabled through hearts circumcised by YHWH.

The wilderness journey began with the affirmation that YHWH brought the children of Israel out of Egypt by his mighty arm. At its end they learned that the Promised Land would not be theirs because of their own merit but only as God's gift. In the meantime they were required to obey the Law and at this they proved to be miserable failures. The covenant was not thereby annulled, however, raising the question of *how much* disobedience would be required to do so. In spite of conforming better to our hypothesis, this narrative still leaves the impression that grace will prevail over disobedience at the end of the day. Partly this can be seen in the wilderness where disobedience led to the death of a generation but the nation itself was sustained. This seems to be a case of "works" at the personal level and grace at the corporate, just to confuse things a little more.

Our formula is front and center during the Conquest. It was made clear that the Land was a gift from YHWH and to retain it the people had to obey the Law, especially separating themselves from the religious practices and beliefs of the inhabitants. In his farewell address Joshua began by telling them that they were incapable of serving YHWH and then made a point of warning them that disobedience would surely lead to destruction. They then insisted emphatically that they would follow YHWH without fail. By this time the reader is betting heavily on Joshua's assessment, in spite of it being a period of relative obedience.

The period of the judges with its cycle of disobedience and deliverance presents a good test of our hypothesis. We saw the "covenant mechanism" at work as the nation disobeyed, fell into difficulties, cried out to YHWH and were delivered. In each case, but most explicitly so in the story of Gideon, it was made clear that the deliverance was from God alone. All of this confirms in a general way the hypothesis that we are saved by grace while maintained by our obedience but "it's complicated," as they say. And the sheer volume of Israel's serial disobediences once again forces the reader to conclude that grace trumps disobedience every time.

In Saul, the first king, we can see our theory working out in his career: chosen and even enabled by YHWH, he fell into disobedience and was rejected. Samuel told the nation that it would not be finally rejected but the present generation would be swept away if disobedient. This was what had happened in the wilderness to the generation that had left Egypt under Moses, adding a personal/corporate complication to our proposal. When we turn to David, grace certainly infused the covenant YHWH made with him regarding his "house," to the point where obedience or disobedience was simply a nonissue in reference to its continuance. The reign of Solomon offered a "for instance" when he fell into serious disobedience and lost half the kingdom but nevertheless did not negate the promise. In an echo of Abraham we are even told that David's previous obedience was partially responsible for this. But David is a rare example of a person who exhibited a heart (almost) fully oriented toward YHWH and this may explain his obedience. It also offers the insight that God is looking for a proper heart, which is something, ironically, only he can provide.

The story of the Northern kingdom of Israel conforms well to our hypothesis. Still covered by the grace that established the family (under Abraham) and the nation (under Moses), the new state was promised a bright future and an eternal dynasty if it only walked in the ways of YHWH. However, their first king, Jeroboam, derailed the whole project and set in motion a train wreck of alienating disobedience. As a result, the nation was destroyed, but even then her prophets proclaimed a coming restoration. Again, grace will prevail.

The Southern kingdom of Judah also exhibited a long slide into disobedience but it was interrupted by several periods of renewed faithfulness. These, however, were not enough and it, too, came under serious judgment, if somewhat less destructive than that suffered in the North. Our hypothesis is clearly working here but at the same time, especially through references to the Davidic covenant, grace is not only present again and again, but seemingly able to triumph over the expected effects of accumulated disobedience.

In the vision of the prophets the glorious eschaton will be both grace-initiated and grace-maintained. It will come about simply because YHWH has declared it so as the fulfillment of his covenants with Abraham and David. The redeemed of Judah, Israel, and even the nations, would come to enjoy an everlasting state of grace, living in perfect Spirit-filled obedience with the orientation of their hearts changed Godward. In the end, obedience will be "required" but will be grace-enabled. Perhaps this is the key to clearing up our earlier confusion over the relationship.

Conclusion

Summary

- Both the original state conditioned upon obedience and the Fall that resulted when the first couple sinned and had to leave the garden conform to the idea that we are saved by grace and maintained in that state by our works.

- Persistent disobedience led directly to the death of almost the entire race in the Flood. Noah was the exception, likely due to his obedience. Although given a second chance after the Flood, humanity only managed to put its wicked heart on public display once again. Clearly YHWH's favor was dependent upon obedience in this era.

- God initiated a new movement toward salvation when he made his unconditional Promises to Abraham. Strangely, Abraham was counted as righteous merely because he believed God's word. But he was still called to walk in obedience even as grace continued to dominate in the birth of Isaac, the son of Promise. Paradoxically, Abraham's radical obedience on Mt. Moriah seems to have placed an unbreakable seal upon the Covenant of grace!

- Isaac, Jacob/Israel, and Joseph seem to have remained in the Covenant on the basis of obedience, not their own, but Abraham's! In fact, Jacob/Israel remained "saved" *in spite of* his questionable character. To him it was grace, but it was grace engendered by someone else's obedience. Where does grace stop and obedience begin?

- In the story of the Exodus things are somewhat clearer. The Israelites are delivered out of Egypt solely by the hand of YHWH and they are explicitly told that they would remain in the covenant only if they obeyed the Law. Our hypothesis is fully at work here, but the narrative contains a strong hint that obedience will be unlikely unless grace-enabled.

- This is borne out in the wilderness where the people established their inability to follow the Law and so many died there, but the covenant was somehow maintained and a new generation promised the Land as a pure gift. A partial explanation is the pattern beginning to emerge of individuals being rejected because of disobedience while the corporate body continues because of grace.

- Their experience during the Conquest adhered to our formula well enough, as the nation seemed both obedient and successful. At the same time it was made clear to them that they would lose the Promised Land if disobedient. And there was reason to anticipate just that.

- Our hypothesis seems to underlie the history of the judges in which YHWH graciously and repeatedly raised up deliverers while disobediences brought judgment. Although they had no mediator like Moses, in spite of their serial unfaithfulness YHWH did not abandon them altogether. The episode contains hints of the need for grace-enabled obedience through the Spirit of God.

- Saul, the first of the kings, is installed by grace and enabled by the Spirit, but disobedience caused him to be rejected. In a new injection of grace, YHWH chose David and then unconditionally promised him a "son" on the throne forever. This was demonstrated in the case of Solomon who went astray but was able to pass the throne on to his son. David's story also strengthened the insight that obedience can only come from a heart set upon YHWH.

- At first the breakaway Northern kingdom appeared to be subject to our hypothesis in its strictest sense and when it fell into persistent sin it ended up being totally destroyed. Even in the face of this, her prophets foresaw restoration ahead. Grace refused to die.

- A similar pattern prevailed in Judah as it too finally came under terrible judgment for disobedience.

- Because Judah was operating under the grace of the Davidic covenant, she had an extra reason to hope for the eschatological blessings promised by the prophets, blessings that would also include the North and the nations. At that time hearts would be changed and the Spirit outpoured, enabling human beings to live as God willed, forever at last.

Conclusion

Our testing formula that we are saved by grace and are maintained in that position by our works, does seem to be reflected in our survey. Certainly the narrative is always clear that it is God who saves us in the first place, not we ourselves. And it is always true that we humans are subsequently obligated to obey YHWH.

So far, so good. The general drift of the narrative, however, makes it clear that such obedience is simply beyond human ability to maintain. Under the strict terms of our hypothesis this should result in the loss of salvation but that is not what happened. Instead, God kept pouring more grace into the equation, upsetting all our calculations.

At the corporate level this happens primarily through the unconditional covenants YHWH establishes with Abraham and David and their descendants. In the end, the grace expressed in these promises will somehow prevail over the many and persistent disobediences of God's people. At the personal level it becomes clear that obedience will finally be achieved, but only through the eschatological endowment of the Spirit, orienting the human heart toward YHWH once and for all.

Thus, in the End, obedience itself will be grace-enabled, and this throws our hypothesis for a loop, literally. We are saved by grace and obligated to obey as before, but now enabled to obey by grace! It is all of grace, from Beginning to End.

CONCLUSION

Another question arises at this point. It is all very well and good to realize that the tensions in the grace/obedience equation will be resolved in the eschaton, when we will be enabled to obey at last. But what about now? For the time being, we must live in the knowledge that our obedience will never be perfect. What can the believer do but throw himself upon the mercy and loving-kindness of YHWH? Which is another way of saying "grace," after all.

The Story sets before us a harrowing account of human misadventure and frailty while simultaneously conveying such a distinct sense of God's being in charge that we are confident that his saving purposes will be accomplished. It's complicated! It's messy! It's familiar! It's really part of that profound mystery we discussed in connection with divine sovereignty and human free will. Throughout the Story we recognize the God of Moses at work in the life of his people:

> Yahweh is slow to anger, and abundant in loving kindness, forgiving iniquity and disobedience; and he will by no means clear the guilty, visiting the iniquity of the fathers on the children, on the third and on the fourth generation. (Num 14:18)

Here again we confront the impenetrable complexity of the divine-human encounter. Coming at this mystery from the grace/obedience angle has perhaps allowed us to probe into it a little deeper. Certainly it has helped us to realize how much it is right at the center of spiritual life.

PART C—A BRIDGE, SO FAR . . .

The central thesis of this book was stated in the Introduction:

> *These pages will attempt to demonstrate that [the Covenant that God made with Abraham] provides the basic framework for God's entire plan. Its provisions will be seen to undergird the sweep of the biblical narrative, supplying its fundamental structure and joining each portion to the others, supplying connective tissue to the entire Story.*[7]

The time has come to evaluate the status of this proposal now that we are about halfway through the biblical narrative. Has the bridge we imagined spanning the gap between the Beginning and the End of the biblical Story made it to mid-river? The evidence, as presented throughout this work, has led us to the following conclusions:

- The Three Promises are found, to varying degrees, in every part of the narrative. In most cases they have arisen naturally from the text itself, once we knew what we were looking for. This one fact provides a basic unity that connects the stories together, demonstrating that it really is one continuous Story after all, its various parts moving together in a definite direction.

7. See 9, above.

- Asking each section of the Story about the Promises has enabled us to see what we had perhaps not seen before. Most especially it has brought out the deep connection between the earliest chapters of Genesis, with their accounts of Creation, Fall, and Flood, to the story of Abraham. This alone would qualify the hypothesis for serious consideration.

- The proposal that all Three Promises are present throughout the Story has led us to dig deeper if one or the other seems to be missing in a particular segment. This is true, for example, of the Blessing to All Nations in the Exodus: it was eventually found in the call of Israel to be a "kingdom of priests," giving this rather enigmatic designation a clearer meaning, especially as the Story developed further.

- While all the Promises are present in all segments of the Story, they are all not equally present in all. It is fair to say that Land dominates most of the time with an occasional appearance of Many Descendants while Blessing to All Nations recedes more or less into in the background after Abraham (and almost disappears) until the prophetic visions of the End come into view. At that point the Promises appear in their fullest and most balanced expression since Abraham first received them.

- In the meantime, the unequal presence of the Promises can serve as a way of measuring how far we are along the Bridge, answering the question, "Are we there yet?" If one appears to be fulfilled, as the Land was on several occasions, the lack of fulfillment of the others is a sign that the answer is "Not yet!"

- The fact that the Story so far has this structure provides us with every reason to expect that the rest of it will be built around the Three Promises as well. Indeed, in the prophetic vision we have now glimpsed the abutment on the far side of the river, the eschaton, and have seen that it will be constructed with the same three elements, gloriously transformed.

- With this vision now fully before us, it has become clearer that, of the Promises, the driving force and ultimate goal is Blessing to All Nations. The Land and Many Descendants derive their significance from the fact that they are part and parcel of Blessing to All Nations. This seems to be the "inner logic" of the Promises.

At this point in the Story, however, the New Creation remains beckoning in the distance, out of reach. Our second volume will pick up the narrative with the children of Israel in Babylonian captivity and take it from there all the way to the End. In other words, we will be filling in the gap, and it will come as no surprise that, as we do so we will find ourselves once again standing on the Promises. Could it be any other way?

From Beginning to End, the Story is embraced in the bosom of Abraham.

Works Cited

Bloesch, Donald G. *Essentials of Evangelical Theology.* Vol. 1: *God, Authority, and Salvation.* San Francisco: Harper and Row, 1978.
Bromiley, G. W., "Sin." In *The International Standard Bible Encyclopedia*, rev. ed, IV:518–525. Grand Rapids: William B. Eerdmans, 1988.
Book of Common Prayer. Toronto: Anglican Book Centre, 1962.
Cundall, A. E., "Baal." In *Zondervan Pictorial Encyclopedia of the Bible* I:431–3. Grand Rapids: Zondervan, 1975.
Dempster, Stephen G. *Dominion and Dynasty: A Biblical Theology of the Hebrew Bible.* Downers Grove, IL: InterVarsity, 2003.
Enns, Peter. *Exodus.* The NIV Application Commentary. Grand Rapids: Zondervan, 2000.
Feinberg, C. L. "Tabernacle." In *Zondervan Pictorial Encyclopedia of the Bible* V:572–83. Grand Rapids: Zondervan, 1975.
Goldsworthy, Graeme. *According to Plan: The Unfolding Revelation of God in the Bible.* Downers Grove, IL: InterVarsity, 1991.
Greidanus, Stanley. *Preaching Christ from the Old Testament: A Contemporary Hermeneutical Model.* Grand Rapids: Eerdmans, 1999.
Hamilton, Victor P. *The Book of Genesis, Chapters 1–17.* New International Commentary on the Old Testament. Grand Rapids: Wm. B. Eerdmans, 1990.
———. *The Book of Genesis, Chapters 18–50.* New International Commentary on the Old Testament. Grand Rapids: Wm. B. Eerdmans, 1995.
Harrison, R.K. "Creation." In *Zondervan Pictorial Encyclopedia of the Bible* I:1020–25. Grand Rapids: Zondervan, 1975.
———. *Introduction to the Old Testament.* Grand Rapids: Wm. B. Eerdmans, 1969.
Henry, Matthew. *Commentary on the Whole Bible.* Vol. I: *Genesis to Joshua.* Toronto: Fleming H. Revell, 1935.
House, Paul R. "Biblical Theology and the Wholeness of Scripture: Steps Toward a Program for the Future." In *Biblical Theology: Retrospect and Prospect*, edited by Scott J. Hafemann, 267–279. Downers Grove, IL: InterVarsity, 2002.
Jewett, P. "Atonement." In *Zondervan Pictorial Encyclopedia of the Bible* I:408–413 Grand Rapids: Zondervan, 1975.
Keil, C. F., and Delitzsch, F. *Commentary on the Old Testament in Ten Volumes.* Vol. 1: *The Pentateuch.* Translated by James Martin. Grand Rapids: William B. Eerdmans: 1986.
Levenson, Jon D. *The Death and Resurrection of the Beloved Son: The Transformation of Child Sacrifice in Judaism and Christianity.* New Haven, CT: Yale University Press, 1993.
———. *Resurrection and the Restoration of Israel: The Ultimate Victory of the God of Life.* New Haven, CT: Yale University Press, 2006.

Works Cited

Montague, George T. *The Holy Spirit: Growth of a Biblical Tradition*. New York: Paulist, 1976.

NIV Study Bible. Edited by Kenneth Barker. Grand Rapids: Zondervan, 1985.

Motyer, J. Alec. *The Message of Amos*. The Bible Speaks Today. Downers Grove, IL: InterVarsity, 1974.

Packer, J.I. *Fundamentalism and the Word of God*. Grand Rapids: William B Eerdmans, 1958.

Pinnock, Clark, ed. *The Openness of God: A Biblical Challenge to the Traditional Understanding of God*. Downers Grove, IL: InterVarstiy, 1994.

Rainey, A.F. "Sacrifices and Offerings." In *Zondervan Pictorial Encyclopedia of the Bible* V:194–211. Grand Rapids: Zondervan, 1975.

Reimer, Andy M. "In the Beginning... Lessons learned in teaching Genesis 1 to evangelical college students." *Canadian Evangelical Review* 29 (2005) 32–44.

Rendtorf, Rolf. *The Canonical Hebrew Bible: A Theology of the Old Testament*. Leiderdorp: Deo, 2005.

Sanders, E.P. *Paul and Palestinian Judaism*. Philadelphia: Fortress, 1977.

Schaeffer, Francis. *No Final Conflict: The Bible Without Error in All that it Affirms*. 5th ed. Downers Grove, IL: InterVarsity, 1979.

Scobie, H.H. *The Ways of Our God: An Approach to Biblical Theology*. Grand Rapids: William B Eerdmans, 2003.

Scroggie, W. Graham. *The Unfolding Drama of Redemption: The Bible as a Whole*. Vol. 1: *The Prologue and Act 1 of the drama Embracing the Old Testament*. London: Pickering and Inglis, 1953.

Selman, Martin J. *2 Chronicles*. The Tyndale Old Testament Commentaries. Downers Grove, IL: InterVarsity, 1994.

Skarsaune, Oskar. *In the Shadow of the Temple: Jewish Influences on Early Christianity*. Downers Grove, IL: InterVarsity, 2002.

Thompson, J. Arthur. "Canaan, Canaanites." In *Zondervan Pictorial Encyclopedia of the Bible* I:1020–25. Grand Rapids: Zondervan, 1975.

———. *The Book of Jeremiah*. New International Commentary on the Old Testament. Grand Rapids: Eerdmans, 1980.

VanGemeren, Willem. *The Progress of Redemption: The Story of Salvation from Creation to the New Jerusalem*. Grand Rapids: Baker, 1988.

Vos, Geerhardus. *Biblical Theology: Old and New Testaments*. Grand Rapids: Wm. B. Eerdmans, 1948.

Walton, John H. *Ancient Near Eastern Thought and the Old Testament: Introducing the Conceptual World of the Hebrew Bible*. Grand Rapids: Baker Academic, 2006.

———. *Genesis*. The NIV Application Commentary. Grand Rapids:, 2001.

Wenham, Gordon J. *Numbers*. The Tyndale Old Testament Commentaries. Downers Grove, IL: InterVarsity, 1981.

Willard, Dallas. *Renovation of the Heart*. Colorado Springs: NavPress, 2002.

Wiseman, Donald J. *1 and 2 Kings*. The Tyndale Old Testament Commentaries. Downer's Grove, IL: InterVarsity, 1993.

Index

Abraham,
  and David, 214–15
  and Moses, 118, 128–33, 238
  and Noah, 66
  bargains with God, 77, 81, 106, 148, 207, 206, 348
  covenant and creation, 34–37, 323–24, 340–41
  covenant central to Bible, 8–15, 18–19
  covenant established, 83–84
  descendants redefined?, 65, 315, 318–19, 339–41, 346
  faith of, 67, 70, 74, 77–78, 83, 357
  father of Islam, 80
  obedience applies to descendants, 87, 90, 93, 106–7, 126, 354–55, 357
  personal relationship with God, 77, 86, 350
  prophet, 210
  reason chosen, 86
  skepticism of, 87, 354
  tested, 83–84
Adam
  and Abraham, 35–37, 73, 83, 340–41
  and animals, 25, 29–30
  and Israel, 262, 292
  and Moses, 129
  and Noah, see "Noah, as Second Adam"
  covenant?, 34–35
  image of God, see "God, image of"
  "in Adam," 36, 47, 49, 53, 143, 317–18, 317–18, 341
  earthy, 29, 35–36
afterlife?, 94
already/not yet, 173–74, 180, 181, 203–14, 330
Amorites,
  encounters with, 158, 163, 169, 177, 178, 182, 198
  sin of, 71, 110–11, 171–72, 178–79, 270–271
angel(s), 23, 71, 108, 120, 149, 159, 191, 195, 251, 281, 328
Ark of the Covenant, 127, 161, 169, 176, 177, 201, 204, 210, 217, 224, 232, 235, 335

Assyria,
  conquers Israel, 241, 245, 247, 258, 259, 260, 266, 269, 271, 279–81, 311, 351
  in general, 255, 278, 282, 296
  policy regarding defeated nations, 247, 330
Athaliah, 266, 269, 275, 276, 292
atonement, 145–46, 149, 151–52, 157, 299, 309, see also "substitute," "substitution," and "sacrifice"

Baal, 195, 198, 240, 241, 245, 249–51, 252, 254, 276
Babylon,
  conquers Judah, 11, 267, 269, 271, 283–86
  description, 60
  fate of, 289
  place of exile, 11, 269, 271, 285–86
  YHWH's instrument, 284–85, 289
Balaam, 158–59, 162
ban, the, 171–73, 185
Beloved Son, death and resurrection of, 77–78, 91, 100, 115, 148, 216, 259, 272, 310, 315, 327, 334, 346
Bethel, 68, 69, 88, 89, 96, 97, 98, 103, 105, 107, 200, 204, 248, 254, 259, 335, 336
Bible,
  as story, 4–8
  harmonization of, 2–4
  unity of, 1–4, 324, 359–60
births, miraculous, 66, 76, 86, 93, 111, 117, 146, 192, 198, 201, 205, 208, also, "God, opens wombs"
blessing the nations principle, 72, 104, 135, 163, 302, 342
Book of the Covenant, 127, 266, 282
both/and, 2, 3, 86, 217, 238

Canaan,
  like Eden, 69, 164, 346
  standing for whole earth, 161, 336–37
circumcision,
  literal, 79, 84, 176, 187

363

circumcision *(continued)*
　of the heart, 131, 132, 139, 189, 239, 301, 329, 355, see also "heart, promise of renovation"
corporate or individualistic thinking?, 80, 168, 236, 264
corporate vs personal, 89-90, 104-5, 113, 146-47, 168, 299, 350, 351, 352, 353, 355, 356, 357
covenant, new, 294, 295, 297-300, 320, 333, 352
covenantal metaphor, 84, 85, 134, 162, 231
covenant mechanism, 129-31, 160, 162, 192, 205, 243, 273, 291, 292, 301-2, 328, 355
covenant renewed, 178, 181-82, 219, 249, 263, 267, 274, 276, 279, 282-83, 292, 332
covenant, sign of, 59, 75, 79-80, 84
creation,
　accounts, 3, 22-23, 23-27, 28-34
　exhibits the Three Promises, 14, 34-38,
　fallen, 21, 40-41
　"for" humanity, 21
　need for transformation, 133
　order out of chaos, 22-23, 24
　promise of transformation, 268, 295-96, 312-13, 315-16, 323-24, 333, 336, 337, 345, 348

David,
　covenant established, 213-15, 224-25
　covenant working, 229, 236-37, 269, 276, 280-81, 292, 356
Day of the LORD, 256, 257, 294, 303-4, 310, 333, 348
demons?, 113
division, seeds of, 194, 200-201, 212, 226
dream(s), 82, 95-96, 100-101, 103, 227, 320

Ebal, and Gerezim, 130, 169, 178, 300, 337
Eden,
　already among the people, 134, 234-35
　embodiment of entire creation, 30, 35, 317-18. 334-36
　and exile, 262, 290-91
　return to, 8, 9, 14, 17, 19, 317
　symbolic elements, 22-23
edom, 158, 254
　edomites, 99, 277
Egypt,
　ally of Israel/Judah, 247, 258, 283
　enemy of Judah, 265, 267, 271, 273, 283
　gods inferior to YHWH, 112-13, 125
　place of captivity, 10, 89, 103, 109-21, 267
　place of refuge, 68-69, 93, 101, 104, 105, 115, 229, 267, 285, 289

Elijah
　compared with Elisha, 245
　compared with Moses, 246, 250
environment as cause of sin?, 47, 54, 238, 326
environment, natural, 24, 26, 29, 41, 45, 52, 53, 57, 58-59, 312-13, 317, 319, 334
eschatology, defined, 295
eschaton,
　continuous *and* discontinuous with present age, 297
　defined, 295
　nature of, 243, 255-57, 259-60, 262-63, 299, 336, 337, 340, 345, 349, 351-53, 356, 358, see also chapter 15
Eve, 36, 40, 43, 46, 47, 49, 52, 60, 61, 67, 71, 83, 143, 145, 262, 292, 326, 333, 334, 338, 341, 344, 345
exile,
　Assyrian, 256, 269, 295, 332
　Babylonian, 10, 132, 267, 269, 286, 293, 309, 311, 313, 314, 315, 321, 334, 339-40, 344, 346, 351
　Egyptian, 91, 117, 183, 285
　from Eden, 48, 61, 326

fall, see "humanity, fall of"
farewell discourse, 144, 146, 159, 160, 181, 188-89, 219, 226-29, 229, 236, 355
forty, 57, 110, 118, 128, 144, 147, 148, 150, 156, 159, 162, 164, 179, 196, 198, 198, 226, 229, 236, 246, 251, 266, 277, 285, 335, 350

Gerezim, see "Ebal and Gerezim"
God,
　appearances of (theophanies), 76-77, 79, 97, 114-15, 138, 147, 149-50, 163, 251, 350
　bargaining with, 75, 77, 81, 86, 97, 106, 148-49, 165, 201, 207
　changes mind?, 62, 77, 97, 148-50, 156, 339
　committed to Israel, 86, 90, 106-7, 143, 165, 207, 263-64, 350, 352
　dangerous, 114, 123-24, 138, 145, 212, 300
　dwelling place, 95, 96, 103, 126-28, 150, 204, 217, 228, 233, 259, 335-36
　evil spirit from, 218, 220, 221
　exasperated?, 206
　forgetful?, 59
　image of, 20, 21, 25, 26, 27, 29, 33, 38, 59
　immanent and transcendent, 41
　judgment?, 54
　opens wombs, 72, 85, 90, 96, 104, 198, 201, 327, 338, 339, see also, "births, miraculous"
　omnipotent, 24-25, 27

Index

omniscient?, 32, 54–55
orientation to love and mercy, 124, 125, 143, 146, 156, 166, 216, 233, 243, 256, 257, 262, 279, 283, 301, 319, 322, 329, 334, 351, 359 – see also "Grace/Obedience" sections
    pain of, 56, 257
    rejected as king, 193, 202
    rest of, 27–28
    silences of, 52, 62, 65, 110, 201, 326, 328
    sovereign over history, 8, 90, 99, 101, 102, 105–6, 159, 195, 207, 254, 327, 350
    Spirit of, 33, 155, 165, 170, 194, 196, 197, 207–8, 218, 220, 221, 222, 235, 239, 245, 264, 275, 306–7, 318, 319–20, 330, 333, 335, 336, 351, 352, 358
    turns evil into good, 91–92, 101, 102, 202
    wrath of, 148, 172, 180, 285, 300, 302, 304, 321
Goliath, 221–22, 280

Hagar, 65, 67, 71, 76, 82, 94
harmonize?, 2–4
heart,
    need of renovation, 47, 54, 56, 58, 59, 63, 107, 116, 144, 147, 166, 188, 220–21, 229, 236, 239, 264, 282, 284, 298–302, 326, 336, 354, 355, 356
    promise of renovation, 131, 132, 139, 189, 208–9, 238–39, 295, 298–300, 320, 322–23, 329, 333, 355, 356, 358
Henry, Matthew, 34
high places, 274, 277, 278
Holy Trinity, 25, 33, 76
Horeb, 109, 114, 117, 128, 134, 241, 246, 251
humankind,
    apex of creation, 22, 26–27, 29–30
    created vegetarian, 27, 58, 312
    fall of, 39, 40–41, 44–48, 49, 56, 60, 86, 161, 244, 338, 340, 344, 346, 348, 349, 354, 357
    having souls?, 29–30
    incapable of obedience?, 53–54, 56, 131–32, 143, 182, 191, 215, 238, 272, 298, 329, 330, 332, 353, 357–58, see also "heart, need for renovation"
    male and female, 26–27, 32–34 mandate to multiply, 20, 26, 36, 56, 57, 60, 61, 62, 70, 338, 340, 341, 346
    mandate to rule the earth, 20, 26, 27, 30, 36, 116, 349
    on probation, 31, 313
Ishmael, 65, 71–72, 76, 79, 80, 82, 85, 94
Israel,
    "Constitution," 125, 126

"Declaration of Independence," 120, 123, 125, 139
    evangelist to the nations, 112, 149, 183, 184–85, 205, 342–43, see also "Blessing to All Nations" sections
    firstborn son of God, 115, 137–38
    kingdom of priests, 122–23, 125, 136, 140, 185, 233, 290, 315, 333, 342, 343, 345, 360
    "one who struggles with God," 97–98, 106, 114, 122, 131, 291
    purpose, 136

Jacob, blessed in spite of behavior, 90, 125
Jeroboam, sin of, 240, 244–45, 248, 254–55, 268–69, 332, 356
Jerusalem,
    besieged, 284–85
    burial place of the kings, 277
    chosen by God, 229, 237
    David's capital, 210, 217
    destroyed, 267, 285, 291, 322
    location of the temple, 217, 230, 247, 248, 336
    plundered, 267, 277
    rebuilt/new, 8, 23, 311–12, 336
    spared, 279–81, 284
Jezebel, 241, 245, 249, 250, 251, 252, 253, 254, 269, 275
Jonah, 255, 260, 343
Joshua, and Moses, 170, 176–77, 179
Judah, blessing of royalty upon, 102, 104, 131, 213–14, 325, 329, 330
judgment/salvation, 54, 121, 304, 310, 328

kings, (see also, "monarchy")
    as servant, 273, 304–10, 333
    narrative focus on, 211, 235, 255, 331
kingdom of priests, see "Israel, kingdom of priests"
Land, ultimate size, 71, 72, 161, 174, 183, 227, 230, 312, 335, 337
law, before the Law, 62, 128
leadership,
    charismatic, 170–71
    monarchy, nature of, 192–93

Machpelah, cave at, 88, 89, 92, 94, 102
marriage, nature of, 32–33
material blessings, 136, 186, 234, 347, see also, "prosperity" as well as "Fruitfulness" sections
messiah, 218, 220–21, 223, 247
Moriah, 76, 78, 83, 85, 87, 90, 107, 116, 143, 152, 231, 355, 357
monotheism, 112–13

Index

Moses,
    as the first prophet, 146
    covenant established, 122–25
    covenant's purpose, 132–33
    covenant at work, see "covenant mechanism" mediator, 148–50, 214, 156, 357
    prophet, 115, 147, 246, 332
    significance of, 146–47
    starting over with, 148, 156, 162, 165, 329

nations, incorporated into Israel, 185, 191, 205, 260–61, 295, 313–16, 336, 340–41, 342–46
Noah, and the exodus, 335
    as second Adam, 52, 56–61, 338
    nakedness, 34, 43, 44, 59
new year, 112, 120, 176, 328

obedience,
    applying across generations?, 237, 255, see also "Abraham," above
    grace-enabled, 139–40, 166, 195, 208–9, 322–23, 355–56, 358
One, the, 56–57, 62, 66, 76, 83, 85, 90, 91, 92, 95, 99, 114, 121, 147, 182, 214, 246, 271, 304, 326–32, 333, 338

Passover, celebrations of, 134, 150, 169, 176, 266, 279, 283, 328
    institution of, 42, 108, 120, 153
Philistines, 80, 105, 179, 191, 198, 199, 201, 203, 210, 218, 219, 220, 221, 222, 223
Presence, the, 8, 43, 48, 49, 103, 113, 122, 145, 148, 150–54, 291, 318, 335, 336, 350, see also "Relationship" sections
problem of evil, 92
Progressive Revelation, 5–7, 66, 70, 72, 76, 79, 173, 214
Promise Keeper, 66, 89, 99, 105, 107, 114, 115, 256, 326, 328, 334
Promise-Fulfillment Dynamic, 8
Promises,
    already fulfilled, 171, 174, 179–80, 181–82, 228, 230, see also "already/not yet"
    transformed, 13, 14
prophecy,
    as "narrative-yet-to-come," 268
    nature of, 296–97 (example, 257)
prophet(s),
    arch-conservatives, 243, 301–2
    covenant prosecutors, 243, 268, 301, 332
    literary, 244, 276, 295, 332
    narrative focus on, 242, 245, 255
    northern vs. southern, 267–68
    role of, 211–12, 242, 255

prosperity, 96, 105, 210, 331, see also "material blessings"

remnant, 101, 247, 251, 271, 288–89, 313, 339
renovation of the heart, see "heart"
rest, edenic, 20, 27–28, 32, 124, 138, 148, 179, 181, 182, 186, 190, 208, 225, 228, 234–35, 287, 312–13, 347
restoration of North, 259, 264
reunion of Israel and Judah, 257, 295, 311, 333, 336, 340, 353
revelation, progressive, 5–7, 66, 69, 70, 76, 85, 113, 173, 214, 324

sacrifice, 70, 76, 77, 78, 83, 85, 116, 120, 126–27, 143, 146, 151–53, 154, 180–81, 218, 219, 228, 250, 256, 279, 299, 300, 308–10, 314, 328, 329, 338, see also "substitute" and "substitution"
    need for a greater, 145–46, 306–7, 328, 329
sacrifice, child, 249–50, 270, 278
salvation,
    and judgment, see "judgment/salvation" as renovation of the heart, 54
    begins with Abraham, 78, 357
    by grace alone, 18, 107, 322–23, 354, 356, 358, see also Grace/Obedience sections
    corporate nature of, 80
    defined, 8–15, 135, 173–74
    through a single person, see "One"
    through Israel, see "Israel, kingdom of priests"
salvation history, 4, 6, 8, 111, 146, 218, 295, 310, 329
Samaria, 240, 249, 252, 258, 259, 268, 271, 276, 295
Samaritans, 247
Samuel, prophet, priest and judge, 201
satan, 6, 39, 42
semitic exaggeration, 107, 179, 180
Serpent Crusher, 6, 45, 52, 66, 76, 89, 91, 102, 111, 147, 170, 174, 192, 214, 216, 246, 305, 308, 325, 326, 327–28, 330, 331, 333
serpent(s), 6, 22, 40, 42, 43, 44, 46, 48, 53, 142, 267, 269, 312, 328, 329, 330, 331, 332, 333, 349
servant-king, see "leadership, king as servant"
Seth, line of, 51, 52, 55, 60, 78, 216, 326
sexuality, 33, 56, 195, 198–200
Sheba, Queen of, 211, 233, 235, 343
Shechem, 64, 68, 72, 98, 170, 182, 183, 198
sin,
    original, 47
    nature of, 40, 53–54, see also chapter 3
    seriousness of, 143, 145–46, 159, 161, 236

Index

Sinai, (see also, Horeb) and burning bush, 123
   as "Place," 17, 115, 123, 128–27, 134, 138
   before and after, 142–43
Solomon, kingdom, glory of, 227–28, 234
   temple, see "temple"
sovereignty and free will, 3, 31–32, 119–20, 289, 295, 353–54, 359
Spirit of God, see "God, Spirit of"
substitute, need for a greater?, see "sacrifice, need for a greater?"
substitution, 76, 78, 83–84, 116

tabernacle,
   described, 126–27
   significance of, 134, 138
   purpose, 151
temple,
   built, 216–17, 228
   dedicated, 217–18, 228, 231, 237, 351
   destroyed, 285, 288, 291
   draws the nations to YHWH, 232–33, 343, 344
   compared/contrasted with tabernacle, 216–17
   house of God, see "God, dwelling place"
   idols in, 270, 276, 278–79
   like Eden, 234–35,
   looted, 265, 266, 267, 273, 277, 278, 284, 285, 289
   rebuilt, 286, 304, 311–12, 314, 318
temptation, nature of, 40
Ten Commandments,
   edenic, 138,
   gift of, 122–25
   Israel's "Constitution," 125
ten lost tribes?, 247, 332
testing, purpose of, 144–45
theocracy, 116, 154, 170, 194, 197, 211, 212, 242
Three Promises in creation, 14–15, 34–38
   tending to be universalized, 35, 49, 65–66, 315–18, 323–24, 345–46
   inner logic, 37, 65–66, 135, 136, 185, 232, 315, 345, 345–46, 360
Tree of the Knowledge of Good and Evil, 20, 22, 30–31, 34, 38, 40, 42–44
Tree of Life, 22, 23, 30–31, 40, 46–47, 49, 60, 145
twelve tribes?, 175

universalism?, 318–19

vegetarian, humankind and animals created as, 21, 27, 30, 51, 312

woman, status of, 32–34

YHWH, use of, 15

www.ingramcontent.com/pod-product-compliance
Lightning Source LLC
Chambersburg PA
CBHW080406300426
44113CB00015B/2420